THE ROUGH GUIDE TO

Fiji

written and researched by

Ian Osborn

This second edition updated by

Helena Smith

roughguides.com

Contents

Introduction to
Fiji

Sun-drenched beaches, turquoise lagoons, swaying palm trees – Fiji supplies all the classic images of paradise. No wonder, then, that every year thousands of travellers come to this South Pacific archipelago for the ultimate island escape. With over three hundred islands to choose from, Fiji is an amazingly versatile destination. Whether you're after a luxury honeymoon retreat, a lively backpacker island or a family-friendly resort you won't be disappointed. You'll also find a warm, hospitable people, an intriguing blend of Melanesians, Polynesians and Indians.

With a reliable tropical climate, a good tourist infrastructure, English as its main language and no jabs or pills to worry about, travelling in Fiji is as easy as it gets. As the hub of South Pacific tourism, the country attracts over half a million visitors a year, mostly from Australia and New Zealand, its largest "neighbours" lying over 2000km southeast. Of the northern hemisphere travellers who arrive, many are backpackers from Europe or surfers and scuba divers from North America.

While it can be tempting to spend your whole time in Fiji sunbathing and sipping cocktails from coconuts, there are plenty of **activities** to lure you away from the beach. Within a ten-minute boat ride of most resorts you can find yourself **snorkelling** with dolphins and manta rays or **scuba diving** at pristine coral reefs. In addition, at the exposed edges of the reefs are some of the world's finest and most consistent **surfing breaks**. **Nature lovers** are also spoilt for choice, both underwater and on dry land, and wildlife-spotting opportunities are plentiful, whether you're seeking turtles, exotic birds or 3m-long tiger sharks.

Away from the resorts is another Fiji waiting to be discovered: a land of stunning mountains, rainforests and **remote villages**. Here you'll find fantastically hospitable Fijians living a similar lifestyle to their tribal ancestors. Staying a night or two at a village homestay will give you an authentic insight into ethnic Fijian culture as well as the chance to sample **yaqona** or *kava*, the national drink. Fiji is also home to a large

ABOVE SURFING MALOLO BARRIER REEF

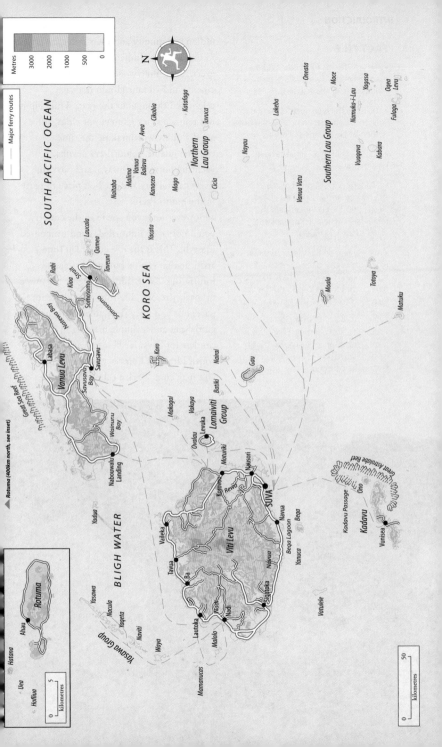

FACT FILE

• Fiji is made up of 333 islands and many tiny islets. Two thirds of Fiji's islands remain uninhabited.

• The name Fiji is an adaptation of the Tongan pronunciation of "Viti", originally written by Europeans as "Feejee".

• Only four of Fiji's 27 airports have paved runways.

• Of a total population of nearly 875,000, around 512,000 are ethnic Fijians, 290,000 Fiji-Indians and the remainder Chinese, Europeans and various Pacific islanders.

• At New Year on the islands, women play a game called *veicaqe moli* – "kick the orange". The winners have to give new clothes to the losers, and the losers' job is to serve the victors *yaqona*.

• Around a fifth of ethnic Fijians live a mostly subsistence lifestyle on tribally owned native land (87 percent of all land in the country).

Indian community and their influence is seen in the delicious Indian food served in almost every town, Bollywood films showing in the cinema and vibrant Hindu festivals celebrated throughout the year. While Fiji is not renowned for its towns or **cities**, three are definitely worth taking the time to explore: quaint, colonial-era Levuka, yachting hotspot Savusavu, and Suva, the lively capital city and the best place to party in the South Pacific.

However long you spend in the country you'll notice an unhurried, good-humoured lifestyle. This is the essence of **Fiji Time** – an attitude that can be both inspiring and infuriating. Away from the highly organized upmarket resorts, life runs at a different pace; bus and ferry timetables serve more as guidelines and a simple meeting in a village can last for days. It's best to leave your inner control freak at home – you never know, you may come back a calmer person.

SIX OF THE BEST RESORTS

Fijian resorts range from simple beachside **bures** (traditional thatched huts) with cold-water showers to opulent **villas** with hardwood floors and private spa pools. With almost a hundred resorts throughout the islands the choice can be overwhelming. To help you decide, we've whittled them down to six of the best, each aimed at a different type of traveller.

Luxury *Vatulele Island Resort*, Vatulele. See p.157
Backpackers *The Beachouse*, Coral Coast, Viti Levu. See p.114
Romance *Matangi Island Resort*, off Taveuni. See p.208
Families *Plantation Island Resort*, Malolo Lailai, Mamanucas. See p.84
Divers *Dolphin Bay*, Vanua Levu. See p.202
Eco-adventure *Tui Tai Cruise*, Vanua Levu and Taveuni. See p.189

Where to go

The vast majority of travellers arrive at Nadi International Airport on **Viti Levu**, the biggest island in the archipelago. Most stay around the suburban tourist hub of **Nadi** for a day or two to organize travels to other parts of the country, or use it as a convenient base for exploring the surrounding countryside and offshore islands. The most popular destination in Fiji lies visible off Nadi's coastline – a gorgeous collection of islands known as the **Mamanucas**. Here you'll find sublime beaches and tiny coral cays with suitably exotic names such as "Bounty" or "Treasure Island". Extending north of the Mamanucas are the **Yasawa Islands**, a string of larger, volcanic islands home to a mixture of budget beach resorts and upmarket boutique accommodation.

Almost as popular as the Mamanucas and Yasawa Islands, especially with families, are the beach resorts of the **Coral Coast** along the south coast of Viti Levu. Around an hour's drive from Nadi, these larger resorts offer good value all-inclusive packages and a great

OPPOSITE VILLAGE CHILDREN, VITI LEVU **ABOVE** MATANGI ISLAND RESORT

UNDERWATER FIJI

A huge part of Fiji's appeal lies below the surface of the waves. Don a mask and snorkel and you will find **coral reefs** shimmering with colourful fish, sea fans dancing in the current and manta rays and reef sharks cruising the lagoons. Throw in crystal-clear water and temperatures that rarely fall below 25°C and you have one of the world's greatest snorkelling and diving destinations.

Fiji's ten thousand square kilometres of coral reef twist and turn around every island, and include the world's third longest barrier reef – the 200km-long Great Sea Reef found off the north coast of Vanua Levu. These amazing structures provide habitats for thousands of species of fish, plants and animals and boast an astonishing biodiversity that's comparable to that found in rainforests.

The three most common types of reef found in Fiji are **fringing reefs**, which are attached to an island and offer snorkelling direct from the shore; **patch reefs**, individual coral reefs found within a lagoon and usually attracting great numbers of reef fish; and **barrier reefs**, which are separated from the shore by a deep channel and feature steep drop-offs and strong currents. There's information on Fiji's best reefs, plus snorkelling and diving advice, on p.35.

Author picks

Our author has island-hopped around Fiji in search of pristine beaches, vibrant markets and memorable sights. She shares her personal highlights here.

Root around the markets No trip is complete without the purchase of *yaqona* from a town market – buy a bunch of tangled roots to take as a gift on a village visit. **See p.40**

Take to the air Tiny planes crisscross the islands, flying low over the atolls and landing on grass airstrips amongst the sugarcane and palms. **See p.24**

Party in Suva After a week or so in the wilds, Suva's restaurant, bar and club scene can seem quite heady. The locals are known for their fondness for a night out. **See p.146**

Go to church Fijians are very musical as well as deeply religious: church services give you the opportunity to hear them belt out harmonious hymns. **See p.67**

Eat like a local Fresh fish, coconut milk, greens and lots of fruit: Fijian food at its best is refreshing and healthy. **See p.29**

Smell the flowers Fiji's orchids and hibiscus flowers (the latter tucked behind your right ear if you're single, the left if you're taken) are wonderfully exotic and colourful. Taveuni has its own rare flower, the Tagimaucia. **See p.66 & p.213**

Break open a coconut Enjoy the cooling milk and soft flesh of the islands' iconic coconut palms. **See p.237**

Discover ancient Fiji Petroglyphs at Vatulele, shards of Lapita pottery embedded in the sands at Sigatoka and huge ocean-going canoes in the Fiji Museum in Suva are just three reminders of the country's early culture. **See p.156, p.110 & p.138**

> Our author recommendations don't end here. We've flagged up our favourite places – a perfectly sited hotel, an atmospheric café, a special restaurant – throughout the guide, highlighted with the ★ symbol.

LEFT DIVING, VITI LEVU **RIGHT FROM TOP** KOKODA (MARINATED FISH); GRASS AIRSTRIP; ORCHID AT THE GARDEN OF THE SLEEPING GIANT

choice of sightseeing tours. Inland is the rugged **rural interior of Viti Levu**. This region was once home to fierce, cannibalistic hill tribes and is crisscrossed with **hiking trails** including the route to Fiji's highest peak, **Mount Tomanivi**. Heading east along Viti Levu's south coast brings you to **Pacific Harbour**, Fiji's adventure tour capital offering whitewater rafting, jet-ski safaris and world-renowned shark dives off the nearby island of **Beqa**. Beyond is **Suva**, Fiji's cosmopolitan capital city and the hub for sea transport throughout the archipelago.

Of the outer islands, the most accessible are in the **Lomaiviti Group**, a short trip by boat from the east coast of Viti Levu. Here you'll find the quirky former capital of Levuka on the island of Ovalau and a good range of budget island resorts – a less commercial alternative to the Mamanucas and Yasawas. Spreading east for hundreds of kilometres is the vast **Lau Group**. Reached by cargo boat from the mainland, these islands provide a true adventure for the intrepid traveller and the chance to sample Polynesian culture. South of Viti Levu is the snaking shape of **Kadavu**, a magnet for scuba-divers thanks to the impressive Great Astrolabe Reef.

Fiji's second largest island, **Vanua Levu**, is in the northern part of the archipelago. On its south coast is the beautiful sailing anchorage of Savusavu while to the east is **Taveuni**, Fiji's lush "Garden Island". Half of Taveuni is protected as a national park and it's the best place in Fiji to hike through rainforest and encounter the country's rare, native birdlife. Offshore is the stunning Rainbow Reef, aptly named after its colourful soft corals. Far north of Vanua Levu, the tiny Polynesian island of **Rotuma** is politically part of Fiji but so isolated it feels like a different country, with its own language, culture and traditions.

When to go

The most comfortable time to visit is during the **dry season** between May and October when temperatures hover around 25°C by day and drop to a pleasant 19–20°C at night. At this time of year the southerly **trade winds** bring cool breezes off the sea and sometimes blustery conditions on the south and eastern coasts. Coinciding with the southern hemisphere winter, the dry season is also the **busiest** time to visit, with holiday-makers from New Zealand and Australia flocking to Fiji to escape the cold. Hotels in the popular resort areas are often booked out months in advance, especially around the **school holidays** between June and July.

The summer months from November to April are known as the **wet season** when temperatures rise to a fairly constant 31°C but with greatly increased humidity. Rainfall during these months is substantially higher, although most of it falls in sudden torrential **tropical downpours**, usually in the mid-afternoon. Mornings and late afternoons generally remain sunny and the sea is often beautifully **calm** – a great time for scuba divers. During the wet season the islands are lush with vegetation and waterfalls are at their most impressive; however, note that walking trails can get slippery and dirt roads impassable. Low pressure between December and April sometimes brings stormy weather from the northwest lasting around five days. In extreme cases **tropical cyclones** can develop. Direct hits on the islands are infrequent and damage quite localized.

Another aspect of Fiji's weather are the **microclimates** found on the leeward and windward sides of the main islands. For example, Nadi, on the dry west side of Viti Levu, has reliably sunny weather while Suva, on the opposite side of the island but barely 100km away is often drenched by showers rolling in off the ocean.

AVERAGE MONTHLY TEMPERATURES AND RAINFALL

	Jan	Feb	Mar	Apr	May	Jun	Jul	Aug	Sep	Oct	Nov	Dec
NADI												
Max/min (°C)	32/23	32/23	31/23	31/22	30/20	29/19	29/18	28/19	29/20	30/21	31/22	32/22
Max/min (°F)	90/73	90/73	88/73	88/72	86/68	84/66	84/64	82/66	84/68	86/70	88/72	90/72
Rainfall (mm)	343	292	341	160	89	65	45	65	70	102	132	178
SUVA												
Max/min (°C)	31/24	31/24	31/24	30/23	29/22	28/21	27/21	26/20	27/21	28/22	29/23	30/24
Max/min (°F)	88/75	88/75	88/75	86/73	84/72	82/70	81/70	79/68	81/70	82/72	84/73	86/75
Rainfall (mm)	371	265	374	366	270	163	136	158	177	221	245	277

15
things not to miss

It's not possible to see everything that Fiji has to offer in one trip – and we don't suggest you try. What follows is a selective and subjective taste of the islands' highlights: from lush rainforests and quaint villages to the best activities on and off the water. All entries have a page reference to take you straight into the Guide, where you can find out more. Coloured numbers refer to chapters in the Guide section.

1 NAVALA VILLAGE
Page 119

Fiji's most picturesque village, set deep in the highlands of Viti Levu and home to over two hundred traditional handcrafted bures.

2 SAVUSAVU
Page 194

Sipping an ice-cold beer overlooking this stunning bay at sunset is hard to beat.

3 FIJI-INDIAN CULTURE
Page 54

Fiji's Hindu temples come alive throughout the year with vibrant festivals, the most spectacular being at Nadi's colourful Sri Siva Subrahmanya Swami Temple.

4 SNORKELLING
Page 35

With vibrant coral reefs found off almost every beach, Fiji is a fantastic place to slip on a pair of fins and dive in.

11 **HIKING, WAYA ISLAND**
Circumnavigate beautiful Waya Island and hike to the summit for stunning views.

12 **MARKETS**
A slice of real Fiji – the bustling markets sell every imaginable type of exotic fruit, vegetable and seafood.

13 **SPENDING A NIGHT IN A VILLAGE**
Get to know the locals over a nightly brew of *yaqona* in one of Fiji's many rural villages.

14 **DIVING WITH SHARKS**
Encounter mean-looking bull sharks and the odd tiger shark at this open-water, shark-feeding dive off Beqa Island.

15 **BOUMA NATIONAL HERITAGE PARK**
This huge tract of protected rainforest on the beautiful island of Taveuni is home to native birdlife, including parrots and the pretty orange dove.

Itineraries

With 333 islands to choose from, you'll need a focus for your Fijian travels, though any itinerary should include at least one boat trip. Desert-island beaches are most people's image of the country, with good reason, but you'll also find densely forested mountain landscapes, lively towns and resolutely traditional villages. These itineraries will help you explore the highlights.

VILLAGE CULTURE AND IDYLLIC ISLANDS

This itinerary starts with a few days exploring the sights around Nadi, before taking the catamaran to island-hop the resorts of the Yasawas. Allow 12–14 days.

❶ Nadi Though it doesn't provide the most thrilling of starts to a Fijian visit, Nadi is a good place to recover from jetlag and organize any logistics. See p.53

❷ Garden of the Sleeping Giant Located just north of Nadi, this hillside tropical garden is a great scenic stop-off, with a spectacular display of orchids. See p.66

❸ Lautoka A run-of-the-mill Fijian town, Lautoka provides a refreshingly non-touristy experience, and has one of the finest markets in the country. See p.68

❹ Navala With its two hundred thatched bures, Navala is the most beautiful place in Fiji to observe traditional life at close hand. See p.119

❺ Waya Allow another night in Nadi before the early start required for the *Yasawa Flyer* catamaran. The choice of island stop-offs is yours if you buy the Bula Pass, but Waya is one of the highlights, with its rocky peaks and white sand shore. See p.92

❻ Naviti The largest of the Yasawas, Naviti features some great snorkelling opportunities, particularly the blue depths and manta rays of the Drawaqa lagoon. See p.94

❼ The northern Yasawas You'll find a good range of accommodation on these low-lying islands, as well as coral reefs, turquoise lagoons and the limestone caves of Sawa-i-Lau. See p.96

AROUND VITI LEVU

The largest island in Fiji has a little bit of everything: townscapes, ancient sites and gorgeous beaches. This route takes you on an anti-clockwise circuit of the island, with a detour to Ovalau. Allow at least eight days.

❶ Nadi Starting out at Nadi, take the coastal bus southeast around the island along the Queens Road. See p.53

❷ Sigatoka Hop off at the national park at Sigatoka and follow the walking routes through secondary forest and onto sand dunes, where ancient burial sites are regularly revealed by storms. See p.108

❸ Coral Coast Continue east, where the Coral Coast provides a gentle start to any trip, with relaxed, long-established resorts edging the warm seas. See p.112

ABOVE LAVENA COASTAL WALK, TAVEUNI; ANEMONE ON A GORGONIAN FAN

❹ Suva The only real city in Fiji, Suva has plenty of metropolitan charm: colonial architecture, some excellent Fiji-Indian restaurants, bars and clubs and a fine museum. **See p.132**

❺ Ovalau This volcanic island with mountain rainforest is a fascinating diversion from Viti Levu. The highpoint is laid-back Levuka, Fiji's former capital and a World Heritage Site. **See p.168**

❻ Kings Road Back on the main island, continue your circuit by heading back to Nadi via the northern Kings Road. If you have time to dawdle, stop off at some resorts on the way. **See p.127**

VANUA LEVU AND TAVEUNI

Small planes, ferries, speedboats and buses provide the transport for this itinerary through northern Vanua Levu and east to the garden island of Taveuni. Allow ten days to give you time to explore the highlights – Savusavu and Taveuni – with as much leisure as possible.

❶ Labasa From Nadi, take a flight to Labasa. The miniscule airport amongst the sugar cane is a sight in itself. **See p.190**

❷ Savusavu Travel by bus to Savusavu, a small town with hot springs, mountain walks, some decent restaurants and a glorious bay. **See p.194**

❸ Buca Bay dive resorts Bus east to the ferry at Natavu. From here a couple of dive resorts can send a speedboat to collect you, and you can enjoy a few days of utter seclusion. **See p.202**

❹ Taveuni Next make the short ferry crossing to verdant Taveuni. There are some great activities here, including natural rock slides, hikes, snorkelling tours, dives and famous surf breaks. **See p.203**

❺ Suva Another small plane – or a cargo boat trip – takes you to the capital for some urban exploration. **See p.132**

❻ Coral Coast Make your way back to Nadi by bus, via the beach resorts of the Coral Coast. **See p.112**

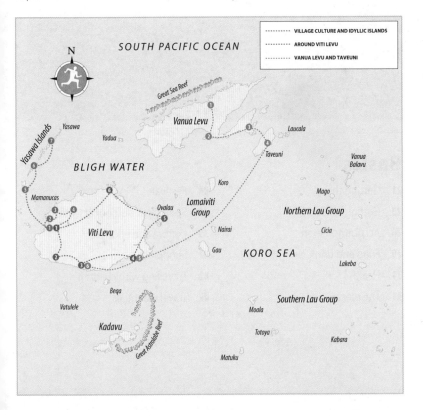

SEA KAYAKING

Basics

Getting there

Fiji is the travel hub for the South Pacific, and a popular stopover on round-the-world tickets. The majority of direct flights arrive from New Zealand, Australia or Los Angeles, and travellers from North America or Europe usually must connect through one of these. Arriving by boat is only possible on a privately chartered yacht, by taking one of the few cruise liners calling in at Lautoka or Suva or by finding passage on a container ship.

If flying from Australia or New Zealand, Fiji's tourism market, you're likely to find heavily discounted airfares and package deals, particularly in the low season between January and April. The majority of travel agents focus on the ever-popular resorts in the Mamanucas, the large hotels along the Coral Coast on the main island and the occasional outer-island boutique retreat.

From North America, the UK or continental Europe, options are more limited, although you should find Fiji as a stopover on many round-the-world tickets. The main tour operators in these regions tend to offer only the large international hotels around Nadi as package holidays. Searching for the best-priced flights, or using frequent-flyer points, then booking more desirable accommodation independently is likely to give you the most options at the lowest price.

Flights from the US and Canada

Fiji-bound travellers from **North America** have two choices for a direct flight to Nadi Airport: Air New Zealand or Fiji Airways. Both have daily flights from **Los Angeles**, with Fiji Airways also having twice weekly flights from **Vancouver via Honolulu**. The eleven-hour nonstop flight from Los Angeles costs from US$850 return, or US$1400 from Vancouver.

Flights from the UK and Europe

From the **UK**, you have the choice of travelling west via North America or east via Asia – it's 16,000km either way. Fares follow the high and low seasons between Europe and North America or Europe and Australia, with June to August and the Christmas holidays being particularly busy, with fewer discounted deals available.

Air New Zealand (W airnz.co.nz) offers a convenient nonstop flight to Fiji **via Los Angeles**

departing daily (except Fri) from Heathrow and costing £1000–1600 – the flight takes 26hr including a four-hour connecting stopover at Los Angeles (unfortunately you have to clear US customs and immigration then re-enter which makes the transit a little frustrating). Air New Zealand also offers a daily eastern route from London Heathrow **via Hong Kong** and New Zealand, although this journey takes 28hr with two stopovers and costs from £1000.

Some of the cheapest direct flights to Fiji from London are **via Seoul** with Korean Air (W korean air.com), costing from £750 if booked via an agent, with the outward journey taking 24hr but the return leg requiring an overnight stop in Seoul with hotel and transfers included in the flight price.

Otherwise, your best option is to find a cheap flight on the route between the UK and **Australia** (costing from £650), and then buy a return flight from either Brisbane or Sydney to Nadi with Virgin Australia, which adds around £300.

Flights from Australia, New Zealand and South Africa

Flights to Fiji are most frequent from **Australia and New Zealand** and both offer competitively priced deals, with reduced fares on the Internet and special offers bundled with accommodation packages.

Two airlines operate flights from **Australia**: Virgin Australia (W virginaustralia.com) and Fiji Airways (W fijiairways.com). Both airlines depart daily from **Brisbane** and **Sydney**, taking about 4hr, with deals often available from A$350 return; Fiji Airways also has four flights a week from **Melbourne** (5hr), costing roughly A$200 more.

> ### A BETTER KIND OF TRAVEL
> At Rough Guides we are passionately committed to travel. We believe it helps us understand the world we live in and the people we share it with – and of course tourism is vital to many developing economies. But the scale of modern tourism has also damaged some places irreparably, and climate change is accelerated by most forms of transport, especially flying. All Rough Guides' flights are carbon-offset, and every year we donate money to a variety of environmental charities.

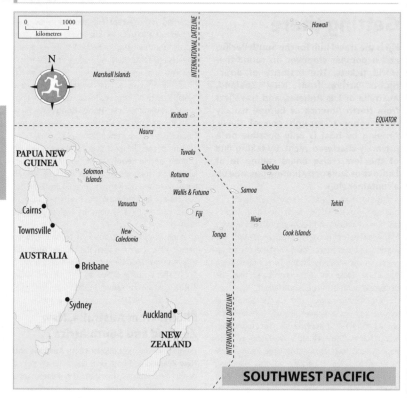

SOUTHWEST PACIFIC

The shorter hop (3hr 5min) from **New Zealand** is generally more expensive, and monopolized by Fiji Airways and Air New Zealand (ⓦairnz.co.nz), with daily flights from **Auckland** starting from NZ$400. There's also a weekly flight from **Christchurch** operated by Fiji Airways taking 4hr (from NZ$500).

The most direct route for travellers from **South Africa** is to fly to Sydney or Auckland and then on to Fiji.

Flights from elsewhere in the Pacific

Flying to Fiji from elsewhere in the South Pacific is not always practical, and often quite expensive, despite Fiji being the main travel hub for the region. Fiji's national airline, Fiji Airways (☎330 4388, ⓦfijiairways.com), flies to Fiji from: Apia, **Samoa** (2 weekly; 1hr 5min; F$485 one way); Funafuti, **Tuvalu** (2 weekly; 2hr 30min; F$780 one way); Honolulu, **Hawaii** (2 weekly; 8hr; F$865 one way); Christmas Island, **Kiribati** (1 weekly; 4hr; F$675 one

way); Tarawa, **Kiribati** (2 weekly; 3hr; F$677 one way); Port Vila, **Vanuatu** (3 weekly; 1hr 30min; F$392 one way); and Nuku'alofa, **Tonga** (2 weekly; 1hr 20min; F$350 one way).

Other regional airlines serving Nadi include: Aircalin from Noumea, **New Caledonia** (ⓦaircalin .com; 3 weekly; 2hr; F$750 one way); Air Vanuatu from Port Vila, **Vanuatu** (ⓦairvanuatu.com; 1 weekly; 1hr 40min; F$390 one way); and Solomon Airlines from Honiara, **Solomon Islands** (ⓦfly solomons.com; 2 weekly; 3hr; F$525 one way). There are no direct flights between Fiji and the Cook Islands, Tahiti or Easter Island – the easiest way to get to Fiji from these eastern Polynesian destinations is via Auckland or Los Angeles.

ONLINE BOOKING

ⓦ **expedia.com**
ⓦ **lastminute.com**
ⓦ **opodo.com**
ⓦ **orbitz.com**
ⓦ **travelocity.com**
ⓦ **zuji.com**

AGENTS AND OPERATORS

Beautiful Pacific Fiji ☎ 672 2600, US ☎ 619 618 0229, UK
☎ 020 8123 8622, Australia ☎ 02 8005 1232, New Zealand
☎ 09 889 0909; ⓦ beautifulpacific.com. South Pacific travel specialist
offering discounted rooms at most beach resorts and adventure retreats.

ebookers UK ☎ 0800 082 3000, Republic of Ireland ☎ 01 488
3507; ⓦ ebookers.com, ⓦ ebookers.ie. Low fares on an extensive
selection of scheduled flights and package deals.

Impulse Fiji Fiji ☎ 672 0600, US ☎ 1-800 953-7595; ⓦ impulse
fiji.com. Postings for last-minute special offers at larger resorts.

North South Travel UK ☎ 01245 608 291, ⓦ northsouthtravel
.co.uk. Friendly, competitive travel agency, offering discounted fares
worldwide. Profits are used to support projects in the developing world,
especially the promotion of sustainable tourism.

Trailfinders UK ☎ 0845 058 5858, Republic of Ireland ☎ 01 77
7888, Australia ☎ 1300 780 212; ⓦ trailfinders.com. One of the
best-informed and most efficient agents for independent travellers.

STA Travel US ☎ 1-800 781-4040, UK ☎ 0871 2300 040, Australia
☎ 134 STA, New Zealand ☎ 0800 474 400, SA ☎ 0861 781 781;
ⓦ statravel.com. Worldwide specialists in independent travel; also
student IDs, travel insurance, car rental and more. Good discounts for
students and under-26s.

Getting to Fiji by boat

Although a romantic proposition, arriving in Fiji **by
boat** is tricky unless on a private yacht – it's a five-
to ten-day journey up from New Zealand
depending on weather, or at least a month's sailing
across the Pacific from the US west coast. Several
large cruise liners visit Fiji but usually spend only a
day at port, either at Lautoka, Suva or Savusavu
before cruising around the islands, perhaps
dropping anchor for snorkelling trips, and then
heading back to the open seas.

Finding passage on a **container ship** was once
one of the great adventures of the Pacific, but most
companies no longer take passengers due to
heightened security concerns. For further information try international shipping agents Andrew Weir
(UK ☎ 020 7575 6480, ⓦ aws.co.uk) or Pacific Forum
Line (NZ ☎ 09 356 2333, ⓦ pacificforumline.com).

If visiting **by yacht**, Fiji has four **ports of entry**:
Suva (☎ 330 2864), Lautoka (☎ 666 7734), Levuka
(☎ 344 0425) and Savusavu (☎ 885 0728). Clearance
must be requested at least 48 hours before arrival:
for the regulations you need to follow go to
(ⓦ www.frca.org.fj/yachts-arrival/). For detailed
sailing info, Yacht Help (☎ 675 0911, ⓦ yachthelp
.com), based at Port Denarau on Viti Levu publishes
the extremely useful and free *Fiji Marine Guide*;
they'll also try and find a yacht charter if you don't
have your own boat. Otherwise, you may find **crew
work** at one of the marinas and possibly passage

on to New Zealand, Australia or California. Most
yachts depart Fiji by September or October before
the start of the hurricane season and start to arrive
again, often having sailed via Tonga or Tahiti, from
May to August.

CRUISES

P&O Cruises Australia ☎ 13 24 69, New Zealand ☎ 0800 951 200;
ⓦ pocruises.com.au. Large passenger cruise ships departing Sydney,
Brisbane and Auckland and visiting various ports including Suva, Lautoka
and Savusavu as well as Beqa and the Yasawas, usually on twelve-day
itineraries.

Soren Larsen New Zealand ☎ 09 817 8799; ⓦ sorenlarsen.co.nz.
New-Zealand-based tall ship adventure cruise broken into twelve
independent legs across the South Pacific. The Fiji leg arrives in Levuka
from Samoa/Tonga in August and spends six days cruising around the
islands before heading on to Vanuatu.

Getting around

**Fiji is spread over a huge area of the
southwest Pacific, covering almost 1.3
million square kilometres. On a map, the
islands may look close enough together
to hop between, but with limited infrastructure this can be a time-consuming
process, often involving back-tracking to
either Nadi or Suva. Viti Levu, the main
island, is extremely well connected by
public transport and easy to explore, as
are the popular beach destinations of
the Mamanucas and Yasawa Islands,
connected by fast catamaran. Exploring
further afield, though, requires patience
and a sense of adventure, with cumber-
some passenger ferries and cargo boats
visiting the outer islands on a weekly or
monthly basis and flights in small
propeller planes landing on gravel and
sometimes even grass airstrips.**

Nadi, on the main island of Viti Levu, is the
nation's tourist hub, home to the international and
main domestic airport and with sea access to the
Mamanucas. **Suva**, 120km away on the opposite
side of the mainland, is the transport hub for all
outer-island shipping, as well as having air access to
ten outer-island airstrips.

On the two largest islands of **Viti Levu** and
Vanua Levu, as well as on **Taveuni**, exceptionally
cheap buses travel around the coast and countryside on a fairly regular basis and carrier vans or taxis
can be hired for private tours. On all other islands,
though, getting around usually involves a boat

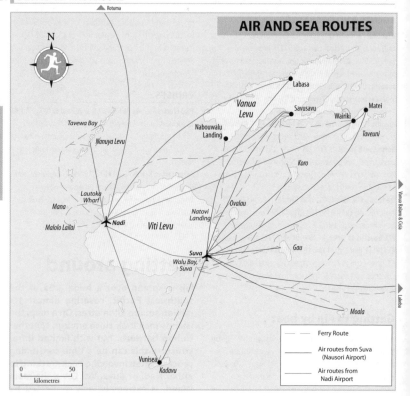

AIR AND SEA ROUTES

N

Rotuma

Labasa

Vanua Levu

Savusavu

Matei

Wairiki

Taveuni

Tavewa Bay

Nabouwalu Landing

Nanuya Levu

Koro

Lautoka Wharf

Mana

Ovalau

Natovi Landing

Nadi

Viti Levu

Malolo Lailai

Suva

Walu Bay, Suva

Gau

Moala

Vunisea

Kadavu

- - - Ferry Route

——— Air routes from Suva (Nausori Airport)

——— Air routes from Nadi Airport

0   50
kilometres

Vanua Balavu & Cicia

Lakeba

journey, often in a small, ten-passenger fibreglass boat with a 60HP single engine, and these, when chartered, are expensive. Hitching a ride with the locals is much cheaper but more often than not boats are filled to the brim, sometimes with as many as twenty large Fijians plus their luggage.

By air

Fiji's **domestic flight network** is dominated by **Pacific Sun**, the domestic arm of the government-owned Fiji Airways (☎330 4388, ⓦfijiairways.com), and served by small twin-propeller planes only. Whilst flying in such aircraft may cause a little nervousness, it is by far the quickest way to get around and there are often excellent **deals** available via the airline's website, with discounts of fifty percent or more available on the main tourist routes. This can make flying almost as cheap as travelling by passenger ferry. **Prices** range from around F\$100 one-way from Nadi to Suva, to F\$400 for the flight from Nadi to far-flung Rotuma. Availability is seldom a problem, except at

Christmas when flights can be booked out months in advance. **Baggage allowance** on internal flights is a meagre 15kg per person. If you plan on travelling with your own scuba diving equipment or surf board check with the airline in advance.

Northern Air (☎992 2449, ⓦnorthernairfiji.com .fj) is based in Waila, Nausori and operates services to Gau, Koro, Levuka, Labasa, Moala and Savusavu.

There are also two **seaplane** companies operating in Fiji: Turtle Airways (☎672 1888, ⓦturtleairways .com) based at Wailoaloa Beach in Nadi, and Pacific Island Air (☎672 5644, ⓦfijiseaplanes.com) based at Nadi Airport. Turtle Airways (☎672 1888, ⓦturtleair ways.com) offers a **daily public flight** to Turtle Island in the northern part of the Yasawas for US\$280 one-way with a minimum of two passengers, but you must pre-arrange a boat to transfer you on to your intended destination – departure times vary and can only be advised the day before based on sea condi-tions. Island Hoppers (☎672 0410, ⓦhelicopters.com .fj) shuttles guests to upmarket resorts by **helicopter**. Baggage allowance on seaplanes and helicopters is 15kg per person, with excess charges thereafter.

For an overview of air routes see the map opposite; details of individual flights are given throughout the Guide.

By passenger ferry and cargo boat

The busy tourist destinations of the Mamanucas are graced by fast **passenger catamarans** offering fabulous views from their upper decks and enclosed air-conditioned seating on the lower levels. By contrast, the bulky and ageing **vehicle and passenger ferries** visiting Kadavu, Vanua Levu, Taveuni and the Lomaiviti Group suffer particularly from sea swell, and often meander around an erratic schedule. Christmas is especially hectic, with over-laden boats common during the summer school break from early December to late January, while rough seas often disrupt schedules between December and April. While the service to the Yasawas is fairly pricey (F$147 for 5 days' travel), it only costs around F$80 for the long trip from Lautoka to Savusavu.

Cargo boats (see box, p.180) have been plying Fiji's waters since the pioneering days of the late nineteenth century, bringing in trade, exporting copra and connecting the people with the outside world. It is still common practice for passengers to join cargo boats supplying the outer islands, usually sitting and sleeping on deck amidst barrels of oil, boxes of tinned meat and bunches of bananas. For those with a little time and a spirit of adventure, it's a chance to rub shoulders with Fijians from all walks of life, and it's cheap and cheerful, too: the route from Suva to Kadavu, for example, will set you back around F$50 one way.

For an overview of sea routes see the map opposite; details of individual ferries and cargo ships are given throughout the Guide.

By bus

With no rail service and few people owning cars, **buses** are the only practical way for the public to affordably get around the large islands of Viti Levu and Vanua Levu. Both islands have reliable, frequent and **exceptionally cheap** bus services operating out of all town centres. Buses usually have open-sided windows and visit almost every rural location imaginable, be it along a dirt road, up a steep mountain or over narrow wooden planks bridging rivers and stopping when requested.

Express buses run between major towns on **Viti Levu**. The five-hour journey between Nadi and Suva costs around F$20. Most buses are rather dated with hard cushioned seats and sliding windows but the tourist operator Coral Sun runs a modern air-conditioned soft-seated coach for double the price. You should also consider the air-conditioned tourist bus operator Feejee Experience (see p.107) which circumnavigates the main island on a four-day adventure journey. A very limited bus schedule operates on **Ovalau** and **Taveuni**, mostly for shuttling kids back and forth from school, but on all other islands buses are non-existent.

Minivans and carrier vans

Also running in urban centres and speeding along the main roads are ten-seater **minivans**, which stop by the roadside to pick up waiting passengers for the same fare as a bus. Many operate illegally and drive carelessly but if your only consideration is to get from A to B quickly and cheaply, they're a good option. More basic **carrier vans**, with an open back usually covered by tarpaulin and with a wooden bench along each side, travel along the rural dirt roads carrying people and their produce between the villages and town markets.

By car

On the main island of Viti Levu **a car** is without doubt the best way to explore the countryside. Although buses and carrier vans travel to most regions, the freedom to stop at will for photos, to chat with locals along the way and simply to travel at your own convenience is both pleasurable and time saving. **Renting a car** is straightforward using your home licence, but you must be aged 21 or older. Rates are relatively cheap, starting at F$65 per day including insurance (twenty percent more on Vanua Levu and Taveuni due to less competition and poor road conditions), but the relatively high cost of fuel makes longer trips quite expensive. Prices are fixed by the government.

It's a good idea to rent a **4WD**, or, at the very least, a car with high clearance – most roads off the coastal highway are unsealed, of compacted dirt and often littered with crater-sized pot holes; with rain (and it often rains in the mountains) these roads become very slippery and sometimes impassable without a 4WD. Rental companies tend to void insurance for breakdowns or accidents on dirt roads so check in detail beforehand.

The same facts apply to Vanua Levu, but renting is not so straightforward, with only a couple of rental firms in Savusavu and Labasa, and these with only a few cars available, so pre-booking is advisable. The only other island where you can rent a car is Taveuni.

Driving tips

Driving between towns along the sealed coastal road of Viti Levu is very straightforward, but turning off this road can be intimidating, with absolutely no **signposts** and roads splitting and veering in every direction. Keep an eye open for the tiny white roadside markers which indicate distance from set points, usually from major towns or turn-offs and the main connecting roads. There are no decent maps available to help navigation in the countryside – the only option is to ask for directions along the way.

The most common **hazards** apart from the potholes are mindless pedestrians and stray animals. Driving is on the left, with the **speed limit** generally set at 40kmph through towns, 60kmph in the suburbs and 80kmph elsewhere. If you **break down**, call your car rental company which should provide you with a 24hr service number – but be warned there are few telephones along the roadside and mobile phone coverage is pretty sporadic in rural areas.

Car rental

The following major **car rental** companies have offices at Nadi Airport, where you can arrange a rental before your trip. Independent local companies are listed throughout the Guide.

CAR RENTAL AGENCIES

Avis US and Canada ☎ 1-800 331-1212, UK ☎ 0870 606 0100, Republic of Ireland ☎ 021 428 1111, Australia ☎ 13 63 33 or 02 9353 9000, New Zealand ☎ 09 526 2847 or 0800 655 111; ⓦ avis.com.

Budget US ☎ 1-800 527-0700, Canada ☎ 1-800 268-8900, UK ☎ 0870 156 5656, Australia ☎ 1300 362 848, New Zealand ☎ 0800 283 438; ⓦ budget.com.

Hertz US & Canada ☎ 1-800 654-3131, UK ☎ 020 7026 0077, Republic of Ireland ☎ 01 870 5777, New Zealand ☎ 0800 654 321; ⓦ hertz.com.

Thrifty US and Canada ☎ 1-800 847-4389, UK ☎ 01494 751 500, Republic of Ireland ☎ 01 844 1950, Australia ☎ 1300 367 227, New Zealand ☎ 09 256 1405; ⓦ thrifty.com.

Taxis

Getting about **by taxi** in Nadi and Suva is cheap and practical, regulated by the government with flag fall set at F$1.50 between 6am and 10pm (F$2 outside these hours), plus 10 cents for every 100m travelled, all calculated by meter. Competition is fierce, with unlicensed minivans scouring the streets and picking up passengers along the way, charging 50 cents for an inter-urban journey.

Hiring a taxi for rural **sightseeing** or travel between towns is a good option if you don't want to drive yourself, and works out as a cheap alternative if travelling with three or more people. Negotiate a rate beforehand and expect to pay around F$30 per hour depending on how far you want to travel.

By bicycle and motor scooter

There are few **cyclists** to be found on Fiji's shoulderless, potholed roads, and good reason for it – cyclists are shown little courtesy from motorists. However, exploring rural Viti Levu or Vanua Levu by bicycle will certainly draw attention and conversation when passing through villages and should be a great adventure for those confident enough to try. Unless you bring your own bike though, you'll have to buy one in Nadi, Suva or Labasa, but don't expect quality. The only place you're able to rent **bicycles** is at a few large resorts, with Denarau Island off Nadi and Malolo Lailai in the Mamanucas being the main contenders.

Motor scooters are extremely rare except in Nadi, where they are something of a novelty. Travelling along the busy town roads is practical, though not particularly safe and you should certainly expect the unexpected with motorists who seem to be blind to anything on two wheels. Travel beyond the town area is not recommended.

Accommodation

For a developing country, Fiji is a fairly expensive place to visit, with room prices and standards closer to those in Australia than Southeast Asia. However, at many budget island resorts and some of the more remote, upmarket boutique resorts, meals and some activities are included, making the price seem more expensive than it actually is. On the outer islands there's usually nowhere else to eat other than the resort restaurant, which can inflate the cost of staying. Nevertheless, there's great diversity around the islands, with some resorts dedicated to scuba diving, surfing or ecotours while others specialize in relaxation and fine dining.

ACCOMMODATION PRICES

Unless noted otherwise, the prices for all accommodation reviewed in this guide refer to the least expensive double or twin room at standard rack rates including all taxes.

Outside of the main towns, almost every place to stay is on a beach or overlooking the sea and called a **resort**, regardless of its amenities. The highest concentrations of accommodation are in Nadi and along the south coast of Viti Levu, which are the **best-value** places to stay, and in the Mamanucas, which are graced with delightful beach resorts from budget to upmarket. There are slimmer but adequate sprinklings of hostels, retreats and boutique resorts around rural Viti Levu and on the outer islands of Kadavu, Ovalau, Vanua Levu and Taveuni, the last of these also being popular for longer stays and holiday homes. Beyond, in the remote outliers of the Lomaiviti Group, the Lau Group and Rotuma, accommodation is scarce and provisions and general infrastructure are basic.

For those travelling on a **budget**, there are plenty of affordable beach resorts all around the islands, with cheap hotel rooms and dorm beds in most towns. Obtaining **discounts** direct from the resorts is difficult, although the large international hotels usually run tempting website promotions. The best bet is to seek out accommodation-only deals via the Internet.

Several companies specialize in diving, kayaking and ecotour holidays in Fiji. See "Sports and outdoor activities", p.35, for information on these niche operators.

Rates

The majority of resorts quote everything in the **local currency** of Fijian dollars (F$), although a few of the upmarket resorts, particularly those focusing on the US market, quote in US$.

All rates in Fiji are quoted **per room** and not per person, unless for dorm beds. Only a few places, mostly urban hotels and hostels, offer single-person room rates. Almost all published prices include local **taxes** which are currently 15 percent for VAT and 5 percent for Hotel Turnover Tax. Once in Fiji, **walk-in rates** at some resorts are given if requested, although seldom at the backpacker hostels. To encourage longer stays, many resorts offer a "stay six/pay five" incentive or similar. Rooms overlooking the beach and ocean are sold at a premium but note that terminology is often ambiguous – a "beachfront" bure may not be right on the beach and an "ocean view" room may only have a partial glimpse of the sea through trees or other buildings.

For the most part, everything from food to activities within a hotel or resort is charged to your room and paid for at the end of your stay by **credit card**, though usually only Visa and MasterCard are accepted, sometimes with a small card-service fee, so check beforehand. Paying **tips** to individuals is not encouraged, but communal staff fund boxes are usually left on reception counters and distributed to staff as a Christmas bonus or used for community projects.

Hotels and inns

On the main island of Viti Levu, particularly on Denarau Island and along the Coral Coast, you'll find a dozen or so large **hotel complexes**. Facilities include air-conditioned rooms with flat-screen TVs, huge swimming pools with swim-up bars, multiple restaurants with international cuisine, souvenir shops, spas, gyms, tennis courts, kids' clubs and jet-skis. Unlike the huge US all-inclusive resorts, the majority are "pay as you go", giving you the freedom to eat where you want and to do as little or as much as you wish. You'll also find smaller, cheaper **hotels and inns** around the Coral Coast, some offering self-catering air-conditioned rooms, others with small restaurants; these usually have few watersports or

BURES

The most common style of accommodation in Fiji is a **bure**, an open-plan traditionally-styled building with high ceilings and thatch roofing ensuring natural ventilation. At the upmarket resorts, bures are exquisite handcrafted palaces, usually with king-sized beds, walk-in showers and wood floors, while at a backpacker resort you can expect thin bamboo walls, a simple foam mattress, no electricity and a shared communal bathroom. At some of the mid-range and larger resorts, a bure is often an A-frame wooden structure split into two or four rooms and referred to as a duplex or quad bure.

TYING THE KNOT

Fiji is a beautiful and relatively stress-free place to get married and most resorts offer **wedding packages** with ceremonies held on the beachfront. For those with large groups in attendance, getting married on the main island of Viti Levu is more convenient, but the atmosphere on the offshore islands is far more intimate and a much better option for smaller parties. Amongst the best options are *Octopus Resort* (see p.94) and *Oarsman's Bay Lodge* (see p.99) in the Yasawas; *Matamanoa Island Resort* (see p.88) and *Treasure Island Resort* (see p.81), in the Mamanuca Islands. If getting married on the **beach**, find out about the tides and sun direction before fixing a time. Early-morning weddings are worth considering as it's not only cooler and less windy, but also less likely to rain – there's nothing more dampening than reciting your vows at a makeshift altar in the resort restaurant.

The practicalities of obtaining a **marriage licence** are very straightforward and all resorts will help with the paperwork. For more information contact ⓦ www.fijinet.com.

---

amenities available except for a swimming pool. Apart from two large beach hotels in the Mamanucas, the majority of places to stay in the outer islands are small, intimate boutique resorts.

Boutique resorts

A small **boutique resort** spanning a secluded beach on a remote island is Fiji's speciality. Some have as few as three bures, others up to fifty, but all focus on providing exceptional service. A few of the more upmarket boutique resorts are all-inclusive affairs, some even including alcoholic beverages in the price. The majority have 24hr reception, small shops, room service, nightly turn-down, restaurants and sunset bars as well as scuba diving and spa/massage facilities. Perhaps the only drawback is the lack of freedom to sightsee or choose where to eat, although for most people this simply makes the experience more relaxing.

Guesthouses and homestays

Guesthouses in Fiji tend to be colonial-style wooden buildings with simple rooms, communal lounges and shared bathrooms. They are usually cheap, with rooms costing less than F$60, and make convenient bases for travellers wanting to explore off the tourist trail; note that guesthouses are often used by government contract workers in the outer islands or remote settlements.

More appealing to tourists are the handful of **bed and breakfasts** around the country. Those in Nadi and Suva on the main island attract business travellers, whilst several charming homestays and self-contained cottages in the small towns on Vanua Levu, Ovalau and Taveuni are mostly operated by expatriates and charge from F$100 per night and up.

Homestays are operated by local families who either open up their homes to travellers (offering absolute immersion into Fijian culture), or build tourist bures just outside the village, which gives both parties a little privacy. Homestays commonly cost F$60 per person per night including meals, sometimes served with the family and laid out on the floor, Fijian style. See p.40 for more about village stays.

Hostels and backpacker resorts

There's a huge amount of **budget accommodation** in Fiji, although those expecting Southeast Asian prices are likely to be disappointed. Although the more shambolic operations don't last for long, standards are variable. Members of the Fiji Backpacker Association (ⓦ fiji-backpacking.com) are usually reliable, as are those promoted by Awesome Adventures (ⓦ awesomefiji.com), although by staying at these established places you'll be missing out on the quirky places which offer a real insight into Fiji. Spending a few days in Nadi and meeting other travellers is a sure way to get on the grapevine and suss out where's new and happening.

The term "hostel" usually refers to a town boarding house aimed specifically at locals. A more common name is "**backpacker resort**", and these can be found throughout the islands and even in Nadi. Most have rooms or lodges crammed with dorm beds, but often the price of a simple double room or bure is the same as two dorm beds.

Student discount cards are not widely accepted – if you've travelled around Australia or New Zealand and already have one you may be able to save yourself around ten percent at certain places. The Australian-operated Nomads

(@ nomadsworld.com) and VIP Backpackers (@ vipbackpackers.com) both have affiliates in Nadi but there's no YHA.

Camping

Wild camping is not encouraged in Fiji – it's perceived by Fijians as an insult, as if you're saying the local village is not good enough to sleep in. However, several backpacker resorts permit pitching of tents within their resort grounds and several organized tours, with the consent of village landowners, make temporary camp on secluded beaches.

Food and drink

Until fairly recently Fiji was a bit of a culinary backwater, with very basic Indian and Chinese restaurants dominating the high streets and most resorts serving unimaginative international cuisine. However much has changed: both Nadi and Suva boast stylish and reasonably priced restaurants serving everything from Italian to Japanese food, and it's also now easier to find well-presented traditional Fijian cuisine. Out on the resorts, internationally acclaimed chefs have been brought in to raise the cooking standards expected by upmarket travellers.

Fijian cuisine

Fijian cuisine includes plenty of locally caught bony reef fish cooked in rich coconut cream, and sometimes *kai* mussels, mud crabs and even lobster, but little meat except for slow-cooked pig

(taro) on a special occasion. When the seas are rough or the season's pickings are slender, Fijians resort to imported fatty mutton and tinned corned beef, the latter perceived as something of a delicacy and often served up by the carton at ceremonial functions.

Appearing at every mealtime is a hefty portion of starchy **rootcrop**, either cassava (a bland and extremely dry tuber), *dalo* (known as *taro* in Polynesia, a large corn) or yams (huge tubers, sometimes two metres long, and the most flavoursome of the three rootcrops). **Vegetables** are less common, with the most popular being *bele*, a green, sometimes slimy, leaf, and *rourou*, the leaf of the *dalo* crop which if cooked too quickly causes an itchy sensation to the throat. The availability of **fruit** is dependent on the season (see p.30).

Traditional Fijian dishes include: **kokoda**, made from a large fish, usually tuna or wahoo, chopped into chunks, marinated overnight in lime juice and chillies, seasoned with coconut cream and served cold; **palusami**, coconut cream wrapped up in the leaf of *dalo* and slow cooked (delicious); and the kids' favourite **vakalolo**, a sticky pudding made from cassava mixed with sugar and thick coconut cream and best served with ice cream and bananas. Fish in *lolo* (coconut cream) with cassava or *dalo* is served as counter food in most high-street restaurants, but finding the more delicate dishes of kokoda, palusami, *vakalolo* or lovo suckling pig is more challenging: *Nadina* in Nadi (see p.62) and *Old Mill Cottage* in Suva (see p.144) are two of the few restaurants serving traditional Fijian cuisine.

Fiji-Indians tend to be more adventurous in taste, relying on home-cooked curries, often made of freshly picked vegetables seasoned with hot chillies and other spices, accompanied by home-made chutney but usually drowned in oil or ghee.

THE LOVO

In pre-European times, the Fijian islanders cooked food in bamboo strips on an open fire but, with increased trade with the Tongans, the underground oven or **lovo** was adopted. To make a lovo, a hole is dug in the soil, laid with wood over which black volcanic stones are placed. A fire is lit, the stones are heated and the food, wrapped carefully in banana leaves or tin foil, is placed on top. The main constituents are usually a whole pig at the bottom with *dalo*, yam, chicken, fish and palusami laid on top in order to give each the correct amount of cooking. The hole is covered with coconut leaves with soil spread on top sealing in the heat and cooking the food slowly (anything from an hour to five hours depending on size). Most Fijian families prepare a lovo early Sunday morning before heading to church so it is ready for eating at lunch. Lovos also form the heart of ceremonial feasting at weddings, funerals and any other communal gathering.

Seasonal fruit and vegetables

While they are available in supermarkets, **imported fresh ingredients** are often too expensive for Fijians and the resorts have been encouraged by successive governments to source more produce locally. The results are slowly being realized, giving Fijians a new source of income.

The availability of **fruit** and some vegetables is determined by the seasons, with local produce extremely cheap when in abundance – **bananas**, **pawpaw** (also known as papaya) and **coconuts** are available year-round. Expensive imports including apples, oranges and melons bolster lows in productivity. The following is a list of fruits grown extensively in Fiji:

January Watermelon, pineapple, vi (Tahitian apple), avocado, vutu (small nut, similar to almond), guava, lemon.

February Pineapple, vi, avocado, guava, lemon, lvi (Tahitian chestnut).

March Guava, lemon, lvi, mandarin, orange.

April Guava, lemon, lvi, mandarin, orange.

May Lemon, mandarin, orange, daruka (Fijian asparagus).

June Mandarin, orange, passionfruit, tarawao (small, round and crunchy with a hard seed), dawa (Fijian lychee), watermelon, soursop (large spiky looking fruit with lots of hard seeds, creamy in texture).

July Passionfruit, tarawao (tiny hard, sour fruit), dawa, watermelon, soursop.

August Kavika (wax apple), soursop.

September Mango, pineapple, kavika, soursop.

October Mango, pineapple, kavika, jackfruit.

November Mango, pineapple, jackfruit, vi (Tahitian apple), breadfruit, vutu.

December Watermelon, pineapple, vi (Tahitian apple), breadfruit, avocado, vutu.

Breakfast and lunch

Breakfast at resorts inevitably includes fresh fruit and a continental-style buffet with freshly baked breads and cereals. In the Fijian home it's often a much heartier affair, with a large plate of boiled rice or cassava, fish if caught the night before, heavy pancakes, sweet tea and plain biscuits.

Lunch is the most commonly overlooked meal in Fiji, and many tourists often find it too hot to consider eating anything substantial, with salads and quick snacks most popular.

Dinner and eating out

Dinner is usually taken early, and you'll find all restaurants open by 6pm and often winding down by 9pm, or perhaps 10pm on busy nights. At independent restaurants mains start from F$9 and seldom rise above F$40 even in Nadi and Suva.

Dinner at **resort restaurants** is always more expensive, and at most island resorts it's your only option, with mains starting around F$15 and often reaching F$50 or more. **Buffet dinners** are popular at the large resorts, particularly the weekly Fijian lovo night (costing from F$50–80 a person), when a suckling pig and root crops are cooked in an underground oven and usually preceded by a traditional dance.

Drinks

Fijians have a reputation for enjoying a **drink**, always in company and often to excess, be it the national drink, **yaqona** (known as kava in Polynesian countries; see box opposite), beer or local dark rum. Drinking sessions are invariably all-male affairs with a single glass or cup passed around in rotation and the contents swallowed in one gulp – a sure way of ending up drunk quickly. If out at a bar or nightclub, **closing time** is usually 1am, although on Saturday everything must close by midnight to avoid being open on a Sunday.

Beer

The four labels of local **beer** are passable, all highly carbonated lagers brewed in Suva under a subsidiary of the Australian Fosters Group. Fiji Bitter (4.6 percent alcohol) is the most palatable. Lighter in taste but of similar strength are Fiji Gold, Fiji Export and Fiji Premium, all more popular with tourists. Fiji Bitter comes in two sizes: 375ml "stubbies" and the larger 750ml "long necks", popular with the locals; Gold comes in stubbies only, Export in cans and Premium in clear bottles. In the shops a stubby costs around F$3, in the local bars it's anything from F$3.50 to F$6 and in the resorts it starts at F$6. Draft Fiji Bitter can be found at the more upmarket bars and resorts and is infinitely better tasting. Imported bottled beer, mostly lagers from Australia, cost a few dollars more. If you thirst for a draught Guinness you'll need to head to O'Reillys Bar in Suva.

Rum and other spirits

Rum, brewed from local sugar in Lautoka, is popularly referred to as "wash down", drunk after a yaqona session to sweeten the palate. The smooth, mellow Bounty Dark Rum brand has won several international awards and costs around F$40 for a 750ml bottle. Both dark and white rum are regular ingredients in the gorgeous **cocktails** concocted by resort barmen – these usually cost anywhere

YAQONA

Also known as *kava* or more simply "grog", **yaqona** is Fiji's national drink. Made from the pounded roots of the pepper plant (*piper methysticum*), it has an earthy, rather bitter taste and resembles muddy water. Although it takes some getting used to, *yaqona* (pronounced "yan-go-na") is refreshing and has a relaxing effect upon the body. Drunk socially by Fijians and Fiji-Indians, it is also used in formal situations and will be offered as part of a **ceremony** to welcome you to a village.

The ritual begins with the presentation of your *sevusevu*, or introductory gift (see p.40), accompanied by a speech by the village herald. After this, the *yaqona* roots are mixed with water in a carved bowl (*tanoa*) while all participants sit in a circle on the floor. Once ready, the drink is served in a half coconut shell known as a *bilo*. It is presented first to the chief and then to any guests. When it's your turn to drink, cup your hands, clap once and say "**bula**" (cheers); you then take the cup and down the contents in one go. Return the cup to the bearer and clap your hands again three times, proclaiming "**maca**", a signal of gratification. The formal ceremony ends when the *tanoa* bowl is empty, indicated by a round of clapping. Throughout the ceremony it's considered bad manners to talk, turn your back on the chief or to point your feet towards the *tanoa* bowl.

After a few cups of *yaqona* you may notice your tongue and lips become numb, a temporary effect caused by the active ingredients in the root. Consuming *yaqona* in large quantities can case **drowsiness**, so avoid driving or going swimming immediately after drinking it.

from F$20 to F$30 although happy-hour prices are substantially discounted. Locally brewed gin and vodka are less appealing.

It's worth noting that you can buy up to 2.25 litres of **duty-free liquor** on arrival at Nadi Airport beside the luggage carousel before clearing customs.

Wine

Wine is usually imported from Australia and New Zealand – a reasonable bottle will cost F$25 in a bottle shop, and perhaps double that in a restaurant. BYO is not a common practice but some restaurants do permit this, with a corkage fee around F$10. In the villages, **home-made wine** made from pineapples, watermelon or oranges is worth trying if offered.

Soft drinks

Despite the abundance of fruit, freshly squeezed **fruit juices** and smoothies can be hard to come by in towns or even resort bars. However, you will find that Fijians are amazingly adept at shinning up tall palm trees, felling a **coconut**, slicing its top off and offering the milky contents as a refreshing drink. Trying one is something of a must-do in Fiji.

Tap water in towns is filtered and chlorinated and on the whole safe to drink, although it's best avoided after heavy rains when sediment often appears. Chilled, sweetened tap water mixed with fresh limes is sold from glass tanks at all town markets. At rural and outer-island resorts, water is

sourced from natural springs or wells, although for drinking purposes **rainwater** collected in tanks is preferable. Brackish well water is sometimes a problem, and in places of scarcity, especially in the Mamanucas, desalination plants have been installed which often give a slightly saline taste to the water and anything made from it.

Bottled water, for which Fiji is globally renowned, costs around F$3 for a large 1.5-litre bottle in the shops, depending on brand, but at least triple that in the resorts. Fiji Water, owned by a private American company and hugely popular in the US, is sourced from a deep well beneath the Nakauvadra Range in northern Viti Levu, with a multi-million dollar bottling plant at Yaqara. Other local brands include VTY, a pun on Fiji Water (*Viti* is Fiji and *Wai* is water in Fijian), Island Chill and Aqua Pacific, all sourced on Viti Levu.

Health

Fiji presents few major health issues for visitors. The most common problems are sunburn and/or heat stroke caused by overexposure to the tropical sun; fungal ear infections from swimming, which are easily cured with ear drops; mosquito or sand fly bites; and on rare occasions, fish poisoning.

No **vaccinations** are required to enter Fiji unless you are coming from a yellow fever area, in which

DENGUE FEVER

Although there is **no malaria** in Fiji, occasionally **dengue fever** outbreaks occur. It's a similar but not nearly as threatening disease – the last widespread outbreak was in early 2014. Outbreaks are usually restricted to urban areas after prolonged heavy rains and are acted upon swiftly by the authorities with spraying to kill the dengue-spreading mosquitoes – it's only the black and white striped **day-biting mosquito** that causes dengue infection. If you become infected, tell-tale signs include **aching joints** accompanied by intense headaches, a sudden high fever, chills, nausea and sometimes a red rash which usually first appears on the lower limbs or chest. The symptoms will last anywhere from five to fifteen days. Although the recommended cure is simple – stay in bed, drink plenty of water and wait it out – it's advisable to consult a doctor. In more severe cases, a doctor will administer intravenous fluids to prevent dehydration and acetaminophen to reduce fever. **Avoid aspirin** as this can often cause complications. Whilst the fever is rarely life-threatening in fit adults, the elderly and children are prone to complications and death can result – if an outbreak is present, take extra precautions against being bitten by mosquitoes.

case you need to have an International Health Certificate indicating that you have been immunized against yellow fever sometime in the past ten years. Vaccination against Hepatitis A is often recommended by independent medical advisories. Isolated outbreaks of typhoid have occurred on Vanua Levu in recent years during the wet season.

Heat stroke

Heat stroke is a serious and sometimes fatal condition that can result from long periods of exposure to high temperatures and high humidity. The wisest approach is to always wear a high SPF **sunscreen** (over 35), even in cloudy weather, not forgetting your lips, ears, feet and back; wear a wide-brimmed hat and sunglasses; **drink plenty of water**, generally a litre every two hours, bearing in mind that room-temperature water is better for you in the tropics and that drinking alcohol is going to add to your dehydration; and **cover up** when out snorkelling by wearing a T-shirt to protect your back, still with sun cream on, and wear a long-sleeve shirt with a collar when out walking. Better still, stay in the shade.

Symptoms of heat stroke include nausea and general discomfort, fatigue, a high body temperature, severe headache, disorientation and/or little or no perspiration despite the heat. Eventually the sufferer can become delirious and fall into convulsions, and rapid medical treatment is essential. First aid is to seek shade, remove the victim's clothing, wrap them in a cool, wet sheet or towels and fan around them.

Drinking water

Although urban **tap water** is filtered, chlorinated and safe to drink, travellers with sensitive stomachs should consider boiling it first or buying bottled water, especially after heavy rains when tap water can appear murky. In rural Viti Levu and the outer islands water is mostly sourced from natural springs which may appear extremely pure but can cause upset stomachs – most travellers are encouraged to buy bottled water or drink rain water which is usually supplied to guests free of charge from large tanks and which is less likely to be contaminated. Drinking from a pristine stream whilst out walking in the forests might be tempting but it's not recommended as water-borne diseases such as bilharzia and leptospirosis can be present.

Bites and stings

Mosquitoes can easily spoil an otherwise perfect evening under the stars. They are most widespread during the **wet season** from December to April, although even during these times you may not be bothered by them. Most resorts spray gardens to keep mosquitoes at bay, but in less-developed parts of the islands they can be voracious, almost unbearable at dusk and dawn when it may be wise to stay indoors or sit by the sea, preferably facing a stiff wind. Most resorts have well-screened windows, but if these are not present, a **mosquito net** and/or mosquito repellent should be used. Mosquito nets are quite romantic to sleep under but do add to the stuffiness, especially in the humid nights of summer. The best type of **repellent** is the Good Knight electric mat heaters which cost around F$4 from supermarkets, plus F$1.50 for a packet of ten mats, one mat being sufficient per night. You'll need constant electricity to use them and when this isn't available, you may have to resort to mosquito coils, which can be slightly noxious on inhalation. **Roll-on mosquito repellent** works for both mosquitoes and sand flies on a temporary basis, and there are now brands that are more environmentally sensitive and safer on your skin – try Rid, an Australian product costing around F$10 a bottle and available from most pharmacies.

Sand flies can cause irritating rashes through their bites, usually spreading over a larger area than a mosquito bite, and are found not surprisingly along sandy beaches, appearing at dusk and dawn. **Sea lice** can also cause a small rash and appear on occasions in sandy-bottom shallow lagoons between December and April.

Ciguatera fish poisoning

Ciguatera fish poisoning is a fairly common ailment amongst rural Fijians and can be caught by **consuming reef fish** which have been feeding on toxic algae. Although seldom life-threatening, the poisoning causes nausea, diarrhoea, vomiting and a numbness or tingling sensation often in the fingers; it usually commences within 24 hours of consumption. If you believe you have the symptoms of ciguatera, head straight to a doctor or local hospital where you can receive treatment via an injection. Although not confined to any particular fish, it is most common in older and larger reef fish, typically grouper, red snapper, Spanish mackerel and barracuda. Most villagers know which fish to avoid at certain times of the year.

MEDICAL RESOURCES FOR TRAVELLERS
US AND CANADA
CDC ☎ 1 877 394 8747, ⓦ cdc.gov/travel. Official US government travel health site.
International Society for Travel Medicine ☎ 1 770 736 7060, ⓦ istm.org. Has a full list of travel health clinics.
Canadian Society for International Health ⓦ csih.org. Extensive list of travel health centres.

AUSTRALIA, NEW ZEALAND AND SOUTH AFRICA
Travellers' Medical and Vaccination Centre ☎ 1300 658 844, ⓦ tmvc.com.au. Lists travel clinics in Australia, New Zealand and South Africa.

UK AND IRELAND
British Airways Travel Clinics
☎ 0845 600 2236, ⓦ ww.britishairways.com/travel/health clinintro/public/en_gb for nearest clinic.
Hospital for Tropical Diseases Travel Clinic ☎ 0845 155 5000 or ☎ 020 7387 4411, ⓦ thehtd.org.
MASTA (Medical Advisory Service for Travellers Abroad) ⓦ masta.org or ☎ 0870 606 2782 for the nearest clinic.
Travel Medicine Services ☎ 028 9031 5220.
Tropical Medical Bureau Republic of Ireland ☎ 1850 487 674, ⓦ tmb.ie.

The media

Fiji's media has often been suppressed under military rule, and tends towards the bland and parochial. When conventional media has been censored, the Internet has proven invaluable in distributing the views of Fijians, notably through blogs often written by critical emigrants living outside of Fiji.

Newspapers and magazines

Of the English-language daily **newspapers**, the *Fiji Times* (ⓦ fijitimes.com), owned by Rupert Murdoch's News Corporation, is the most dominant, with the broadest international coverage. Its closest rival is the locally owned *Fiji Sun* (ⓦ fijisun.com.fj), a slightly more tabloid-style publication.

Radio

The part-government-owned Fiji Broadcasting Corporation (ⓦ fbc.com.fj) operates six **radio stations**, two each in Fijian, Fiji-Hindi and English; of these, one focuses on news and community issues, the other music and chat. For Fijian music try Bula FM (FM102.4 in Nadi) – all stations have varying FM frequencies depending on location. The independent Communications Fiji Limited (ⓦ www .cfl.com.fj) broadcasts five mostly music stations, two Fiji-Hindi, one Fijian and the popular English music and gossip stations – FM96 and Legend FM (FM106.8).

Television

Fiji has three free-to-air **television** channels. Fiji One's programming is almost exclusively in English, with only a few locally produced shows, the rest being sourced from the US, UK and New Zealand.

The one-hour *Fiji News* is shown daily at 6pm, with mostly local content and a smattering of international headlines. Mai Television is sports orientated, and FBC TV has attempted to raise the standard of local news broadcasting.

Festivals

Ethnic Fijians tend to express their culture in day-to-day life rather than through specific festivals. By contrast, Fiji-Indians celebrate most events with gusto, whether it's a local wedding, religious festival or one of the many fascinating firewalking ceremonies held around the country. The country enjoys twelve public holidays; the most likely of these to feature traditional dance and other public displays are Ratu Lala Sukuna Day on May 30 and Fiji Day on October 10.

The main **towns** of Nadi, Lautoka and Suva each have a commercially driven week-long **festival** (see calendar below) with fairground rides, food stalls, parades, beauty-queen crowning and an alternative Priscilla night when gays and transvestites take centre stage. The town festivals held in Levuka and Savusavu are more culturally inclined.

Indian festivals are commonly celebrated in public and with great fanfare, with Diwali the biggest and loudest for Hindus and Eid a serious affair for Muslims – towns with a large Fiji-Indian population are naturally the best, especially Lautoka and Tavua on Vanua Levu or Labasa on Vanua Levu. There are over forty Indian **firewalking** ceremonies held around the country between April and September. These are fascinating and very spiritual experiences – ask around at local temples to find out where one is being held. The two largest are listed below.

JANUARY

Coconut Tree Climbing Competition 1 Jan. Held at Denarau Island, this zany event tests the skills of Fiji's most daring personalities.

Thaipusam Festival End Jan with main day being the last Sat. This ten-day Hindu festival at the Nadi temple (see p.54) has devotees piercing their bodies and dragging chariots using meat hooks.

MARCH

Holi One day after full moon, usually early March. Hindu festival celebrated with throwing of coloured turmeric powder, feasting and the singing of religious poems.

APRIL

Indian fire walking First Sun after the full moon. Held at the Malolo Temple south of Nadi, with devotees walking across a pit of burning wood embers.

MAY

Rotuma Day 13 May. Dance and feasting amongst Rotumans throughout Fiji to celebrate Rotuma's cession to Fiji and Britain.

Ratu Sir Lala Sukuna Day 30 May. Public holiday remembering statesman Ratu Sukuna (see p.224), sometimes with organized dance and fundraising events in urban centres, but generally a family holiday with *lovo*.

JULY

Bula Festival Mid to end of the month (☎ 670 0133). Nadi's yearly week-long celebrations at Koroivoli Park.

Fiji Swims 🌐 fijiswims.com. Three ocean races from 1km to 18km centred around Beachcomber Island in the Mamanucas.

AUGUST

Indian firewalking First Sun after the full moon. The largest of the Fiji-Indian firewalking event is held at the Mahadavi Temple on Howell Rd, Suva.

Hibiscus Festival Mid-Aug, coinciding with school holidays (☎ 331 1168). Suva's yearly week-long celebrations at Albert Park.

SEPTEMBER

Fiji Regatta Week Musket Cove Marina, Mamanucas (🌐 musket covefiji.com). Pirate trips, races (in small hobie-cat boats) and general yachty hoo-ra.

Sugar Festival Usually the first week of Sept (☎ 666 8010). Lautoka's yearly week-long celebrations at Churchill Park.

OCTOBER

Fiji Day 10 Oct. Public holiday celebrating the day when Fiji was both ceded to Britain (1874) and given independence (1970). Dance performances are sometimes held in Albert Park, Suva.

Back to Levuka Week 10 Oct. Traditional re-enactments of cession, art displays and agricultural shows.

Diwali Late Oct to mid-Nov, depending on lunar calendar. Fireworks and lights are the star attractions of this Hindu celebration.

Rising of the Balolo Mid-Oct to mid-Nov, depending on moon. Naturally occurring event at a dozen or more coral reefs around the islands – the tail of a mysterious worm rises to the surface, is collected and eaten as a delicacy (see p.234).

NOVEMBER

Savusavu Music Festival 🌐 fiji-savusavu.com. Local musicians and dance troupes perform throughout this week-long event.

DECEMBER

Fara 1 Dec to mid-Jan. Door-to-door dancing and merry-making on the outer island of Rotuma, known as *fara* (see p.215). Sometimes indulged in by Rotumans living in urban centres, particularly Suva.

Sports and outdoor activities

With endless beaches, teeming coral reefs and water temperatures averaging 27˚C, Fiji is renowned for its scuba diving, snorkelling, surfing and other watersports. But adventure also awaits in the sultry tropical rainforests with fabulous hiking, river rafting and ecotours on offer.

Scuba diving and snorkelling

Fiji offers superb **scuba diving** and **snorkelling**, with exceptionally colourful and easily accessible reefs as well as plenty of diverse fish species including sharks. Diving is excellent year-round, with visibility usually at least 30m – the very best months are October and November, after the trade winds have subsided and before the tropical wet season begins.

Almost all resorts offer scuba diving, with dive sites normally between five and forty minutes by boat. Many resorts offer **dive training**, with PADI Open Water courses the most popular, costing F$650–900 for a three- to four-day package. For the more tentative, introductory scuba lessons offer a few hours learning the basics in a swimming pool – these cost around F$200. Advanced Courses (F$650) and Rescue Diver (F$850) are also widely available. The only place to dive using Nitrox is in the Mamanucas with Subsurface (see p.79) or on one of the live-aboard cruises (see opposite).

For scuba divers, the **soft corals** for which Fiji is renowned are most prolific along the Great Astrolabe Reef, which twists its way around Kadavu, and the northern islands of Vanua Levu and Taveuni, where many fabulous reefs are found including the Rainbow Reef between Taveuni and Vanua Levu, Noel's Wall off Matagi Island, Namena

Marine Reserve, E-6 and Hi-8 in the Koro Sea and the Great Sea Reef off north Vanua Levu. For many divers these are dream sites, with outstanding coral formations and drop-offs, although currents can be too strong for the inexperienced. The Mamanucas offer fun and easy dives for **beginners** as well as more challenging dives for the enthusiast including wrecks, caves and reef shark dives. The Beqa Lagoon off Pacific Harbour is renowned for its pelagics, particularly **sharks**, including two of the three most dangerous sharks in the world, bulls and tigers, while pilot **whales** and minke whales can be seen off Ovalau. For exploratory diving, **live-aboards** ply the remote reefs around the Koro Sea to the north of Ovalau.

DIVING CONTACTS

Dive Worldwide UK ☎ 0845 130 6980, ⓦ diveworldwide.com. Specialist dive holidays from the UK, with an extensive selection of Fiji itineraries.

Fiji Recompression Chamber ☎ 885 0630 or ☎ 330 5154. Fiji's only recompression centre is on the corner of Amy St and Brewster St in the Suva suburb of Toorak, with administration and enquiries handled from Savusavu on Vanua Levu.

PADI Australia ☎ 02 9454 2888, ⓦ padi.com. The Professional Association of Diving Instructors provides basic information on diving, courses and certification, as well as list of all PADI-registered companies in Fiji.

LIVE-ABOARDS

Fiji Aggressor US ☎ 1 800 348 2628, Fiji ☎ 336 2930, ⓦ aggressor .com. US-based company with two sleek vessels (10- and 18-passenger) operating in Fiji, visiting the Koro Sea including E-6, Hi-8 and Namena Marine Reserve. From US$2995 per person for a one-week charter.

Nai'a US ☎ 1 888 510 1593, Fiji ☎ 345 0382, ⓦ naia.com.fj. Seven and ten-day charters on a serene 40m sailing yacht for 18 passengers. Visits the Koro Sea, diving E-6, Mount Mutiny and Namena Marine Reserve. From US$3340 per person for a one-week charter.

Snorkelling

For **snorkellers**, the great beauty is that most reefs start just a few metres from the shoreline.

FIJI'S TOP DIVE SITES

Jacques Cousteau put Fiji on the diving map when he declared it "the soft coral capital of the world". Divers will also find big shark encounters, exciting drift dives and plenty of wrecks to explore. The following are some of the islands' top-rated dive sites:

Beqa Lagoon, Pacific Harbour The best open-water shark dive on earth. See p.116.

Rainbow Reef, Taveuni Gorgeous soft corals and fast drift dives. See p.207.

E-6, Bligh Water The photographer's favourite, accessed by live-aboard boat. See above.

Naiqoro Passage, Kadavu Beautiful drift dive on the Astrolabe Reef. See p.160.

The Salamander, Mamanucas A 36m wreck now home to puffer fish. See p.79.

RESPECTING THE REEF

Lying at the crossroads of the Pacific, Fiji's reefs are recognized as a globally important area of **biodiversity** and make up four percent of the world's total area of coral reefs. As well as attracting thousands of tourists, they protect the islands from hurricanes and provide an income for fishermen. Despite their often vast size, coral reefs are fragile and complex ecosystems that require care and respect from snorkellers and scuba-divers. It's imperative you **do not touch** the reef, or try to stand or tread water close to coral heads. Even a brief contact is likely to destroy the delicate coral polyps which can take years to grow back. Brushing against the reef is also likely to result in cuts or grazes which can take weeks to heal.

Although they make tempting souvenirs, **shells** should not be removed from the reef as they play a vital role in providing homes for invertebrates. Avoid buying shells from the village markets, especially tritons, or trumpet shells, the only natural predators of the coral-destroying crown of thorns starfish.

For information on reef wildlife, see p.234.

Some of the best **shore sites** are off the rocky west coast of Taveuni where the waters drop off dramatically, along Lesiaceva Point in Savusavu, in the Mamanuca-i-Cake Group and along the entire Yasawa chain of islands. Resorts which don't have good shore snorkelling provide **boat trips** to bommies, passages and outer reefs where marine life and corals are prolific. Of these, Vesi and Naiqoro passages in Kadavu and Caqalai and Toberua reefs in the Lomaiviti Group are particularly outstanding.

Manta rays congregate at Galoa and Vuro islands off Kadavu and around Drawaqa in the Yasawas between May and October. The best places to swim or snorkel with **spinner dolphins** are at the slightly remote regions of Natewa Bay in Vanua Levu or at Moon Reef off East Viti Levu.

It's worth investing in your own mask, snorkel and fins. Snorkel gear provided by resorts may not fit and masks often leak.

Surfing

Fiji is a regular venue for international **surfing** competitions, with over a dozen extremely challenging but reliable reef breaks. For the casual surfer, perhaps an even greater attraction is uncrowded waves. The only **beach breaks** for novices are at Sigatoka (see p.110); otherwise all surfing breaks are **reef breaks** over shallow razor-sharp coral with a wipe-out bound to graze, but more likely cause serious injuries – this is for experienced surfers only. The dozen or so breaks along the Malolo Barrier Reef (see p.59) are the most accessible, although several of the biggest breaks are reserved under exclusive agreements with upmarket surf resorts that sell only via the US. More isolated surfing destinations include Nagigia

off Kadavu, Wilkes in Beqa Lagoon and Kia off northern Vanua Levu.

Windsurfing and kite surfing

The best place for **windsurfing** is from *Safari Lodge* (see p.127), facing the trade winds on the exposed east beach of Nananu-i-Ra island off north Viti Levu; you can take week-long courses here or rent equipment by the hour. Other good locations include Matamanoa Island where winds can sometimes be stiff, or Plantation Island which features a sandy-bottomed shallow lagoon ideal for beginners, both in the Mamanucas. The optimum time for windsurfing is when the trade winds are blowing strongest between June and September.

Kite surfing is also offered at *Safari Lodge*. If you have your own equipment the flat lagoon between Malolo and Malolo Lailai in the Mamanucas is another good kitesurfing spot; the winds funnelled through the channel create ideal conditions.

Sailing

Although Fiji is a paradise of stunning islands and bays, treacherous reefs make **sailing** a challenging experience. Unless you have your own yacht, it's unlikely you'll find anyone prepared to offer boats for hire, with the few **sailing charters** operating from the marinas below on a skipper and crew basis only. The country's six **marinas** with full facilities are Port Denarau, Vuda Marina and the Royal Suva Yacht Club, all on Viti Levu; Musket Cove in the Mamanucas; Levuka on Ovalau; and Savusavu on Vanua Levu.

Yachties arrive in Fiji between May and August, usually sailing with the trade winds from California

WATER SAFETY

Swimming and snorkelling in Fiji's waters is pretty safe but there are a few precautions to be aware of. Wave action on the beaches is generally very sedate – the only places you may face danger are around river passages on the larger islands where **rip tides** can pull you out to sea. In the event of this happening, never fight it – go with the rip and try swimming sidewards to get out of the current, then swim parallel with the beach for 100m before trying to swim back to land.

When snorkelling, avoid contact with coral – apart from killing the delicate polyps you're likely to cut or graze yourself, which can cause painful infection. If you can, avoid snorkelling at low tide – with less water between you and the reef, collisions can be common. If you do get a **coral cut**, clean it immediately, preferably using iodine, and apply an anti-bacterial cream regularly.

Reef sharks are present in the lagoons – if you're lucky enough to see one it's very unlikely to stir unless you aggravate it persistently when it might swipe a bite in protest. Stinging jellyfish and crocodiles, which often spoil waters in other tropical countries, are not present in Fiji. Perhaps the greatest danger is the **sun** and without the protection of a UV swimming vest, or at the very least a high-factor sunscreen, sunburn is inevitable, even on a gloomy overcast day.

via Tonga and heading onwards to Australia or New Zealand, via Vanuatu or New Caledonia, no later than October when the trade winds subside and dangerous storms can occur. Popular regions for exploring include Vanua Balavu in the Lau Group, the islands off Taveuni and the idyllic lagoons and bays of the Mamanucas. See the section "Getting to Fiji by boat" for more information about immigration and customs.

Most resorts in the Mamanucas have small **sailing catamarans** for mucking around in the lagoons, while the best facilities for casual sailing are at Vuda Marina.

Sea kayaking

Every resort seems to have **sea kayaks** for guest use, usually as a complimentary activity; note that it's always wise to wear a life jacket and inform somebody of your intended journey in case you get caught in a dangerous current or a squally storm suddenly descends. Two companies (see below) offer week-long **kayaking expeditions** between May and October, snorkelling in the lagoons and camping on beaches or overnighting in remote fishing villages. Another good option is the half-day trip along the Lavena Coastline (see p.210) within the Bouma National Heritage Park on Taveuni.

KAYAKING OPERATORS

South Sea Ventures ☎ 02 8901 3287 in Australia, ⊛ southernseaventures.com. Australian-run group trips exploring the northern Yasawas in either single or twin sea kayaks. Eight-day packages from A$2130.

Tamarillo Tropical Expeditions ☎ 360 3043, ⊛ tamarillo.co.nz /fiji. New-Zealand-based company exploring the rugged and remote coastline of Kadavu with support boats. Seven-day packages from NZ$2295 per person.

Fishing

Fishing is a way of life for many Fijians, using nets, spear guns and fish traps in the shallow lagoons and simple hand lines along the river banks as a matter of subsistence. Commercial fishermen with small wooden fishing boats head to the deeper waters for tuna, mahi-mahi and wahoo. For tourists, **game fishing** is an exciting prospect, particularly in pursuit of **billfish** in the deep waters off Taveuni and Savusavu in the north and in the rich fast-flowing currents between Beqa and Kadavu in the south. Fishing licences aren't required but you'll need to find a reputable fishing charter with a proper game-fishing boat, good equipment and most importantly, a knowledgeable skipper – charters are usually available at Savusavu on Vanua Levu and at Pacific Harbour on Viti Levu, with more casual game fishing from Port Denarau in Nadi; otherwise, recommended resorts include *Matangi Island Resort* (see p.208) off Taveuni; *Makaira* (see p.206) on Taveuni; or *Matava* (see p.163) on Kadavu; rates start from F$750 for half a day.

Casting into the fringing reefs from small boats is usually excellent, with snapper, barracuda and trevally the prize catches; fly fishing in the shallow lagoons is good in places although there are few opportunities to land the highly prized bone fish, prolific in other parts of the South Pacific, and you'll definitely need to bring your own gear. Fishing in the **rivers** is seldom practised as a sport, although a couple of lodges along the south coast of Vanua Levu are idyllically set up for this.

Hiking and horseriding

Compared to its South Pacific neighbours, Fiji stands out as a great **hiking** destination. There are fine tropical rainforest walks in the Namosi Highlands, mountain treks on Viti Levu and Kadavu and stunning coastal walks on Waya island. Of the national parks, Koroyanitu and Bouma on Taveuni are the best for hiking. For less avid walkers, there are usually short trails leading to hilltop lookouts overlooking islands and lagoons. Resorts offering excellent local hikes include *Matamanoa Island Resort* (see p.88), *Botaira Beach Resort* (see p.95), *Naveria Heights Lodge* (see p.198) and *Matangi Island Resort* (see p.208).

Horseriding hasn't really developed as an attraction, although the potential is excellent. You can hire saddled horses along the wild beachfront at the Sigatoka Sand Dunes (see p.110).

River rafting and adrenaline sports

River rafting is a fun way of exploring the remote regions of Viti Levu, with the Grade III rapids of the upper Navua River on the south coast of Viti Levu the only place with established operators (see p.107).

For adrenaline seekers there's **skydiving** available from Nadi Airport (see p.58), **waterskiing** from Port Denarau (see p.58), **canopy zip lines** in the rainforest at Pacific Harbour (see p.118) and just north of Nadi at the Sleeping Giant (see p.66) and **paddleboarding** in the Mamanucas (see p.82) and off Ovalau (see p.176).

Golf

Fiji is beginning to establish itself as a major **golfing** holiday destination, thanks to its great year-round weather and affordable green fees. There are championship golf courses at Denarau (see p.58) and Pacific Harbour (see p.142).

Ecotours and village visits

Fiji is well positioned as an ecotour destination, with **village-based cultural visits** and **marine biology** the main focus. There are no specific ecotour holiday packages but most resorts, especially those in the outer islands, can organize village visits, plantation tours and guided hikes.

Visiting a village is more often than not an overwhelmingly positive experience. Apart from relishing the tourist-orientated *yaqona* ceremony (see box, p.40), travellers can usually visit people's homes, sample foods, learn to weave, go fishing and generally immerse themselves in daily Fijian life. Several villages have set up **community resorts**, usually located at the parameters of the village so as not to disrupt village affairs. For more background on village visits see box, p.40. For a more thorough introduction into Fijian life, consider joining one of the internationally organized **gap-year education programmes** where you assist in teaching at a remote village school and live with the people (see opposite for details).

Boasting numerous diverse and unchartered coral reefs, Fiji is also the focus for several global institutions conducting scientific **marine research**.

NATIONAL PARKS AND HERITAGE PARKS

Fiji's first official national park, protected by law, is the fascinating **Sigatoka Sand Dunes National Park** (see p.110) on the southwest coast of Viti Levu. The fragile sand-dune ecosystem, scattered with ancient bones and pottery, has an informative visitor centre and two managed trails for exploring.

Otherwise, the lush **Bouma National Heritage Park** (see p.208) encompasses almost half of Taveuni; and **Koroyanitu National Heritage Park** (see p.70) sits inland from Lautoka on Viti Levu. Both offer managed walking trails to waterfalls, village interaction and community-run accommodation.

Other projects managed by the **National Trust of Fiji** (❼ nationaltrust.org.fj) include Momi Guns (see p.65), south of Nadi; Levuka Town (see p.169) on Ovalau; Yadua Taba Island (see p.194); and Waisali Reserve in Vanua Levu (see p.199).

It's possible to join one of these groups on a working holiday, volunteering in research and gathering information, often on remote islands.

Research your trip thoroughly though: there are reports that some for-profit organizations fail to feed and house volunteers adequately, turning what should be a rewarding break into an ordeal.

ORGANIZATIONS FOR WORKING HOLIDAYS

American Institute for Foreign Study US ☎ 1 866 906 2437, ⓦ aifs.com. Language study and cultural immersion combined with Australian programmes.

Earthwatch Institute US ☎ 1 800 776 0188 or 978 461 0081, UK ☎ 01865 318 838, Australia ☎ 03 9682 6828, ⓦ earthwatch.org. Scientific expedition project that spans over fifty countries with environmental and archeological ventures worldwide.

Frontier UK ☎ 020 7613 2422, ⓦ frontier.ac.uk. English teaching project based in Suva. £1195 for four weeks includes a weekend of TEFL training. They also run medical, marine, journalism and animal welfare projects.

Gap Year Diver UK ☎ 0845 257 2392, ⓦ gapyeardiver.com. Four- to ten-week marine conservation projects off the south coast of Vanua Levu costing from £2660.

Greenforce UK ☎ 020 7470 8888, ⓦ greenforce.org. Six- to ten-week programme assisting in the survey of coral reefs on behalf of the World Conservation Society. From £2200 per person. No dive experience required.

Madventurer UK ☎ 0845 121 1996, ⓦ madventurer.com. A range of opportunities based around Lautoka on Viti Levu, from teaching sport to working in healthcare. Two weeks from £600.

Peace Corps US ☎ 1800 424 8580, ⓦ peacecorps.gov. Over fifty volunteers work all around Fiji assisting in a wide scope of community projects, from environmental and health awareness to teaching information technology.

Culture and etiquette

Any discussion of Fijian culture must take account of the split between ethnic Fijians and their Fiji-Indian adopted neighbours. Fiji-born Indians are forbidden by law to call themselves Fijians, with an almost apartheid-styled constitution being the country's greatest barrier to building a unified nation. On the street level, the two races get on well enough, but with vastly different cultures and aspirations they tend not to mix socially. Considering them as a whole is thus difficult, although you'll find Fiji's peoples are generally extremely hospitable, generous and forgiving. They tend also to be deeply religious with church, temple and mosque well attended.

In **rural areas**, both amongst Fijians and Fiji-Indians, men and women have distinct roles and seldom mix in social settings. Macho behaviour is common and women travellers may find they experience unwanted attention. Amongst indigenous Fijians a strong heritage of tribal customs influences day-to-day life. For more information on these traditional customs see p.40.

Smoking is socially acceptable in public places, although it has been officially banned on public transport. Some restaurants and a few bars have self-imposed smoke-free zones. **Public toilets** are few and far between.

As for **dress codes**, local women dress modestly. Shorts, sleeveless tops and short skirts are quite acceptable in town centres although they may draw undesired attention. Bikinis are fine at the pool or the beach, but not out and about. Bathing topless in public is strictly forbidden. Most restaurants and resorts are pretty casual but upscale eateries generally expect you to dress for dinner by donning trousers and a collared shirt for men; trousers, skirts or dresses for women. The most conservative environment for dress is in the villages where it's expected for women to cover shoulders and for both men and women to wear *sulus* or at least shorts covering the knees – sunglasses and hats should also be removed.

Fijians tend to go to bed early and wake up early so don't expect much to be going on after 9pm. When meeting, locals are eager to shake hands and ask you where you're from, and usually exchange pleasantries when passing – a hearty "**bula**" being almost mandatory in rural areas, although in town centres this greeting is usually a ruse for selling you something. Fijians do not, as a rule, shout at each other or demand service. Visitors often become frustrated at the often glacial speed at which things move and the detached attitude when a problem arises – **sega na leqa** rules, a mix of *mañana* of Latin America and the "no worries mate" of Australia. There is little you can do about it and the more anxious or frustrated you get the less sympathy or assistance you'll be shown. Slow down, relax and take it Fiji time.

VISITING A FIJIAN VILLAGE

Visiting a traditional village is one of the highlights of a trip to Fiji. As soon as you arrive at a village, excitable kids call out "bula!", elders take the time to shake your hand and you'll invariably receive offers to stay for a meal or longer. To do so will provide a unique insight into Fijian culture.

TOURS AND HOMESTAYS

Most resorts offer **village tours**, often including a trip to a craft market and a simple *yaqona* ceremony (see box, p.31). While these can be a good option for those short on time, you may end up with a rather sanitized experience, as resorts tend to visit nearby villages which have become over commercialized. The best tours visit the more remote, traditional villages and are often combined with adventure activities such as rafting or kayaking. Look out for tours running from Nadi (see p.50) or try a trip to Kadavu (see p.157).

There's nothing to stop you visiting a village **unaccompanied**, providing you follow the tips given below. For a fuller immersion into Fijian life consider staying overnight at a village **homestay**, which involves staying with a family, usually in a traditional bure. Homestay accommodation is listed throughout the guide.

VILLAGE ETIQUETTE

When visiting a village there is a certain amount of **etiquette** to be aware of. As an outsider, locals won't expect you to follow all the rules but the more you pick up the more you'll be respected. The following are a few useful pointers:

- Dress conservatively – men and particularly women should cover shoulders and knees, and preferably wear a **sulu** (Fijian sarong) around the waist.
- Avoid visiting a village on a **Sunday**, which is a special day for religion, family and rest.
- Before entering a village, remove your hat and sunglasses and carry any backpacks in front of you – don't hide them as this arouses suspicion.
- On arrival, ask to see the **turanga ni koro** (village headman) to whom you should present a **sevusevu** or introductory gift. *Yaqona* is the most appropriate form of *sevusevu* and can be bought at all town markets, either in root form or ready prepared as *waqa* (powder) – about half a kilo or F$30 worth of roots is appropriate.
- Other appreciated **gifts** include books and magazines; food (if staying overnight); school stationery for children or toys such as balloons or balls.
- On entering a home, remove your shoes, crouch when passing through the door and sit cross-legged with your head a little stooped as a sign of respect. It is polite to shake hands with anyone already present and introduce yourself simply by name, town and country.
- As part of the ceremony to welcome you to the village, you will be invited to drink **yaqona**, Fiji's national drink, with the chief. For more details on this ceremony, see box, p.31.
- Taking **photos** is acceptable in almost all instances except the initial *yaqona* ceremony. Fijians take pride in being photographed and will often ask you to take their picture and to see it afterwards. Sending printed photographs is a nice follow-up gesture.
- If invited to **eat**, sit cross-legged and wait until everybody has sat down. The head of the house will say grace (*masu*) after which you can start eating, normally using your hands. You may find yourself the only person eating, with someone fanning the food for you – don't be put off, this is a common gesture reserved for guests.

TOP 5 VILLAGES

Yalobi, Waya, Yasawa Islands (see p.93)
Navala, inland Viti Levu (see p.119)
Nataleira, east coast Viti Levu (see p.128)
Arovudi, Ovalau (see p.174)
Lavena, Taveuni (see p.210)

Shopping

Fiji is not a great shopping destination, hindered by its isolation and heavy import duties and starved by lack of individual creativity in design and fashion. With a dearth of boutique shops and art galleries, your best bet is to head to the urban municipal markets, which ooze character, overflow with local produce and have the most authentic collection of handicrafts.

Both Nadi and Suva have special **handicraft markets**, although both are burdened with pushy sales people – try to pick out the artisan traders who are often busy weaving, polishing or sewing their wares. Woodcarving items include beautifully polished and patterned rimmed *tanoa* bowls, war clubs, cannibal forks and totemic items such as turtles and face masks. Bags woven from *pandanus* leaves and styled with *tapa* cloth are often eye-catching, as is jewellery made from coconut shells. Hand-woven mats costing from F$60 and up, depending on the fineness of the weave, make practical souvenirs.

The best places to buy **local crafts** direct from the artisans are from the Flea Market in Suva (see p.137) or, if your timing is right, at one of the craft fairs in Nadi organized by the Western Arts & Craft Society every few months. Otherwise, Jacks Handicraft has quality crafts, a large variety of scented **coconut oils**, creams and soaps, locally harvested **black pearls** (see p.41), colourful ranges of clothing and other knick-knacks often sourced from overseas – they also provide a shipping service.

The shopping experience can be hampered by shopkeepers standing in their doorways pestering tourists to come in and look, particularly in Nadi. You'll need to **haggle** at all small Indian-owned shops – even at the big chain stores if you ask politely for a discount you'll probably get something off. Bargaining, though, is not a Fijian custom so if buying from an indigenous Fijian the asking price will invariably be realistic. You should avoid buying **shells**, especially turtle and triton shells which are both banned as export items, as is the *tabua* **whale's tooth**.

Shops are few and far between on the outer islands so it's wise to **stock up** on provisions before you depart Viti Levu. In an emergency, most outer-island resorts have small shops selling sun cream and other essentials at greatly inflated prices.

Travelling with children

Often viewed as a romantic escape for couples, Fiji is in fact a popular family holiday destination, especially amongst Australians and New Zealanders. With enormous empathy and affection for children, Fijians make fabulous hosts and those with infants will find the locals eager to entertain your children at every opportunity. Most resorts have complimentary kids' clubs and plenty of family-orientated water activities.

Soft sand and gentle waves are a great formula for family holidays, with the beach resorts along the **Mamanucas** a particular favourite, notably *Treasure Island* (see p.81), *Plantation Island* (see p.84), *Castaway Island* (see p.86) and *Amunuca Island* (see p.88) in the Mamanucas; and the more budget-orientated *Octopus* (see p.94), *Korovou* (see p.95) and *Oarsman's Bay* (see p.99) in the Yasawas. The large resorts along the **Coral Coast** (see p.112) are also popular, with several good family attractions including the Kula Eco Park as well as adventure activities around **Pacific Harbour** for older children.

Most resorts allow kids under a certain age to **stay for free** if sharing a room with their parents – some even offer free meals as incentives. The exception are the upmarket boutique resorts which often have a strict **no-child policy** to ensure a romantic atmosphere for their guests; the exception is *Jean-Michel Cousteau Resort* (see p.198) on Vanua Levu which is one of the very best luxury resorts for families; others may allow kids only during dedicated holiday periods. Other outer-island resorts which actively encourage families are *Naigani Island Resort* (see p.176) in the Lomaiviti group and *Papageno Resort* (see p.163) on Kadavu. For those on a budget, many of the backpacker resorts have family rooms, especially in Nadi.

Rural **villages** are a fascinating environment for children of all ages and they'll most likely be enthusiastically welcomed by the village kids, encouraged to play and generally well looked after.

Minor **health issues** are the greatest concern for parents travelling with young children, especially from the adverse effects of high humidity, intense sun and mosquito bites. Medicated baby powder for the prevention of rashes and sores is an essential item to carry. In the main towns, high-quality baby formula, nappies and children's medications imported from Australia are readily available. **Breast feeding** in public is fairly commonplace, especially so in rural environments, although baby-changing facilities are rarely offered.

If travelling by car or taxi, seat belts, let alone dedicated infant **car seats**, are difficult to find, although the major car rental companies do provide them. **Prams** in general are not that practical to travel with: pathways are sandy at many of the resorts, and even around towns pavements are not pram friendly.

Travel essentials

Costs

For travellers most items will appear very affordable, especially public transport, dining out and buying local food. If frugal, you can survive on F$70 (£22/€27/US$37) per day, staying in dorms, preparing your own meals and travelling on public transport. Stay in private rooms and eat out regularly and you'll need around F$180 (£60/€70/US$96), although extras such as alcohol, car rental, scuba diving and sightseeing tours will all add to your costs. Travelling around the two largest islands of Viti Levu and Vanua Levu offers the best value, with prices on the outer islands usually inflated by at least 20 percent. Note that **tipping** is not expected and in traditional Fijian society causes embarrassment.

Hostel **accommodation** will set you back around F$40 a person for a dorm bed, or F$85 per person including meals at the popular Yasawa backpacker resorts. Town hotel rooms start from around F$70, with double or twin rooms often the same price as a single. A moderate beach resort starts from F$200 for a room, the more popular holiday resorts cost from F$350 and a luxury boutique resort will set you back anything from F$500 to over F$2000 per night.

Food on the whole is reasonably cheap, with local produce offering by far the best value, especially when purchased from the roadside or at municipal markets. Supermarket shelves tend to be dominated by more expensive imported food items, mostly canned and restricted in

---

EMERGENCIES

☎ 917 is the free **emergency** telephone number to summon the police. Call ☎ 911 for ambulance or fire service.

---

variety. Dining out is affordable, with cheap restaurant counter food costing from F$5 a serving, and main dishes ordered from a menu from F$9 to F$25; resort restaurants are invariably more expensive.

Travelling around Viti Levu by public transport is especially cheap, with the five-hour journey from Nadi to Suva costing just F$22, and local journeys starting from 80 cents. Visiting the offshore or outer islands is going to eat up a larger chunk of your budget. For example, the hop-on, hop-off boat pass along the Yasawas costs F$191 for seven days; and a domestic flight to Taveuni can cost up to F$250 one way, although discounted fares are usually available via airline websites and can almost match passenger ferry rates, which cost from F$65 between Suva and Taveuni.

Every traveller over twelve years of age departing Fiji pays a **departure tax** of F$200, although this is pre-paid in the cost of your airline ticket.

Crime and personal safety

As in any society, **crime** exists in Fiji but it's certainly not rife and not nearly as common as in most European or North American cities. **Petty theft** stems from a cultural trait where the individual owns few possessions, shares everything freely and is bound by the beliefs of *kerekere*, a form of asking for something with the owner being obliged to give. It's especially common among hotel workers and you may find clothes or small change frequently going missing from bures and communal resort areas. Bring in clothes and shoes at night and certainly don't leave money or jewellery lying about as an invitation.

With machismo entrenched in Fijian culture, **sexual harassment** can be an issue for female travellers – a firm "not interested" should ward off any unwanted attention while all the usual precautions apply, such as avoiding walking alone at night. If in need of assistance contact the Fiji Women's Crisis Centre (ⓦ fijiwomen.com) in Nadi (☎ 670 7558), Ba (☎ 667 0466), Suva (☎ 331 3300) or Labasa (☎ 881 4609). Domestic violence, or "**wife bashing**" as it's rather crudely known in Fiji, is also disturbingly prevalent, and a bruised eye is seldom concealed or reported to the authorities. At the same time Fijians are a respectful society and treat each other and especially visitors with kindness.

Although commonly smoked by young urban Fijians, **marijuana** possession is strictly illegal and is strongly discouraged in more traditional rural areas where it is perceived as a dangerous evil – if a village youth is caught smoking more than once, public floggings may result. The official penalty for marijuana possession is three months in jail, so consider wisely before indulging.

The **Fijian police** are for the most part helpful, with police stations in all towns and major settlements. Larger towns have additional posts in busy areas. See the "Directory" sections of towns for local contacts.

Electricity

Fiji's electrical current is 220–240 volts (50Hz) with a **three-pin plug** common with Australia and New Zealand. Fluctuation in current and surges are common, especially in the outer islands where electricity is run by diesel generator, so it's advisable to have a **surge protector** if using electrical equipment. In many resorts, 110 volt outlets for shavers and hairdryers are provided.

Entry requirements

All visitors to Fiji must hold a valid passport for at least six months beyond the intended period of stay, and proof of onward travel to another country. Adhering to the above, a four-month **tourist visa** is issued on arrival to most nationals including those of Australia, New Zealand, South Africa, the US, Canada and EU member states. For a complete list, check the Fiji Visitor Bureau website (**W** fiji.travel).

A maximum **two-month visa extension** may be made on application with the Immigration Department at Nadi Airport or Suva, but there are no provisions for stays beyond six months for any overseas nationals unless obtaining resident status or work/student visas.

All visitors are required to fill out standard immigration cards upon arrival. The card must be surrendered to Fiji immigration authorities upon departure.

FIJIAN EMBASSIES ABROAD

Australia High Commission of the Republic of Fiji, 19 Beale Crescent, Deakin, ACT 2600 **☎** 06 260 5115.
Belgium Embassy of the Republic of Fiji, 92–94 Square Plasky, 1030 Bruxelles **☎** 32 2 736 9050.
New Zealand High Commission of the Republic of Fiji, 31 Pipitea St, Thorndon, Wellington **☎** 04 473 5401.
UK and Ireland High Commission of the Republic of Fiji, 34 Hyde Park Gate, London SW7 5DN **☎** 020 7584 3661.
US Embassy of the Republic of Fiji, 2000 M St NW, Suite 710, Washington DC 20036 **☎** 202 466 8320.

EMBASSIES AND CONSULATES IN FIJI

Australia High Commission, 37 Princes Rd, Tamavua, Suva **☎** 338 2211.
European Union Commission, 4th floor, Development Bank Centre, Suva **☎** 331 3633.
Federated States of Micronesia 37 Loftus Rd, Suva **☎** 330 4566.
Kiribati 38 McGregor Rd, Suva **☎** 330 2512.
New Zealand Pratt St, Suva **☎** 331 1422.
Tuvalu 16 Gorrie St, Suva **☎** 330 1355.
UK High Commission, 47 Gladstone Rd, Suva **☎** 322 9100.
US Embassy, 158 Princes Rd, Tamavua **☎** 337 1110.

Gay and lesbian travellers

Gay and lesbian travellers shouldn't feel any sort of discrimination in Fiji, especially within resort environments where many openly homosexual staff work. However, gay behaviour is far more evident than lesbian and open affection between women may generate curiosity. In urban areas, homosexuality and cross-dressing are quite open, although it's frowned upon in the conservative Christian-dominated village environment where discretion is advisable.

Insurance

You should always have **travel insurance** that covers you against theft, illness and injury. Most policies exclude so-called dangerous sports unless

ROUGH GUIDES TRAVEL INSURANCE

Rough Guides has teamed up with WorldNomads.com to offer great travel insurance deals. Policies are available to residents of over 150 countries, with cover for a wide range of adventure sports, 24hr emergency assistance, high levels of medical and evacuation cover and a stream of travel safety information. Roughguides.com users can take advantage of their policies online 24/7, from anywhere in the world – even if you're already travelling. And since plans often change when you're on the road, you can extend your policy and even claim online. Roughguides.com users who buy travel insurance with WorldNomads.com can also leave a positive footprint and donate to a community development project. For more information, go to **W** roughguides.com/travel-insurance.

an additional premium is paid: in Fiji this can mean snorkelling, surfing or scuba diving. If you need to make a claim, you should keep all receipts for medicines and treatment as well as transport and any additional accommodation bills whilst recuperating. In the event of having anything stolen, you must obtain an official statement from the police confirming this.

Internet

Almost all large hotels and boutique resorts offer **Internet access** – a few of the larger hotels around Viti Levu also have wireless (Wi-Fi) access or broadband sockets in rooms. On the outer islands, Internet access is not always available, especially at the budget resorts in the Yasawas; when it is available it's generally slower and more expensive than elsewhere. Prices are typically at least F$25 an hour at the luxury hotels and outer-island resorts, F$4 to F$8 an hour at the backpacker hostels and around F$2 to F$4 an hour at private **Internet cafés**. Internet cafés can be found in most town centres – especially in Nadi, Lautoka and Suva – where competition is fierce and prices sometimes fall below F$2 an hour, usually charged by the minute. "Directory" sections in the Guide contain addresses for local internet access points.

Laundry

Most hotels and resorts provide a **laundry service** for guests, although self-service machines are seldom available. Independent laundries, which tend to be better value, can be found in the larger towns, or at several of the larger marinas.

Living in Fiji

Due to high levels of unemployment, it is difficult to obtain a **work permit** for Fiji. Many expatriates work in the hospitality industry and if you have relevant work experience or **specific skills** such as languages or scuba diving qualifications, you may find resort work. A prospective employer in any field must demonstrate that they have conducted an exhaustive but unsuccessful search for a qualified Fijian candidate and must post a bond to cover the costs of shipping you home if you become incapacitated. Few are willing to go through this process unless your skills are particularly desirable.

International students may apply for enrolment at the University of the South Pacific (Ⓦwww.usp .com.fj, ☎323 1000) on either a cross-credit semester or a full-time course, providing you have attained a High School certificate pass or similar from your home country. There's no age limit for enrolment and a student visa is granted to all successful applicants providing a clean police record and clear medical including a negative HIV test.

Alternatively, a variety of marine conservation organizations offer unpaid or even you-pay **internships** for periods lasting a week to several months; see p.39.

Otherwise, if you have a large chunk of money you're willing to invest and you can find a local partner who must hold at least a fifty-percent shareholding, you can set up or purchase a **business**. Specific questions should be addressed to Investment Fiji (☎331 5988; Ⓦinvestmentfiji .org.fj), headquartered at Civic Tower on Victoria Parade in Suva, with another office on Naviti Street in Lautoka.

Mail

Post Fiji operates all **post offices** (Mon–Fri 8am–4pm, Sat 8am–noon). All post offices have telephones and sell phone cards for calling internationally and locally; larger branches sell stationery and postcards.

ADDRESSES

Fijian **addresses** are something of an enigma. There is no door-to-door postal service so anybody wanting to receive mail uses a PO Box number; consequently few people know their residential address or display a house number. In towns, the majority of shops and businesses don't have a shop number, although street addresses are mostly signposted. On Viti Levu, the main road around the island – called the Queens Road along the south coast and the Kings Road along the north coast – passes through most towns where it more commonly reverts to "Main Street" or "High Street". On outer islands, addresses are a complete unknown except identifying a village or settlement. Directions are equally vague and you shouldn't necessarily take someone's earnest advice as fact.

Post can be slow, especially **posting items to Fiji** and it's not uncommon for letters to take three weeks from North America or Europe, with delivery to the outer islands often taking an additional week. **Posting items from Fiji** is cheap and somewhat quicker, with letters to Europe commonly taking less than ten days. All letters and postcards should be labelled with an airmail sticker otherwise they may go by boat, taking months to arrive. UPS, DHL and Federal Express all have offices in Suva and Nadi, although Post Fiji's in-house **courier service**, EMS, is considerably cheaper.

Stamps are available from most hotels and gift shops, as well as some bookstores. Public mail boxes are very rare, and you should always find the nearest post office to mail important items; most resorts, especially those on the outer islands, will post letters for you.

Poste restante is available at all post offices. Letters should be marked "General Delivery, Poste Restante", followed by the location of the post office and your name. Letters will be held for two months – for post sent to Nadi, be sure to specify either Nadi Town or Nadi Airport. To receive a parcel in Fiji, you must clear it through the post office's customs counter (Mon–Fri 10am–11am & 2pm–3pm), and pay a service charge plus any customs or import duty.

Maps

Navigating between towns is very straightforward, with just one or two main roads on each island. General-purpose town or island **maps** are hard to come by, the most useful being the free Jason's Travel Media map available from most hotel tour desks. A slightly more detailed folded sheet map is published by Hema and available in bookstores and large chain stores around Nadi and Suva for F$12.95.

For 1:250,000 **topographical maps** of the individual islands and 1:15,000 town maps (around F$8–9 each), contact the Lands and Survey Department (☎321 1395, ⓦwww.lands.gov.fj) or visit the Map Shop on the ground floor and at the back of Government Buildings in Suva, or the Government Bookshop on Rodwell Road, also in Suva.

EXCHANGE RATES (NOTE THAT RATES ARE VARIABLE)

F$1 = US$0.54, £0.32, €0.39, AUS$0.59, NZ$0.64

PUBLIC HOLIDAYS

The following are **public holidays** in Fiji, when government offices, banks, schools and most shops are closed. Note some public holiday dates vary from year to year – see ⓦfiji.gov.fj for official dates.
New Year's Day January 1
National Youth & Commonwealth Day March 10
Prophet Mohammed's Birthday March 17
Good Friday
Easter Saturday
Easter Monday
Ratu Sir Lala Sukuna Day May 30
Queen's Birthday Third Monday in June
Fiji Day October 10
Diwali Late October/early November
Christmas December 25
Boxing Day December 26

Money

Fiji's currency is the **Fiji dollar** (F$) divided into 100 cents. Notes come in F$2, F$5, F$10, F$20, F$50 and F$100 denominations; F$100 notes are hard to trade with, especially at small shops. All notes proudly feature Queen Elizabeth II along with other traditional and iconic symbols. Any foreign currency should be exchanged at one of the five bank chains, including ANZ and Westpac, or with one of the many currency exchange outlets found in the main towns and at Nadi Airport.

Travellers' cheques tend only to be accepted by hotels or cashed at banks, but **credit cards** are widely accepted, although only Visa and Master-Card, and very occasionally AMEX; all usually incur a service charge of around 4 percent. If visiting the Yasawas, bear in mind some resorts are cash-only environments whereas others insist everything is payable by credit card at the end of your stay; check with the resort beforehand.

ATM machines are available in all towns on Viti Levu except Tavua and Korovou, in Levuka on Ovalau, at Savusavu and Labasa on Vanua Levu and at Naqara on Taveuni, as well as at Nadi Airport, the Nadi branch of *McDonald's*, the shopping mall in Port Denarau and several of the large hotel chains in Nadi and along the Coral Coast. If you plan on using your debit card or credit card at an ATM, make sure you have a personal identification number (PIN) that's designated to work overseas.

> ## CALLING HOME FROM FIJI
>
> Note that the initial zero is omitted from the area code when dialling the UK, Ireland, Australia and New Zealand from abroad.
>
> **Australia** 00 + 61 + city code.
> **New Zealand** 00 + 64 + city code.
> **Republic of Ireland** 00 + 353 + city code.
> **South Africa** 00 + 27 + city code.
> **UK** 00 + 44 + city code.
> **US & Canada** 00 + 1 + area code.

Having **money wired** from home is never convenient or cheap and should only be considered as a last resort. The post office acts as general agents for Western Union (🌐 westernunion.com), which has branches at Nadi Airport, Nadi Town, Lautoka and Suva; MoneyGram (🌐 moneygram .com) operates via Westpac Bank and some Morris Hedstrom supermarkets. Direct bank transfers are also possible but you'll need the address and swift code of the bank branch where you want to pick up the money and the address and swift code of the bank's Suva head office which will act as the clearing house; money wired this way usually takes two working days to arrive and costs around £25/US$40 per transaction.

Opening hours

Business hours at government and private offices are Monday–Friday 8am–5pm, with offices generally closed for at least an hour for lunch, sometimes two. Regular **banking hours** are Monday–Friday 9am–4pm, although banks have slightly varying times on Mondays and Fridays; specific bank details are listed throughout the Guide. Most high street shops are open Monday–Friday 8.30am–5pm, although some, particularly the larger hardware shops, close on Saturday at noon; some **supermarkets** and local grocery shops open as early as 7am and don't close until 8pm. Most **restaurants** are open seven days a week, the most likely time of closure being Sunday lunch and for a couple of hours from 3pm to 5pm.

Phones

Before travelling, contact your mobile network provider to ensure you can use your phone in Fiji. It will almost certainly work out cheaper **buying a SIM card** for your phone along with pre-paid calling time, available from many retail outlets around the islands; even if you don't have a mobile you can pick up a simple model with SIM card in Nadi for under F$100. Mobile phone **coverage** around the main islands of Viti Levu and Vanua Levu is poor once outside the main urban areas and certainly in the highlands; in the Mamanucas you will probably have to climb a hill to get the faintest of signals.

The cheapest option of all though, is taking advantage of **VoIP** (Voice over Internet Protocol) calls (for example 🌐 skype.com) from an Internet café.

Public phones and phone cards

Public phones remain a good option for calling, with over 1500 distinctly styled *drua* phone booths around the country operated by **TeleCard**. Cards, available in F$3, F$5, F$10, F$20 and F$50 denominations, can be purchased from all post offices and many retail outlets, and can be used from private landlines, although they are often barred from being used in hotel rooms.

Local calls have become substantially cheaper in recent years. If calling overseas, landline costs remain prohibitive, with most destinations costing 75¢ per minute, often with a hefty surcharge billed when calling from hotel rooms. Consider buying a **telephone charge card** from your phone company back home. Using a PIN number, you can make calls from most hotel, public and private phones that will be charged to your account, but check to see Fiji is covered and bear in mind that rates aren't necessarily cheaper than calling from a public phone.

Photography

Fiji is a photographer's paradise, with wonderful scenery and vivid colours. If in a village, it's polite to ask before taking photographs. As Fijians tend to pose for the camera it can be difficult to get natural and spontaneous expressions – after snapping a few posed pictures, wait until the scene becomes more natural before shooting again. The most dramatic **light** is experienced early in the morning and late in the afternoon, although taking pictures of beaches and lagoons is good when the sun is high in the sky and the blues are pronounced. Film and **memory cards** are available in Nadi, Lautoka and Suva, although at higher prices than in the US or Europe.

Time

Fiji has a single **time zone**, being twelve hours ahead of Greenwich Mean Time (GMT), an hour ahead of Sydney and twenty hours ahead of Los

Angeles. The sun has a minimal variation from summer to winter, rising between 5am and 6am and setting from 6pm to 7pm, always with only a brief period of twilight.

Tourist information

Almost every hotel, resort and hostel in Fiji has its own privately operated tour desk offering brochures and a booking service.

The government-funded **Fiji Visitor Bureau** (FVB) provides basic tourist information through its website ⓦfiji.travel. Its head office is sited in an obscure location at the Colonial Plaza in Namaka, Nadi (Mon–Thurs 8am–4.30pm, Fri 8am–4pm; ☎672 2433); you can pick up several useful tourist publications here, including *Affordable Guide* and *Fiji Dive Guide*, but there are no staff on hand to help with travel enquiries or bookings.

Two of the outer-island regions have established their own privately funded tourism organizations: the Savusavu Tourism Association (ⓦfiji-savusavu .com); and the Taveuni Tourism Association (ⓦpuretaveuni.com).

VISITOR BUREAU OFFICES OVERSEAS

Australia Level 12, St Martin's Tower, 31 Market St, Sydney ☎02 9264 3399.

New Zealand 35 Scanlan St, Grey Lynn, Auckland ☎09 376 2533.

UK Albany House, Albany Crescent, Claygate, Esher, Surrey KT10 0PF ☎0800 652 2158.

US 5777 West Century Boulevard, Suite 220, Los Angeles, CA 90045 ☎310 568 1616.

USEFUL WEBSITES

ⓦ **fijiguide.com** Information on travelling around the islands, including sections on diving and surfing, as well as entertaining anecdotes.

ⓦ **fiji.travel** The official Tourism Fiji website.

ⓦ **islandsbusiness.com** Current events and issues affecting Fiji and its Pacific Island neighbours.

ⓦ **roughguides.com** Post any of your pre-trip questions – or post-trip suggestions – in Travel Talk, our online forum for travellers.

ⓦ **spto.org** Useful website for sourcing hotels, tours, travel agents and cultural events throughout the South Pacific.

GOVERNMENT SITES

Australian Department of Foreign Affairs ⓦ dfat.gov.au, ⓦ smartraveller.gov.au.

British Foreign & Commonwealth Office ⓦ fco.gov.uk.

Canadian Department of Foreign Affairs ⓦ dfait-maeci.gc.ca.

Irish Department of Foreign Affairs ⓦ foreignaffairs.gov.ie.

New Zealand Ministry of Foreign Affairs ⓦ mft.govt.nz.

US State Department ⓦ travel.state.gov.

Travellers with disabilities

Fiji has a poor infrastructure for **travellers with disabilities**. There's no provision for wheelchairs on public transport and pavements are rarely in a fit state for wheelchairs or the visually impaired – holes, ledges and cracks are all too common and there are few ramps at street corners. Moreover, many resort pathways are made of sand, making mobility extremely difficult. Fortunately, Fijians will go out of their way to make your travels comfortable, assisting whenever possible and even building temporary ramps for disabled guests at resorts. The Fiji National Council for Disabled Persons, at Qarase House on Brown Street in Suva (☎331 9045, ⓦfncdp.org), can offer general advice and information.

Nadi and around

NADI MUNICIPAL MARKET

1

Nadi and around

Almost all of Fiji's 600,000 annual visitors get their first glimpse of the country descending towards Nadi International Airport. Tiny tropical islands glint in the ocean off Nadi Bay while Viti Levu's spectacular mountains loom inland. Given this introduction, Nadi (pronounced *Nan-dee)* itself can come as an anticlimax. Despite boasting Fiji's third largest population, it's not really a city, more a loose collection of villages surrounded by sugarcane fields, and you may be forgiven for thinking you've arrived at a quaint, tropical suburbia. Where Nadi is useful, though, is in its choice of accommodation, with everything from five-star resorts to beachside backpackers dotted along the nearby coastline. You'll also find all the facilities you need to plan the rest of your trip including banks, travel agents and a good range of shops, as well as a few excellent restaurants.

Nadi Airport, 10km north of the Downtown area, features a small cluster of hotels but otherwise it provides a low key and verdant arrival point, surrounded by farmland. Heading south along the congested Queens Road from here you come to **Namaka**, a frenetic shopping parade, while further south in the suburb of **Martintar** there are several ethnic and international restaurants, Nadi's best nightlife and a couple of affordable hotels. South again, scruffily active **Downtown Nadi** is the terminal for buses, and home to the municipal market, internet cafés, boutique shops and cheap Chinese restaurants but virtually no accommodation. The southern point of town, where sugarcane fields take over, is guarded by Nadi's sole iconic attraction, the riotously colourful **Sri Siva Subrahmanya Swami Temple**, or more simply "Nadi Temple". A few kilometres west off the Queens Road lie the beaches of **Nadi Bay**, home to the budget hotspot of **Wailoaloa Beach** as well as **Denarau Island**, an exclusive luxury enclave.

Inland, there are tropical waterfalls, traditional villages and some breathtaking walking trails in the serene mountains of the **Nausori Highlands** and **Koroyanitu National Park** – the latter accessed via the utilitarian port of **Lautoka**, twenty minutes' drive north of Nadi Airport.

Brief history

Nadi before the 1870s was a wild, uncharted region, seldom visited by the tyrants of Eastern Viti or Lau and hardly documented by European explorers or missionaries. In 1870, a small British community, known as the **Nadi Swells** for their broad-brimmed hats and affluent demeanour, set up cotton and cattle farms along the Nadi River. Soon after, with the establishment of **sugarcane** as a viable crop and with indentured labourers from India, the region began its transformation to an Indo-Fijian dominated market centre. During World War II,

Highlights

❶ Sri Siva Subrahmanya Swami Temple
The largest Hindu edifice in the Southern
Hemisphere is a riot of colours and
beautiful carving: follow up a visit with
lunch at the simple temple restaurant.
See p.54

❷ Wailoaloa Beach Take a sunset stroll
along the beach at this travellers' hotspot and
grab a cool beer at the *Bamboo Travellers* bar.
See p.54

❸ Day cruising Enjoy a day under sail cruising
around Nadi's offshore islands. **See p.58**

❹ Garden of the Sleeping Giant Wander
amongst the orchids and forest plants in this
lush botanical garden. **See p.66**

❺ Lautoka market The provincial town isn't a
hotspot in itself, but it does feature one of the
country's most dramatic markets – a huge
concrete dome overhanging stalls crammed
with colourful fresh produce. **See p.69**

❻ Koroyanitu National Heritage Park Make
an overnight trek to this stunning region and
sleep in a small hut on the top of Mount
Batilamu. **See p.70**

HIGHLIGHTS ARE MARKED ON THE MAP ON P.52

1

THE MAMANUCAS AND YASAWA ISLANDS

The **Mamanucas and Yasawa Islands** are covered in the next chapter (see p.74), but day-trips to the offshore islands of the Mamanucas from the Nadi area (which depart from Port Denarau) are detailed in this chapter (see p.58).

the Royal New Zealand Air Force lengthened and strengthened the tiny Nadi airstrip, the US military constructed a major **airbase** and two large British gun batteries were erected either end of Nadi Bay to protect the surrounding waters of the Navula Passage. The Japanese invasion never came, but the paved runway was certainly big enough to receive the first jet planes and, with a slight expansion in the 1960s, Nadi established itself as the **tourist hub** of Fiji.

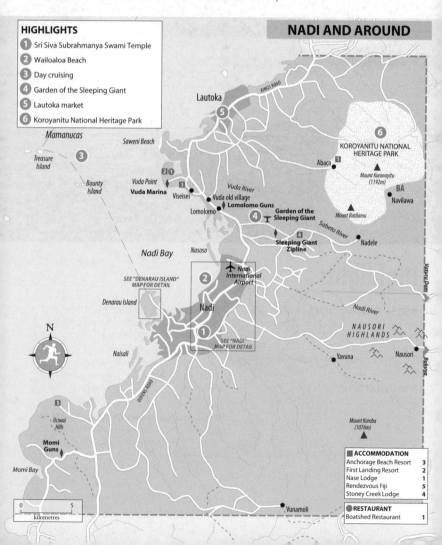

NADI AND AROUND

HIGHLIGHTS

1. Sri Siva Subrahmanya Swami Temple
2. Wailoaloa Beach
3. Day cruising
4. Garden of the Sleeping Giant
5. Lautoka market
6. Koroyanitu National Heritage Park

ACCOMMODATION

Anchorage Beach Resort	3
First Landing Resort	2
Nase Lodge	1
Rendezvous Fiji	5
Stoney Creek Lodge	4

RESTAURANT

Boatshed Restaurant	1

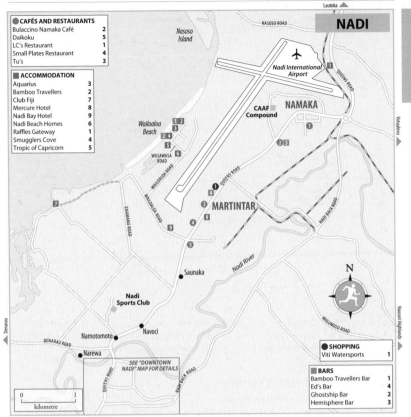

● CAFÉS AND RESTAURANTS	
Bulaccino Namaka Café	2
Daikoku	5
LC's Restaurant	1
Small Plates Restaurant	4
Tu's	3

■ ACCOMMODATION	
Aquarius	3
Bamboo Travellers	2
Club Fiji	7
Mercure Hotel	8
Nadi Bay Hotel	9
Nadi Beach Homes	6
Raffles Gateway	1
Smugglers Cove	4
Tropic of Capricorn	5

● SHOPPING	
Viti Watersports	1

■ BARS	
Bamboo Travellers Bar	1
Ed's Bar	4
Ghostship Bar	2
Hemisphere Bar	3

Downtown Nadi

With a population of around twelve thousand, split almost evenly between indigenous Fijians and Fiji-Indians, **NADI** has a laid-back rural charm, enhanced by an almost constantly sunny climate. The twin Fijian villages of Navoci and Namotomoto and the murky Nadi River separate **Downtown Nadi** from its northern suburbs. South of here, the congested Queens Road is referred to as **Main Street**, lined with fashion and accessory shops and with a lively market square off to one side. East of the market and beyond the **bus stand** is a tiny grandstand overlooking Prince Charles Park, venue for Nadi's football and rugby games.

The **northern side** of town is by far the most pleasant, with several excellent restaurants serving Indian dishes, and some interesting boutique handicraft stores, although persistent taxi drivers vying for attention distract from its charm. The further south you walk along Main Street, the seedier things become and by **Westpoint Arcade** beyond Hospital Road, the sidewalk touts take over, hassling tourists with "Bula mate!" or "Best prices in my shop!" From here on, the road is dominated by *kava* saloons where the locals gather to play pool.

The markets

The busiest part of Nadi is off Main Street, down Clay Street and into Market Road towards the lively covered **Nadi Municipal Market** (see p.64), an attractive place to

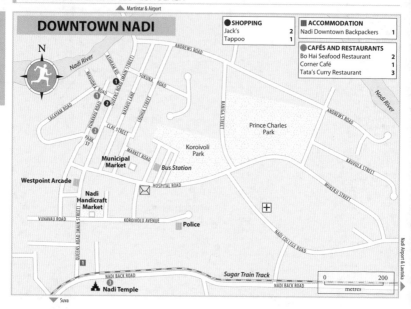

escape the sun, pick up local produce and *yaqona* roots and mingle with the locals.

A few hundred metres south in the Children's Park are 25 wooden stalls that make up the **Nadi Handicraft Market** (see p.64); you'll need to negotiate on prices.

Sri Siva Subrahmanya Temple

Nadi Back Rd • Daily 6am–7pm • F$5 • Remove your shoes before entering.

In 1994, the impressive **Sri Siva Subrahmanya Swami Temple** moved from beside the flood-prone Nadi River to the southern end of town, where an evocative three-tower Hindu complex was created over a ten-year period by eight specialist craftsmen brought in from India. A leaflet for visitors details the stories behind the vividly coloured murals. The Dravidian temple is dedicated to the deity Murugan, whose statue, specially carved in India, is housed within the 12m-high main pryramidal *vimanam* with a rectangular toped roof. The two towers at the rear of the temple with colourful domed shaped roofs are dedicated to Ganesh and Shiva.

The best time of year to visit the temple is during one of its festivals, the most striking of which is the **Thaipusam Festival** (see box, p.64), held in January/February. The festival attracts worshippers from around the world, and sees pierced devotees dragging chariots using meat hooks inserted through their flesh.

Wailoaloa Beach

Although **Wailoaloa Beach** has neither gleaming white sands nor an aquamarine lagoon, it does have a tranquil ocean outlook and stunning views towards the mountains, and makes an excellent spot for a **beach stroll**; it's a reasonably tranquil place to spend a couple of nights recovering from a long flight and planning onward travel, but there nothing to keep you here longer.

The picturesque beachfront stretches for 3km in the heart of Nadi Bay but has surprisingly little development. Backpacker hostels and budget apartments (see p.60) congregate around Wasawasa Road in Newtown and here you can enjoy a quiet beer, grab a meal or watch Polynesian dancing at weekends. The sea is good for **swimming**, although the murky lagoon is rather off-putting, blackened from the surrounding muddy mangrove estuaries.

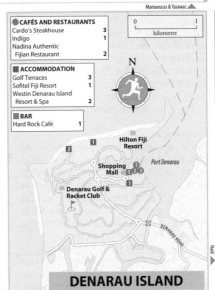

● CAFÉS AND RESTAURANTS	
Cardo's Steakhouse	3
Indigo	1
Nadina Authentic Fijian Restaurant	2

■ ACCOMMODATION	
Golf Terraces	3
Sofitel Fiji Resort	1
Westin Denarau Island Resort & Spa	2

■ BAR	
Hard Rock Café	1

DENARAU ISLAND

Denarau Island

Denarau Island was once a swampy mangrove forest but with substantial landfill, reclamation and landscaping, and, more recently, hotel and residential development, it is now a picturesque but heavily manicured environment. The island now boasts large resorts – including global giants *Hilton*, *Sofitel*, *Westin*, *Sheraton* and *Radisson* – standing in a line along a sombre grey beach, which in places has been powdered white with imported sand. The beachfront is divided by a rocky point: **west beach**, facing Malolo Island, has the *Sheraton* and *Radisson* resorts and is good for beachcombing, with stronger waves and often littered with driftwood; the **north beach** faces Nadi Bay, with tranquil views overlooking the Sleeping Giant, a shapely mountain feature separating Nadi and Lautoka. The man-made lakes, canals and inlets of an eighteen-hole championship **golf course** (see p.58) take up much of the island, with several holes hemmed in either side by hotel apartments and premium residential properties.

Port Denarau

The latest development to grace Denarau is **Port Denarau**, a modern and sterile shopping centre and marina complex built from corrugated iron and resembling an industrial sugar mill. The complex boasts half a dozen **restaurants**, some with views overlooking the silvery waters of Nadi Bay towards the stunning mountains. You'll also find tour operators, car rental outlets, a beauty and massage outlet and **shops** including a branch of ubiquitous emporium Jack's (daily 7.30am–9pm); a beauty and massage outlet; Newsagency (Mon–Thurs 7am–7pm, Fri–Sat 7am–9pm), good for books and with a Post Fiji counter; and Yee's Deli, an expensive supermarket selling gourmet food. Port Denarau is the departure point for most day-trips and transfers to the Mamanucas and Yasawas (see Chapter 2).

ARRIVAL AND DEPARTURE   NADI

As a tourist hub, **Nadi** is a major centre for travel, with the international and domestic airport, and the main ferry terminal for the Mamanucas and Yasawa Islands at Port Denarau. The easiest way of **moving on** from Nadi is by bus, with frequent services heading north to Lautoka and south to Suva from Downtown Nadi and Nadi Airport.

BY PLANE

Nadi International Airport (☎ 672 5777, ⓦ www .afl.com.fj) handles both international and domestic flights in a single terminal building located to the north of town.

Airlines Most airlines are based at the arrivals

1

concourse, including Fiji Airways (☎672 0888, ⊛fijiairways.com); Air New Zealand (☎672 2472, ⊛airnz.co.nz); and AirCalin (☎672 2145, ⊛fj.aircalin.com).

Destinations Kadavu (daily; 45min); Labasa (daily; 1hr 5min); Malolo Lailai (4 daily; 10min); Mana (4 daily; 15min); Matei, Taveuni (2 daily; 1hr 25min); Nausori, Suva (10 daily; 25min); Savusavu (5 daily; 1hr).

INFORMATION

Tourist information There is no official tourist information at the airport. However, just after passing customs on the right-hand side, you'll find an accommodation bulletin board where you can make free calls to advertised hotels around Nadi. Once inside the general public area, a help desk manned by Airport Fiji Limited can point you in the right direction for taxis, buses, tour operators and travel agents. The airport has a reputation for accommodation touts – a firm "no" should suffice if being pestered. If you need booking assistance, call in on the reliable Sun Vacations (☎672 4273; open 24hr) to the right of Western Union currency exchange.

Facilities The airport has free basic showers at both the domestic and arrival concourse toilets and you can leave luggage in a secure 24hr storage room at the far corner of the departures concourse (F$10 per day per suitcase or backpack).

GETTING INTO TOWN

Bear in mind most hostels and hotels offer complimentary pick-ups for international flight arrivals; arrange this in advance when you book your accommodation.

By bus Express buses running between Lautoka and Suva call in at the departures concourse and will drop you in Downtown, 20min to the south (F$1.30). Regular local buses stop along the Queens Rd opposite *Raffles Gateway Hotel*, a 2min walk from the arrivals concourse, between 6am and 6pm and cost F$1.10 into town.

By taxi Taxis wait directly outside the arrivals concourse and charge around F$9 to Martintar, F$13 to Wailoaloa or Downtown or F$25 to Denarau Island or Vuda.

BY BUS

Arriving in Nadi, buses or minivans will drop you at the main terminus in Downtown, with many continuing on to the airport. Once at the bus station, you buy tickets from the booths run by the individual companies.

Express buses Of the express buses, easily the most comfortable is the a/c Coral Sun (☎672 3105 or ☎672 6392; daily departures from Nadi Airport to Suva at 7.30am & 1pm; 30min later from Downtown Nadi; F$22; 4hr), with large cushioned seats and big windows. Other options include Sunbeam Transport (☎666 2086; 6 daily from Nadi Airport to Suva, 9am–2.15pm; F$15.70; 5hr) and Pacific Transport (☎670 0044; 5 daily from Nadi Airport to Suva, 6.50am–5.50pm; F$15.10; 5hr). There's roughly one express bus every hour to Lautoka (7am–6pm; 45min; F$2.80).

Local buses Local buses (F$2.80) depart every 10–15min, stop frequently along the Queens Rd and take double the time of express buses.

Minivans Minivans can be substantially quicker than buses but are often hair-raising experiences and you won't get to see much of the scenery along the way. They cost F$17 to Suva, departing from Raniga St beyond the bus stand in Downtown Nadi.

Destinations Lautoka (40 daily; 45min–1hr 45min); Sigatoka (18 daily; 1hr–1hr 45min); Suva via Pacific Harbour (13 daily; 4–5hr).

BY FERRY

Arriving by sea you will likely be pulling into Port Denarau (see p.55), served by fast catamarans from the Yasawas or Mamanucas, or if travelling by yacht, Vuda Marina (see p.67).

Destinations from Port Denarau Beachcomber (4 daily; 45min); Bounty (4 daily; 35min); Castaway (3 daily; 1hr 50min); Mana (3 daily; 1hr 25min); Malolo (3 daily; 2hr); Malolo Lailai (3 daily; 55min); Matamanoa (2 daily; 1hr 30min); South Sea (4 daily; 30min); Tokoriki (2 daily; 1hr 45min); Vomo (daily; 1hr 15min); Yasawa Islands, Kuata to Nacula (daily; 2–5hr).

Destinations from Wailoaloa Beach Mana (2 daily; 50min).

BY TAXI

A taxi will set you back around F$60 to Lautoka or F$250 to Suva; negotiate in advance.

INFORMATION

Tourist information There's no formal tourist office in town – the best source of information will be your accommodation. Beware of several shops on Main St disguised as "tourist information centres" – these are manned by pushy sales agents trying to sell private tours or timeshare units.

Touts Given its constant supply of freshly arrived tourists, Nadi is a magnet for touts trying to flog woodcarvings and masks. While they can be aggressive, a firm "No thanks" should stop you being followed around all day.

Services You'll find ATMs dotted along Main Street in Nadi, and the Queens Rd. There's a useful Westpac Bank with ATM machine at Port Denarau.

GETTING AROUND

A constant stream of cars, minivans and buses impatiently dart along the main Queens Rd between Nadi Airport and Downtown, and picking up **public transport** here is a breeze. Travelling off the main road, though, usually involves taking a **taxi**, with only an infrequent bus service to the busy tourist areas of Wailoaloa and Denarau, and these only from Downtown. The suburban layout of Nadi, with gaping farmland between attractions, makes exploring by foot impractical. You can bypass the whole of suburban Nadi by taking the **Nadi Back Road** from the roundabout south of Nadi Airport to the southern end of Downtown, a journey that takes less than 10min.

BY BUS

Along Queens Rd Local buses operate between 6am and 6pm travelling every 15min or so along the Queens Rd between Downtown Nadi and Nadi Airport, costing F$1.10 a ride, with about half of these travelling on to Lautoka and the other half diverting off the Queens Rd to rural settlements.

To Wailoaloa. There are six buses daily from Downtown to Wailoaloa between 7.10am and 5pm, costing 80 cents.

To Denarau Island There are nine buses daily from Downtown Nadi between 8am and 5pm, costing F$1.10. Once on the island, the hotels, Golf and Racket Club and Port Denarau are all connected by the complimentary Bula Bus (6am–11pm, departs every 15min).

BY MINIVAN

Minivans, many of them illegally operated, run constantly along the Queens Rd picking up passengers by the roadside for 80 cents a trip – the legal operators usually have a business name and telephone number stencilled on their bodywork.

BY TAXI

Taxis are based at most hotels, or can be called by reception staff. Otherwise, you can hail a cab on the street with an outstretched arm and a flap of a hand. Nadi International Airport taxis are painted yellow and wait immediately outside both the international and domestic arrivals concourses at all hours.

Taxi firms Airport Taxi (☎ 670 3249) at Nadi Airport; Taxi 2000 (☎ 672 1350) in Martintar; Safeway Tours (☎ 670 3280) in Downtown.

Fares Although bound by law to charge fares by the meter, with a flag fall of F$1.50 (F$5 from the airport) plus 10 cents for every 100m travelled, not all do. Instead journeys are charged a fixed rate, which is often inflated for tourists. Make sure you know the price before you get in the taxi, and bargain down if necessary. Downtown Nadi to Denarau

or the airport should be F$15, to Wailoaloa Beach F$11, or to Martintar F$6.

BY CAR

If you're planning to explore Nadi and Viti Levu, renting a car is more economical than hiring a taxi and a lot more convenient than waiting for sporadic buses along the Queens Rd, especially in rural locations. Rates range from F$65 to F$150 per day (plus F$15–20 a day for insurance); all agencies will drop the car off for free at any hotel in the Nadi area.

To Denarau Island From the Queens Rd roundabout just before Downtown, the route to Denarau winds 5km along a narrow road that eventually bridges a small mangrove estuary onto the island; there's a large public car park (F$1 for 1hr, F$20 for 24hr) beside Port Denarau.

Rental firms Avis, Nadi Airport (☎ 672 2233); Aims, Shortlane St, Namaka (☎ 672 8310); Budget, Nadi Airport (☎ 672 2735), also at Denarau Island (☎ 675 0888); Carpenters Rentals, Waqadra (☎ 672 2772); Hertz, Nadi Airport (☎ 672 3466); Khans, Nadi Airport (☎ 672 3506) also Downtown (☎ 995 1738); Satellite, Queens Rd, Martinar (☎ 670 2109); Sharma's, Nadi Airport (☎ 672 1908), also Downtown (☎ 670 1055); Thrifty, Nadi Airport (☎ 672 2935).

BY SCOOTER

Scooter rental is offered by Westside Motorbike (☎ 672 6402; F$99/24hr) in Namaka Industrial Estate and is OK for buzzing around town but is neither pleasant nor safe on the main highways.

BY BIKE

Excellent off-road cycling day-tours and general bike rental are offered by Stinger Bicycles (☎ 992 2301, ⊛ stingerbikes.com; bike F$50 per 24hr including bike delivery to Nadi hotels; mountain tour including pick up, fruit, juice and helmet from F$140, depending on the number of cyclists).

TOURS AND ACTIVITIES

Nadi offers a huge range of **tours** and **activities**, allowing you to sample the nearby islands of the Mamanucas and Yasawas, hike inland to remote villages, or try out scuba diving or deep-sea fishing, all within a day. If you just need to kill a few hours, Denarau Island offers excellent golf and tennis. You'll be able to book day-trips and activities at your accommodation but note that hotel and resort **tour desks** always give preference to operators, paying them the highest commissions, or even promote private tours with family and friends. If in doubt,

1

contact the operators listed below direct or try Sun Vacations at Nadi Airport. Tour operators offer complimentary pick-up and drop-off from all Nadi hotels. Bear in mind that if you're staying near the airport, the journey to Port Denarau (departure point for island trips) takes over an hour meandering around the suburbs and town picking up other guests; to save time, you may want to travel by taxi, which will cost F$22 one-way and take 20min.

ADRENALINE SPORTS

Adrenalin Watersports Denarau Island ☎675 1111, ⓦadrenalinfiji.com. Parasailing (F$259/1hr), wakeboarding (F$215/1hr), waterskiing (F$215/1hr) and more, from the beach in front of *Sofitel Fiji*.

Tandem Skydive Nadi Airport ☎672 8166, ⓦskydivefiji.com.fj. Tandem freefall from over 4000m with a pro sky diver, landing on the beach at Wailoaloa or Denarau. F$495–735 depending on height jumped.

DEEP-SEA FISHING

The Malolo Barrier Reef, 20km southwest of Port Denarau, is a great spot for deep-sea fishing, best in the early hours of the morning. Sailfish, tuna and walu are the prize game, with giant trevally and barracuda good casting fish.

Adrenalin Watersports Denarau Island ☎675 1111, ⓦadrenalinfiji.com. Half-day, full-day and overnight charters from Port Denarau, plus reef fishing and jigging for dogtooth tuna. From F$280 for 4hr.

★**Malolo Fisher Sports** Port Denarau ☎672 3770, ⓦgamefishingindenarau.com. Predominantly fishing charters to the Malolo Barrier Reef; the fleet includes a 14m boat, the fastest in Port Denarau. They use braided lines from 40lb to 80lb, meaning you feel every movement of the fish. They also operate sightseeing charters, snorkelling and dolphin-watching trips, night-fishing excursions and island hopping. Half-day from F$790, full day from F$1880, including all gear, lunch and soft drinks.

DIVING AND SNORKELLING

Nadi Bay's murky waters, spoiled by run-off from the surrounding hills, are unsuitable for diving or snorkelling. For both, you need to travel at least 20min offshore, which takes you to the excellent dive sites of the Mamanucas – the further away from the mainland, the better the water clarity and more vibrant the coral reefs. Dive boats depart from Port Denarau, Wailoaloa Beach and Vuda Marina.

★**Coral Cats** Port Denarau St ☎936 4840, ⓦcoralcatssailing.com.fj. Small catamaran which heads to the Malolo Barrier Reef for dolphin watching and snorkelling, plus an excellent BBQ lunch on Malolo Lailai. The super-friendly and attentive crew makes the experience outstanding. Bring sun protection. 10am–5pm; F$175 includes lunch.

Viti Watersports Corner of Queens Rd & Kennedy St ☎670 2413, ⓦvitiwatersports.com. Operating fast covered boats from Denarau with state-of-the-art dive gear. They also sell snorkel and dive equipment.

PADI open-water course F$695, 2-tank dive F$225, snorkelling F$70.

GOLF AND TENNIS

Denarau Golf Club ☎675 9711, ⓦdenaraugolf .fiji-golf.net. A long, flat course, well-manicured with virtually no rough but lots of fish-shaped bunkers, canals coming into play and large fast greens. Book ahead in high season. Daily 6.30am–6.30pm; F$145 including compulsory golf cart, club hire F$65, shoe hire F$15; slightly discounted rates for guests staying at any of the Denarau resorts. The club also has four all-weather synthetic tennis courts and six grass courts, with lessons available by the hour. Daily 7am–9pm; F$35 per hr.

ISLAND CRUISES

Exploring the offshore islands of the Mamanucas on a day-trip can either be experienced aboard an elegant yacht or by zooming out to the island resorts by fast catamaran.

SAILING CRUISES

PJ's Ultimate Sailing & Snorkelling Experience Port Denarau ☎672 5022, ⓦpjfishsailfiji.com. Sailing, snorkelling, island-hopping and fishing on board three-masted yacht *Pelorus Jack*. The crew point out seahorses and stingrays, as well as singing traditional songs and entertaining kids with face painting. 9.30am–5.15pm; F$185 includes BBQ lunch and soft drinks.

Ra Marama Port Denarau ☎670 1823. Most affordable of the sailing cruises, aboard a charming square-rigged vessel which cruises along the Viti Levu coast to the tiny coral island of Tivua, where you can spend five hours day-dreaming, lounging in the lagoon and snorkelling. 10am–5pm; F$97 includes BBQ lunch.

Seaspray Port Denarau ☎675 0500, ⓦssc.com.fj. Two-part tour, with the first leg catching the *South Sea Cruise* fast catamaran to Mana Island, where you transfer to a double-mast schooner venturing to the outer Mamanucas. It takes almost 3hr travel time from Nadi, but you do get to walk on the fine white sands of Modriki, one of the locations of the film *Castaway*, starring Tom Hanks. You also visit the traditional fishing village of Yanuya, where a shell market and *kava* ceremony are put on by the locals (daily except Sun). 9am–6pm; F$209 includes BBQ lunch, local beer and wine.

★**Whale's Tale** Port Denarau ☎670 2443, ⓦwhalestale.com.fj. This beautiful 33m schooner offers a day of indulgence – sipping wine whilst sightseeing around the protected waters of the inner Coral Islands and anchoring at an uninhabited island for a gourmet lunch and snorkelling. 10am–6pm; F$199 includes champagne breakfast, lunch and all drinks.

MOTORBOAT CRUISES

★**South Sea Combo Cruise** Port Denarau ☎675 0500, ⓦssc.com.fj. Good sightseeing introduction to the small island resorts of the Mamanucas – the best views are from the top-level open-air deck, and you pull up sufficiently close to three tiny coral cays to see into the bures. A BBQ lunch is served on South Sea Island before heading back. 9am–5.45pm; F$180 includes lunch and all drinks.

SCENIC FLIGHTS

★**Island Hoppers** Nadi Airport ☎672 0410, ⓦhelicopters.com.fj. The best views of the islands and mountains are on large-window scenic helicopter flights: F$417 per person for 20min, F$540 per person for 30min, or you can try the "tag-along" deal where you can join resort transfers to an unspecified destination for F$417. You can also buy packages, where you're dropped off at various islands including Castaway (from F$612).

SURFING

Surfing on the Malolo Barrier Reef is easily accessible from Momi Bay or Uciwai (see p.65), where there are two surf-oriented budget resorts for experienced surfers.

Fiji Surf Co Corner of Hospital Rd, above Raniga Jewellers ☎670 5960, ⓦfijisurfco.com. Transfers to surfing breaks, surf equipment rental and surf instruction at Natadola Beach or Sigatoka Sandunes (good for beginners as both breaks are accessible from the beach and don't crash over hazardous coral reefs). Surf lessons F$250, surf tours F$150, surfboard/bodyboard rental F$50.

★ **Fiji Surf School** Nadi ☎997 0216, ⓦfijisurfschool .com. Highly recommended surf lessons at all levels, plus one-day or tailor-made "surfaris", where you can combine surfing, diving and spearfishing. From F$150.

VILLAGE TOURS

★**Fiji Eco Tours** Lot 13, ATS Subdivision, Votualevu ☎672 4312, ⓦfijiecotours.com.fj. The 2hr drive to delightful Navala Village is well worth the effort just to walk amongst the 200 traditional thatch houses (Mon–Sat 9am–4pm; F$220 includes picnic lunch, min 2 people), but there's also pleasant sightseeing along the way. A shorter half-day tour visits Nalesutale Village, a 30min drive from Nadi along the Sabeto Valley, with a short forest hike to a small waterfall and village lunch (Mon–Sat departs 9am & 1pm; F$99 includes lunch). You can add a therapeutic visit to the Tifajek mud pools and hot springs for F$21 extra. Full-day tours which take in the Garden of the Sleeping Giant or additional activities like horseriding, mat weaving and river fishing cost F$178 (daily 9am–5pm). There are also various village stay options, for a more in-depth cultural experience.

Pehicle ☎672 4086, ⓦpehicle.com. For those interested in Indian culture, Pehicle run the only tour visiting an Indian settlement, where you can make and sample curries, roti and chutneys (daily on demand; F$45; 2hr 30min). There's also a full-day tour to Lauwaki Villageon the road to Lautoka, with a *kava* ceremony, lovo lunch and dancing (Mon–Sat 9.30am–2.30pm; F$145; min 2 people). On the Mystery Dinner Tour, the mystery is whether the dinner will be in a Fijian or Indo-Fijian home (Daily 6.30–8.30pm; F$76; min 2 people).

Rosie Holidays Rosie House, Martintar ☎672 2755, ⓦrosiefiji.com. A four-day/three-night immersion in village life, trekking through the forest and grassland of the Central Highlands (Mon & Wed departs 8am). You stay overnight in bures, eat food cooked in a lovo, swim in natural pools and ride horses.

ACCOMMODATION

There are a handful of affordable hotels along the bland and overdeveloped main road between **Nadi Airport** and **Downtown**. However, to get a view of the ocean, you need to stay at either Wailoaloa Beach or Denarau Island, off the Queens Rd on Nadi Bay. **Wailoaloa Beach**, the budget and backpacker centre, is the most central of these and has a laid-back atmosphere with stunning views along the coast, but the greyish beach itself is by no means postcard-worthy. The opulent man-made creation of **Denarau Island**, 5km west of Downtown, with its five-star resorts, luxury homes and a modern shopping centre has an intuitively hollow, plastic feel. **Vuda Point** (see p.67), a 20min drive north of the airport, features a couple of mid-range boutique beach resorts and is closer to Lautoka. For **longer stays**, try *Nadi Beach Homes*

STAYING AT PORT DENARAU – OR NOT

Port Denarau is the jumping-off point for trips to the Mamanucas; **accommodation** at the port is expensive (see p.60), so many visitors stay in Nadi and take advantage of the efficient free bus service that links resorts and hotels with the hydrofoil service on request.

1

(☎ 672 7999, ⊛ nadibeach.com), with excellent-value weekly and monthly rates in three-bedroom private holiday homes with swimming pools, modern one- and two-bedroom a/c beach apartments, or studio-style homestays.

NADI AIRPORT AND DOWNTOWN

★**Mercure Hotel Nadi** Queens Rd, Martintar ☎ 672 2255, ⊛ mercure.com; map p.53. Great location for dining out and visiting a few of Nadi's local bars that are within walking distance. The 85 modern rooms are bland in design but very comfortable, located in two blocks, each three storeys high, overlooking a small central swimming pool. F$130

Nadi Bay Hotel Wailoaloa Rd, Martintar ☎ 672 3599, ⊛ fijinadibayhotel.com; map p.53. The largest backpacker hostel in Nadi is set in a mundane suburban location just off the main Queens Rd. Once inside, though, it's a pretty oasis with a large swimming pool. Cosy restaurant Antoinette's serves the best food of all the backpacker places in a plant-filled courtyard with wooden decking and murals. Dorms, standard rooms and apartments are all a bit pokey however, and light sleepers will curse at being directly in the flight path of the early morning 747s. Breakfast voucher included. 14-bed dorm F$37; a/c 4-bed dorm F$40; rooms F$160

Nadi Downtown Backpackers Queens Rd, Downtown Nadi ☎ 670 0600, ⊛ fijidowntownhotel.com; map p.54. One of the few options in Downtown Nadi, this poky building is located along the seedier southern end of the main street. The eight-bed dorm rooms and double rooms are identical in size, each with en-suite cold-water bathrooms, but bedding is grubby; unless you have a particular yen to be downtown it's not recommended. Dorms F$25; rooms F$85

Raffles Gateway Queens Rd, Nadi Airport ☎ 672 2444, ⊛ rafflesgateway.com; map p.53. Smack opposite Nadi International Airport, with a spacious garden setting, tennis courts and a large family pool with water slide, this is a good choice for families. Rooms boast floral decor and wicker furniture but are clean and with a/c. The family rooms can sleep two children who, if under 16 and accompanied by two adults, stay for free. Day rooms (available between 6am and 6pm) are handy for late flights. F$195

WAILOALOA BEACH

Aquarius Wasawasa Rd, New Town Beach ☎ 672 6000, ⊛ aquariusfiji.com; map p.53. A converted homestead facing the beach and ocean, this place feels homely, with hammocks, a small pool, communal lounge and a wide staircase leading to the slightly old-fashioned rooms. The cramped dormitories (with two, four or twelve beds) are squashed at the back but have a/c and en-suite bathrooms. Dorms F$30; rooms F$120

★**Bamboo Travellers** 33 New Town Beach ☎ 672 2225, ⊛ bamboobackpackers.hostel.com;

map p.53. Pitch-perfect backpackers right on the beach, with a warm atmosphere, *kava* nights in the bar, Fijian language lessons and excursions. Some of the basic double rooms are set back from the beach across the road. The restaurant/bar (see p.62) is a good place to meet fellow travellers. *Bamboo* operates the popular North Fiji Backpacker Project, an adventure-orientated trip to their sister hostel on Taveuni (see p.205) and the remote neighbouring island of Qamea. Dorms F$12; rooms F$60

Club Fiji Enamanu Rd, Wailoaloa South ☎ 670 0150, ⊛ clubfiji-resort.com; map p.53. Quiet beach setting at the secluded southern end of Wailoaloa; the restaurant and bar has a gentle, island-style atmosphere. Accommodation is in beachside bures with timber floors and verandas, plus there's a self-contained one-bedroom apartment with lounge and kitchen. Bures F$142; apartment F$174

Smugglers Cove Wasawasa Rd, New Town Beach ☎ 672 6578, ⊛ smugglersbeachresort.com; map p.53. This stark modern cement building hides one of Wailoaloa's liveliest beachfront spots. Guitarists and *kava* drinking keep the bar humming, the open-sided kitchen serves probably the best food on the beach, while a small pool and large deck area face the sand. Modern a/c rooms are clean, albeit small, and most have tiny bathrooms. The large mixed dorm is partitioned into four-bed areas with lockers; there's also a four-bed mixed dorm and an eight-bed female dorm. Internet, laundry and a 24hr reception make this a popular choice, and it's often full. Rates for double rooms include a light breakfast. Large dorm F$33; 4- and 8-bed dorms F$42; doubles F$145; family rooms F$265

Tropic of Capricorn 11 Wasawasa Rd, New Town Beach ☎ 672 3089, ⊛ tropicofcapricornresort-nadi.com; map p.53. Modern three-storey cement building facing the beach, with clean simple rooms and good balcony views, especially the deluxe ocean-view rooms at the top. The dorm rooms in the old building at the back are a bit basic though. Dorms F$30; rooms F$130

DENARAU ISLAND

Golf Terraces Port Denarau ☎ 675 0557, ⊛ theterraces .com.fj; map p.55. Fully equipped and spacious one-, two- and three-bedroom apartments overlooking the golf course and mountains, a 2min walk to Port Denarau's shops, restaurants and marina. F$478

★**Sofitel Fiji Resort** North beach ☎ 675 1111, ⊛ www.sofitelfiji.com.fj; map p.55. Beautifully landscaped five-star resort, with most of the 296 rooms having ocean views, although they are small for the price.

The beach outlook is pretty, with plenty of watersports available, and there's a serene spa centre. The V Restaurant dishes up gourmet international food. **F$377**

Westin Denarau Island Resort & Spa North beach ☎ 675 0000, ⓦ westindenarauisland.com; map p.55.

Classically designed resort with traditional architecture, dark timber and a streamlined swimming pool. Like all resorts on Denarau, rooms are in three-storey cement blocks. Half the resort faces a sea wall, with the other half on black sand. **F$225**

EATING

Being a tourist town, Nadi's **restaurants** offer almost every style of international cuisine, though there's just one traditional Fijian restaurant, in Denarau. Prices at all independent restaurants are very reasonable, with mains seldom topping F$40, although resort restaurants tend to be overpriced. Most of the resorts on Denarau Island offer themed buffet dinners for between F$55 and F$75 per person; you can also experience a **Fijian lovo night** (around F$60 per person), traditional food cooked in an underground oven at the *Sofitel Fiji Resort* on Thursday and *Sheraton Fiji Resort* on Saturday. For lunch, the **Downtown** area has plenty of good affordable restaurants, especially for sampling Indian dishes; one of the best options is the free lunch provided by the **Sri Siva Subrahmanya Swami Temple** – head towards the trestle tables at the rear of the temple (visitors can make a donation but there's no obligation). The most popular places for dining out at night are along the Queens Rd between **Namaka** and **Martintar**, an otherwise dull light industrial area, and at **Port Denarau**, with its fine-dining restaurants, marina views and inflated prices.

NAMAKA AND MARTINTAR

★**Bulaccinio Namaka Café** 7 Queens Rd, Namaka ☎ 672 8638, ⓦ bulaccinio.com; map p.53. This chic café is a great place to treat yourself to coffee and cake as well as sumptuous lunchtime meals. The grilled fish in a subtle lemon sauce (F$19.50) is divine. Mains from F$14. Mon 6am–5pm, Tues–Sun 6am–11pm.

★ **Daikoku** Corner of Queens Rd & Northern Press Rd, Martintar ☎ 670 3622; map p.53. Attractive temple-style decor and fabulous Japanese food, with nine *teppanyaki* tables upstairs where food is cooked in front of you and a sushi bar downstairs. Try the seafood combination (F$51.50), or Max chicken (F$40.50), a whole chicken cooked and served as five distinct dishes. Sashimi lovers will relish tuna, giant clam and red snapper, all caught locally. Mon–Sat noon–2pm & 6–9.30pm.

LC's Restaurant Hillside Rd, Namaka ☎ 672 8181; map p.53. Most reliable of the many Chinese restaurants in Nadi and the locals' favourite, although it's a little hard to find, located upstairs and behind the Morris Hedstrom supermarket in Namaka. Well-cooked Cantonese food and good service; F$25 will get you two courses and drinks. Mon–Sat 11am–3pm & 6–10pm, Sun 6–10pm.

★ **Small Plates Restaurant and Bar** Queens Rd, Martintar, opposite Capricorn Hotel ☎ 672 3888; map p.53. Delightful little place in a garden setting serving tapas-style Chinese dishes with a Fijian twist; each costs only F$6–8, so you can mix and match choices such as salt and pepper squid or stir fry. Well-priced imported beer and wine by the glass. Daily 11.30am–2pm & 6–10pm.

Tu's Queens Rd, Martintar ☎ 672 2110; map p.53. Simple but colourful and engaging Fijian-owned place

where the big breakfast (F$22) and pancake stacks (F$19.50) will definitely keep you going. The broad menu includes several Indonesian dishes and the best fish and chips in town, with most mains from F$22. Daily 9am–9pm.

DOWNTOWN NADI

Bo Hai Seafood Restaurant Main St, above Naginda's Store ☎ 670 0178; map p.54. Reliable Chinese restaurant in a utilitarian Main St location that's very popular with locals, including Chinese families. They serve dishes such as seafood wonton soup (F$10) and an intriguing bêche-de-mer hotpot, with the odd samosa on the menu for good measure. Large round tables make it good for groups. Daily noon–9pm.

Corner Café Back of Jack's Complex, Wavudra Rd ☎ 670 1233; map p.54. If you're looking for well-presented European food, this modern a/c restaurant is the best in town. The big breakfast is filling, and the lunchtime menu has burgers or salads (F$13) and mains including prawn curry (F$19) and pan-seared tuna (F$22), as well as fresh juices (F$7), good coffee and home-made cakes. Mon–Sat 8am–4pm, Sun 8am–2.30pm.

Tata's Curry Restaurant Nadi Back Road; map p.54. Set at the back of the Nadi Temple, this simple raised shack with tables and stools serves typical Fiji-Indian curries – not too hot, quite oily and with meat on the bone. Most dishes are F$5–8, including dhal soup, goat curry and roti, making this the best-value food in town. Mon–Sat 7.30am–9pm.

DENARAU ISLAND

Cardo's Steakhouse Port Denarau ☎ 675 0900; map p.55. Fantastic location overlooking the placid bay surrounding Port Denarau, with lots of outdoor tables under flame trees. As well as well-presented, tender steaks (a touch expensive at around F$40), *Cardo's* makes the best thin-crust pizzas (F$20) in Nadi. It's also a good spot for coffee and a cooked breakfast. The bar usually creates a lively atmosphere in the evenings, especially at weekends. Daily 8am–10pm, bar closes 11pm.

Indigo Port Denarau ☎675 0026, ⓦindigofiji.com; map p.55. Classical Indian restaurant with contemporary interior and plain outdoor tables overlooking the canal to residential homes. Try the subtly spiced duck curry, slow cooked on the bone (F$27), or the creamy lamb korma

(F$26). Also offers vegetarian dishes (under F$20). Daily 11am–10pm.

★**Nadina Authentic Fijian Restaurant** Building C, Shop R1 & R2, Port Denarau ☎679 0290; map p.55. An appealing shack-style waterfront place that's a good local alternative to the international hotel restaurants, Nadina serves up Fijian fish classics such as kokoda (F$16) and pan-fried walu steak (F$35). You may also be treated to an impromptu *kava* ceremony and some live music. Daily 7am–10pm.

DRINKING, NIGHTLIFE AND ENTERTAINMENT

For most tourists, Nadi's nightlife revolves around quiet **resort bars**, with happy hours usually running from 5.30pm to 6.30pm. To immerse yourself in the local after-hours culture you have to head to either Martintar, popular with Nadi office workers, or the south end of Downtown where pool bars, *kava* saloons and a couple of raucous **nightclubs** are the hangouts for urban and rural Fijians. Apart from these two areas, and the resort enclaves of Denarau Island and Wailoaloa Beach, Nadi after dark is pretty much a ghost town and roaming around on your own isn't recommended. Traditional **dance shows** are held at several resorts and are usually free to watch, with a blend of animated Fijian war mekes (see box below), elegant Polynesian-style hula and enthralling Samoan fire dancing; some are combined with lovo buffet dinners. Times may vary, so it's worth calling ahead. There's a multiplex **cinema** next to the *Capricorn Hotel* in Martintar.

BARS AND CLUBS

★**Bamboo Travellers** 33 New Town Beach ☎672 2225, ⓦbamboobackpackers.hostel.com; map p.53. The best option for beach-bound travellers to meet for a drink, with friendly staff, *kava* sessions, guitar playing and a decent selection of beers, wines and spirits, as well as good Fijian food to soak it up. Daily 10am–late.

★**Ed's Bar** Queens Rd, Martintar ☎672 4650; map p.53. Unchallenged as Nadi's only trendy night spot for at least twenty years, this place is popular with more affluent locals and it's still a great place to meet over a F$4 beer early on, or to shuffle onto the packed dancefloor as the night progresses. Bouncers try to keep a tight lid on things and there's occasional live music, when admission is F$5. Daily 5pm–5am.

Ghostship Bar Smugglers Cove Resort, Wailoaloa Beach ☎672 6578, ⓦsmugglersbeachfiji.com; map p.53. Delightful spot for a quiet afternoon beer, with wooden tables beside the beach, ocean breezes, sunset views and happy hour from 5pm to 7pm. Every night there's musical entertainment from Tai and the Kavaholics, plus Polynesian and Fijian hulas and knife and fire-dancing shows. Daily 10am–11pm.

Hard Rock Café Port Denarau ☎675 0032; map p.55. Hard Rock's 126th outlet features the usual international rock memorabilia – though disappointingly no mention of any Fijian musicians. Staff are the hippest in town, ensuring a lively atmosphere. There's draught beer for F$4.50 and decent but expensive hamburgers and nibbles. Daily 11am–11pm.

THE FIJIAN MEKE

One element of Fijian life that seems to have changed little since the 1800s is the **meke**, a performing art of dance and song. Legends and tales have been passed down the generations through meke and it remains Fiji's most prominent form of artistic expression.

Traditionally, music was created only by chanting and rhythmic clapping, often with the addition of a *lali* (hollowed wood) drum hit with bamboo sticks. More recently the guitar and ukelele have been introduced. Mekes are generally performed by male-only or female-only groups, although a modern introduction, the *vakamalolo*, combines the two.

At formal mekes, men may perform club and spear dances and the women perform fan dances. In village mekes, the practice of *fakawela* involves presenting the dancers with a gift in appreciation of their performance, often fine cloth or fabric. At times of weddings or other celebrations bringing two parties together, this usually involves encircling the dancers with long rolls of cloth. Otherwise money is collected as they perform.

SRI SIVA SUBRAHMANYA SWAMI TEMPLE (P.54) >

1

THAIPUSAM FESTIVAL

The bizarre **Thaipusam Festival** at Nadi's Sri Siva Subrahmanya Swami Temple calls together thousands of Hindu worshippers to celebrate the birthday of Subrahmanya, or Lord Murugan, the god of war worshipped amongst South Indians. During the ten-day festival held over the full moon between January and February, devotees arrive at the temple to pray and cleanse their spirits. Some prove their faith with multiple **body piercings** on the chest, arms, face and tongue while others drag **chariots**, or *kavadris*, attached by sharpened meat hooks to their backs. It's a fascinating and highly photogenic festival and you'll be offered free food and invited to join in the celebrations, which are accompanied by dancing musicians. Be sure to observe common courtesies such as removing shoes before entering the temple grounds and not attending if you have recently drunk alcohol.

Hemisphere Bar 7 Queens Rd, Namaka ☎ 672 8638, ⓦ bulaccino.com; map p.53. Set at the back of the popular Bulaccino café, the garden-set Hemisphere Bar is a classy spot for an evening drink, with cocktails and imported wines and beers, plus a tapas-style food menu. Daily 11am–11pm.

DANCE SHOWS

These shows generally feature fire dancing and song as well as meke – traditional dance – and cost around F$25 per person.

Hilton Fiji Resort Denarau Island ☎ 675 6800; map p.55. Fijian meke is performed beside the pool for diners at the swish if anodyne surroundings of this Denarau resort. Sat 8.30pm.

★ **Smugglers Cove** Wailoaloa Beach ☎ 672 6578, ⓦ smugglersbeachfiji.com; map p.53. Informal beach setting with a mix of Fijian and Polynesian dance, plus enthralling fire dances performed by the Helava Group. Wed, Fri & Sun nights from 7pm.

Westin Denarau Resort Denarau Island ☎ 675 0777; map p.55. Impressive Fijian fire walking set in a staged amphitheatre, combined with a meke, featuring the country's fabled songs of love and loss. Wed 7.30pm.

SHOPPING

Nadi has a decent selection of **shops** and its department stores are handy for stocking **electronic goods** such as memory cards for digital cameras. General shopping hours are from 8.30am to 5.30pm weekdays, and 8.30am to 1pm on Saturday. Most shops at the open-air Port Denarau shopping centre are open daily including Sundays from 7am to 7pm, closing at 9pm on Friday and Saturday.

CRAFTS AND JEWELLERY

When looking at craft items, be aware that war clubs, printed designs on *masi* (bark cloth), *tanoa* drinking bowls and priest dishes are authentic Fijian designs, while face masks are simply tourist gimmicks and mostly imported from Asia.

Handicraft Market Koroivulo Ave, Downtown; map p.54. If you're good at haggling, this attractive little strip of stalls is the place to pick up reasonably priced wooden carvings, woven baskets and sarongs. Mon–Sat 8am–5pm.

Jack's Queens Rd, Downtown ☎ 670 0744, ⓦ jacksfiji .com; map p.54. Dependable department store which sells Fijian crafts in a faux-rustic setting. Good-quality workmanship, and they will pack and post worldwide. Mon–Sat 8am–5.30pm, Sun 9am–4.30pm.

Tappoo Queens Rd, Downtown ☎ 670 1022, ⓦ tappoo .com.fj; map p.54. Department store that's a good source of black and multi-hued pearls. These are harvested at several places in Fiji and make fine necklaces and earrings, but quality and prices vary immensely: the cheapest disfigured pearls cost as little as F$20; perfect ones – opaque, smooth and of a deep colour – fetch as much as F$1000. Some pearls are imported from the Cook Islands and Tahiti, the biggest producers of black pearls in the world. Daily 8am–5pm.

FOOD

Municipal Market Between Market Rd & Hospital Rd, Downtown; map p.54. Atmospheric covered market, with enticing piles of fresh seasonal fruit and veg and a whole section dedicated to the sale of *yaqona* roots – an essential purchase if you're making a village visit (see p.31). If you're after a snack, Indian boys usually sell inexpensive peanuts, curried beans and roti parcels at the main entrance on Market Rd. Mon–Sat 7am–5pm.

SNORKELLING AND DIVING EQUIPMENT

It's worth buying your own set of snorkelling gear, especially as many budget island resorts either don't supply them or have rather old leaky kit. When you're done, the gear makes a fantastic gift to a local villager, which also saves lugging them home. It will set you back about F$65 for a snorkel and mask and F$45 for a pair of fins. As well as

Viti Watersports (see below), Jack's and Tappoo (see opposite) also sell snorkelling gear.

Viti Watersports Martintar ☎670 2413, ⓦ vitiwatersports.com; map p.53. Stocks a good range of dive and snorkelling equipment, plus they have a repair and maintenance facility. Mon–Fri 8am–5pm, Sat 8am–noon.

DIRECTORY

Banks All the following have ATM machines, but expect lengthy queues on Thursday afternoon and Friday after payday, and also on Saturday morning: Westpac, corner of Main St and Vunivau Rd (Mon–Thurs 9.30am–3pm, Fri 9.30am–4pm), also at Namaka Lane and Port Denarau; ANZ Bank, Queens Rd (Mon 9.30am–4pm, Tues–Fri 9am–4pm), also at Namaka Lane and Nadi International Airport Arrivals Concourse (24hr). Machines sometimes run out of cash, in which case try the ATM inside *Macdonald's* in Saunaka Village between Martintar and Downtown, or beside the boat transfer check-in counter at Port Denarau.

Hospital Nadi Hospital, Nadi College Rd, Downtown (☎670 1128).

Internet access Tappoo's Internet Shop, Queens Rd, adjacent to the department store (Mon–Fri 8.30am–5.30pm, Sat 8.30am–3.30pm, Sun 8.30am–2.30pm; F$2/hr).

Medical centres Namaka Private Medical Centre, Namaka (Mon–Fri 9am–6pm & 7–9pm, Sat 9am–1pm & 7–9pm, Sun 10am–1pm & 7–9pm; ☎672 2288), can perform some surgical procedures. Zens Medical Centre, 30 Lodhia St, Downtown Nadi (doctor 24hr, dentist Mon–Fri 8am–6pm, Sat 8am–1pm; ☎ 670 3533), is best for minor ailments.

Pharmacy Island Pharmacy Shop 1, Main St, Downtown Nadi (Mon–Sat 8am–7pm, Sun 9am–2pm; ☎670 6506).

Police Emergencies ☎917. The main police station is at Koroivolu Lane in Downtown (☎670 0222). There are suburban stations at Nadi Airport (☎672 2172) and Totogo Lane in the CAAF Compound, Namaka (☎672 2222).

Post office At Koroivolu Lane, Downtown and at Nadi Airport (Mon–Fri 8am–4pm, Sat 8am–noon). Both offer Poste Restante (see p.45).

Telephone There are public phones at Nadi Airport and in front of the post office in Downtown.

Around Nadi

The area around Nadi offers access to Viti Levu's rural interior as well as the surfing breaks of the nearby **Malolo Barrier Reef**; the latter can be sampled by staying at *Rendezvous Fiji* (see below). Inland, the flats of the Nadi River eventually yield to the alpine **Nausori Highlands**. North towards Lautoka, the Queens Road passes the scenic **Sabeto River Valley** and **Vuda Point**. A few kilometres further on, the busy industrial port of **Lautoka** offers good shopping and access to the north coast. In the distance, the shapely **Koroyanitu National Park** beckons through the haze.

Uciwai Hills and the Momi Guns

Twenty minutes' drive south of Nadi along the Queens Road is the turn-off to **Uciwai Hills**, the closest spot on the mainland to the surfing breaks along the Malolo Barrier Reef (see p.58). Just before the turn-off for Momi Bay, a small track leads to the **Momi Guns** (daily 9am–5pm; F$3; ☎997 1580), two six-inch World War II coastal artillery guns aimed at Navula Passage in anticipation of Japanese invasion. The site is administered by the National Trust and has a lovely view of the southern Mamanuca Islands.

ARRIVAL AND DEPARTURE   UCIWAI HILLS AND THE MOMI GUNS

By taxi Few buses run out here so your best bet is to take a taxi from Nadi (15min; F$15).

ACCOMMODATION

Rendezvous Fiji Uciwai Hills ☎628 4426, ⓦ surfdivefiji.com; map p.52. Budget surf resort run by a local Fijian surfer and his Japanese wife. Accommodation is clean and simple, either in private en-suite rooms sleeping up to four, doubles with shared facilities or a six-bed dorm. Daily surf trips (F$140, minimum 2 people) take just 20min to get to Malolo Barrier Reef and spend 2–4hr surfing; both short and long boards can be rented, with a few secondhand boards normally for sale. Rates include meals. Camping F$20; dorms F$28; rooms F$52

1

The Nausori Highlands

Towering over the coastal flats of Nadi are the high peaks of Koromba to the south and Koronayitu in the north, both over 1000m and forming part of the spectacular **Nausori Highlands**. With your own transport, a stunning **drive** starts from halfway along the Nadi Back Road at the turn-off known as Mulomulo Road. Head inland along this road for 14km, and after a steep hairpin bend, keep an eye out for a walking track on the left-hand side (you can park 50m beyond at a roadside clearing on the right); the track leads up past a triangular survey marker to a steep cliff with superb views over the Sabeto River Valley and out over Nadi to the offshore islands.

The road continues climbing through pine forests to Nausori village. Five kilometres beyond is a fork in the road – the left track marked Natewa Road heads over to Vaturu Dam (see below), but it's a rough 4WD trail.

North to Lautoka

The most scenic region around Nadi lies along a rural stretch of the Queens Road running north towards Lautoka, dotted with palm trees, timber churches, grazing horses and tranquil villages and backed by forested hills. Inland is the **Sabeto River Valley**, the botanical **Garden of the Sleeping Giant** and the **Sleeping Giant Zipline** adventure park; further on the road passes through the historic villages of Lomolomo and Viseisei before reaching the tranquil coastal setting of **Vuda Point**, halfway between Nadi Airport and Lautoka.

Sabeto River Valley

The lush **Sabeto River Valley**, 4km north of the airport, is accessed along a 5km sealed road, which thereafter turns to dirt for another 30km. The valley is flanked on its north side by the distinct outline of the **Sleeping Giant** rock formation with its pointy nose facing the sky. The road turns to dirt just beyond Masimasi Hindu Temple, and continues on winding its way up the steep Sabeto Hills to the utterly remote **Vaturu Dam**.

Garden of the Sleeping Giant

Take the Wailoko dirt road, which turns inland off the Queens Rd 1km beyond the Sabeto Valley turn-off; the entrance is 2km further on • Mon–Sat 9am–5pm, Sun 9am–noon • F$16 • ☏ 672 2701, ⓦ gsgfiji.com

Founded by actor Raymond Burr (aka Perry Mason), the **Garden of the Sleeping Giant** boasts a wonderful collection of orchids and other flowering plants as well as several trails meandering through the landscaped grounds and into the lowland rainforest abutting the Sleeping Giant escarpment. The entrance fee includes a tropical juice which you can enjoy on their lovely terrace.

Sleeping Giant Zipline

Free return transfers from Nadi Downtown hotels and Port Denarau, with pickups at 8.30am & 1pm • F$189, children (4–12yrs) $94.50, includes unlimited zips, Orchid Falls, jungle safari, deli lunch and fruit juice • ☏ 666 7935 or 999 6360, ⓦ ziplinefiji.com

The **Sleeping Giant Zipline**, a 35-acre rainforest adventure park, features an array of ziplines, allowing you to whizz across the terrain. You can also can bathe at the Orchid waterfalls (remember to bring swimming costumes), swing on jungle vines and spot parrots in the forest canopy.

ACCOMMODATION   SABETO RIVER VALLEY

★**Stoney Creek Lodge** Just beyond Masimasi Hindu Temple ☏ 672 2206, ⓦ stoneycreekfiji.net; map p.52. This delightful rural retreat, with dreamy views looking north up the valley, is only 15min from Nadi Airport and boasts a lovely swimming pool, excellent restaurant and quiet bar. Activities on offer include mountain treks and a trip to hot springs. Camping F$55; dorms F$55; rooms F$150; bures F$190

1

Lomolomo

Eight kilometres north of the airport, the rocky tongue of the Sabeto Hills descends dramatically to the base of **LOMOLOMO** village. From here, you can explore a delightful **walking track** over the hills and back to the Wailoko dirt road. The trail starts from the unsignposted Esivo Road, 1km beyond the village just beyond the timber mill. Three hundred metres down this dirt road, a small track leads uphill following the ridge inland towards the seldom-visited **Lomolomo Guns**. It takes thirty minutes to walk to these World War II artillery guns from the main road, and there's a fine view overlooking Nadi Bay and the surrounding mountains. For a longer two-hour trek, continue walking along the ridge, bearing right towards the telecommunication antennae. From here, the trail meanders around boulders and overhanging caves to the rocky summit of Khan's Farm where you'll notice plenty of goats. From the summit, you can follow the access road south to Wailoko Road, 3km inland from the Queens Road and close to the Garden of the Sleeping Giant (see opposite).

Viseisei

Village visit $5

Heading north towards Lautoka and just after the Vuda River, the old Queens Road branches off left through the chiefly village of **Viseisei**. According to Fijian legend this was where **Lutunasobasoba**, the first inhabitant of Fiji, landed his canoe, the *Kaunitoni*, having sailed all the way from Tanganyika (modern-day Tanzania). Today, Fijians around much of the country still claim descent from Lutunasobasoba.

Park up on the roadside at the near end of the village – local women at the seafront **craft stalls** will arrange a village visit. This takes in the **Methodist church**, the exterior of the chief's thatched house and the totemic breadfruit tree. Arrive at 10am on Sunday to hear wonderful a cappella singing in the church (service 10.30am–noon).

Vuda

Turn right off the Queens Rd just before the Vuda River, along the Vuda–Vaivai Rd; the site is signposted on the right • F$8 fee (if someone on duty), includes guided tour; otherwise free

Vuda, the ancient village that Lutunasobasoba is said to have founded, is a couple of kilometres inland along the Vuda River at the foot of a massive boulder. As you explore the overgrown paths around the old village site, keep an eye out for the ancient **rock platforms** where homes were built and for clearings with accumulated pottery shards and *kai* shells where the common people cooked. The high chiefs, and supposedly Lutunasobasoba himself, lived atop the rocky bluff for added security; any invaders would have to pass through a rock doorway guarded by warriors.

Vuda Marina and around

☎ 666 8214, ⓦ vudamarina.com.fj

On the brow of the hill past Viseisei village, a scenic road turns left and runs for 3km to **Vuda Point**, home to a marina and two small boutique resorts. A kilometre further down the road, and beyond the unattractive oil storage tanks, is **Vuda Marina**, considered the safest anchorage for yachts in Fiji. There's a general store and café (daily 7.30am–4pm) here, as well as a restaurant (see p.68).

ARRIVAL AND DEPARTURE

VUDA MARINA AND AROUND

By ferry Ferries from Vuda Marina run to *Beachcomber Island* (daily; 25min), *Nanuya Island Resort* (daily; 2hr 15min), *Octopus Resort* (daily; 1hr 30min) and *Treasure Island* (daily; 20min).

By bus The city bus to Lautoka arrives at the Vuda Marina police post. Arriving by bus from Nadi, get off at the Vuda Point junction.

1

ACCOMMODATION AND EATING

Anchorage Beach Resort Vuda Point ☏ 666 2099, ⓦ anchoragefiji.com; map p.52. Perched on a hillside, this resort has great views of the offshore islands and inland to Mount Koroyanitu. The resort rooms are colourfully decorated with spa bathrooms, while the beachside villas are spacious, albeit in duplex fashion. Between June and November, sugar trains run right past the resort swimming pool. F$275

Boatshed Restaurant Vuda Marina ☏ 666 8214; map p.52. Elegant, open-plan restaurant well placed for sunset views, serving dishes such as "island-style" poached chicken and coconut-crusted walu fish (both $18). Daily 10am–10pm.

★**First Landing Resort** Vuda Marina ☏ 666 6171, ⓦ firstlandingfiji.com; map p.52. Adjacent to the marina and fronting a pretty coral-sand beach, this luxurious resort has magnificently mature gardens boasting huge rain trees and decorative mosaic pathways. Bure accommodation is in 33 duplex plantation-style cottages with dark interiors and polished wood floors. The luxury two-bedroom holiday villas have plush, modern furnishings and private swimming pools; villa rates include cooked breakfast. There's an excellent restaurant overlooking the beach serving wood-cooked pizzas. Bures F$199; villas F$599

Lautoka

Half an hour's drive north of Nadi, **LAUTOKA** is Fiji's second largest city and an important port. It's a surprisingly low-key affair – the city centre doesn't feel any bigger or busier than Downtown Nadi, with most of the 53,000 population living amongst the light industrial suburbs. Although there is little to admire architecturally, Lautoka is a good place to wander, with plenty of leafy avenues and diverting **Fiji-Indian stores** and market stalls – the latter a far cry from Nadi's touristy souvenir shops.

Lautoka established itself around the **sugar industry**. In 1903, the Australian-owned Colonial Sugar Refinery Company set up headquarters here, attracted by a deep-water harbour that almost rivals Suva's. The **sugar mill** they built is still the largest in Fiji and employs more than a thousand people, mostly from the surrounding Fiji-Indian sugarcane farms. The rambling corrugated sheds and chimney stacks of the mill are fed by an endless parade of cane trucks and trains between June and December, eventually pumping raw molasses along pipes to container ships moored at **Lautoka Port** – it's not a place to linger, with the stench of sugar sludge filling the air.

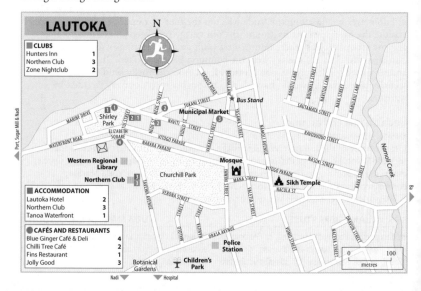

LAUTOKA ORIENTATION

Approaching from Nadi, the Veitari roundabout, full of mango sellers from August to December, splits the **Queens Road** in two. The right fork, along **Drasa Avenue**, passes through Lautoka's residential area, bypassing downtown and joining the Kings Road to Ba Town at the north end of the city. The left fork heads down **Navutu Road** along the industrial section of Lautoka into downtown; the road passes South Pacific Distilleries (where Fiji's famous rum is concocted), the fishing port and the sugar mill.

In recent years, Lautoka has become a second home for the indigenous people of the **Yasawas** who, without secondary schools or work opportunities, send their children here for education. Today, more Fijians live in the city than Fiji-Indians.

The city centre

The organized city centre is laid out in a grid pattern with one-way streets, flanked by beautiful tree-lined Vitogo Parade and parallel Naviti Street. A walk around this one-square-kilometre centre takes in the majority of **shops**, the municipal market and an impressive **mosque**. Opposite the mosque, there's an endless parade of fashion stores along **Vitogo Parade** selling suits, saris and costume jewellery. Most of the shops along **Naviti Street** sell a bizarre array of odds and ends, mostly cheap imports from China, but you'll find plenty of colourful **fabrics** sold by the roll as well as tailors who can make you up clothes at bargain rates. Across Naviti Street under a Brutalist concrete dome is the **Municipal Market** (Mon–Fri 7am–5.30pm, Sat 5am–4pm), one of the most spacious and least claustrophobic markets in Fiji.

For a pleasant detour away from the downtown shopping area, head south of Elizabeth Square down Tavewa Avenue. Midway down you can stop for a swim or a beer at the colonial-style **Northern Club** (see below) before continuing on past the government offices and elegant Hari Krishna Temple to Lautoka's superbly kept **botanical gardens** (Mon–Fri 8am–6pm, Sat & Sun 10am–6pm; free). Opposite the gardens is the **Children's Park**, busy with swings, slides and monkey bars.

ARRIVAL AND DEPARTURE
LAUTOKA

By bus and minivan Arriving by bus or minivan, you'll be dropped at the bus stand between Tukani and Naviti streets behind the Municipal Market in the heart of the city.

Destinations Ba (16 daily; 30min–1hr); Nadi (40 daily; 25–50min); Suva via Rakiraki (6 daily; 6hr); Suva via Nadi and Sigatoka (20 daily; 5hr 30min).

ACCOMMODATION

Lautoka Hotel Corner of Naviti & Tui streets ☎ 666 0388, ✉ ltkhotel@connect.com.fj. Handy location, and the best spot for backpackers. The budget rooms and ten-bed dorms are simple windowless boxes with plywood walls, but the deluxe rooms surrounding the pool are pretty and good value, and come with a/c and Sky TV. Can get noisy at weekends when two nightclubs operate in the premises. Dorms F$17.50; standard rooms F$65; deluxe rooms F$85

★**Northern Club** 11 Tavewa Ave ☎ 666 2469, ✉ northernaccom@yahoo.com.au. This pleasant colonial-style establishment is a bit of a gentleman's

watering hole and popular with families at weekends, but it's close to downtown and set in nice landscaped gardens with a pool. The six studio units in a separate two-storey cement building are a bit old-fashioned and the bathrooms are tiny, but with a/c, TV, cooking stove and fridge they're excellent value. F$120

Tanoa Waterfront Marine Drive ☎ 666 4777, ⊕ tanoahotels.com/waterfront. Located adjacent to Shirley Park and across the road from the ocean, this is Lautoka's only upmarket hotel. It features a large landscaped swimming pool but it remains predominantly frequented by business people. Rooms F$140; poolside suites F$220

EATING, DRINKING AND ENTERTAINMENT

CAFÉS AND RESTAURANTS
Blue Ginger Café & Deli Elizabeth Square ☎ 907 6553. This endearing and friendly Indian-run café is brightly

coloured inside and out, and serves the town's best coffee and cakes (F$4), as well as healthy salads and juices. Daily 7.30am–5pm.

1

Chilli Tree Café 3 Tukani St ☎665 1824. Lautoka's best option for a simple breakfast or sandwich lunch, serving cakes for around F$4, good coffee for F$5.50, a full breakfast for F$15.90 or kebabs and wraps for F$14. Mon–Fri 7.30am–5pm, Sat 7.30am–4pm.

Fins Restaurant At the Tanoa Waterfront hotel, Marine Drive ☎666 4777. Lautoka's only fine-dining restaurant has a handful of outdoor tables boasting ocean views, although the modern interior is café-style. The broad but overpriced menu includes beer-battered fish and chips (F$22.50), grilled local market fish (F$25), curry of the day (F$27) and local beef fillet (F$45). Daily 6.30–9.30am, 11.30am–2.30pm & 6–10.30pm.

Jolly Good Corner of Naviti & Vakabale streets. Convenient café if you're after a quick bite, with counter-cooked food served from a large trailer and covered outdoor tables opposite the market. The fish and chips are excellent value at F$6.75 and the F$1.30 ice cream is worth savouring. Mon–Wed 9am–9pm, Thurs–Sat 8am–10pm, Sun 8am–9pm.

BARS AND CLUBS

Hunters Inn At the Lautoka Hotel, Tui St ☎666 0388. This dark, dungeon-like nightclub has free entry throughout the week and plays popular Fijian-style hits. Mon–Sat 8pm–1am.

Northern Club 11 Tavewa Ave ☎666 0184. The bar of this social club is a good place to meet a few locals over a cheap draught beer, or play snooker on a full-sized table for 50 cents a game. Also serves bar snacks and meat pies. Daily 2pm–midnight.

Zone Nightclub Naviti St ☎927 0623. Popular with a young, predominantly Fiji-Indian crowd. There are DJs on Fri & Sat nights, pool tables and satellite TV showing sports or music. Entry F$3. Mon–Sat 8pm–1am.

CINEMA

Village Four Cinemas 25 Namoli Ave ☎666 3555. Shows the latest Hollywood blockbusters. Tickets F$6.50. Daily 10am–11pm.

LISTINGS

Banks All banks listed have 24hr ATM machines. ANZ Bank, 165 Vitogo Parade (Mon 9.30am–4pm, Tues–Fri 9am–4pm, Sat 9am–1pm), also with Currency Express; Westpac, 175 Vitogo Parade, fronting Shirley Park (Mon–Thurs 9.30am–3pm, Fri 9.30am–4pm).

Internet access Rohit's, 2nd floor Kamil Building on Narara Parade just off Elizabeth Square (Mon–Sat 8am–6pm; F$1 per hr), is the cheapest in town. Click Internet opposite the market on Naviti St is the largest, with 20 terminals (Mon–Sat 8am–6pm, Sun 9am–5pm; F$2 per hr).

Library Western Regional Library, Tavewa Ave off Elizabeth Square (Mon–Fri 10am–5pm; ☎666 0091).

Medical care Lautoka Hospital off Thompson Crescent (☎666 0399) caters for emergencies. Alternatively, several general practitioners are based at the Bayly Clinic, 4 Nede St (Mon–Fri 8am–1pm & 2–4.30pm, Sat 8am–1pm for private doctor or dentist; ☎666 4598).

Pharmacy Hyper Pharmacy, 101 Vitogo Parade (Mon–Sat 8am–8pm, Sun 9am–2pm & 6–8pm; ☎665 1940).

Police At Drasa Ave opposite Yawini St (☎666 0222). There's also a police post in the city centre on Tui St beside Shirley Park.

Post office Elizabeth Square (Mon–Fri 8am–4pm, Sat 8am–noon).

Sports Northern Club, 11 Tavewa Ave (☎666 0184). Social club with swimming pool (F$3), tennis (F$1.50/30min) and squash (F$1/30min).

Telephone At the post office on Elizabeth Square.

Koroyanitu National Heritage Park

Around 10km southeast of Lautoka, **Koroyanitu National Heritage Park** has the most accessible walking trails of Fiji's two National Heritage Parks. The park was created in 1992 to preserve the area's natural forests and endemic birdlife from clearing for pine forest and encroaching grasslands.

THE STORY OF ABACA

Abaca got its name by accident. The original village was called Nagara but in 1931 a **landslide** hit the village, leaving only three survivors. Thankful to be alive, the three went in search of a new home. On their journey they came across a large stone emblazoned with the letters ABC. The letters had been painted by a missionary in the 1830s while teaching the alphabet to the people of Nagara. Inspired by this prophetic sign, the survivors decided to name their new village "Abaca", an acronym in the local dialect for "the beginning of eternal life after a miracle".

1

At the **Abaca visitor centre** you can pick up pamphlets and local information, and you'll find two **walking tracks** from here. The most challenging is the Batilamu Track, which snakes uphill through forest for two hours until it reaches the summit of the 1163m **Mount Batilamu**. The mountain forms the belly of the Sleeping Giant (see p.66), and from the summit you can see all the way back to Lautoka and across to the Yasawa Islands. Alternatively, an easy two-hour loop trail follows a grassy ridge to **Savuione Falls**, which tumbles 80m in two tiers to a deep swimming pool. From the falls, the trail descends into thick dakua forest back to Vereni Falls close to Abaca village.

If you're interested in exploring the park further, guides from Abaca can accompany you on an **overnight trail** deep into the forest. This involves a tough five-hour walk to the remote village of Navilawa.

ARRIVAL AND DEPARTURE   KOROYANITU NATIONAL HERITAGE PARK

By car Access to the park is by 4WD from Lautoka via Tavakubu Rd off Drasa Ave; it takes 30min to reach Abaca village, travelling up a steep dirt road past the dramatic volcanic escarpment of Castle Rock. If you've not got your own transport, contact George Prince (☎ 664 5431, 860 5406 or 991 6956, ✉ george_prasad@hotmail.com), who operates transfers from Lautoka to Abaca (F$30/60 one way/return per person).

By bus A carrier van from opposite Lautoka bus stand will cost F$35.

INFORMATION AND TOURS

Entry fee F$12, plus compulsory guide: Savuione Falls F$15; Mt Batilamu day-trip F$25; Mt Batilamu overnight F$40.
Visitor centre ☎ 664 5431/ 992 1517. Mon–Sat 8am–5pm, Sun 8–10am & noon–5pm.

Tours Guided trekking tours are offered by Mount Batilamu Trek, based in Lautoka (☎ 664 5431/ 992 1517). A two-and-a-half-day trek costs F$460 and includes meals, transfers and all fees.

ACCOMMODATION

To stay with a family in Abaca village, contact the visitor centre; it will cost around F$80. An overnight stay in the hut at the peak of Mount Batilamu with your guide will set you back F$150.

Nase Lodge Arrange via the visitor centre (see above); map p.52. Colonial-style lodge in a remote wilderness setting within the park. There are two large bunk rooms, a communal lounge and a kitchen – you're likely to be the only guest unless there's a school group in residence. Order meals at the village: breakfast F$13, lunch F$13/dinner F$25. Camping F$35; dorms F$50

The Mamanucas and Yasawa Islands

REEF IN THE MAMANUCAS

The Mamanucas and Yasawa Islands

Extending in an arc off the coast of Viti Levu, the Mamanucas and Yasawa Islands are a chain of beautiful palm-fringed islands with perfect white sandy beaches, placid lagoons and picturesque resorts. This is Fiji's tourism gem, attracting thousands of visitors, especially from Australia and New Zealand. Thankfully, though, the islands remain remarkably undeveloped – no building rises higher than a coconut palm and even on the most popular islands it's possible to wander a short distance to find a secluded stretch of beach. The focus here is on relaxation. Most visitors spend their days sunbathing, snorkelling or scuba diving, with sightseeing limited to hiking between small villages or trekking to a hilltop to see the sunset. Evenings are spent around the resort bar and restaurant which, apart from at a couple of backpacker resorts, tend to wind down around 10pm – this is no Bali or Ibiza, though there are plenty of opportunities to try *yaqona* (*kava*).

The thirty or so small islands of the **Mamanucas** lie just off the coast from Nadi making them the most popular day-trip destination in Fiji. Budget accommodation and small **boutique resorts** are scattered evenly around the group, some on tiny uninhabited **coral islands** and the majority in secluded bays. Honeymooners, families and singles flock here between June and October when Australia and New Zealand are gripped by winter; finding accommodation can be difficult during this time.

Extending to the north of the Mamanucas is a long, thin string of fifteen volcanic masses that make up the **Yasawa Islands**. These islands are slightly larger and more dramatic in appearance than their southern neighbours and, being further out from the tourist hub of Nadi, are less commercialized. The **beaches** here are exquisite and the best way to see them is by hopping on and off the fast *Yasawa Flyer* catamaran – the most popular **backpacker trail** in Fiji – and staying at the many locally owned budget resorts along the way. For a little more luxury, consider taking an overnight or week-long **cruise**, putting ashore at secluded beaches and anchoring at fabulous coral reefs for snorkelling.

Brief history

Before the arrival of tourists, the Mamanucas were used as fishing and egg gathering grounds by the people of Viseisei and Nadi on Viti Levu. The majority were never inhabited due to the intense sun and lack of fresh water. Only three of the larger volcanic islands – Malolo, Yanuya and Tavua – supported **fishing villages**. With poor farming conditions, life was extremely tough and the majority of islanders sought out new opportunities on the mainland. Today, with a reversal of fortunes, every village household earns money through hotel land rent and has at least one family member

WAYA SAND SPIT

Highlights

❶ Mystery Island Spend a romantic night stargazing on this tiny uninhabited coral island. **See p.81**

❷ Musket Cove Marina Light a barbecue overlooking the beach, grab a cocktail and watch the yachts sail by. **See p.83**

❸ Monuriki Island Take a trip to Monuriki Island with its high volcanic rocks, deep lagoons and coral reefs. The little island was the setting for Tom Hanks' desert island solitude in the movie *Castaway*. **See p.90**

❹ Overnight cruises Splash out on a multi-day cruise to the Yasawas with fabulous sightseeing, snorkelling and village visits along the way. **See p.92**

❺ Waya and Wayasewa Explore these stunning volcanic islands along scenic coastal and ridge trails. **See p.92**

❻ Drawaqa Lagoon Snorkel amongst beautiful coral gardens with a good chance of spotting manta rays in the reef passages. **See p.94**

❼ Blue Lagoon Bay Island-hop between beach resorts based around this turquoise lagoon. **See p.96**

HIGHLIGHTS ARE MARKED ON THE MAP ON P.76

MAMANUCAS AND YASAWA ISLANDS

HIGHLIGHTS

1 Mystery Island
2 Musket Cove Marina
3 Monuriki Island
4 Overnight cruises
5 Waya and Wayasewa
6 Drawaqa Lagoon
7 Blue Lagoon Bay

N

Yasawa-i-rara

Vawa

Yasawa
Island

Teci

Nabukeru

Sawa-i-Lau Caves

4 Nacula

Tavewa

Nacula

7 Nanuya Lailai

Matacawa
Levu

Yaqeta

Yasawa Islands

Soso

Naviti

Drawaqa

6

Naivalavala Passage

BLIGH WATER

Waya

5

Yalobi

Wayasewa

Kuata

White Rock

PACIFIC OCEAN

Sacred Islands

Vomo

Viwa

Tokoriki

3

Matamanoa-i-Cake

Mystery 1

Lautoka

Matamanoa

Beachcomber

Bounty

Mana

Mamanucas

Navini

Vuda River

Malolo

Yaro

2

Mololo
Lailai

Nasoso

Nadi Bay

Malolo Barrier Reef

Denarau
Island

Nadi

Namotu

Tavarua

Naisali

Momi Bay

Viti Levu

Yasawa Flyer
South Sea Cruises
Malolo Cat

0   10
kilometres

working in the tourist industry. Food supplies are now shipped in on fast boats from the mainland.

Conditions were better on the larger Yasawa Islands. Thanks to the presence of natural spring water and more fertile soils, a greater number of coastal villages established here. The southernmost islands of the chain, Kuata and Wayasewa, are aligned to the mainland village of Viseisei, being part of its *yavusa* or district. All other islands give allegiance to the high chief or **Tui Yasawa** who resides in Yasawa-i-rara Village at the northernmost tip of the group. Little is known about the early history of the Yasawa people except that they were deeply feared as warriors by the inhabitants of eastern Fiji. In 1789 **Captain William Bligh** (see p.218), having been cast adrift in a small rowing boat by the *Bounty* mutineers, rowed through the Yasawas and was chased by several war canoes. Fortunately for him, a squall blew in and the pursuing Yasawans retreated. The passage through which he escaped is known as Bligh Water.

The Mamanucas

Clearly visible from Nadi, the **MAMANUCAS** are a stunning collection of 32 small islands surrounded by 35 square kilometres of translucent ocean strewn with coral reefs. Situated in the lee of the main island of Viti Levu, the islands boast the finest weather in Fiji – year-round sunshine, calm seas and gentle breezes. Given the ease of travel and the wide choice of resorts this is the prime beach holiday destination in the South Pacific.

The **coral islands**, lying immediately offshore from Nadi and Lautoka, comprise a dozen picturesque tiny **coral cays**, which feature heavily in the tourist brochures and boast several world-class surfing breaks. More prominent, though, from the mainland are the larger volcanic islands of the **Malolo Group**, with rolling grassy hills framing beautiful **beaches** and the surrounding seas bobbing with yachts and ferries. There are plenty of **activities** here to keep tourists busy, including game fishing, jet-skiing and kayaking, as well as excellent **scuba diving**.

Forming the western border of Fiji, the remote **Mamanuca-i-Cake Group** is also volcanic in appearance but has more rugged coastlines and steeper hills covered in light forest. Being further from the mainland – it takes ninety minutes by boat from Nadi – these islands are less busy, with just three small boutique beach resorts appealing mostly to the honeymoon market. They are also a popular stop on **overnight cruises**.

ARRIVAL AND GETTING AROUND   THE MAMANUCAS

The bulk of visitors arrive on the **fast catamarans** running from Port Denarau at the southern end of Nadi, although there are also **water taxis** and a dedicated service to Mana from **Wailoaloa Beach**. To make the most of fantastic sightseeing along the way you could also consider transferring out to the islands by seaplane or helicopter. Once in the Mamanucas, all resorts have speedboats for **inter-island transfers**, but these are expensive – the short 10min hop between Malolo and Malolo Lailai, for example, will set you back F$90 one-way. It's a lot cheaper catching one of the fast catamarans between the islands; South Sea Cruises have the most frequent connections. Day-trips from Nadi are covered on p.58. For information on visiting the Mamanucas as part of a longer Yasawas cruise, see p.92.

BY FAST CATAMARAN

The following companies all offer free hotel pick-ups and drop-offs in the Nadi area; some resorts operate their own speedboat transfers and this will be arranged when you book. Note that the Mamanuca-I-Cake Group lies beyond the fast catamaran route from Port Denarau,

---

DAY-TRIPS FROM NADI

Those looking to save money on their accommodation might consider staying in Nadi – where rooms are far more competitively priced – and visiting the islands on a series of **day cruises** (see p.58).

2

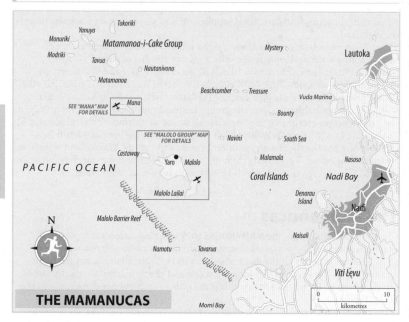

THE MAMANUCAS

although there are regular connections by smaller outboard boats.

Awesome Adventures (Yasawa Flyer) Port Denarau ☎ 675 0499, ⊛ awesomefiji.com. The 200-passenger *Yasawa Flyer* departs Port Denarau daily at 8.30am, calling in at South Sea Island, Bounty Island and Beachcomber Island, before heading up to the Yasawas. They are keen to push the Bula Pass (see p.91) and don't feature or sell short hops online; enquire by phone or book at the office in Port Denarau.

Leeward Services Port Denarau ☎ 675 0205, ⊛ malolocatfiji.com. Operates the fast *Malolo Cat I & II* between Port Denarau and Malolo Lailai for *Plantation Island Resort* and *Lomani Resort*. Services depart Port Denarau at 7.30am, 10.30am, 2pm & 5.30pm (F$70 one-way; 1hr) and leave Musket Cove Marina on Malolo Lailai at 5.45am, 8.45am, 12.15pm & 4pm. Guests staying on adjacent Malolo Island will be picked up from Musket Cove Marina.

South Sea Cruises Port Denarau ☎ 675 0500, ⊛ ssc.com.fj. Runs services to most Mamanucas resorts. Their large catamaran ferry departs Port Denarau at 9am, 12.15pm & 3.15pm calling at: South Sea, Bounty, Treasure and Beachcomber islands (F$93 one-way); Malolo Island (F$123); Castaway Island (F$123); and Mana Island (F$125). A second fast catamaran departs Port Denarau at 9.15am & 3.30pm for Matamanoa and Tokoriki (F$158). A/c seating in the Captain's Lounge will set you back an additional F$30.

Destinations from Port Denarau Beachcomber (4 daily; 45min); Bounty (4 daily; 35min); Castaway (3 daily; 1hr 50min); Mana (3 daily; 1hr 25min); Malolo (3 daily; 2hr); Malolo Lailai (3 daily; 55min); Matamanoa (2 daily; 1hr 30min); South Sea (4 daily; 30min); Tokoriki (2 daily; 1hr 45min); Vomo (daily; 1hr 15min).

Destinations from Wailoaloa Beach Mana (2 daily; 50min).

BY WATER TAXI OR SMALL BOAT

Mana Flyer Wailoaloa Beach ☎ 997 1885, ⊛ manaflyerfiji.com. Small covered wooden boat serving the backpacker resorts in the Mamanucas, departing Wailoaloa Beach at 9.30am and returning from Mana around 12.30pm (F$75 one-way). Travellers heading on to the Yasawa Islands can arrange transfers from Mana to Beachcomber Island in order to meet up with the *Yasawa Flyer*.

Sea Fiji Port Denarau ☎ 672 5961, ⊛ seafiji.net. A 24hr water taxi service from Port Denarau to all island resorts, in distinctive bright orange catamarans and mono-hulls. Transfers to the inner islands start from F$445 for up to eight people.

BY PLANE

Island Hoppers Nadi Airport ☎ 672 0410, ⊛ helicopters.com.fj. Helicopter flights to most islands in the Mamanucas from Nadi Airport, Denarau Island and various resorts along the Coral

SCUBA DIVING IN THE MAMANUCAS

With fast boat transfers and a wide choice of dive operators, **divers** can easily sample all dive sites in the Mamanucas while staying at a single resort. The islands are a great spot to **learn to dive** with sheltered lagoons, water temperatures seldom dropping below 24°C and excellent visibility, usually at least 30m.

The dozen or so shallow patch coral dive sites in the northern **coral islands** are ideal for beginners. More advanced divers come here for the two popular **wrecks** – a partially intact World War II B26 bomber at 26m; and the 40m-long cruise ship, *Salamander*, lying at 12–28m and covered in soft corals and anemones. In the southwest of the Mamanucas, the 30km-long **Malolo Barrier Reef** has several deep drop-offs suitable for experienced divers – turtles, lion fish, rays and large sharks are common. The reef is a fifteen-minute boat ride from Malolo Lailai.

The reefs surrounding **Mana** have some exceptional sites for beginner to intermediate divers. The most raved about site is "Supermarket", offering regular **shark encounters** from white tips to greys, as well as a drift dive along a wall with an abundance of lionfish and moray eels. Other sites include "Gotham City", named for its abundance of batfish, and "Barrel Head", a wide bommie where you can drift along a wall with massive sea fans and plenty of turtles. Heading west to the Mamanuca-i-Cake Group, **Tokoriki** has several interesting sites with gorgonian **sea fans** featuring prominently at "Sherwood Forest", along with a fine selection of soft corals, nudibranchs and anemones.

DIVE OPERATORS

AquaTrek Mana ☎ 666 9309, ⒲ aquatrekdiving .com. Highly organized outfit based at *Mana Island Resort*. Four-day PADI Open Water Course F$930, two-tank dive F$250.

Ratu Kini's ☎ 666 9309. Budget operator for the backpackers on Mana Island. Four-day PADI Open Water Course F$750, two-tank dive F$230.

Reef Safari ☎ 675 0950, ⒲ reefsafari.com.fj. International operator with bases at South Sea Island and Barefoot Island. Four-day PADI Open Water Course F$700.

Subsurface Fiji ☎ 666 6738, ⒲ subsurfacefiji.com.

Dominant dive operator with bases at Malolo, Malolo Lailai, Musket Cove, Likuliku, Plantation Island, Lomani, Tavarua, Namotu and Tropica. One-tank dive for day-trippers F$145, two-tank dive for resort guests F$270, three-day PADI Open Water Course F$974.

Viti Watersports Port Denarau Marina ☎ 670 2413, ⒲ vitiwatersports.com. Based at Matamanoa, but also operates fast covered boats for day-trippers from Denarau Island to the Malolo Barrier Reef. From Denarau single-tank dive F$160, PADI Discover course F$240; from Matamanoa two-tank dive F$386, PADI Open Water course F$1049.

Coast. Prices start from F$799 per person return (min 2 passengers).

Pacific Island Seaplanes Nadi Airport ☎ 672 5644, ⒲ pacificislandair.com. Four- and eight-seater seaplanes, taking off from Nadi Airport and splashing down in the resort lagoons. Prices start from F$350 per person one-way, and you're allowed 20kg of luggage.

Turtle Airways Wailoaloa Beach, Nadi ☎ 672 1888,

⒲ turtleairways.com. Turtle Airways offers low-flying seaplane transfers and scenic flights. Resort transfers depart every other hour, and service the Mamanuca (15min) and Yasawa (30min) Islands primarily. Prices start from F$280 per person one-way (min 2 passengers). Departure times are tailored around International flights, to ensure fast same-day transfers.

The coral islands

The **CORAL ISLANDS** comprise twelve tiny cays, surrounded by a shallow lagoon. These islands seldom rise more than 5m above sea-level, are covered with light scrub vegetation and until recently were all uninhabited. Apart from the resorts that are now built on them, there's not an awful lot to distinguish one from another, except for Namotu and Tavarua in the southeastern tip of the Malolo Barrier Reef, which have world-class **reef surfing**. The northern coral islands are the most accessible, with transfers from both Port Denarau and Vuda Marina in less than twenty minutes.

2

ISLAND NAMES

Resorts on the smaller coral islands have a higher profile than the islands themselves and in most cases the **traditional Fijian name** has been ditched in favour of an alluringly exotic title. We've used the **resort names** throughout, as this is what you will see on transport information and timetables.

RESORT NAME	FIJIAN NAME
Beachcomber Island	Tai
Bounty Island	Kadavu
Castaway Island	Qalito
Mystery Island	Tivua
South Sea Island	Vunivadra
Treasure Island	Elevuka

South Sea Island

The tiny speck of **South Sea Island** is the smallest of the coral islands and takes just 25 minutes to reach from Port Denarau. This is the first stop on both the South Sea Cruises and the *Yasawa Flyer* routes, making it a busy little place with both day-trippers from Nadi and backpackers heading to and from the Yasawas. It's a rather cramped island, not even a hundred paces in width, and takes less than five minutes to walk around. If you like snorkelling you'll be disappointed: this close to Nadi Bay the reefs have been damaged by runoff from the sugarcane farms and rivers on Viti Levu. There's not much to do except bask on the beach and cool off in the resort's swimming pool – **day-trippers** are enticed by the offer of unlimited beer or house wine.

ACCOMMODATION   SOUTH SEA ISLAND

South Sea Island Resort ☎ 675 0500, ⊛ ssc.com.fj. Youth-orientated option on the miniscule island: accommodation is in one large wooden dorm room above the restaurant, with two toilets and an open sink smack in the middle making it devoid of privacy. Rates include meals. **F$147**

Bounty Island

Five minutes northwest of South Sea Island is **Bounty Island**, the largest of the coral cays in the Mamanucas at 48 acres, and the best for exploring; it was the idyllic location for reality TV show *Celebrity Love Island*. Bounty is a popular spot for **backpackers** heading back and forth from the Yasawas. Kayaks and catamarans are available for rent, and **kayakers** can circumnavigate the island in an hour paddling in a crystal clear lagoon. The north lagoon facing the resort has reasonable **snorkelling**, with shallow waters good for beginners, and there are several massive coral heads with plenty of small reef fish barely 30m from shore. You'll also find **walking** trails meandering under light scrub (good for bird-spotting), and interesting **beachcombing** with lots of shells, driftwood, hermit crabs and wonderful views looking back to Vuda Point and the mountains of Viti Levu.

ACCOMMODATION   BOUNTY ISLAND

Bounty Island Resort ☎ 666 7461, ⊛ fiji-bounty.com. A laidback resort on Bounty Island's north beach. The 22 simple wooden and bamboo huts come with a/c and en-suite bathrooms and are strung out along the beachfront, whilst dorm rooms are set back from the sea in a large cement building and share hot-water showers. There's a restaurant and swimming pool with wooden decking beside the beach, with kayaks and catamarans for rent. Dorms **F$42**; island bures **F$162**; beachfront bures **F$222**

Treasure Island

Three kilometres to the west of South Sea Island is fourteen-acre **Treasure Island**, home to family-orientated *Treasure Island Resort*. There's a **turtle sanctuary** (see box opposite)

SEA TURTLES IN THE MAMANUCAS

Three of the world's seven species of **sea turtle** can be found in Fiji and all three lay their eggs on the small coral islands of the Mamanucas. The green and hawksbill are very similar in appearance and average around 1.2m in length whilst the endangered leatherback can reach over 2m. Female turtles reach sexual maturity around the age of 25 and return to the same beach where they hatched to lay their eggs, burying them deep in the sand in batches of up to two hundred. This happens at night, some time between September and January. After sixty to seventy days, the eggs **hatch** en masse, again at night, and the hatchlings make their way to the sea. As few as one in a thousand reach full maturity, and the odds of survival are being reduced further by light and noise pollution from resorts.

Despite a national ban on **hunting turtles** for their meat – which for Fijians is both a delicacy and an essential ingredient in ceremonial feasting – locals in the outlying islands continue to do so. In an effort to revive populations and promote ecological awareness, *Treasure Island Resort* has set up a small **turtle sanctuary** to nurture baby sea turtles for a year before releasing them back into the ocean. If your timing's right you may be able to participate in their feeding and release which generally occurs between November and March.

2

in the centre of the island and a few hundred metres off the south beach sits a tiny sand islet with some good snorkelling.

ACCOMMODATION — TREASURE ISLAND

Treasure Island Resort ⊕ 666 6999, ⓦ treasureisland-fiji.com. Accommodation is in 66 a/c family rooms set 30m back from the beach. There's a fantastic all-day kids' club, plus mini-putt golfing. Same-day transfers from the airport. F$750

Beachcomber Island

Facing Treasure Island, less than a kilometre to the west, is **Beachcomber Island**, home to the hedonistic *Beachcomber Island Resort*. Organized party nights with pumping music, limbo dancing, crab races and lots of young gap-year travellers may not be everyone's idea of fun but the island raves past midnight, something of a rarity in Fiji. There are also plenty of activities to fill the days, including parasailing, sailing, waterskiing, jet skis and banana-boat rides, all of which can be sampled on an action-packed day cruise.

ACCOMMODATION — BEACHCOMBER ISLAND

Beachcomber Island Resort ⊕ 666 1500, ⓦ beachcomberfiji.com. Accommodation is in two stuffy 84-bed dormitories and 22 more comfortable bures with en-suite hot-water bathrooms. Not for nothing is it known as the party island – it's loud, raucous and you don't come here for a good night's sleep. The reasonable rates include simple meals, but beware: drinks are pricey. Dorms F$126; rooms F$385; bures F$506

Mystery Island

Ten kilometres northeast of Beachcomber and just a few kilometres off Lautoka on the Viti Levu coast is **Mystery Island**. Leased by Captain Cook Cruises, the island is used as a picnic stop on its three- and seven-day small ship cruises up to the Yasawas (see p.92). The snorkelling reefs are at least 300m from the beach and best accessed on the organized snorkelling boat trips.

ACCOMMODATION — MYSTERY ISLAND

Beach huts ⊕ 670 1823, ⓦ captaincook.com.fj. For a slice of sheer escapism those on one of Captain Cook Cruises' all-inclusive cruises (see p.92) can arrange to stay in one of the two beachside huts, giving you an uninhabited island almost to yourself. The wooden huts have simple furnishings, a basic cold-water bathroom and a wooden deck looking out over the ocean. The island caretaker will cook meals, mix *kava* and serenade you under the stars.

2

SPOTTING THE SOUTHERN CROSS

Free from excessive ambient light, southern hemisphere **stargazing** is quite outstanding in Fiji, especially on small islands such as the Mamanucas. As dusk fades, look toward the south and slightly east to see the **Southern Cross** as it rises above the horizon. It's a small series of five stars, most easily located by Alpha and Beta Centauri, the two brightest stars low on the horizon. Draw an imaginary line from the lower star to the upper one and extend it a little in an arc to the lowest star of the horizontal cross. Be careful not to confuse it with the false cross, slightly higher in the sky, of about the same size but not as bright.

Navini Island

A tiny coral cay encircled by a white sandy beach, **Navini Island** is set off the regular ferry route in a secluded spot between Beachcomber and Malolo. With just ten beachfront bures, no day-trippers and extremely attentive staff, it makes for a perfect **honeymoon destination**. Just offshore is a great snorkelling lagoon.

ACCOMMODATION   NAVINI ISLAND

Navini Island Resort ☎ 666 2188, **☻** www.navini fiji.com.fj. Deluxe bures come with spa baths and a private courtyard overlooking the beach. Fishing trips, village visits and use of watersports equipment are included in the price. **F$625**

Namotu and Tavarua

At the southern end of the Mamanucas, on the eastern edge of the Malolo Barrier Reef and facing Momi Bay on Viti Levu, are two coral cays, **Namotu** and heart-shaped **Tavarua**. Each island is home to an upmarket **surf resort** run by US-based companies with exclusive access to the Malolos' best surf breaks.

As well as the world-class surfing breaks, this section of the Malolo Barrier Reef is also a popular playground for pods of bottle-nose **dolphins**, which can be seen on organized dolphin-watching cruises from Malolo Lailai (see p.84) and Nadi (see p.58).

ACCOMMODATION   NAMOTU AND TAVARUA

Namotu Island Resort ☎ +1 310 584 9900, **☻** namotuislandfiji.com; book direct online or via their California-based office. US-run resort offering all sorts of water-related activities: surfing, paddleboarding, kitesurfing, game fishing, diving and more. Accommodation is in rustic beachfront bures, more luxurious bures, or a plush villa which sleeps six and has its own pool. Seven-night all-inclusive package (per person) **US$2375**

Tavarua Island Resort ☎ 670 6513, **☻** tavarua.com. Operated by a US company, this comprises sixteen timber beachfront bures with verandas and a/c. You can surf, dive and fish for yellowfin tuna, wahoo and trevally. Seven-night all-inclusive package (per person) **US$2919**

Vomo

A far-flung northern outpost of the Mamanucas, palm-cloaked **Vomo** island is a tiny chunk of paradise, with excellent snorkelling, a high ridge and two pristine beaches. It's home to the luxury *Vomo Island Resort*, which will take you the short distance to private and uninhabited **Vomo Lailai** (Little Vomo), with its twin rocky bluffs.

ACCOMMODATION   VOMO

Vomo Island Resort ☎ 666 7955, **☻** vomofiji.com. With 28 attractive bures tucked under the palm trees and climbing the ridge, this resort offers desert-island luxury but – unlike other high-end places – it's very child-friendly. Watersports are a must, including some of the best snorkelling in the islands, and you can also play golf, tennis, croquet and volleyball. There's a weekly meke and lovo night, incorporating a *kava* ceremony. Excellent food is supplemented by produce from their herb and vegetable garden. Rates include meals. **US$1850**

The Malolo Group

Twenty kilometres from Nadi, the coral cays give way to four large volcanic islands making up the **MALOLO GROUP**. This is the heart of the Mamanucas tourism experience, boasting the most popular and busiest resorts. **Malolo**, the largest island in the group at just over 2400 acres, and its little sister **Malolo Lailai** have a scattering of resorts, a **marina** and the chiefly village of **Yaro**. Along with beautiful **Castaway Island** these islands form a cluster protected to the south by the stunning Malolo Barrier Reef. Surfing in the passages is a fifteen-minute boat ride away and advanced scuba divers will enjoy the challenging wall dives on the outer edges of the reef. Six kilometres to the northwest of Malolo is **Mana**, the liveliest island for backpackers, with lovely **beaches** to explore.

2

Malolo Lailai

The third-largest island of the Mamanucas, **Malolo Lailai** is surrounded by picturesque sandy beaches. On its west side is a sheltered bay separating the island from its larger sister, Malolo. Tucked into the bay are several resorts, restaurants and the **Musket Cove Marina** (daily 8am–1pm & 2–5pm; ☏666 2215, VHF CHL 68). In mid-September the Fiji sailing season culminates here in the week-long **Musket Cove Regatta**, featuring race days as well as plenty of partying. The low grassy hills on the north side of Malolo Lailai are crisscrossed with walking tracks with stunning views looking back to Viti Levu and out over the Mamanucas.

When Australian prospector **John Thompson** sailed to Fiji in 1872 he purchased Malolo Lailai for fifty muskets and five hundred pieces of gold from the landowners on the neighbouring island of Malolo. In 1903 the island was leased to the Won Ket family who worked the land as a successful copra plantation for 63 years using Chinese labourers – a **Chinese cemetery** can be seen in the hills. In 1966, with the collapse of copra prices, the island was sold to its present owners, the Smith and Raffe families, both of whom pioneered the region's tourism industry building successful **holiday resorts**.

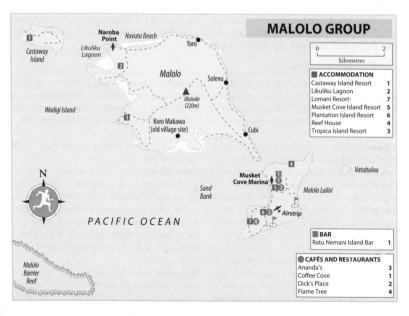

2

ACTIVITIES ON MALOLO LAILAI

Activities at both *Musket Cove Resort* and *Plantation Island Resort* are available to non-guests and include waterskiing, parasailing, banana rides, sport fishing, island-hopping trips and surfing. Subsurface Fiji (see p.79) offers a full range of **scuba diving** courses including PADI Bubblemaker for kids and Nitrox. Thousands of tiny reef fish congregate around the sand bar, a kilometre offshore in Malolo Bay, but you'll need to join the **snorkelling trip** by boat to get there, organized by all resorts on Malolo Lailai.

For **sailing** or speedboat charters, the best option is Take a Break Cruises (☎925 9469, ⓦtakeabreakcruises.com; F$60 per person, up to six people), based at Musket Cove Marina. They also offer organized **dolphin-watching cruises** on board the luxury sailing catamaran *Take A Break* (Mon–Thurs 9.30am–12.30pm; F$90, minimum 4 people).

The activity bure (daily 8am–5pm) beside Musket Cove Marina rents out **bicycles** for F$20 per day. There's a flat nine-hole **golf course** behind *Plantation Island Resort* (F$16 a round or F$27 including golf clubs and balls). Several holes run parallel to the beach (the longest is only 329 yards) and with nice sea views it makes for a pleasant walk.

ACCOMMODATION   MALOLO LAILAI

Lomani Resort ☎666 8212, ⓦlomaniisland.com. With just 26 Mediterranean-style whitewashed suites and a lovely swimming pool with decked outdoor restaurant, this is a good choice for honeymooners. The serene plantation-style setting with open lawns is at the quieter end of Malolo Lailai's main beach, with a lagoon deep enough for swimming and snorkelling. **F$705**

Musket Cove Island Resort ☎666 2215, ⓦmusketcovefiji.com. Varied accommodation, from standard hotel rooms, to traditional thatched bures with hammocks, to villas on an artificial island with over-water decks. There's a large pool with lanes, and free snorkelling excursions. Rooms **F$290**; bures **F$570**; villas **F$790**

Plantation Island Resort ☎666 9333, ⓦplantationisland.com. Large resort bustling with young families. The palm-fringed beach is stunning and there's a specially cordoned-off lagoon area as well as three swimming pools; windsurfing boards and kayaks are available to borrow. As well as restaurants and bars, there's a snack bar, shops and an espresso and juice bar. Rooms are slightly dated, but the resort is friendly and kids are welcomed. **F$465**

Reef House ☎664 0805, ⓦafijiholiday.com. Secluded three-bedroom bungalow tucked behind a hill on the northern point of the island along a rocky coastline. The pine-panelled rooms are small and distinctly unfashionable, with pastel furniture, but as the bungalow sleeps up to eight people it can be excellent value. There's a grocery store on the island, so you can self-cater, making this a good option for independent travellers. You can rent kayaks, bicycles or snorkel equipment from *Musket Cove Resort*, a 5min walk away and use their swimming pools free of charge. **F$633**

EATING AND DRINKING

One of the delights of staying on Malolo Lailai is its choice of **restaurants**. For **food shopping**, *Ananda's* (see below) has a small supermarket (daily 7am–8.30pm), and The Trader (daily 8am–7pm), beside Musket Cove Marina, stocks a good selection of groceries but no alcohol. Expect to pay double mainland prices. You can buy ready-to-cook meat and fish packs (F$20) at The Trader and wander over to *Ratu Nemani Island Bar* (see opposite) to cook on the supplied wood-fired BBQs.

Ananda's Plantation Island Resort ☎666 9333. Located on the beach midway between *Plantation* and *Musket Cove*. The Fijian chef's F$35 three-course BBQ is a winner, with a choice of fish fillet, boneless chicken or sirloin steak cooked in front of you – but with a long line of diners waiting in turn behind. Otherwise there's a blackboard full of alternatives, from fettuccine to curry chicken. Come early to ensure a beachside table. Daily 6pm–10pm.

Coffee Cove Musket Cove Marina, accessed from The Trader ☎666 2215. A pretty setting overlooking the marina, but the staff are rushed off their feet so don't expect a quick snack. The pie of the day is good value at F$10 including chips and salad, or try the F$14 gruyère quiche. Otherwise, sit admiring the view over a F$3.50 cappuccino. Daily 10am–6.30pm.

Dick's Place Musket Cove Resort ☎664 0805. This resort restaurant has an excellent menu, from delicious New Zealand lamb shanks to *ika vakalolo* (traditionally cooked fish in coconut cream) to risotto, with mains around F$30. If you're here on Thurs you'll be treated to the sumptuous Pig on the Spit for F$36. The kids' menu portions are huge and very reasonably priced. Daily 7.30am–10pm.

Flame Tree Lomani Resort ☎666 8212. This is a good choice if you want to get away from the hordes, and kids – it's adults only here. The food is excellent and the setting thoroughly romantic with just fourteen candlelit tables under a large flame tree. Mains are around F$32, with the lamb rack an excellent option, and there's a choice of fourteen wines. It's a good 20min walk along the beach from Musket Cove, but if you call ahead they'll happily pick you up by golf cart. Daily noon–10pm.

Ratu Nemani Island Bar Musket Cove Marina ☎ 666 2215. Atmospheric bar on an artificial island connected to the marina by pontoon and overlooking Malolo Bay. A great spot to sip a beer, wine or local spirit (all F$4) or try one of the multicoloured exotically named cocktails (from F$12). Daily 10.30am–11pm.

Malolo

2

Malolo is the largest island in the Mamanucas, home to two budget resorts as well as one of the most luxurious resorts in the region. The 220m-high hill fort of Uluisolo looks down on the island's rich vegetation and white beaches.

The north and east coast

On the island's **north coast**, backed by grassy sunburnt hills with patches of ironwood trees, is the chiefly village of **Yaro**. Twenty minutes' walk along the tidal beach down the **east coast** is **Solevu**, promoted as "shell village" to tour groups although many of the shells on sale here are imported from Asia. Fifteen minutes further south is the tiny settlement of **Cubi**, inhabited by a community from Fulaga (see p.182) in the Lau Group – the men are renowned wood carvers and you should be able to find fine samples of *tanoa* bowls and war clubs. From Cubi, you can follow the inland trail to Uluisolo (see below) or it's a ten-minute walk to the southern lagoon (see below).

The southern lagoon

The southern point of Malolo juts out into a shallow **lagoon** almost touching Malolo Lailai – you can walk between the two islands at low to mid-tide. Although not practical for swimming or snorkelling (the reefs have been extensively damaged by fishing), the southern lagoon is great for **kitesurfing**, with southeasterly trade winds creating almost perfect conditions between May and October.

Inland Malolo

The real beauty of Malolo lies inland. There are plenty of **walking tracks** around the island including several ascending to the 220m-high **Uluisolo**. At the summit is a US-built World War II **lookout post** offering fabulous views of the entire Mamanucas and as far north as Matacawalevu in the northern Yasawas. It takes just under an hour to reach the top, although note that there is little shade along the way.

There's also an excellent walking track along the fire break at the northwestern point of the island. The path winds its way over several bluffs with lovely panoramas from **Naroba Point** and looks down on the exclusive *Likuliku Lagoon* resort (see p.86). From

---

THE DESTRUCTION OF SOLEVU VILLAGE

In July 1840 a flotilla of six **US Navy warships** was sent to the South Pacific to survey the islands and assure the safety of American whalers in the region. Having toured Tonga, Samoa, New Zealand and most parts of Fiji, the ships arrived at Malolo island. A small boat was sent to Solevu Village to bargain for much needed food provisions but the crew was ambushed and two officers killed. Outraged by this unprovoked attack, the captain of the flotilla, John Wilkes, set about revenge. First, the bodies were recovered and buried in an unmarked grave on tiny Kadavu island (presently home to *Bounty Island Resort*); then the village of **Solevu** was swiftly burned to the ground, garden plantations ripped apart, canoes sunk and 57 men slaughtered. The attack proceeded to neighbouring Yaro where the village elders hastily surrendered by prostrating themselves as a sign of humility. Wilkes ordered the villagers to supply his ships with water, yams, a dozen pigs and three thousand coconuts – a huge task considering the damage caused by the attack and the poor farming conditions of the region. Wilkes was subsequently court-martialled for his severe actions – the first military strike in Fiji carried out by Western forces.

2

SURFING MALOLO

Surfing at **Malolo Barrier Reef** is exceptional, with waves up to 5m high, crystal-clear water and smooth right- and left-hand breaks. The most famous breaks are the left-handers "Cloudbreak" and "Restaurants", the right barrel of "Wilkes" and "Desperations".

One of the best ways to experience them is by visiting the activities hut at *Plantation Island Resort* on Malolo Lailai (see p.84). Their boat departs every day during high tide (sometimes twice daily). Choose one of seven breaks, according to the conditions and your level of ability; the trip takes around four hours (F$70–90).

Other resorts offering boat trips to the reefs include *Castaway Island* (see p.86) and *Mana Island* (see opposite). There's also direct access from *Rendezvous Fiji* on the mainland, a twenty-minute drive south of Nadi (see p.65).

Note that most of the breaks are at their best in the **morning** before the winds freshen up and the prime season for monster waves is between April and November. Surfing here is not for beginners – waves can be huge and, with **sharp coral heads** just a few metres below the surface, any untimely wipeout could lead to severe cuts or grazes.

Naroba Point, you can scramble down to shimmering **Navutu Beach** and walk east along the north coast all the way to the southern point of Malolo past Yaro and Solevu villages (see p.85); if coming from Yaro the track ascending Naroba Point is difficult to find.

ACCOMMODATION   MALOLO

★ **Likuliku Lagoon ☏** 672 0978, **🌐** likulikulagoon .com. In a delightful crescent-shaped bay with tidal beach, this resort oozes elegance. The eighteen hand-crafted beachfront bungalows are exquisite, with massive bathrooms with indoor and outdoor showers plus plunge pools and daybeds. The very pricey and dramatic overwater bungalows have good snorkelling direct from the steps leading down into the lagoon but are a long

walk from the main resort area. **F$1790** includes meals
★ **Tropica Island Resort ☏** 665 1777, **🌐** tropicaisland .com. A boutique beachfront resort with 14 rooms, 12 beachfront bures and 4 beachfront suites. The whitewashed, thatch-roof bures, with their swing benches and hammocks, are a delight. Food is outstanding, there's an indulgent spa and activities include watersports, basket weaving and crab races. **F$549**

Castaway Island

Lying less than a kilometre off the northwest tip of Malolo, steep rocky **Castaway Island** has a stunning powdery sand point and gorgeous turquoise lagoon. The island also boasts one of the best **walking trails** in the Mamanucas. Starting at the back of *Castaway Island Resort* (see below), a narrow path climbs for five minutes before levelling out and meandering through light natural forest. After twenty minutes, the trail emerges on the rocky slopes of the east side of the island where you're graced with wonderful **views** overlooking the small uninhabited Mociu Island and beyond to Mana and Matamanoa. The trail ends here but it's worth continuing for ten minutes, picking your way over the boulders until you reach the eastern tip of the island. Here there's another stunning view overlooking Likuliku Lagoon and the western end of Malolo Island.

You can return via the north beach – look out for a trail on the right within a minute's walk back down through the forest. Follow this to the beach and then continue north and around Monkey Rock, which resembles a monkey's head, and back to the resort.

ACCOMMODATION   CASTAWAY ISLAND

Castaway Island Resort ☏ 666 1233, **🌐** castawayfiji .com. A popular choice for families as well as older couples, with 66 traditional thatch bures located on the beautiful

sand point. There's a tennis court, two swimming pools (one for families) and a spa in the landscaped gardens as well as exceptional snorkelling from the beach. **F$1080**

Mana

Mana is one of the best islands in the Malolo Group to explore, with several hilly peaks and outstanding views of the surrounding islands. Flanked by gorgeous sweeping

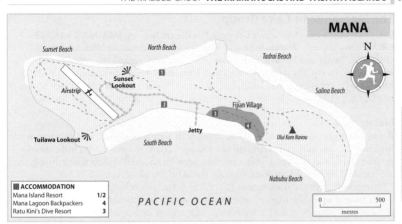

MANA

N

Sunset Beach   North Beach   Tadrai Beach

Sunset Lookout   [1]   Salina Beach

Airstrip

Fijian Village

[2]

[3]

Jetty   [4]   Ului Koro Navou

Tuilawa Lookout   South Beach

Nabubu Beach

PACIFIC OCEAN

■ ACCOMMODATION	
Mana Island Resort	1/2
Mana Lagoon Backpackers	4
Ratu Kini's Dive Resort	3

0   500
metres

2

beaches, this 569-acre island is home to the largest resort in the Mamanucas, plus four small backpacker resorts. It lies on the outer edges of the Malolo Group, 25 minutes by boat from Malolo and Castaway Island. The island is split by the *Mana Island Resort*, which occupies the entire western side of the island, and the **backpacker hostels** squashed in amongst the Fijian village on **South Beach**.

Around the coast

Past the rocks enclosing either side of South Beach are fine stretches of secluded sand. It's possible to **walk** around the entire island in about two hours, mostly along the beachfront, but make sure it's close to low tide as crossing the rocky points between beaches when wet can be difficult.

The **lagoon** off South Beach has copious amounts of seaweed, but swim 50m out and you'll reach a nice drop-off with great visibility for **snorkelling**, coral heads teeming with fish and the chance to spot the occasional turtle. The beaches on the north side of Mana have even better snorkelling, with a steep drop-off 50m from shore, particularly off **Dream Beach**.

Inland Mana

There are several nice walks along the hilly ridges inland. Signposted trails depart from the *Mana Island Resort* to **Sunset Lookout** and **Tuilawa Lookout**, both fifteen-minute ambles through light forest to viewpoints with great sunset views. Another trailhead starts behind the blue lodge at *Ratu Kini's* and follows the eastern ridgeline to the 60m summit of **Ului Koro Navou**, with superb views overlooking the rocky islands of the Mamanuca-i-Cake Group.

ACCOMMODATION   MANA

Mana Island Resort ☎ 665 0423, ⓦ manafiji.com. With 150 rooms and bungalows, this is the largest of the Mamanuca resorts, though you wouldn't know it, as it's spread out over three hundred acres of landscaped gardens, fronting both South and North Beaches. There are loads of amenities and water activities on offer, and a wide range of accommodation options from rooms, apartments and bungalows. F$420

Mana Lagoon Backpackers ☎ 929 2337, ⓦ mana lagoonbackpackers.com. Cheerful backpackers with a large and lively sand-floor beachfront restaurant and two

rather stuffy dorm lodges at the back. Rates include meals. Dorms F$40; rooms F$99

Ratu Kini's Dive Resort ☎ 672 1959, ⓦ ratukinidive resort.com.fj. Long-established backpacker hostel. The restaurant and bar are right on the beach, with the units set in a cement building 30m behind and the lodge rooms and dormitory right at the back of the village abutting the hill. Interiors are clean and there's a lively atmosphere at night, with themed entertainment including fire dancing. They also have a fully equipped dive shop. Dorms F$35; rooms F$250

The Mamanuca-i-Cake Group

Only two of the thirteen islands belonging to the enchanting **MAMANUCA-I-CAKE GROUP** have resorts – **Matamanoa** and **Tokoriki** – and there are traditional fishing villages on **Tavua** and **Yanuya**. Otherwise, the islands are completely uninhabited. **Modriki** and its equally stunning neighbour **Monuriki** were made famous in the 2001 film *Castaway* starring Tom Hanks, but the remote **Sacred Islands** remain well off the tourist trail, only visited briefly by an overnight cruise company or by private yachts.

2

Matamanoa

Rocky **Matamanoa** is covered in thick forest, with a gorgeous beach on its eastern flank. Bird Rock, a few hundred metres off the southern coast, teems with seabirds, mostly noddies, terns and frigates, and is a fantastic spot for snorkelling and scuba diving; trips are operated by Viti Watersports, who are based on the island (see p.65).

A steep **trail** from the *Matamanoa Island Resort*, starting behind the tennis court, winds its way up to the island's summit where several huge boulders seem to balance precariously; it's easy to scale these for one of the most impressive **views** in Fiji – a 360-degree panorama with small islands in all directions. Directly north is **Tavua**, the third-largest island in the Mamanucas with a single village on its west coast, lined with lush coconut trees which stick out amongst its sunburnt barren hills. If you come in the evening or early morning, there's a good chance of spotting fruit bats and doves, which feed in the forests, and possibly the elusive crested iguana, which is usually well camouflaged in the canopy.

ACCOMMODATION   MATAMANOA

★**Matamanoa Island Resort** ☎672 3620, ⓦmatamanoa.com. If you're looking for a good-value romantic getaway this is the place to stay. The resort's twenty spacious thatch bures are raised slightly from the beach, giving fabulous ocean views; there are also fourteen a/c rooms at the back in a single-storey cement block. Rooms F$495; bures F$795

Tokoriki

Surrounded by a fringing reef, hilly **Tokoriki** has two resorts either side of a rocky outcrop that divides a long stretch of beach on the west side of the island. In recent years the island has suffered from beach erosion and large amounts of seaweed washing up on certain tides, although the resorts remove it before it gets too whiffy. The offshore reefs are unaffected by the seaweed and **snorkelling** is excellent about 200m from the beach at both resorts. From May to July the lagoon teems with tiny bait fish, attracting both **seabirds** which circle and dive bomb from above, and locals from the neighbouring villages casting fishing nets from small boats.

ACCOMMODATION   TOKORIKI

Amunuca Island Resort ☎664 0640, ⓦamunuca .com. Overlooking a turquoise lagoon, this resort has a contemporary feel, and its affordable one- and two-bedroom whitewashed units are perfect for families. Wakeboarding, banana-boat rides and parasailing are all available. F$371
★**Tokoriki Island Resort** ☎672 5926, ⓦtokoriki.com. This upmarket retreat for honeymooners has a gorgeous infinity pool overlooking the ocean and several beach bures. Perched against the hillside at the far end of the property are a series of private villas ranking amongst the most delightful in Fiji, each with handcrafted wooden interiors and their own plunge pools. F$1170

Yanuya, Monuriki and Modriki

Tokoriki is owned by the people of neighbouring **Yanuya**, a long thin island with several knolls. The village here is renowned for its **pottery making** and you can visit on a day-trip from either resort, or on the daily *Seaspray* sailing cruise from Mana Island (see p.86) which comes ashore for a traditional *kava* ceremony and village craft market.

CASTAWAY ISLAND (P.86) >

2

THE LEGEND OF THE SACRED ISLANDS

The **Sacred Islands** are owned by the people of Tavua. In their oral history, the **legend** of the canoe *Rogovaka*, arriving with Fiji's first inhabitants led by Tui Na Revurevu, is still recalled in dance. The new arrivals are said to have settled on the largest of these islands and called it Vanua Levu, translating to "big island" (not to be confused with its much larger namesake in northern Fiji). The legend goes on to tell of a second wave of immigrants who, finding Vanua Levu already settled, continued on to Vuda on Viti Levu (see p.67). A village thrived on Vanua Levu for a while, but as the island has no source of spring water, it was later abandoned. An archaeological excavation revealed ancient **Lapita pottery** which seems to justify the legend's authenticity. The people of Tavua hold the island sacred and to this day, it's expected that anyone setting foot on Vanua Levu should lay a traditional gift of *yaqona* roots in a small cave found behind the row of coconut palms on the eastern side of the sand spit.

Off the west side of the village are the islands of **Monuriki** and **Modriki**, used as the setting for the 2001 film *Castaway*. With steep craggy rock faces and thick forests, it's difficult to explore these islands, but with a guide you can reach the summit of the long flat rock face of Modriki from where Tom Hanks looked out in despair seeing nothing but ocean (though in reality there are six islands directly in front of you to the east, the Sacred Islands and the southern Yasawas to the north, as well as most islands in the Mamanucas). The beaches on the eastern side of both islands are beautiful, with fine white sand piled deep on a point backed by tall palm trees.

The Sacred Islands

Ten kilometres north of Tokoriki, the seven uninhabited **Sacred Islands** (or Mamanuca-i-Ra) rise out of the ocean in breathtaking splendour. Between May and September a handful of yachts are usually anchored in the protected bays here enjoying the solitude. Apart from the weekly visit by Captain Cook Cruises (see p.92) on its way up to the Yasawas, few other people venture this way except the occasional TV crew who have filmed four series of *Survivor* on the islands.

The reef alongside the picturesque 200m-long sand spit on **Vanua Levu** has fantastic **snorkelling**, with extensive coral gardens, but the beach is difficult to land on. Neighbouring **Navadra** is more accessible, with a good swimming beach. The islands are important nesting grounds for migrating seabirds, particularly terns and noddies.

The Yasawa Islands

The volcanic **YASAWA ISLANDS** attract thousands of visitors, drawn to their dramatic jagged peaks, tranquil bays and stunning beaches. Connected by a fast daily catamaran service from Nadi, the islands are easy to hop between and have developed into a popular **backpacker trail**.

The group of thirty islands has three distinct zones. **Kuata**, **Wayasewa and Waya**, in the southern part, are similar in nature to the outer Mamanucas, with high mountain peaks, dramatic rock faces and fantastic walking tracks. These three islands are the closest to the mainland, only two hours by fast catamaran, and are by far the most interesting to visit, with deep bays and pretty villages providing regular stops for **overnight cruises**. To the north is the largest island in the group, **Naviti**, with rolling grassy hills and a dozen small offshore islands where **manta rays** congregate between May and October. Fifteen minutes' sailing north of Naviti are the **northern Yasawas**, home to a cluster of budget resorts and three super-exclusive retreats.

THE RISE OF THE BACKPACKER RESORT

Thirty years ago, travellers who wanted to explore the Yasawas had to obtain a special visitor pass from the District Office in Lautoka. However, in 1987, the government decided to open up the region to independent travel. A few **backpacker resorts** initially sprang up on Tavewa, and these were soon followed by similar developments on Waya and Wayasewa. Passage to the islands was by small fishing boat, usually without radio or life jackets and often with dubious engines. Having witnessed the success of these early resorts, the government opened an **ecotourism** start-up fund offering F$50,000 worth of materials to local landowners. The result was an explosion of budget resorts. Since 2001, with the introduction of the *Yasawa Flyer* catamaran service, the region has changed dramatically and the romantic days of exploratory tourism have given way to a thriving commercial industry with over thirty resorts now operating across the area.

2

SERVICES, HYGIENE AND FOOD

The majority of backpacker resorts in the Yasawas are run by the islanders themselves, either as individual businesses or as community projects. **Services** and **hygiene** have improved over the years, although you're still likely to run into the odd creepy-crawly, especially in the thatch bures. **Meals** at the more basic resorts can be a disappointment – it's definitely worth bringing some snacks.

COSTS

Compared to the mainland, **costs** are inflated. Most resorts charge F$80 for a dorm bed including three meals, while a small bottle of beer costs around F$5. Snorkelling gear costs F$6 a day to rent so it's definitely worth bringing your own set. There's little else to spend money on – organized **activities** are limited to fishing trips and village visits and work out at F$20–50 per person.

ARRIVAL AND GETTING AROUND — THE YASAWA ISLANDS

The efficient *Yasawa Flyer* **catamaran** serves the majority of the Yasawa Islands. While a few resorts try to compete with the *Flyer* by offering quicker direct transfers from Lautoka on the mainland for around the same price, these boats are often too small for the somewhat choppy waters and best avoided. Taking a multi-day **cruise** may not appeal to everyone, but it can be the most convenient way to experience the Yasawas; all the cruises listed below anchor at sublime open-water snorkelling reefs, take time out at secluded beaches and visit traditional villages, with great sightseeing from the boat along the way.

BY CATAMARAN

YASAWA FLYER

Services and tickets The *Yasawa Flyer* catamaran (Ⓣ675 0499, Ⓦawesomefiji.com), operated by Awesome Adventures, departs from Port Denarau daily at 8.30am and returns at 6pm, stopping in either direction at all Yasawa resorts as far north as Nacula, as well as several islands in the Mamanucas. Tickets start at around F$100 for a one-way trip to Kuata (2hr). Note that you and your luggage will be transferred from the *Yasawa Flyer* to your resort by a small outboard-motor boat; mostly it's free, but some resorts charge F$10–20 for the service.

The Bula Pass You can buy transfers between islands on the *Flyer*, although if you're going to island-hop, the best option is to purchase the Bula Pass (F$147 for 5 days, F$191 for 7 days, F$251 for 10 days, F$277 for 12 days, F$302 for 15 days or F$332 for 21 days), which allows unlimited trips on the *Flyer* until you return to Port Denarau.

Destinations from Port Denarau Yasawa Islands, Kuata to Nacula (daily; 2–5hr).

BY PRIVATE TRANSFER

Resort boats The only resort boats worth taking are the comfortable speedboats that ferry guests to *Navutu Stars* or *Nanuya Island Resort* in the northern Yasawas. These boats reach their respective islands in about 2hr 30min, half the time of the *Yasawa Flyer*. Once in the northern Yasawas, the only way to get around is by resort outboard boat. These can be expensive for private charter, costing around F$90 for the short 10min hop between Tavewa and Nacula.

BY PLANE

To Yasawa Island The only airstrip in the Yasawas is on the northernmost island, Yasawa Island, but the grass runway is used exclusively by the upmarket *Yasawa Island Resort*.

To Nanuya Levu Turtle Airways (Ⓣ672 1888; daily, times vary; 35min; F$299 one way) provides seaplane transfers between Wailoaloa Beach in Nadi and Nanuya Levu in the northern Yasawas, but you must pre-arrange with your chosen resort for them to pick you up by boat from Nanuya Levu.

2

ON A CRUISE TRIP

Blue Lagoon Cruises ☎ 666 1622, ⓦ bluelagoon cruises.com. Offers a range of trips to the Yasawas, from the three-night "Explorer Cruise" (from F$2250 per person) to the seven-night "Paradise Cruise" (from F$5600 per person including all meals). Cruises depart Port Denarau every Fri at 3pm on board the *Fiji Princess*.

Captain Cook Cruises ☎ 670 1823, ⓦ captaincook .com.fj. Spanning four levels and with a maximum of 90 guests, this cruise ship is surprisingly spacious on board. The ship has a swimming pool, sauna and sun deck and lively entertainment. A four-night Northern Yasawa Cruise departs Port Denarau every Tues at 2pm (from F$1068 per person for cabin bunks includes all meals).

ISLAND TOURS

Sightseeing trips Most resorts offer organized island sightseeing trips or village visits for around F$30 per person.

Kuata, Wayasewa and Waya

The three volcanic islands of **Kuata**, **Wayasewa** and **Waya** are the most striking of the Yasawa Islands and on a clear day can be seen from Nadi jutting out on the distant horizon. The 50km journey by boat from Port Denarau takes just under two hours.

Kuata

Kuata, the most southerly island of the Yasawas, has been designated a **nature sanctuary** by its owners on adjacent Wayasewa. Pleasant **walking trails** meander around the oddly shaped hills and rocky outcrops but, unless you're very lucky, you're unlikely to see any of the **crested iguanas** that hide in the forest trees. A deep ocean wall immediately off the island's west coast has fantastic **scuba diving**, and there's an unusual figure-of-eight swim through pinnacles and caves off the east coast. There are dive operators at both *Kuata Natural Resort* and neighbouring *Waya Lailai Ecohaven Resort* on Wayasewa (see below), or you can dive with Captain Cook Cruises (see above). Snorkelling is also very good here and there's a popular reef, reached by boat, where you're likely to see quite a few reef sharks.

Wayasewa

Across the passage from Kuata, **Wayasewa** (also known as Waya Lailai) is dominated by the towering 350m-high twin peaks of Vatuvula and Vatusawalo, with the old village of **Namara** sitting precariously beneath. In 1985, after heavy rain, a landslide brought several huge boulders tumbling down the hillside to within inches of people's homes. The village was declared unsafe and relocated to the north side of the island at **Naboro**. It didn't take long, though, for a few stubborn families to return and when the adjacent backpacker resort reopened, more villagers moved back. Today, over half of the houses are occupied, although most families with young children prefer living close to the new primary school at Naboro.

Inland Wayasewa

The forty-minute **hike** from the back of *Waya Lailai Ecohaven Resort* to the summit of **Vatuvula** is a must, especially at sunset. The well-trodden track ascends steeply through forest and up a narrow crag before opening out onto a rocky escarpment that leads to the summit. It's hard going after rain and crossing the 10m-long boulder to reach the sheer-cliff summit is a little nervy, but for conquerors there are fabulous views looking directly down on the resort and over the bay to Kuata and the Mamanucas. The return leg passes another island icon, the **wobbling rock**, a giant boulder you can rock from side to side.

Waya

Dramatic **Waya** has a strange, contorted appearance, with knife-edge ridges, monumental rock protrusions and several unbelievably photogenic **beaches**. From its western coast, a giant's face seems to peer out from the island, slanting back as though

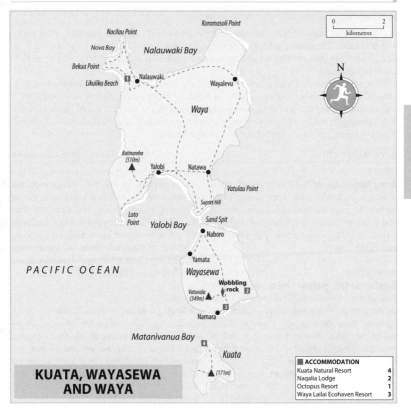

KUATA, WAYASEWA AND WAYA

■ ACCOMMODATION	
Kuata Natural Resort	4
Naqalia Lodge	2
Octopus Resort	1
Waya Lailai Ecohaven Resort	3

floating in the sea. Four fishing villages lie around the coast, all connected by **walking trails**, making it a paradise for hikers (remember etiquette codes for dress and behaviour when visiting villages; see p.31). Although Waya is connected to Wayasewa by a 200m-long **sand spit** exposed at low tide, the islands' inhabitants have very different roots: the people of Waya look north to the high chief of Yasawa Island, while Wayasewa is inhabited by the people of Vuda from Viti Levu.

The south side of the island

For hikers, **the southern side** of Waya is a great base from which to explore the island. From here **walking trails** head along the cliff edge and into the undulating hills, and it's possible to scale the pointed 510m Mount Batinareba. Local **guides** (around F$35 per half day) are essential for all but the short twenty-minute trail to Sunset Hill, as the paths can be difficult to follow and are treacherous after rainfall; the locals also believe dangerous spirits lurk in the hills; make sure you carry plenty of water.

   Directly north of the sand spit, curved beach extends to either side, with pretty **coral reefs** in both bays although the west side is more sheltered. A twenty-minute walk from the sand spit along the west beach brings you to **YALOBI**, one of the most stunningly located villages in Fiji. Set in a deep bay, fronting a sandy beach, it's backed by a series of massive contorted cliffs almost 500m high, with green veins of rainforest growing in the fissures and valleys. Yalobi is the chiefly village of Waya Island, home to around five hundred people, a health centre and a primary school.

The west coast

Along the **west coast** of Waya are the pretty twin bays of Liku and Likuliku, each with a small resort. The most established of these, *Octopus Resort* (see below), faces a delightful long crescent-shaped beach backed by coconut palms, with extensive coral gardens offshore.

There's a great coastal **hike** from here. From the north end of **Likuliku Beach**, walk around the rocky ledge of Bekua Point to secluded Nova beach. At low tide, you can rock-hop around Nacilau Point for a sweeping view of the north coast of Waya Island. Just before you reach Nalauwaki Village climb over the hills and back down to *Octopus Resort* – the complete circuit takes two to three hours.

2

ACCOMMODATION   **KUATA, WAYASEWA AND WAYA**

KUATA

Kuata Natural Resort ☎ 666 9020, ⓦ kuatanatural resort.com. This lively backpacker resort is popular among the Bula Pass crowd. The thatched-roof dorms are a tad tired looking, but the en-suite bungalows with tiled floors are spacious and clean. Rates include meals. Dorms F̲$̲5̲5̲; bures F̲$̲1̲5̲9̲

WAYASEWA

Naqalia Lodge Naqalia Point ☎ 977 4696, ⓦ naqalialodge-yasawa.com. Run by local villagers, with traditional and simple bures and a twelve-bed dorm. Great swimming above the coral, and a pleasant relaxed atmosphere. Limited cold water and electricity, and the evenings are tranquil: it's not one for the party crowd. Rates include meals. Dorms F̲$̲1̲0̲0̲; bures F̲$̲2̲5̲0̲
★**Waya Lailai Ecohaven Resort** Namara ☎ 651 2292, ⓦ wayalailairesort.com. One of the more organized backpacker resorts in the Yasawas, with a lot of

activities, yet it's managed to retain a charming laid-back Fijian atmosphere. Set over three terraced levels with spacious lawns, the two dorm lodges sit at the top overlooking ten small en-suite bures which gaze down onto the beach. There's a large deck restaurant abutting the hill, with stunning views over to Kuata and unobscured stargazing. Activities include summit walks and swimming with reef sharks. Rates include meals. Camping (with own tent) F̲$̲5̲5̲; dorms F̲$̲7̲0̲; bures F̲$̲2̲0̲0̲

WAYA

★**Octopus Resort** Nalauwaki ☎ 666 6337, ⓦ octopusresort.com. Appealing to families, couples and the more refined backpacker, this resort has a gorgeous beach location, a swimming pool and excellent food selected from a blackboard menu. There's a coral reef offshore, and a good range of activities including hikes. Book in advance. Rates include meals. Dorms F̲$̲4̲0̲; bungalows F̲$̲2̲0̲0̲; bures F̲$̲3̲0̲0̲

Naviti

Less intriguing than Waya Island but blessed with delightful secluded beaches, **Naviti** is the largest of the Yasawa Islands, home to five villages and the region's only boarding school. The island is shaped somewhat like a lobster with two elongated arms reaching out to the north and a cluster of small islets forming a tail to the south. The best of the **beaches** is alongside *Botaira Beach Resort* on the southwest side.

Drawaqa Island lagoon

A gradual climb from the *Botaira Beach Resort* into the hills and along a grassy ridge to the southern point of the island presents an inspiring view looking down on the lagoon around **Drawaqa Island** with its thousand hues of blue. The lagoon offers excellent **snorkelling**, and between May and October it's possible to swim with **manta rays**, which feed around the rich current-fed passages. Your best chance of seeing them is one hour after high tide. You can visit from *Botaira Beach Resort*, a ten-minute boat ride away, or swim directly from *Barefoot Lodge* on Drawaqa Island or from the aptly named *Mantaray Island Resort*, on the adjacent island of Nanuya Balavu.

The west coast of Naviti

A little over halfway along the west coast of Naviti is **Natuvalu Bay**, a beautiful long stretch of sandy beach peppered with tall coconut trees and a couple of resorts. The lagoon here is very shallow, but if you walk ten minutes over the point at the north end

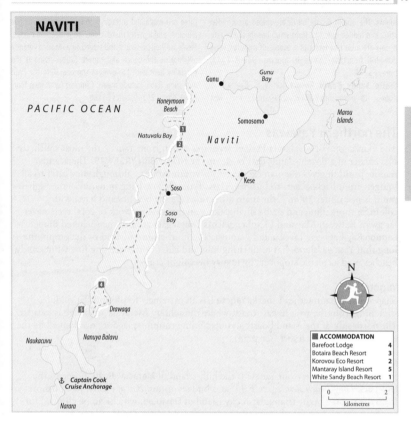

NAVITI

PACIFIC OCEAN

Gunu
Gunu Bay
Honeymoon Beach
Somosomo
Marou Islands
Natuvalu Bay
N a v i t i
Kese
Soso
Soso Bay
Drawaqa
Nanuya Balavu
Naukacuvu
Captain Cook Cruise Anchorage
Narara

2

■ ACCOMMODATION	
Barefoot Lodge	4
Botaira Beach Resort	3
Korovou Eco Resort	2
Mantaray Island Resort	5
White Sandy Beach Resort	1

0   2
kilometres

of the bay you'll find **Honeymoon Beach**, a great swimming and snorkelling spot. For even more seclusion, continue walking north around the rocky bluff to find a series of charming sandy cove beaches. On your way back, just past the summit of the small hill leading down to the resorts, a track on the right leads off along a promontory which after ten minutes opens out to a lookout with fabulous **views** of both Natuvalu Bay and Honeymoon Beach.

ACCOMMODATION   NAVITI

Barefoot Lodge Drawaqa ☎670 3040, ⓦbarefootislandfiji.com. Set on a stunning point with beaches on both sides, lined with thatch bures. Amongst the usual activities – lovo dinners, volleyball, night fishing – you can swim with manta rays on safaris held between May and Oct. Good food and a non-party atmosphere. Rates include meals. Dorms F$115; bures F$310

★**Botaira Beach Resort** Soso ☎603 0200, ⓦbotaira .com. Welcoming *Botaira* couldn't have a nicer beach, with hammocks strung between palm trees, deep white sand and good snorkelling. The fourteen thatch bures feature thatched roofs and varnished timber floors. Rates include meals. F$498

Korovou Eco Resort Natuvalu Bay ☎665 1001, ⓦkorovouecotourresort.com. A tad too many cement pathways and an ugly seawall spoil the appearance of this place, but a swimming pool and affordable lodge rooms and bures with private bathrooms (albeit with cold water) make it popular with both backpackers and families. Rates include meals. Dorms F$120; bures F$290

★**Mantaray Island Resort** Nanuya Balavu ☎664 0520, ⓦmantarayisland.com. Lively backpacker resort with lots of activities including game fishing, scuba diving and waterskiing. The restaurant and bar is perched on a hill overlooking Drawaqa Lagoon and has satellite TV and themed party nights. The quaint jungle bures are raised on wooden stilts and hidden amongst light scrub beside the beach; dorms are a bit box-like and a couple of minutes' walk downhill from the shared bathrooms. Dorms F$41; bures F$275

White Sandy Beach Resort Natuvalu Bay ☎ 666 4066, ✉ whitesandy_diveresort@yahoo.com. Just three self-contained cottages – one sleeping up to five people – and a pretty thatch dorm lodge sleeping twelve. Meals are well presented and served on a wooden veranda overlooking the beach and sunset. Scuba diving is the speciality here with the owner's son operating the PADI dive shop. Rates include meals. Camping (with own tent) F$70; dorms F$240; bures F$480

The northern Yasawas

The 5km choppy Naivalavala Passage separates Naviti from Yaqeta, the most southerly of a cluster of a dozen islands that make up the **NORTHERN YASAWAS**. The islands' remote position gives them an exotic, exclusive atmosphere, although they cater to all budgets from backpackers to business class. Typically low-lying in nature – the highest point is just under 300m – the main attractions are the beaches and bays, with colourful snorkelling and scuba diving along an intricate network of coral reefs never far away. Between May and October, **yachts** congregate around the sheltered **Blue Lagoon Bay** between Tavewa and Nanuya. The northernmost island of the group, the long thin **Yasawa Island**, has undulating hills and cliffs, with sweeping fine white sandy beaches used as picnic stopovers by luxury overnight cruises.

Yaqeta

Shaped like a hammerhead shark, **Yaqeta** has an extremely fertile and flat middle, stretching from the west to east coast, where the solitary Matayalevu Village is located. The **north side** of the island boasts an outstanding turquoise lagoon, overlooked by the elegant *Navutu Stars* resort (see p.98).

Matacawalevu

Just across the lagoon from Yaqeta is the hilly island of **Matacawalevu**, home to the laid-back *Long Beach Resort* (see p.99) and budget option *Bay of Plenty*. Just offshore from the resort sits the triangular rocky island of **Deviulau**, which can be climbed for fantastic views of the beach and bay; it also offers good snorkelling along its southern point. You can walk to the island at low tide, though look out for sting rays lurking in the water.

A twenty-minute track from the resort leads across to the east coast village of **Vuake**. The village's picturesque **Catholic Church**, perched on a hill overlooking the shallow tidal waters of Nasomo Bay, is a wonderful place to experience the full volume of a Fijian Sunday church service. From Vuake, walking tracks lead up into the hills, where village gardens are planted with *dalo* and *yaqona*, or you can walk north to the island's second village, the Methodist enclave of **Matacawalevu**, also on the east coast.

Blue Lagoon Bay

Flanking the north and east coast of Matacawalevu are the small islands of Nanuya and Tavewa, with the larger island of Nacula to the north forming the **Blue Lagoon**

KAYAKING IN THE NORTHERN YASAWAS

A fantastic way of seeing the remote side of the northern Yasawas is to join one of the **kayaking trips** run by South Sea Ventures (☎ 02 8901 3287 in Australia, ⓦ southernseaventures.com; 7 nights for A$2130). Group trips run between May and October, and involve between three and four hours of paddling a day in either single or twin sea-kayaks. On the eight-day trip, five days are spent paddling between Matacawalevu and Sawa-i-Lau, camping on beaches in two-man tents. Trips are equally suitable for novice or experienced kayakers, although a reasonable level of fitness is expected.

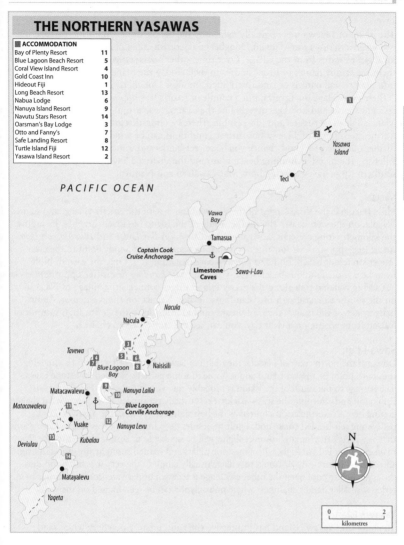

THE NORTHERN YASAWAS

■ ACCOMMODATION

Bay of Plenty Resort	11
Blue Lagoon Beach Resort	5
Coral View Island Resort	4
Gold Coast Inn	10
Hideout Fiji	1
Long Beach Resort	13
Nabua Lodge	6
Nanuya Island Resort	9
Navutu Stars Resort	14
Oarsman's Bay Lodge	3
Otto and Fanny's	7
Safe Landing Resort	8
Turtle Island Fiji	12
Yasawa Island Resort	2

PACIFIC OCEAN

Yasawa Island

Teci

Vawa Bay

Tamasua

Captain Cook Cruise Anchorage

Limestone Caves *Sawa-i-Lau*

Nacula

Nacula

Tavewa

Blue Lagoon Bay

Naisisili

Matacawalevu *Matacawalevu*

Nanuya Lailai

Blue Lagoon Corvile Anchorage

Vuake *Nanuya Levu*

Deviulau *Kubalau*

Matayalevu

Yaqeta

N

0   2
kilometres

Bay. The bay is named partly for its dream-like turquoise waters but also to capitalize on the semi-erotic 1980 film *The Blue Lagoon*, starring Brooke Shields, filmed partly on Nanuya Levu. Around this sheltered bay is the highest concentration of **backpacker resorts** in the Yasawas, making it a handy place for island-hopping.

Nanuya Levu and Nanuya Lailai

Nanuya Levu (big Nanuya) is strictly off-limits unless staying at the ultra-exclusive *Turtle Island Resort* (see p.99). There's more down-to-earth accommodation on **Nanuya Lailai** (little Nanuya), the northern of the two islands. The **best beach** on Nanuya Lailai is on the sheltered west coast, and there's decent snorkelling a hundred metres offshore along a 30m coral wall drop-off.

2

Tavewa

The island of **Tavewa** was originally owned by the people of neighbouring Nacula, but was given as a dowry to William Dougherty, a Scottish copra planter who married a local girl of status from the village. Over time, other Scots settled here, bringing with them the family names of Bruce and Campbell. Today the island has been subdivided into many small parcels of land distributed amongst Dougherty's descendants.

There's no village on Tavewa, but a couple of resorts (see opposite) and a handful of resident shacks and holiday cottages line the eastern beachfront. The west coast, as with Matacawalevu, is rugged and inaccessible. There's a fantastic **coral wall** around the northeastern point of Tavewa but surface conditions can be windy. If you head a little further out, there's a good chance you'll see reef sharks and sometimes tons of harmless jellyfish. The nicest swimming beach is around the sheltered **Savutu Point**, at the southern tip of Tavewa facing both Matacawalevu and Nanuya.

Nacula

Hilly **Nacula** is the third largest of the Yasawa Islands with the chiefly village, also named Nacula, on the west coast. The southern side of the island has lovely beaches, including the kilometre-long crescent sands alongside *Oarsman's Bay Lodge* and *Blue Lagoon Beach Resort* (see opposite). At low tide you can walk south around **Sandy Point** to the even longer stretch of beach, home to *Nabua Lodge* (see opposite). Over the eastern bluff from here is the fabulous beach setting fronting *Safe Landing Resort* (see opposite).

A scenic **walking trail** along the grassy inland ridges connects the village of Naisisili on the southeast coast with the island's namesake, Nacula, on the west coast. About halfway across the island, the trail breaks off and leads up to the 238m-high summit of **Naisau** from where, on a clear day, you can see the entire Yasawa chain.

Sawa-i-Lau

Lying off the north coast of Nacula, the island of **Sawa-i-Lau** lies in a pretty bay hugging the south point of Yasawa Island and is home to some partially flooded **limestone caves**. The passage to the south of the island is probably the windiest place in Fiji, with gusts ripping in and churning the seas – backpackers usually get drenched and somewhat shaken getting here. Nevertheless, it's touted as the best sightseeing trip in the Yasawas. Locals believe the ten-headed **snake god**, Uluitini, resides deep inside the caves and folklore warns that any pregnant woman, however slight, will be unable to fit through the entrance. The main chamber is 15m high, with limestone pillars and natural sunlight streaming in from above. Boys from nearby Nabukeru Village usually climb to the very top and jump into the crystal-clear **pool** here; the other challenge is to swim underwater for ten seconds to a series of smaller darker chambers where **petroglyphs** can be seen incised on the walls.

Yasawa Island

The long thin **Yasawa Island** has impressive **cliffs** and pristine powdery white sand beaches along the west coast, several of which are leased to one of the two cruise companies which visit almost daily (see p.92). The island is synonymous with the luxury *Yasawa Island Resort* (see opposite), which is beautifully positioned on a secluded stretch of beach on the northeast coast.

Six traditional villages are found on the east coast. The fishing village of **Teci** is one of the most authentic in Fiji, with over half its homes being traditional thatch-roof bures. At the northern tip of the island is the chiefly village of **Yasawa-i-Rara**; you can stay nearby at small budget retreat *Hideout Fiji* (see opposite), close to Vulawalu Beach.

ACCOMMODATION   **THE NORTHERN YASAWAS**

YAQETA

Navutu Stars Resort ☎664 0553, ⊛navutustarsfiji.com. Run by a young Italian couple, the food here is superb,

using herbs and fruits grown in the organic gardens. There are little corners of solitude everywhere, including a treehouse-style yoga platform and a simple spa hut. The contemporary whitewashed villas have a Balinese feel and the grand bures on the hill have beautiful sunken spa baths and wonderful views of the bay. Closed Feb. F$700

MATACAWALEVU

Bay of Plenty Resort ☎ 967 3696, ⊚ bayofplenty -yasawa.com. A small and modest resort for budget travellers, offering a nice slice of Fiji life with village trips including school visits. The hillside bures have lovely views, and the fruit and local dishes are abundant. Rates include meals. Dorms F$90; bures F$170

★**Long Beach Resort** ☎ 666 0198, ⊚ longbeachfiji .com. This small, laid-back retreat, located along a beautiful 1km stretch of powdery white sand, is run by welcoming hosts from the local village. You can stay overlooking the beach either in a quaint thatch bure (quite small and with shared outdoor bathrooms about 50m away) or opt for one of the reasonably priced modern en-suite cottages with ceiling fans and tiled floors. One of the cottages is used as an eight-bed dorm. Cash only; rates include meals. Dorms F$105, bures F$250, cottages F$280

BLUE LAGOON BAY

NANUYA LEVU

Turtle Island Fiji ☎ 672 2921, ⊚ turtlefiji.com. The fourteen handcrafted and ultra-luxurious bures at this exclusive resort are offered to couples only on an all-inclusive minimum five-night package costing over US$9999

NANUYA LAILAI

Gold Coast Inn ☎ 776 0212, ⊚ goldcoastinn-yasawas .com. This family-run resort features just seven rooms – six bungalows plus a dormitory. The timber bures are fairly basic, but the welcoming Fijian family who own the resort provide visitors with three organic meals a day from their garden plus a solar lamp at night. Rates include meals. Dorms F$100; bures F$240

★**Nanuya Island Resort** Blue Lagoon Beach ☎ 666 7633, ⊚ nanuyafiji.com. Fantastic value on the northern end of Blue Lagoon Beach. The centrepiece here is its huge restaurant and lounge bar, where delicious meals are served. Simple wooden treehouse bures are perched on a steep hillside, or there are beachfront cottages sleeping up to four people. Bures F$330; cottages F$F498

TAVEWA

Coral View Island Resort ☎ 666 2648, ⊚ coralview .com.fj. A wide range of activities are on offer at this resort, including dance lessons, game fishing, snorkelling, kayaking and *kava* drinking. There's also a scuba dive centre (⊚ prodivers-world.com). Accommodation is in serried ranks of palm bures. Dorms F$42; bures F$130

★**Otto and Fanny's** ☎ 666 6481, ⊚ ottoandfanny .com. A terrific budget option with five thatch bures set

slightly back from the beach. Two are big enough for families and there's a small eight-bed dorm appealing to the more sedate budget traveller. Fanny's home-cooked meals have a good reputation and her chocolate and banana cakes draw in the backpackers from along the beach. Rates include meals. Dorms F$40; bures F$108

NACULA

Blue Lagoon Beach Resort Reservations NZ ☎ +64 3442 9998, ⊚ bluelagoonbeachresort.com.fj. Very high-quality dorm accommodation, with bedside lamps and beach towels provided. Budget rooms are bright and attractive, while the villas are in a cosy bungalow style. The resort also has a dive shop and offer a range of courses. Dorms NZ$47; budget rooms NZ$197; villas NZ$229

Nabua Lodge ☎ 666 9173 or 990 7294, ⊚ nabualodge -yasawa.com. A delightful family-run budget retreat with nine bures; six of them overlook the beach, three of them have en-suite bathrooms and sleep up to four people. Dorms F$100; bures F$240

Oarsman's Bay Lodge ☎ 672 2921, ⊚ oarsmanbayfiji .com. This picturesque resort with wonderfully accessible snorkelling is popular with backpackers, couples and families. The simple wooden cottages are excellent value, though beginning to show signs of wear and tear, and the wooden-decked restaurant serves decent food. A twelve-bed dorm, located above the restaurant, has low slanting ceilings and is usually packed and stuffy. Rates include meals. Camping (with own tent) F$38.50; camping (with hired tent) F$55.50; dorms F$38.50; bures F$205

Safe Landing Resort ☎ 632 0309, ⊚ safelandingfiji .com. Some of the nicest budget bures in Fiji: they're fairly basic, with limited electricity, but there's good fishing and snorkelling as well as jewellery making and language classes. Rates include meals. Camping (with own tent) F$40; dorms F$100; bures F$320

YASAWA ISLAND

Hideout Fiji Yasawa-i-Rara ☎ 628 3803, ⊚ hideoutfiji .com. A small budget retreat close to Vulawalu Beach. It takes over an hour by outboard boat to reach the resort from the *Yasawa Flyer* drop-off point at Nacula (which adds F$300 onto the transfer cost). Depending on the seas, this transfer can either be a glorious adventure with lovely scenery or an endurance test; however, it's worth it for those looking to escape the well-trodden backpacker path further south. Rates include meals. Dorms F$80; bures F$160

★**Yasawa Island Resort** ☎ 672 2266, ⊚ yasawa .com. Superb high-end resort with eighteen a/c bures with elegantly minimal interiors and outdoor showers. There's a spa offering body treatments and facials, and the resort will tailor-make private picnic excursions for you. Rates include meals; air transfers extra. Bures F$850

Rural Viti Levu

FIJIAN WOMEN MAKING POTTERY

Rural Viti Levu

Given that Fiji is renowned for its tiny coral islands, many visitors are struck by the sheer size of its main island, Viti Levu or "Big Fiji". Covering just over ten thousand square kilometres, it's roughly half the size of Wales and offers a wide range of scenery, from sunburnt yellow sugarcane fields along the dry north coast to the verdant blanket of rainforest spread over the eastern half of the island. With the exception of the Nadi to Lautoka corridor and the urban sprawl between Suva and Nausori, Viti Levu is distinctly rural in character, with only a handful of small market towns along the coastal road circling the island. Most such towns are found at the mouths of rivers, which in turn connect the isolated and seldom visited mountainous interior.

3

Viti Levu can be hastily explored in two days, either by public bus or rental car, but a week is recommended to have a chance to meet some of the exceedingly hospitable characters who will welcome you along the way. More time will allow you to branch off the main roads to explore and **hike** amongst some of the most beautiful countryside in the South Pacific.

The Queens Road, the main artery connecting Nadi and Suva, travels along **South Viti Levu**, a relatively well developed tourist region. The first stop is the small town of Sigatoka, close to the absorbing Sigatoka Sand Dunes National Park. Further east are the beach resorts of the Coral Coast and the adventure sports capital of Pacific Harbour. By contrast, **North Viti Levu** appears rather barren, its scenery dominated by sugarcane farmland interspersed with the market towns of Ba, Tavua and Rakiraki. Inland, however, is Fiji's most attractive village, Navala, as well as the country's highest point, Mount Tomanivi; offshore are the budget resorts of Nananu-i-Ra island. **East Viti Levu** is the least developed area on the mainland, still mostly covered in rainforest; its main attraction is the picturesque Tailevu Coast, accessed by remote dirt road.

Climate

Viti Levu's **climate** splits into two zones. The area around Suva catches the brunt of the southeasterly trade winds, which roll in off the warm ocean and cause cloud build-up over the mountains. Consequently, everything east of a fairly distinct line extending from Rakiraki to Sigatoka lies in the **wet zone**, with high rainfall, dense forests and often-unbearable humidity. Once the clouds have blown over the mountain range – the highest point of which reaches 1323m at Mount Tomanivi – they fall, cool and dissipate, leaving the other half of the island with almost perpetual sunshine. This is the **dry zone** or "Burning West", as it is ridiculed by umbrella-clad Suva-ites.

GETTING AROUND   **RURAL VITI LEVU**

The easiest way to travel around Viti Levu is **by road**, with the busy single-lane Queens Rd connecting Nadi and Suva along the south coast (4hr), and the less-travelled Kings Rd connecting Nadi and Suva via Lautoka along the

NAVALA VILLAGE

Highlights

❶ Sigatoka Sand Dunes National Park
Explore the wild beachfront where ancient
Fijians once lived, and go surfing on the waves.
Shards of bone and ancient pottery are regularly
revealed by the wind. **See p.110**

❷ Shark diving, Pacific Harbour Extreme
adventure fans can come face to face with
tiger and bull sharks on this world-famous dive.
See p.116

❸ River rafting Journey along the lush
waterfall-lined rapids of the Navua River either
by kayak, longboat or river raft. **See p.118**

❹ Navala village Fiji's sole-surviving traditional
thatch village on the Ba River is truly
breathtaking and on a grand scale. **See p.119**

❺ Tavua Charming Fiji-Indian market town off
the tourist trail. **See p.121**

❻ Mount Tomanivi Climb Fiji's highest peak for
a spectacular view of the surrounding forests.
See p.122

❼ Tailevu Coast Travel along the remote and
seldom-visited east coast with winding bays and
delightfully friendly Fijian villages. **See p.128**

HIGHLIGHTS ARE MARKED ON THE MAP ON PP.104–105

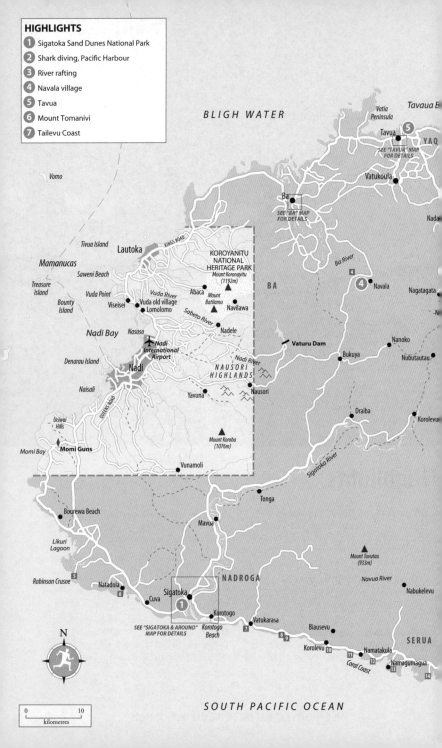

HIGHLIGHTS

1. Sigatoka Sand Dunes National Park
2. Shark diving, Pacific Harbour
3. River rafting
4. Navala village
5. Tavua
6. Mount Tomanivi
7. Tailevu Coast

BLIGH WATER

Vomo

Vatia Peninsula

Tavaua E

Tavua **5**

YAQ

SEE "TAVUA" MAP FOR DETAILS

Vatukoula

Ba **4**

SEE "BA" MAP FOR DETAILS

Nada

Tivua Island

Lautoka

KINGS ROAD

KOROYANITU NATIONAL HERITAGE PARK

Mount Koronqyitu (1192m) ▲

Ba River

BA

Nada

Mamanucas

Saweni Beach

Abaca

Mount Batilamu ▲

Navilawa

4 Navala

Nagatagata

Treasure Island

Vuda Point

Vuda River

Vuda old village

Lomolomo

Bounty Island

Viseisei

Sabeto River

Nadele

Nanoko

Nubutautau

Nadi Bay

Nasoso

Nadi International Airport

NAUSORI HIGHLANDS

Nadi River

Vaturu Dam

Bukuya

Denarau Island

Nadi

Draiba

Korolevu

Naisali

Yavuna

Nausori

QUEENS ROAD

Uciwai Hills

Momi Bay

Momi Guns

Mount Koroba (1076m) ▲

Sigatoka River

Vunamoli

Tonga

Bourewa Beach

Mavua

Mount Tuvutau (933m) ▲

Likuri Lagoon

NADROGA

Navua River

Nabukelevu

Robinson Crusoe **5**

Natadola **6**

Cuva

Sigatoka **1**

Korotogo

Vatukarasa

Biausevu

SEE "SIGATOKA & AROUND" MAP FOR DETAILS

Korotogo Beach

7

8 **9**

Korolevu **10**

11

Namatakula

12

SERUA

Namagumagua

13

14

Coral Coast

N

0   10
kilometres

SOUTH PACIFIC OCEAN

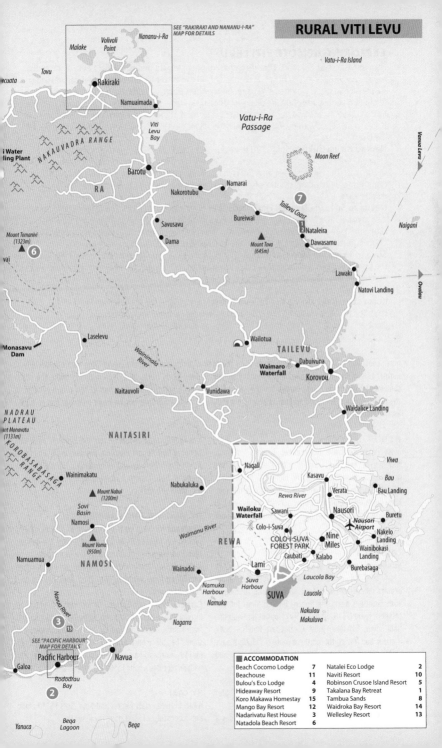

RURAL VITI LEVU

SEE "RAKIRAKI AND NANANU-I-RA" MAP FOR DETAILS

Nanan-i-Ra

Malake
Volivoli Point

Tovu

cuata

Rakiraki

Namuaimada

Vatu-i-Ra Island

Vanua Levu

i Water
ling Plant

NAKAUVADRA RANGE

Viti Levu Bay

Vatu-i-Ra Passage

Moon Reef

7

Barotu

RA

Nakorotubu

Namarai

Taileru Coast

Savusavu

Bureiwai

Dama

1
2 Nataleira

Naigani

Dawasamu

Mount Tomanivi (1323m)

6

Mount Tova (645m)

Lawaki

vai

Natovi Landing

Ovalau

Laselevu

Wainimala River

Wailotua

TAILEVU

Monasavu Dam

Dabuivuna

Waimaro Waterfall

Korovou

Naitauvoli

Vunidawa

Waidalice Landing

NADRAU PLATEAU

nt Monavatu (1131m)

KOROBASABASAGA RANGE

Wainimakatu

NAITASIRI

Nabukaluka

Nagali

Viwa

Kasavu

Bau

Rewa River

Verata

Bau Landing

Mount Nabui (1200m)

Wailoku Waterfall

Sawani

Buretu

Sovi Basin

Nausori

Namosi

Colo-i-Suva

Nausori Airport

Nakelo Landing

Mount Voma (950m)

Waimanu River

REWA

COLO-I-SUVA FOREST PARK

Nine Miles

Wainibokasi Landing

Namuamua

NAMOSI

Wainadoi

Caubati

Kalabo

Burebasaga

Lami

Suva Harbour

Laucola Bay

Navua River

Namuka Harbour

SUVA

Laucola

3
15

Namuka

Nagarra

Nakulau Makuluva

SEE "PACIFIC HARBOUR" MAP FOR DETAILS

Pacific Harbour

Navua

Galoa

2

Rododrau Bay

Yanuca

Beqa Lagoon

Beqa

ACCOMMODATION

Beach Cocomo Lodge	**7**	Natalei Eco Lodge	**2**
Beachouse	**11**	Naviti Resort	**10**
Bulou's Eco Lodge	**4**	Robinson Crusoe Island Resort	**5**
Hideaway Resort	**9**	Takalana Bay Retreat	**1**
Koro Makawa Homestay	**15**	Tambua Sands	**8**
Mango Bay Resort	**12**	Waidroka Bay Resort	**14**
Nadarivatu Rest House	**3**	Wellesley Resort	**13**
Natadola Beach Resort	**6**		

3

EXPLORING REMOTE VITI LEVU

Four less-travelled dirt roads provide a really genuine insight into **rural Viti Levu**. None of the routes below is served by buses, and although all can be navigated by a regular car with good suspension in good weather, 4WD is recommended. Before you leave, check your tyres (including your spare) and take plenty of drinking water – *yaqona* roots are also good to carry as a *sevusevu* in case you decide to visit a village. Each of the following routes takes around five hours to drive but with overnight options in villages along the way it's worth taking longer to explore:

Nadi to Ba via Bukuya Start from the Nadi Back Road, climbing into the grassy hills of the Nausori Highlands. The scenery is barren and very remote, with panoramic views along most of the road. The route passes through two fascinating villages: Bukuya; and Navala with over a hundred traditional thatch bures (see p.119). Overnight stopover: *Bukuya Homestay* and *Bulou's Lodge*.

Navua to Suva via Namosi Highlands Start from Namosi Rd along the Queens Rd, 11km east of Navua Town. The road meanders through dense tropical forest into the Namosi Highlands (see p.118), past traditional villages with stunning mountain views along the way. Overnight stopovers: *Namosi Homestay* and *Raintree Lodge*.

Suva to Tavua via Monasavu Dam This route journeys through the heart of Viti Levu, past the lush Sovi Basin and Monasavu Dam towards Mount Tomanivi, Fiji's highest mountain, before heading downhill into the farming valleys surrounding Tavua. Overnight stopovers: *Nadarivatu Rest House* (see p.122).

Korovou to Rakiraki via the Tailevu Coast Travels along the secluded and winding coastline of Tailevu, passing rivers, seldom-visited villages and scenic bays. Overnight stopovers: *Natalei Eco Lodge* (see p.129), *Takalana Bay and Retreat* (see p.129).

north coast (6hr). Between them the roads cover the 460km circumference of the island. Stray cattle (especially at night), kids playing on the roadside, speeding minivans, over-laden trucks and deep potholes make the roads somewhat hazardous. Public **buses** are the safest way to travel and offer lovely views of the countryside from the high windows. There are no **trains** apart from industrial sugar train lines and no **boat** service between towns around Viti Levu.

BY BUS

Most buses originate from either Lautoka or Suva, travelling between the two cities on the Kings Rd along the north coast, or on the Queens Rd along the south coast, stopping at towns and most large hotels along the way. Local buses stop frequently between destinations – to hail one on the roadside simply put out your arm and flap your fingers.

COMPANIES

Sunbeam Transport ☏ 666 2086 in Lautoka, ☏ 338 2704 in Suva, ⓦ sunbeamfiji.com. Operates regular express services between Lautoka and Suva, running in both directions along the Queens Rd and Kings Rd. The southern route (F$18; 10 daily; 5hr) stops at Nadi Airport, Nadi Town, Sigatoka, most Coral Coast hotels, Pacific Harbour and Navua; the northern route (F$15.70; 8 daily 6hr) stops at Ba, Tavua, Rakiraki, Barotu, Korovou and Nausori.

Pacific Transport ☏ 670 0044 in Nadi, ☏ 330 4366 in Suva. Serves the Queens Rd only (F$20.25; 5hr; 6 daily).

Coral Sun ☏ 672 3105, ⓦ coralsunfiji.com. Provides a more comfortable and direct tourist bus service each way between Nadi Airport and Suva, stopping at all Coral Coast hotels, Pacific Harbour and terminating at Holiday Inn Suva (departs Nadi Airport 7.30am & 1pm; Suva 7.15am & 3.30pm; F$22; 4hr).

BY MINIVAN AND CARRIER VAN

Minivans Minivans operate between all towns, usually picking up passengers at bus stands. They are quicker than buses and cost approximately the same, but can be a hair-raising experience, especially at night when overtaking large vehicles, with their horn blaring and lights flashing.

Carrier vans Open-backed carrier vans travel to all interior villages along dirt roads, bringing produce to and from market – ask amongst the market vendors and you should be able to hitch a bumpy ride squashed in the back for F$3–7 depending on the distance. To hire a carrier van with driver costs around F$50 for a 1hr journey.

BY TAXI

A taxi between Nadi Airport and Suva costs F$250 along the Queens Rd, or F$300 along the Kings Rd.

BY CAR

Car rental You can rent a car in north Viti Levu in Ba (see p.120), and in south Viti Levu in Sigatoka (see p.108).

BY PLANE

The only domestic airports are at Nadi (see p.55) and Nausori (see p.141), the latter a 30min drive north of Suva. Flights between the two take 30min and are operated by Pacific Sun (3 daily; around F$135 one-way).

ON A TOUR

In addition to the operator listed below, numerous day-tour companies also explore inland Viti Levu from Nadi (see p.59).

Feejee Experience ☎ 672 3311, ⓦ feejeeexperience .com. Can arrange round-island bus tours which take four days to travel around Viti Levu, overnighting at the Coral Coast, Suva and Rakiraki. Sightseeing and activity stops along the way include sand surfing down the Sigatoka Sand Dunes and tubing down the Navua River. Transport pass only F$479; departs Nadi Mon, Tues, Wed & Sat.

South Viti Levu

The scenic Queens Road passes through countless fishing villages alongside the winding bays of **South Viti Levu**. A fabulous beach, **Natadola**, lies within an hour's drive south of Nadi. To the east is the region's main town, **Sigatoka**, a rather uninspiring market centre. However, in its immediate vicinity are several worthy attractions, including the **Sigatoka Sand Dunes National Park** and **Tavuni Hill Fort**. Beyond Sigatoka the sunny climate and sugarcane fields give way to cloud-clad mountains, which descend towards the picturesque lagoons of the **Coral Coast**. Graced by white sandy **beaches**, this was where tourism first began in Fiji and it's still home to a wide range of resorts, from large family-friendly complexes to budget resorts tucked away in secluded bays. Further east is **Pacific Harbour**, with the fabulous **Beqa Lagoon** offshore for scuba diving and game fishing, and the oppressive virgin rainforest of the **Namosi Highlands** offering remote riverside villages, pristine waterfalls and whitewater rafting. From here, the bustling, rain-drenched capital city of Suva (see Chapter 4) is just forty minutes' drive along the coast.

Natadola Beach and around

One of Viti Levu's most picturesque white sandy beaches, **Natadola**, is found hidden off the Queens Road less than an hour's drive south of Nadi.

A long sweeping crescent, blessed with regular waves, it is one of the few **body surfing** beaches in Fiji. There's even a small surfing break on the south side close to the river mouth which is popular with local kids. It's an excellent day-trip from Nadi, despite the persistent touts from the local village who will try to sell you handicrafts or a ride on a mangy horse (around F$25). It's also the departure point for transfers to the lively backpacker resort, **Robinson Crusoe Island** (see below).

ARRIVAL AND DEPARTURE

NATADOLA BEACH AND AROUND

By car The initial journey from Nadi passes through flat featureless sugarcane fields for 17km before cutting inland through dense pine forests just after the Momi Bay turn-off. The longer, winding old coastal road from Momi Bay to Likuri Harbour is far more scenic. When the old coastal road rejoins the Queens Rd, it's only another 4km to the Natadola turn-off.

By bus Paradise Transport buses connect Natadola with Sigatoka (4 daily; 1hr; F$3.25).

ACCOMMODATION

Natadola Beach Resort ☎ 672 1001, ⓦ natadola .com; map pp.104–105. A no-kids resort with just eleven "suites" set in tropical gardens, each with its own private courtyard. Close to the beach and with friendly, warm service. F$250

Robinson Crusoe Island Resort ☎ 628 1999, ⓦ robinsoncrusoeislandfiji.com; map pp.104–105. Lively resort with attractive traditional-style bures and lodges. Features lots of organized activities and pseudo tribal entertainment (which may not be everyone's cup of tea), but there's good snorkelling on the outer reef. Rates include meals. Dorms F$31; bure F$115; lodge F$149

Sigatoka and around

Often incorporated into the tourist region of the Coral Coast, the busy market centre of **SIGATOKA** marks the southern boundary of the dry leeward side of Viti Levu. The town itself is located 4km inland on the banks of the Sigatoka River and acts as a hub for the region. To the west is the **Sigatoka Sand Dunes National Park**, where ancient Lapita pottery shards lie buried in the sand; walking trails criss-cross the dunes, and there's good surfing offshore. Inland, the Sigatoka River, the longest in Fiji, winds north for 120km to Nadarivatu at the foothills of Mount Tomanivi (see p.122). The lower portion of the river valley makes for good exploring by car, but there are no designated walking trails other than the steep track weaving around **Tavuni Hill Fort**. Eight kilometres east of Sigatoka is **Korotogo Beach**, a pleasant resort area with a variety of accommodation, several restaurants and the **Kula Eco Park**, a good place to see native Fijian wildlife.

Sigatoka town

Central Sigatoka is dominated by Indian traders and several restaurants specializing in hot curries. It's certainly not a place to stay, but quite a few people visit either en route to somewhere else or whilst visiting nearby attractions. The bus stand and adjacent **market** are rather grimy, with belching bus fumes lingering in the air and market vendors furiously pushing their souvenirs on tourists. By contrast, the smart air-conditioned **boutique shops** found further along the Valley Road have fixed but somewhat inflated prices.

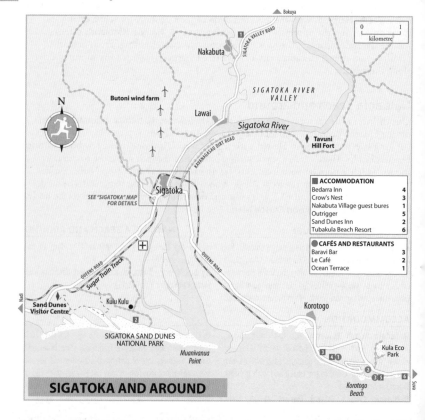

SIGATOKA AND AROUND

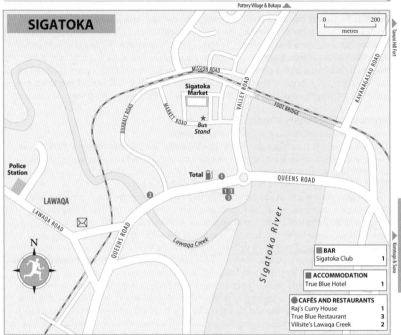

SIGATOKA

Pottery Village & Bukuya

Tavuni Hill Fort

0   200
metres

MISSION ROAD

Sigatoka Market

VALLEY ROAD

FOOT BRIDGE

KAVANAGASAU ROAD

MARKET ROAD

DUIBALE ROAD

★ Bus Stand

Police Station

Total

QUEENS ROAD

3

LAWAQA

LAWAQA ROAD

QUEENS ROAD

Lawaqa Creek

Sigatoka River

Korotogo & Suva

N

BAR
Sigatoka Club   1

ACCOMMODATION
True Blue Hotel   1

CAFÉS AND RESTAURANTS
Raj's Curry House   1
True Blue Restaurant   3
Vilisite's Lawaqa Creek   2

Nadi

ARRIVAL AND DEPARTURE

By bus Sunbeam Transport and Pacific Transport buses pass through Sigatoka several times daily on the south coast route.
Destinations Lautoka (14 daily; 2hr); Nadi (15 daily; 1hr 20min); Navua (15 daily; 2hr); Pacific Harbour (15 daily; 1hr 30min); Suva (15 daily; 4hr 50min).

SIGATOKA TOWN

By car Car rental is available at Budget (☎650 0986), Queens Rd, 1km west of town just beyond the Mosque; Coastal Rental (☎652 0228, ⓦcoastalrentalcars.com.fj), Korotogo Back Rd, Korotogo; and Sharmas (☎650 1680, ⓦsharmasrental.com), beside Total petrol station on Queens Rd, Nadi side of bridge.

INFORMATION

Banks Westpac and ANZ banks (Mon–Fri 9.30am–4pm) both have ATMs on Market Rd.
Hospital ☎650 0455. On a side road off the Queens Rd, 1km west of town towards Nadi.
Internet access Net Café (Mon–Fri 9am–4.45pm, Sat

9am–12.45pm, 20 cents a minute) has broadband.
Police ☎650 0222. The main station is at Lawaqa, west of the town centre, but there's a police post on the Valley Rd opposite Morris Hedstrom.

ACCOMMODATION

True Blue Hotel Queens Rd, on the roundabout beside the road bridge ☎650 1530, ⊜truebluehotel @connect.com.fj; map above. The pick of a dire bunch: top floor en-suite rooms are adequately furnished with

ceiling fans and some with a/c; on the middle floor are three dorm rooms, while the *Sigatoka Club* graces the bottom floor. Dorm F$30; rooms F$79

EATING AND DRINKING

Raj's Curry House Queens Rd, beside the Total Station ☎650 1470; map above. This is the locals' favourite, tiny and a little grubby, but with goat or duck curry on the bone costing F$16 and six simple vegetarian dishes for around F$9 you get a good sample of Fiji-Indian food here. Avoid

the pre-cooked meals from the counter. Mon–Sat 8am–9pm.
Sigatoka Club True Blue Hotel, Queens Rd; map above. You can play snooker with the locals here on a full-sized table (20 cents a game) or enjoy a F$4 beer. Daily 7am–11pm.

True Blue Restaurant Queens Rd ⊙ 650 1530; map p.109. Situated beneath the *True Blue Hotel*, this large restaurant has direct access from beside the Sigatoka bridge. Mostly Indian flavours, but some Fijian and Chinese dishes too. The delicious masala crab will set you back F$47; alternatively the chicken biryani or vegetarian thali are around F$17 and filling. There are tranquil views overlooking the river, plenty of tables and a bar. Daily 7am–11pm.

Vilisite's Lawaqa Creek ⊙ 650 1030; map p.109. Don't let the naff interior put you off – the seafood here is pretty good, especially the fried octopus in coconut cream and the curry prawns (both around F$35). Cheaper blackboard specials range from F$15 to F$25. Licensed. They also operate the neighbouring ice cream and drink shack. Daily 9am–9pm.

Sigatoka Sand Dunes National Park
Visitor centre Mon–Fri 8am–4.30pm, Sat & Sun 8am–4pm • F$10 • ⊙ 652 0243

Two kilometres east of Sigatoka Town, the **Sigatoka Sand Dunes National Park** makes for an inspiring outing. The dunes cover an area of 650 hectares, stretching for 3km and petering out to a sand spit at the mouth of the Sigatoka River. In places they rise to 80m with fantastic views of the crashing surf along the beach.

The **visitor centre** has an informative display highlighting the fragile ecology and archeological importance of the region, and can also provide guides. There are two designated **walking trails** from here: an hour's stroll through forest to the beach; and a two- to three-hour walk which takes you along the ridge of the dunes. Along the beachfront you'll find plenty of driftwood and, if you look carefully, you'll come across small shards of **Lapita pottery**, evidence of human settlement from over two thousand years ago. Unusually large human bones are regularly found here, suggesting that the fish diet and lifestyle of the early settlers was very healthy. Circling back round to the forest you'll encounter "treehuggers" sculpted from dead wood, symbolizing the need to protect the environment, and there's a clearing just beyond noisy with flying foxes.

Good **surfing** can be had around the Sigatoka River mouth at the southern end of the beach, although the sea can be ferocious at times with strong currents – locals can advise the safest entry points for both surfers and swimmers. You can rent boards at the *Sand Dunes Inn* (see below).

ACTIVITIES   SIGATOKA SAND DUNES NATIONAL PARK

Horseriding You can go horseriding along the beach with Sand Dune Horseriding (⊙ 972 0386; daily 8am–5pm; F$25 per hour), based at Yadua village, 1km towards Nadi from the visitor centre. It's run by Arthur Ratuva, a member of the Fijian 2007 Rugby World Cup team.

Surf board rental The *Sand Dunes Inn* rents surf boards (F$25 a day), body boards and sand boards (both F$20 a day).

ACCOMMODATION

Sand Dunes Inn Queens Rd ⊙ 627 9064; map p.108. This budget hotel has direct access to the dunes and is only a 10min walk along the beach from the surfing break. The owners from adjacent Kulu Kulu Village offer four basic

---

FIJIAN POTTERY

The single most important item identifying the migration of people across the South Pacific is **pottery**. For Fijians, the trail commences with the introduction of **Lapita pottery**, a distinct form of geometric patterning impressed on clay pots by finely saw-toothed blades prior to firing. The oldest examples of Lapita, dating back to 1220 BC, were found at Bourewa Beach on the southeast coast of Viti Levu. The highest concentration of the pottery is found at Sigatoka Sand Dunes National Park (see above).

In pre-European times, pottery formed the basis of Fijian homewares, with clay vessels used as water containers, *yaqona* bowls, and pots for baking, steaming and frying food. Today, potters around the islands retain traditional motifs, some using woven mats to create patterns, others using carved paddles or leaves. The potters, almost exclusively **women**, knead the clay with fine sand using the heels of the feet, beat it into shape using a wooden mallet, crudely fire the pots and then glaze them for waterproofing by rubbing over with the hot wax-like gum of the *dakua* tree which was also used as a candle in pre-European times.

shared rooms in the main house, and a large fourteen-bed dorm in a separate lodge; they will cook simple meals on request (around F$10). The hotel is a little tricky to find. Coming from Nadi on the Queens Rd, turn right onto the dirt road immediately after passing under the railway bridge beyond the Sand Dunes visitor centre; keep right when the road divides after about 200m – the inn is 1.5km further on at the end of the track. Alternatively you can catch the Sunbeam bus from Sigatoka to Kulu Kulu. Dorms **F$29**

Sigatoka River Valley

Early morning mists rising from the **Sigatoka River** fill the surrounding valley, giving it a surreal atmosphere. Along the river's banks is some of the most fertile farming land in Fiji, with plantations of fruit, vegetables and sugarcane. A dirt road travels either side of the river from Sigatoka Town. The west side of the valley, known as the Valley Road, extends from Sigatoka Town all the way to Bukuya Village (see p.106); here the road branches off to Nadi, or continues across the centre of Viti Levu to Ba on the north coast. The east side of the valley is less travelled and goes only as far as Mavua village.

The Valley Road

The **Valley Road**, on the west side of the river, makes an excellent **walking track** and passes many villages and viewpoints along the way. The initial 6km from Sigatoka Town is sealed, passing immediately through Sigatoka Village and hugging close to the river. After 2km, just beyond Lawai, you'll come to the Butoni Wind Farm, with 37 wind turbines lined on the hill ridge. A further kilometre leads to **Nakabuta Village** (tour by donation – approx F$5 – anytime from 8am to 5pm; ☎ 650 0929), where a *yaqona* ceremony, **pottery-making** demonstrations and Fijian dance are performed for impromptu arrivals.

Tavuni Hill Fort

Beside the village of Naroro, 5km from Sigatoka Town, accessed via the Kavanagasau Rd on the Suva side of the Sigatoka bridge • Mon–Fri 8am–5pm, Sat 8am–4pm • F$12, guide additional F$3

Five kilometres up the rough dirt road on the east side of the valley is **Tavuni Hill Fort**, a fascinating example of Fiji's tribal past. In the eighteenth century, Tongan invaders began to push further into Fijian territory and established a base on this fantastically steep hill overlooking the Sigatoka River. They waged wars on the surrounding settlements until 1876 when they were subdued by native troops under British control. What remains is a well excavated and easily accessible hill fort with stone foundations, rock barricades, ceremonial grounds and the chilling *vatu-ni-bokola*, or killing stone, where victims' heads were smashed with a war club. The **views** from the hilltop are worth the visit alone.

GETTING AROUND   SIGATOKA RIVER VALLEY

By bus Valley Buses (☎ 650 0168) from Sigatoka Town travel up the Valley Rd for two hours to Draiba (5 daily; F$4.50), before turning back around.
Tours Sigatoka River Safari (☎ 650 1721, ⓦ sigatokariver.com) offers entertaining jet-boat tours (F$239) of the Sigatoka River Valley, including village visits with *kava*, Fijian food and dance.

ACCOMMODATION

Nakabuta village guest bures Valley Rd ☎ 650 0929; map p.108. You can stay in one of the four basic and seldom-used guest bures beside the village. Rate (per person) includes breakfast and Fijian meals can be purchased from the villagers. **F$40**

Korotogo Beach and Sunset Strip

Eight kilometres beyond Sigatoka Town, past the final stretch of sugarcane fields, is **Korotogo Beach**. The beach itself is ordinary and not great for swimming but the pleasant 2km-long road towards it, known as the **Sunset Strip**, has a few restaurants, budget motels and holiday homes and makes a convenient base for exploring the sights around Sigatoka.

Kula Eco Park

Just across the Queens Rd from the Sunset Strip • Daily 10am–4pm • F$30 • ☏ 650 0505, ⌨ www.fijiwild.com

The absorbing **Kula Eco Park** holds Fiji's largest collection of native wildlife, and is nicely situated in a temperate forest with self-guided boardwalks meandering through aviary cages, reptile enclosures and a reef fish aquarium. Large crested iguanas (see box, p.194) are its highlight: endemic to Fiji, they are rarely seen and limited to only a couple of islands off Vanua Levu and Yasawa.

ACCOMMODATION	KOROTOGO BEACH AND SUNSET STRIP

Bedarra Inn Sunset Strip ☏ 650 0476, ⌨ bedarrafiji .com; map p.108. Twenty spacious en-suite rooms in a two-storey block, with views overlooking the pool and gardens, plus a bar, excellent restaurant and tour desk. Overall, great value for money, and guests get a complimentary foot spa. F$184

Crow's Nest Sunset Strip ☏ 650 0230, ⌨ crowsnestresort fiji.com; map p.108. Attractive individual wooden villas set into the steep grassy terrace facing the sea. The nautical theme permeates throughout, and there's even a little museum of whaling and sailing memorabilia. Their restaurant specializes in Italian food and seafood dishes. F$135

Outrigger Queens Rd ☏ 650 0044, ⌨ outrigger.com; map p.108. Five-star resort set in forty acres of beautifully landscaped grounds. The reception and most of the 207

rooms are perched on a hill overlooking the deluxe bures below – the latter all come with a butler to pamper you. Rooms have all the mod cons you could expect and there are three fabulous restaurants on site. The beach is not great, close to a swiftly flowing passage with rip tides – instead guests relax around a massive swimming pool. Rooms F$324; bures F$680

Tubakula Beach Resort Queens Rd ☏ 650 0097, ⌨ fiji4less.com/tuba.html; map p.108. Quiet retreat for backpackers looking to wind down. Very plain and simple A-frame bungalows with kitchens – some set up as rooms and others as dorms – neatly set in gardens alongside the beach and pool. Nothing fancy, but great value for money, and the food, though simple, is nourishing. Dorms F$28; rooms F$70; bungalow F$125

EATING

Baravi Bar At The Outrigger on Queens Rd ☏ 650 0044; map p.108. Offers a "culinary journey" through India, Thailand, Singapore and China. For more intimate evening dining, the *Ivi Restaurant* offers Pacific/Continental cuisine starting from F$35, but children under 13 are not permitted. Daily noon–9.30pm.

★ **Le Café** Sunset Strip ☏ 652 0877; map p.108. Cosy café-bar with a courtyard garden and happy hour (5–8pm). Offers a varied menu with thin-crust pizzas, fish curry and

grilled catch of the day; mains are around F$18. The pancakes and ice cream are a winner. Licensed and BYO. Tues–Sat 3–10pm, Sun noon–10pm.

Ocean Terrace At Bedarra Inn on Sunset Strip ☏ 650 0476; map p.108. A good choice for a romantic night out, with candlelit dining upstairs on the terrace. Delicious and elegantly presented mains include valley pork fillet (F$34) and seared tuna (F$30), and there's a daily chef's special. Licensed and BYO (F$5 corkage). Daily 6–9.30pm.

The Coral Coast

Driving along the **Coral Coast**, loosely defined as the 60km section of the Queens Road between Korotogo Beach and Pacific Harbour, is perhaps the most pleasant drive in Fiji. The name, inspired by the exposed offshore reefs, was used to market Fiji's first collection of tourist resorts, which were set up here in the 1960s. The Coral Coast begins in the province of Baravi, passing through the small settlement of **Korolevu**, where Fiji's first tourist hotel once stood; along the coastline here are a dozen **beach resorts**. Beyond Korolevu, the scenery becomes more intense as the highway climbs inland over the mountains of **Serua**, which shield several deep bays with secluded budget retreats. There are few specific attractions on the Coral Coast apart from its scenery, but its situation, midway between the sites of Sigatoka and the activities of Pacific Harbour, makes it a good base.

Korotogo Beach to Vatukarasa

Beyond Korotogo Beach, the Queens Road hugs the coastline for 30km all the way to Namatakula village. One of the finest coastal views is found 15km beyond Sigatoka, past Malevu village, overlooking the peaceful **Sovi Bay** with its pounding surf. There's plenty of roadside parking and you can scramble down the rocks to the grey sandy beach for a walk (though with unpredictable currents, swimming is not advisable). On the far side of the bay is the pretty setting of **Vatukarasa**, once settled by Tongans and with several beautifully thatched bures surrounding the village green, plus a couple of excellent handicraft shops (see p.114).

Korolevu, Biausevu and around

At **Korolevu**, 15km east of Vatukarasa, there's a BP petrol station with a small shop. Visible in the undergrowth behind is a small airport control tower, evidence of the old airstrip that served guests heading to the *Korotogo Beach Hotel*. The hotel was the pinnacle of tourism in the early 1970s before the Queens Road was tar-sealed. The hotel, the first tourist resort in Fiji, closed in 1983. A dirt road running parallel to the disused grass runway leads inland for 5km through lush tropical forest to **Biausevu Village** (F$10 entry fee). From the village, there's a thirty-minute relatively flat trail which crosses over a small stream half a dozen times and ends at the pretty **Savunamatelaya Waterfall**, where you can swim in the natural pool.

Beyond Korolevu

Nine kilometres beyond Korolevu is the village of **Namatakula** in the province of **Serua**. Here the Queens Road cuts inland for 20km to climb over steep hills draped in thick **rainforest**. On the first ascent, a small dirt road leads to *Mango Bay Resort*, with a beach backed by incredibly tall coconut palms. There's another pretty beach with good snorkelling at **Namagumagua**, accessed down a 4km dirt road signposted to *The Wellesley Resort*, 10km further along the Queens Road.

For a wonderful view of this **mountain scenery**, take yet another dirt road signposted towards *Waidroka Bay Resort* at the 69km roadside marker, and go past the Dogowale Radio Station track, turning left on Retreat Road. Walk up the first steep driveway on your left for a panoramic lookout – you can keep on walking for ten minutes up to the tower but the views at the top are sometimes obscured by long grass.

ACCOMMODATION

THE CORAL COAST

KOROTOGO BEACH TO VATUKARASA

★**Beach Cocomo Lodge** ☎ 650 7333, ⓦ beachcocomo .com; map pp.104–105. Set on a small hill overlooking the ocean and with steps leading down to a secluded sandy beach, this little-known spot is a real gem for those seeking seclusion. The two wooden cottages with polished wooden floors are tastefully decorated and have hot-water en-suite bathrooms; the only downside is that they back onto the main road. Delicious meals are served in a breezy thatch bure overlooking the sea. **F$168**

VATUKARASA TO KOROLEVU

Hideaway Resort ☎ 650 0177, ⓦ hideawayfiji.com; map pp.104–105. Once you're behind the prison-like walls which barricade this large resort from the highway, the atmosphere is rather quaint, albeit cramped. The duplex and quad bures are prettily painted and set in landscaped grounds. Interiors are bright and airy, most with a/c and some with outdoor courtyard showers. The beach is adequate, and there's good reef surfing in the passage 1hr either side of high tide. **F$369**

Tambua Sands ☎ 650 0399, ⓦ warwicktambuasands .com; map pp.104–105. With just 25 bures, some interconnecting, this is the smallest of the Coral Coast resorts, sedate but slightly dated. The ocean and garden bures are comfortable, with high roofs, ceiling fans and plenty of open spaces between them. If you're looking for something simple, with a small swimming pool and good restaurant, this pretty beachfront resort is great value. Includes continental breakfast. **F$180**

KOROLEVU

Naviti Resort ☎ 653 0444, ⓦ warwicknaviti.com; map pp.104–105. Liveliest of the large hotels in Fiji, probably thanks to the excellent-value meals-and-drinks-inclusive packages which cover alcohol. Within the resort's 38 acres there are 220 a/c rooms, five tennis courts, a nine-hole pitch and putt golf course and two swimming pools. The staff are very attentive, especially with children, and there's also a kids' club and babysitting service. **F$270**

3

BEYOND KOROLEVU

★**The Beachouse** ☎0800 653 0530, ⓦfijibeachouse.com; map pp.104–105. The location is pretty good, with tall coconut palms and a white sandy beach, and it's great if you're after a party atmosphere – you're made to feel instantly at home. There's a good swimming pool and bar, the food is tasty and there's loads to do, from waterfall hikes to sea kayaking. Rates include breakfast. Dorms F$55; rooms F$189

Mango Bay Resort ☎653 0069, ⓦmangobay resortfiji.com; map pp.104–105. Marketed as a "flashpacker" resort, this is a fun place to party, although it may be a little expensive for budget travellers. The four seven-bed dorms have individual bamboo screens and lockers, whilst the smart safari tents, also set back a fair way from the beach, have polished timber floors and en-suite bathrooms. The ten beachfront bures are best suited to young couples and come with outdoor courtyard showers. There's a good restaurant, lively bar and nightclub and even an outdoor cinema. Game fishing and scuba diving are organized daily, with PADI Open Water dive courses available for F$595. Rates include continental breakfast. Dorms F$36; cabins F$200; bures F$280

Waidroka Bay Resort ☎330 4605, ⓦwaidroka .com; map pp.104–105. This place is distinctly laid-back, as you'd expect from a surfing and scuba diving retreat. It's tucked 4km down a dirt road, screened by thick jungle but without a beach. The five simple terrace rooms are set on a hill with fine views, and six cosy bures and a swimming pool are scattered in gardens overlooking the sea. The Beqa Lagoon dive sites are 20–30min away by one of the five fully equipped fast boats; Frigates Passage surfing is a 45min trip, while three local surf spots are within 10min of the resort. There's a handsome variety of boards to rent. Rooms F$275; bures F$375

Wellesley Resort ☎650 0807, ⓦwellesleyresort .com.fj; map pp.104–105. One of the few chic yet affordable small resorts on Viti Levu. The fifteen suites are set some way back from the beach, with heavy wood decor set off by colourful Gauguin prints. The restaurant serves excellent European-inspired cuisine, served overlooking the pool and beyond to the ocean. The beachfront is pretty, with long strolls along the white sands in both directions, and the snorkelling is pretty good for the mainland. F$219

SHOPPING

VATUKARASA

Baravi Vatukarasa ☎652 0588; map pp.104–105. On the Suva side of the village, this is the larger and more commercial of Vatukarasa's two handicraft shops, with a wide range of wood carvings and jewellery made from all around Fiji. Mon–Sat 7.30am–6pm, Sun 8.30am–5pm.

Kuki's Handicrafts Vatukarasa; map pp.104–105. Tiny Kuki's, on the Nadi side of the Queens Rd, sources items mostly from Kuki's friends and relatives, and also serves coffee, cake and cold drinks. Mon–Sat 8am–5pm.

Pacific Harbour and around

Renowned as Fiji's adventure sports hub, **PACIFIC HARBOUR**'s suburban setting seems rather dull on first acquaintance: the town was purpose-built in the early 1970s, drained from swampland and laid out meticulously with suburban driveways and intermittent luxury villas. The surrounding environment, however, is something quite special. The **Navua River**, some 10km to the east, offers stunning waterfall hikes and longboat excursions, whilst further inland, the high mountains of the mysterious **Namosi Highlands** offer fantastic 4WD driving, whitewater rafting and remote village treks. Offshore is the phenomenal **Beqa Lagoon**, with world-class scuba diving, including the raved-about shark dives (see box, p.116), and serious game fishing.

The Arts Village

Hibiscus Drive · **Cultural Centre** Tours depart every 30min, 9am–4pm · Day pass F$60, day tour with lovo lunch F$125; prebooking essential · ☎ 345 0065, ⓦ artsvillage.com.fj

Apart from its offshore activities, Pacific Harbour's main attraction is the **Arts Village**, an atmospheric colonial-style shopping centre with thirty boutique shops selling quality clothes and crafts and restaurants (plus an ATM machine, Internet café – at no 18 – massage place and supermarket). Also here is the kitsch but fun **Cultural Centre**, a mock-traditional Fijian village with an artificial lake that you can

TRADITIONAL FIJIAN COSTUME >

3

BEQA LAGOON SHARK DIVES

Beqa Lagoon, 12km south of Pacific Harbour, is renowned for its **shark-feeding dives**, which attract divers from across the world. On a good day you may see up to a hundred sharks over the two dives, including reef sharks, silvertips, tawny nurse sharks, sicklefin lemon sharks, menacing-looking bull sharks and the occasional tiger shark, as well as schools of other large fish taking advantage of the free food (mostly tuna heads from a nearby factory). The best dive sites are on the western tip and north side of the lagoon, best accessed from Pacific Harbour, where accommodation is more affordable and dining more diverse than on the island of Beqa itself.

DIVE OPERATORS

Both of the companies below claim an excellent safety record, but if you fancy a more sedate experience there are also soft coral and wreck dives available in the lagoon on the days that the sharks are not fed.

Aqua Trek Beqa The Pearl ☎345 0324, ⓦaquatrek.com. Professional dive operator with top-of-the-range gear and boats. Shark dives cost US$200 and depart Pacific Harbour 8.30am on Mon, Wed, Fri and Sat, with reef diving around Beqa Lagoon available on other days for US$130.

be punted around in a canoe. You can also explore the replica *bure kalou*, or scared temple, to hear about ancient customs and legends. The highlight, though, is the theatrical **fire walking** ceremony (Mon–Sat 11am), performed on an island in the middle of the lake.

ARRIVAL AND DEPARTURE
PACIFIC HARBOUR

By bus Sunbeam Transport and Pacific Transport buses pass through Sigatoka several times daily on the south coast route.

Destinations Lautoka (14 daily; 3hr 30min); Nadi (17 daily; 2hr 50min); Navua (24 daily; 30min); Sigatoka (15 daily; 1hr 30min); Suva (15 daily; 1hr 20min).

ACTIVITIES

GAME FISHING

Xstreemfishing Shop 11a, Arts Village ☎361 2188, ⓦxstreemfishing.com. With an HQ in the Arts Village, this operation organizes fishing charters (F$1200 per day, max 8) for game fish such as tuna, wahoo and Spanish mackerel. Bring sunglasses, sun screen, drinks and snacks.

Xtasea ☎345 0280, ⓦxtaseacharters.com. Game fishing charters aboard a 20m well-equipped game fishing boat (F$1860 for full day; max 4 anglers but up to 8 people). Heads south of Beqa to the deep channels trawling for billfish and tuna. Includes breakfast and lunch.

GOLF

Golf course Great Harbour Rd ☎990 8125, ⓦthepearlsouthpacific.com/golf.asp. One of Pacific Harbour's star attractions is its underutilized championship golf course (daily 9am–6pm; F$75 green fee; carts, caddies and rental equipment available). The 18-hole mostly flat course has stunning views.

JET-SKIING

Jetski Tours Pacific Harbour ☎345 0933, ⓦjetski-safari.com. Guided jet-ski tours circumnavigating Beqa island (daily 9am–1pm; solo ride F$530, dual ride F$580). The tour includes a picnic lunch on one of Beqa's deserted beaches and a snorkel on one of the stunning reefs.

SCUBA DIVING

For information about Beqa shark dives, see box above.

WHITEWATER RAFTING

★**Rivers Fiji** The Pearl, Pacific Harbour ☎345 0147, ⓦriversfiji.com. American-run operator offering thrilling year-round whitewater rafting on the Upper Navua River (Mon, Wed, Fri & Sat; departs 6.45am; US$219). The 4hr journey downstream passes over exciting Grade II-III rapids and through a stunning canyon with sheer rock walls overflowing with waterfalls. They also offer more sedate inflatable kayak tours heading down the Luva River (Tues, Thurs & Sat; day tour US$179; two-day camping tour US$335).

Beqa Adventure Divers ☎345 0911, ⓦfiji-sharks .com. Local operator conducting staged shark dives departing 8.30am Mon, Wed, Fri & Sat; two-tank dive F$300.

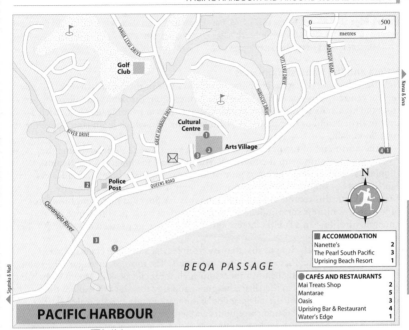

PACIFIC HARBOUR

▼ Beqa Island

ACCOMMODATION

Nanette's 108 River Drive ☎ 345 2041, ⓦ nanettes.com.fj. An attractive homely option: a villa with four en-suite bedrooms, a mahogany-ceilinged lounge and kitchen. Available for full rental, or on a B&B basis. Decent sized pool. Room F$187; whole villa F$750

The Pearl South Pacific Queens Rd ☎ 345 0022, ⓦ thepearlsouthpacific.com. An iconic Pacific Harbour resort with a fresh contemporary look – the six lavish suites are something else, draped in exotic linens and with themes from French provincial to India. There's an intricately designed pool and it's right on the beach with views of Beqa and breezes off the ocean. Rooms F$334;

suites F$624

★**Uprising Beach Resort** Off Queens Rd ☎ 345 2200, ⓦ uprisingbeachresort.com. This affordable beachside resort fits in seamlessly with Pacific Harbour's adventure label, offering plenty of activities. There's also a funky restaurant, and the curved bar is a popular locals' hangout although it can get rowdy at weekends. The large 20-bed grand-looking dorm is set back from the beach, with male/female showers and lockers. The pine-panelled bures with polished wood floors vary in size, sleeping between two and four, with cute bathrooms and outdoor showers, and the villas are on a grand scale with all mod cons. Dorms F$40; bures F$235; villas F$335

EATING

★**Mai Treats** Shop 6a, Arts Village. A little corner café serving smoothies, juices and sandwiches, plus sweet treats such as carrot cake (snacks from F$3.50); it's a pleasant stop in the Arts Village. Daily 7.30am–5pm.

Mantarae At The Pearl South Pacific ☎ 345 0022. Soothing contemporary fusion dishes (around F$30) with European, Indian and Asian flavours. There's an extensive wine list with some pretty pricey labels. Daily 6–10pm.

Oasis Shop 7, Arts Village ☎ 345 0617. Large airy dining restaurant serving hearty meals, with a secondhand book exchange and Internet access. The Asian dishes are around

F$15, the catch of the day F$30 and a whopping T-bone steak F$40. Mon–Sat 6.30am–2pm & 6–9.30pm, Sun 10am–3pm & 6–9.30pm.

Uprising At the Uprising Beach Resort, off Queens Rd ☎ 345 2200. This resort restaurant has a funky atmosphere, with light jazz playing in the background. The lunchtime quick snacks are filling and include handmade burgers, burritos and classic fish and chips, all around F$15. The dinner menu is Modern European but with some curries, mostly around F$15, plus there are three 3-course blackboard specials from F$25, usually with fish and local vegetables. Daily 7am–9.30pm.

Water's Edge Shop 86, Arts Village ☎ 345 0145. This happening place on the edge of the pond in the Arts Village is run with style by an ex-New Yorker. Super-friendly staff serve pizza, pasta (both from F$15), burgers (F$12) and snacks, and there's live jazz at weekends. Mon–Thurs 8.30am–3pm, Fri & Sat 8.30am–9pm.

Navua and the Namosi Highlands

NAVUA, 10km east of Pacific Harbour on the Suva side of the Navua River, is a dusty market centre with a mix of Fiji-Indian rice farmers from the delta and Fijian villagers from the highlands selling their produce. The only reason to come here is to catch a boat to Beqa Island or to explore the Namosi Highlands, which loom large above the river floodplain.

At the north end of town, between the market and bridge, longboats line the riverbanks and journey up the murky **Navua River** to the villages of the **Namosi Highlands**. A local operator offers guided longboat trips (see below), and Rivers Fiji (see p.116) offers whitewater rafting through stunning scenery towards Wainimakatu; this remote region fronts the massive **Sovi Basin**, an amphitheatre of lowland rainforest surrounded by mountain ridges with an abundance of endemic birdlife – this is Fiji's largest and most important protected nature reserve.

With a 4WD vehicle, it's possible to drive from Navua along the Namosi Road, following the Waidina River through remote forests. The most picturesque village along the road is **Namosi**, sitting beneath the 950m-high sheer cliff peak of **Mount Voma**. You could present a *sevusevu* to the village headman and stay the night to explore the stunning environment with a village guide. Climbers can quite easily scale Mount Voma without ropes in around three hours and will be graced on a clear day with sweeping views of the surrounding mountains.

ARRIVAL AND GETTING AROUND
NAVUA AND THE NAMOSI HIGHLANDS

By bus Most buses between Nadi and Suva stop at the bus stand in Navua for a 15min rest stop.
Destinations Lautoka (14 daily; 4hr); Nadi (15 daily; 3hr 20min); Pacific Harbour (15 daily; 30min); Sigatoka (15 daily; 2hr); Suva (24 daily; 50min).
By boat Boats leave from Navua to Namuamua and Nukusere (from 10am; 2hr; $15). Bear in mind that you may not be able to return till the next day.
By car Driving from Navua along the Namosi Rd, bear right at the three-road junction to follow the Waidina River to Naqali. From Naqali, the road heads south to

Suva (4hr from Navua), or north to Monasavu before eventually connecting with Tavua on the north coast of Viti Levu.
Tours Guided longboat trips (F$125) are offered by Discover Fiji Tours (☎ 345 0180, ⊛ discoverfijitours.com), an enterprising local operator, based just before the market stalls in Navua when coming in off the Queens Rd. If you fancy floating on a traditional *bilibili*, a raft of bamboo poles strapped together using vines, or tubing down the mild rapids, opt for the less commercial overnight tour (from F$160 a day), staying in a local village.

ACCOMMODATION

Koro Makawa Homestay 4km north of Navua ☎ 345 0180, ⊛ discoverfijitours.com/accommodation.html; map pp.104–105. Discover Fiji has its own accommodation beside the Navua River in traditional bures. Rates include meals, and visitors can join local men to fish, as well as participating in adventure activites. **F$140**

Wainadoi

Leaving Navua, the main Queens Road continues east through the sparse flats of the river delta, dotted with ancient pandanus trees and massive banyans whose roots descend from its branches like balls of rope. Beyond, on the mountain side of the highway, is **WAINODOI**, home to **Spices of Fiji** (Mon–Sat 9am–4pm, Sun noon–4.30pm; F$10; ☎ 336 2851, ⊛ spicesfiji.com), which offers 45-minute walking tours around the gardens, taking in various local spices in production. Alternatively you can zoom through the forest canopy 30m up on a zip line operated by **Zip Fiji** (daily 8am–8pm; F$225 per person; ☎ 930 0545, ⊛ zip-fiji.com).

North Viti Levu

At first glance **North Viti Levu**, with its rolling sunburnt hills and succession of dusty inland towns, might appear rather dreary. But delve a little deeper and you'll discover some charming unexpected sites. The raw **Ba hinterland** boasts Fiji's most spectacular traditional village, Navala, while further east and also inland is Fiji's highest mountain, Tomanivi, which can be conquered on a pleasant but arduous half-day hike. Off the undulating coast of **Rakiraki**, the tranquil island of **Nananu-i-Ra** has fabulous diving and is a popular retreat with budget travellers. Further east, the most scenic roadside views in Fiji are to be found around **Viti Levu Bay**, with the high peaks of the Nakauvadra Range rising from the flat sugarcane fields.

The Ba hinterland

The most scenic road from Nadi to North Viti Levu heads inland along a dirt track through the **Ba hinterland**. The road passes the remote village of **Navala** with its traditional thatch houses before rejoining the Kings Road five hours later at the dusty town of **Ba**. Further east, the charming one-street Indian-dominated town of **Tavua** is a wonderful place to soak up the region's friendly rural atmosphere. Inland is the high plateau around **Nadarivatu**, base camp for exploring the 1323m **Mount Tomanivi**. South of here you can traverse the **Nadrau Plateau** to visit the historically infamous village of **Nubutautau**.

3

Navala

Home to almost two hundred traditionally thatched bures, the village of **NAVALA** is an iconic symbol of Fiji. Back in 1950, the community decided to reject modern building materials and to encourage all school leavers to learn the art of traditional bure making (see box below). The result, sixty years on, is the last remaining **thatch village** in Fiji. The only cement structures are the church, school and a few generator huts.

To visit the village, introduce yourself to the first person you come across on the roadside – they will take you to the village headman where you pay a F$25 village entry fee. The money represents a *sevusevu* and helps with the upkeep of the village. Strolling around is a delightful experience. The chiefly bures have elaborately designed rooftops and are set in a neat line facing the village green. The more disorganized clusters of bures on the lower slopes of the Ba River are where the ordinary people live. The village is surrounded by grass-covered mountains full of secret caves where the people once retreated in times of war.

BURE BUILDING

Traditional Fijian homes or **bures** are usually built communally by members of the same *mataqali*. The main wooden structure is made from a hardwood tree, often *vesi*. Bure shapes vary slightly between regions: most are broadly rectangular although in Lau they have rounded ends similar to those found in Tonga. The wooden posts are joined together with *magimagi* (see p.183), a fibrous coconut string, rather than nails or bolts. There is no central post, ensuring a large open-plan living area and a high ceiling for ventilation. The walls are usually made from bamboo, sliced and woven together. A raised platform makes up the floor, and this is laid with straw as a cushion and woven mats for decoration. The roof is thatched using a reed called *sina* and lasts for around five years before being replaced. Across the top of the roof, or piercing either side, is a black post known as the *balabala*. This is the trunk of a fern tree and is decorated with white cowrie shells to indicate various forms of chiefly status. Roofs of lesser huts or kitchens are made from the leaf of the coconut tree and will last from three to ten years depending on the skill in weaving. Bures are usually laid out around a central *rara*, or village green, used for ceremonial events and daily rugby practice.

ARRIVAL AND DEPARTURE   NAVALA

By bus The only way to reach Navala by public transport is from Ba town. Buses (F$4.40; 1hr 30min) leave from the bus stand at 12.30pm, 4.30pm and 5.15pm, although the last of these reaches Navala after dark. The bus heads back to Ba at 6am, 7.30am and 1.45pm.

By carrier van or day tour A private carrier van from beside Ba market costs F$45, or you can visit on a day tour from Nadi (see p.59).

ACCOMMODATION

Bulou's Eco Lodge ☎628 1224 or 666 6644 after beep dial 2116, ✉sipirianotui@gmail.com; map pp.104–105. Perched on the banks of the Ba River a 5min walk south of the village, the ten-bed dorm lodge forms part of Bulou's house and is a bit cramped, but you're likely have it to yourself (bring a small *sevusevu*). The two en-suite bures are set down a small trail on a hillside clearing overlooking the river. The lodge can arrange guided walks in the hills with the energetic Tui, likely to be a highlight of your visit. Rates include bountiful Fijian meals and altogether it provides a great local experience. Dorms F̲$̲6̲5̲; bures F̲$̲1̲8̲0̲

Ba

3

Located just south of the Kings Road and separated from the ocean by a huge mangrove estuary, **BA** can easily be missed. The town has a population of around 15,000 – mostly Indians – making it the fifth largest town in Fiji. Many of the residents are Muslim and the town **mosque** is a major landmark. The only other significant building is the large sugar mill south of the centre. Apart from stopping for a meal or visiting the **market** (on the south side of town off Rarawai Road, near the bus stand), few tourists pass this way. There is one quirky sight on the way out of town – a giant soccer ball sitting on the pavement at the western entrance of Main Street, a reference to the town's obsession with the beautiful game.

ARRIVAL AND DEPARTURE   BA

By bus A local bus service runs between Nadi and Ba several times daily (F$2.80). You can also reach Ba on the plusher Sunbeam Transport and Pacific Transport services, which pass through Ba several times daily on the north coast route.

Destinations Lautoka (20 daily; 45min); Rakiraki (8 daily; 1hr 45min); Suva (7 daily; 6hr 10min); Tavua (8 daily; 45min).

By car Car rental is available at Singh's Rental on Main St (☎667 4988).

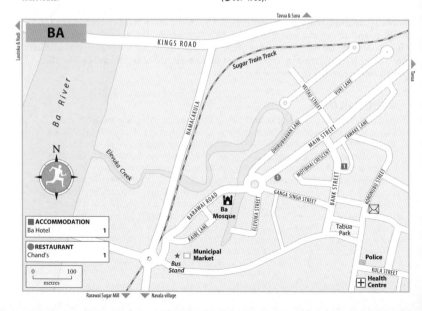

PATHWAYS OF THE SPIRITS

Viti Levu, particularly the grasslands between Ba and Rakiraki, is crisscrossed with **ancient pathways** known as *tualeita*. Dating back centuries before European contact, most of the paths run along the highest ridges allowing walkers to spot enemy war parties and to avoid being followed. The paths played an important role in the Fijian colonization of Viti Levu, linking pioneer settlements to the main chiefly villages. Before the widespread conversion to Christianity, *tualeita* also held a religious importance. It was believed that the spirits of the dead followed the trails on their journey back to their origins, and thence on to the afterlife. Most walking tracks today follow *tualeita*.

INFORMATION

Banks Westpac and ANZ banks (Mon–Fri 9.30am–4pm) both have ATMs on Bank St.
Internet access IT Intelligence Ganga Singh St (Mon–Fri

8am–5.30pm, Sat 8am–1pm; 50 cents for 10min) has broadband.

ACCOMMODATION AND EATING

Ba Hotel Bank St ☎ 667 4000. The only accommodation in Ba can be found at this slightly seedy hotel, which doubles as a bar, nightclub and bottle shop; there are thirteen spartan rooms with bouncy beds, tiny bathrooms and a/c. **F$85**

Chand's Main St, near the roundabout. The locals' favourite restaurant, located one floor up with views down onto the street, offers excellent South Indian curries from F$15. Mon–Sat 7.30am–9.30pm, Sun noon–2.30pm.

Tavua and around

A forty-minute drive east from Ba brings you to **TAVUA**, a smaller, more intimate market centre set slightly inland from the coast. The Kings Road passes straight through town, making it feel busier than it is. The roadside is lined with twenty or so tiny shops packed with all sorts of odds and ends while the cramped **town market** is found at the eastern end. You can easily spend an idle day here chatting with the locals without being pressured to buy anything.

Eight kilometres inland from Tavua, the Vatukoula **gold mine** was once Fiji's largest, until the Australian-owned Emperor Mines Limited closed it in 2006, claiming it was no longer profitable. The mine's workers, mostly from Tavua and its sister town of Vatukoula, became instantly unemployed and many left the region altogether.

ARRIVAL AND DEPARTURE   TAVUA AND AROUND

By bus The Sunbeam Transport Kings Rd bus service connects Tavua with Ba and points east.

Destinations Ba (7 daily; 45min); Lautoka (8 daily; 1hr 20min); Rakiraki (9 daily; 1hr); Suva (9 daily; 4hr 40min).

INFORMATION

Banks ANZ bank, Vatukoula Rd (Mon–Fri 9.30am–4pm), and Westpac, eastern end of Kings Rd.
Internet access Internet Kona in H. Bilimoria building,

corner of Kings Rd and Nabukulu St (Mon–Sat 8am–1pm & 2–6pm; F$1.50 per hr).

ACCOMMODATION AND EATING

Fu Lee's Beside the market on Kings Rd; map p.122. One of the better places to eat in Tavua, a step up from the canteens serving dubious pre-cooked counter food; this place has a blackboard menu offering decent-sized servings of chow meins and curries with dhal soup for F$6.50. Mon–Sat 7am–5pm.
Tavua Hotel Nabua Rd ☎ 668 0522, ☎ 668 1225; map p.122. What really gives Tavua an edge over its

neighbours is this charming whitewashed colonial-style hotel, a 5min stroll uphill from town. Its eleven airy en-suite rooms come with a/c, ceiling fans and TVs. Around the swimming pool are three cottages sleeping five, each with a kitchen. The restaurant serves the best food in town, with a big breakfast and a lunch and dinner menu serving curry of the day for F$12 and a locally produced surf and turf for F$18. **F$150**

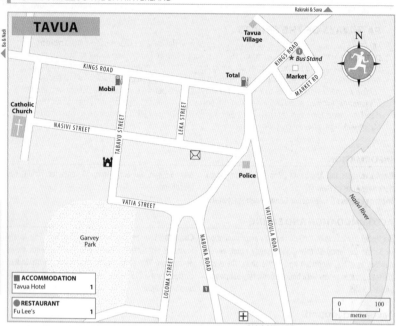

Nadarivatu

The old colonial settlement of **NADARIVATU**, once the penal colony for Fiji, lies around 25km inland from Tavua and is one of the access points for climbing Mount Tomanivi (see p.122). It's a wonderfully cool and peaceful setting, located in a large depression surrounded by mountains and pine forests above the heat of the coast. The journey up here is quite spectacular, accessed 3km east of Tavua town via a dirt road. The trip can be done in fifty minutes but with wonderful views along the way, particularly on the steep ascent from pretty Waikubukubu village, it will probably take longer. Nadarivatu translates as "the stone bowl", which refers to a small black stone found beside the road close to the health centre – legend tells of water sprouting from the stone in times of drought and its being the source of the mighty Sigatoka River.

ACCOMMODATION
NADARIVATU

Nadarivatu Rest House ⊕628 0477; map pp.104–105. Two serene cottages with stone fireplaces, wooden floors and three bedrooms (sleeping up to six people), each with kitchen, cold-water showers and 24hr electricity. The fireplaces are stocked with logs, which is a good thing as at almost 1000m, it gets pretty chilly up here at night, even in summer. The caretaker can advise on a remote two-day walking track crossing the Nadrau Plateau to the south side of Viti Levu. Cottages **F$50**

Mount Tomanivi

Mount Tomanivi, also known as Mount Victoria, is the highest point in Fiji standing at 1323m. Unfortunately, at this high elevation, the mountain appears to be nothing more than a hill, although the two-hour hike to the top is certainly strenuous. The **trail** starts from **Navai village**, 8km south of Nadarivatu. You'll need to hire a guide (F$20) and pay a F$20 admission fee which goes towards village projects; you can also enquire in the village about homestays. The walk is best attempted on a dry day, setting off from Navai around 8am – any later and the trail becomes swelteringly hot, any earlier and the summit is likely to be obscured by morning mist. The lower part of the trail is extremely muddy, passing plantations and crossing a couple of streams. About halfway up, it enters the government-leased **Tomanivi Nature Reserve**, where you'll probably see masked shining parrots, long-legged warblers and hear whistling doves. From here on up the route follows an exceptionally steep ridge over boulders and contorted tree roots – it's quite a scramble but thankfully the trail is hemmed in by thick forest. There are a couple of clearings along the way with glimpses of the surrounding countryside, and the panorama from the top is exceptional. On a clear day you'll see the stark contrast between the dry valleys in the distant north and the rugged tropical mountains draped in rainforests to the south.

ARRIVAL AND DEPARTURE MOUNT TOMANIVI

By carrier van Other than rental car, the only way to get to Navai village, where the trail to Mount Tomanivi begins, is by carrier van from beside the market in Tavua. Shared carriers cost F$6, usually heading out in the morning around 6.30am and in the afternoon at 1pm. If staying overnight in Nadarivatu, arrange for the Navai carrier van to pick you up for F$16 – otherwise it's a good 2hr walk south along the Monasavu Rd. Two kilometres past Nadarivatu, the road splits in two – the left-hand track goes to Navai and on to Monasavu; the right-hand track to Nagatagata (see p.123).

Nubutautau and the Nadrau Plateau

It's possible to head deep into the Viti Levu interior on a **two-day trail** traversing the Nadrau Plateau and visiting the notorious village of Nubutautau. The trail starts from **Nagatagata village**, 15km south of Nadarivatu, at the end of a dirt track which branches off to the right from the Monasavu Road just south of Nadarivatu.

Nagatagata to Nubutautau

Walkers should aim to arrive at Nagatagata in the morning and ask for a **guide** (expect to pay around F$40) for the three-hour trek to remote **Nubutautau**. It was here in 1867 that the Reverend Thomas Baker was killed and devoured by the

REVEREND BAKER AND THE CURSE OF NUBUTAUTAU

In 1867, having spent eight years in Fiji and speaking the language fluently, the English clergyman the **Reverend Thomas Baker** was appointed Missionary of the Interior. His job was to persuade the fierce hill people of Viti Levu to convert (or *lotu*) to the Christian faith. The odds were stacked against Baker as the hill people, or *Colo*, were great enemies of Cakobau, King of Fiji (see p.149) who had already converted to Christianity, making them suspicious of the new religion.

By 20 July, Baker had reached the village of **Nubutautau**. Wishing to cross over to western Viti Levu, he presented a *tabua* to the chief, Nawawabalavu, requesting safe passage. However, Nawawabalavu had already received a *tabua* from the people of Naitasiri village, lower down the valley, requesting him to kill the missionary. The following morning, while leaving the village, Baker and his party of nine men were ambushed by Nawawabalavu's warriors, clubbed to death and then eaten. Another version of the story maintains that the attack was in revenge for Baker insulting the chief by removing a comb from his hair, although there is no evidence that this happened. News of the event reached the European stronghold of Levuka, and pressure was put on **Cakobau** to punish the murderers. Reluctantly, eight months after Baker's death, Cakobau led his forces towards Nubutautau but was ambushed, losing almost a hundred men including several influential chiefs.

The people of Nubutautau eventually succumbed to Christianity but for many years it was believed their land was **cursed** as drought consumed the hills. It wasn't until November 2003 that reconciliation was complete, with the invitation of Reverend Baker's relatives to a formal *soro*, or forgiveness ceremony, conducted by the then Prime Minister, Laisania Qarase.

villagers (see box, p.123) – the steel axe used in the attack is still kept in the village. If you wish to continue along the trail you should present a *sevusevu* in order to stay the night.

Nubutautau to Korolevu

After overnighting in Nubutautau, you'll be guided the following morning by a lad from the village along the difficult but scenic six-hour walk to the highlands village of **Korolevu** (not to be confused with Korolevu on the Coral Coast), crossing the **Sigatoka River** a dozen times along the way – it's really only practical during the dry winter months from May to October, and then best in stable weather. Once at Korolevu, you can catch the daily early morning carrier van for the 75km journey down to Sigatoka on the south coast.

Nanoko

From Nagatagata, it's also possible to head east across the interior to **Nanoko village**. The route takes six hours on foot or ninety minutes by 4WD vehicle and is only possible in dry weather – ask the Nadarivatu district officer (☎651 0756) about the state of the road before heading out. From Nanoko it's a short drive to Bukuya in the Nausori Highlands, from where you can head down to Nadi.

ARRIVAL AND DEPARTURE   **NUBUTAUTAU AND THE NADRAU PLATEAU**

By bus A bus operated by Nadan (☎668 0150; F$5) departs Tavua for Nagatagata via Nadarivatu at 3.30pm on Mon, Tues, Thurs and Fri.

Tavua to Rakiraki

The journey east along the Kings Road from Tavua to **Rakiraki** passes through the vast cattle farmland of Yaqara. The scenery here resembles a mini Wild West, with cowboys rounding up the herds and the rugged mountain scenery of the **Nakauvadra Range** in the background. Further along the coast is the small market town of **Rakiraki**, also known as Vaileka Town. Nearby is the pretty coastal setting of **Volivoli Point** and the beautiful offshore island of **Nananu-i-Ra**, both featuring some lovely holiday cottages.

The Nakauvadra Range and around

Around 25km east of Tavua is the turn-off for the impeccably sterile bottling plant for **Fiji Water** (⌨fijiwater.com), which since its inception in 1996 has become Fiji's most recognized global brand. The company was set up by Canadian billionaire David Gilmour and sold for a massive profit in 2004 to an American investor. Water is sourced from an artesian well fed from the legendary **Nakauvadra Range**, said to be the home of Degei, the most powerful of Fijian gods (see box below).

DEGEI, GOD OF GODS

Near the summit of Uluda, the northern peak of the Nakauvadra Mountains, is a cave. It is no ordinary cave, for it is said that **Degei**, the most important god in Fijian folklore, resides here. To the early Fijians, Degei was the creator of the world, creator of men and god of anger and war. He took the form of a **snake** and, when he moved, the earth shook. Noise irritated him so the bats were chased away from the cave, birds were ordered to sleep away from the summit and the waves crashing onto the nearby reef were silenced. Throughout Fiji, and particularly on Viti Levu, the snake god ruled supreme and was offered the first bowl of *yaqona* as a matter of respect. In the hills of Viti Levu you may still see the first bowl of grog poured outside in his honour.

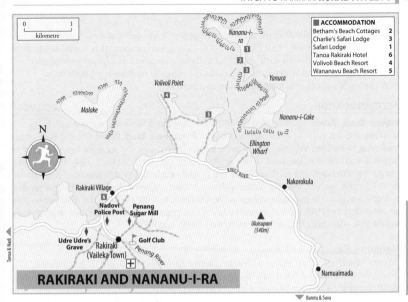

■ ACCOMMODATION	
Betham's Beach Cottages	**2**
Charlie's Safari Lodge	**3**
Safari Lodge	**1**
Tanoa Rakiraki Hotel	**6**
Volivoli Beach Resort	**4**
Wananavu Beach Resort	**5**

RAKIRAKI AND NANANU-I-RA

Navatu Hill

Seven kilometres before Rakiraki is a fabulous roadside viewpoint overlooking the rocky volcanic plug of **Navatu Hill** with an ancient fortification perched on its summit – there's a rough trail on the east side of the hill leading to the top with its panoramic view. The multi-unit **hill fort** was used as a defence from the fearsome **Udre Udre**, a chief from Rakiraki who folklore recalls ate nothing but human flesh. You can see Udre Udre's **grave** beside the Kings Road, 100m on the right before the Nadovi Police Post – the 872 stones placed here supposedly represent the number of people he ate.

Rakiraki (Vaileka Town)

Vaileka Town, usually referred to as just **RAKIRAKI**, evolved from a tiny village site with the expansion of the **Penang Sugar Mill**, the oldest of Fiji's four working mills, built in 1880. The town of around 1500 residents remains dominated by sugarcane farming and, apart from a small market, it has little to entice tourists.

ARRIVAL AND INFORMATION   **RAKIRAKI (VAILEKA TOWN)**

By bus The Sunbeam Transport bus service connects Rakiraki with other towns on the Kings Rd.
Destinations Ba (8 daily; 1hr 45min); Lautoka (8 daily; 2hr 10min); Suva (9 daily; 3hr 40min); Tavua (9 daily; 55min).

Banks There are ATM machines at both ANZ and Westpac banks on Rakiraki Rd opposite Vaileka Market, but tellers only open on Tues & Thurs 9.30am–3pm.
Internet access *Lal's Net Cafe* next to Westpac bank on the main street has slow broadband access.

ACCOMMODATION

Tanoa Rakiraki Hotel Kings Rd, Rakiraki Village ☏ 669 4101, ⊛ tanoarakiraki.com. The only local accommodation is in the original village of Rakiraki, 3km from the town centre. The hotel is surprisingly large, with 36 a/c rooms with en-suite bathrooms, ten basic rooms with shower and a sixteen-bed dorm that is seldom used except for groups. There's a pleasant swimming pool and good restaurant but it's a bit out of the way if you don't have your own transport. Dorms <u>F$30</u>; rooms <u>F$150</u>

Volivoli

The placid hills of **Volivoli** mark the northern point of Viti Levu and look out on the offshore islands of Malake and Nananu-i-Ra. Taking advantage of this serene landscape are two small resorts, both with good scuba diving operators. The beach at Volivoli Point at high tide is non-existent but as the tide retreats, an 80m-long **sand spit** emerges with a small area for sunbathing and bonfires.

ACCOMMODATION VOLIVOLI

Volivoli Beach Resort Volivoli Rd ☎ 669 4511, ⊛ volivoli.com. This plush family-friendly resort is a good option for snorkellers and divers, with Ra Divers, a long-established dive operation based at the resort, offering Open Water courses for F$750 and 2-tank dives for F$270; there are also dive and accommodation packages available. Full-day game-fishing charters are also available for F$1800. Access to the resort is 5km east of Rakiraki Village on the Kings Rd then 4km along the

extremely scenic Volivoli Rd towards the coast. **F$309**

★**Wananavu Beach Resort** Kings Rd ☎ 669 4433, ⊛ wananavu.com. The restaurant here takes pride of place, with delightful views along the coast and serves excellent food. Accommodation is in one of 31 bures, mostly duplex lodges with pine-panelled interiors, or in the more luxurious Mediterranean-style villas in the hills. Rates include buffet breakfast. Bures **F$450**; villas **F$770**

Nananu-i-Ra

Fifteen minutes by boat across a choppy passage from Ellington Wharf (see below) takes you to delightful **Nananu-i-Ra**, a small hilly island surrounded by beautiful white sandy beaches. There are plans for luxury holiday homes and a *Hilton* resort development on the northern side of the island but until these appear it remains blissfully down to earth, with just three family-owned **budget resorts**.

Lomanisue Beach

The long curving palm-fringed **Lomanisue Beach** fronting the east side of Nananu-i-Ra is accessible along a two-minute trail from behind *Charlie's* (see below). Swimming on this side of the island is good but it's constantly buffeted by winds; while this may not suit sunbathers, it's probably the best spot in Fiji for **windsurfing**.

North side of the island

From the north end of Lomanisue Beach, you can walk around the rocky headland at low tide to the secluded bay on the **north side** of the island – the centuries-old stone wall formations lining the shore here were built to catch fish on the outgoing tide. From the bay several walking tracks lead up the lightly wooded hills and head back to Sekoula Point.

ARRIVAL AND DEPARTURE NANANU-I-RA

TO ELLINGTON WHARF

By bus Nananu-i-Ra is accessed from Ellington Wharf, 10km east of Rakiraki along the Kings Rd (15min). Sunbeam Transport express buses between Lautoka and Suva will drop you at the junction for the wharf, as will Flying Prince (☎ 669 4346; 8 daily; F$2.80), a local bus service from Rakiraki which heads on to Namuaimada and Barotu. Note that it's a 2km walk from the junction to the wharf.

By taxi If you have heavy luggage your best bet is to hire a taxi to Ellington Wharf from Rakiraki (F$15).

TO NANANU-I-RA

By boat A small well-supplied shop and café beside the wharf run by Safari Lodge coordinates boat transfers to the island on request (F$20 one-way), or arrange in advance through your resort.

ACCOMMODATION

Betham's Beach Cottages ☎ 669 4132, ⊛ www .bethams.com.fj. The pick of Nananu-i-Ra's resorts offers five simply furnished beachfront cottages, a four-bed dorm and a few private rooms; the on-site *Anchor Restaurant* knocks up the usual mix of burgers, noodles and the like.

Dorms **F$35**; rooms **F$110**; cottages **F$160**
Charlie's ☎ 669 4676, ⊛ charliescottages.com. The cottages at *Charlie's* are spacious but rather sparsely furnished, with big windows and even bigger views overlooking frangipani trees and the ocean. There's no

restaurant but Louisa will cook meals on request. Dorms **F$35**; cottage **F$125**

Safari Lodge ☎ 669 3333, �🌐 safarilodge.com.fj. Set on the beachfront, *Safari Lodge* is a simple and sustainable option, with a range of affordable accommodation: power is provided by a wind turbine. They offer windsurfing lessons and kite-surfing. Camping (with own tent) **F$10**; dorms **F$30**; room **F$95**; bures **F$200**

East Viti Levu

The hilly, tropical countryside of **East Viti Levu** is the least-visited part of the big island. Here you'll find some of the prettiest roadside landscapes in Fiji, particularly around **Viti Levu Bay** along the northeast coast. South of the bay, from the village of **Barotu**, the Kings Road cuts 20km inland through deep tropical rainforest alongside the Wainibuka River. An alternative track from Barotu heads over the high Nakorotubu Range to the undulating hills and bays of the remote **Tailevu Coast**. The two roads meet again at **Korovou** town, from where the route descends into the fertile flat farming land of the mighty Rewa River, eventually rejoining the urban world at Nausori, just north of Suva.

3

Viti Levu Bay

Ten kilometres west of Rakiraki, the Kings Road loops south around the northeastern corner of Viti Levu. From here there are impressive views of the Nakauvadra Range tapering off into deep **Viti Levu Bay**. Thanks to volcanic activity, the coasts to the north and south of the bay are steep and irregular, with numerous promontories.

Namuaimada

Dwarfed by the high mountains, and hugging the exposed northerly point of the bay, is the pretty beachside village of **Namuaimada**. Lodged between two bluffs the beach here bears the brunt of the trade winds and is a renowned **kite-surfing spot**. The village is a little rough around the edges but it's a friendly place, with a pleasant mix of traditional thatch bures, wooden lodges and modern cement buildings surrounding the church. Guides from the village offer **trekking** in the mountains as well as hand-line **fishing** on the reef (both around F$10).

St Francis Xavier's Catholic Church
Naiserelagi village, 8km south of Namuaimada

At the base of the bay, buffered by mangrove forests, **St Francis Xavier's Catholic Church** lies perched on a hilltop overlooking the school in Naiserelagi village. Inside are three beautiful **murals** painted by Jean Charlot in 1962. Challenging European colonization and superiority of the time, the centrepiece, a 10m-high fresco, depicts a crucified Black Christ wearing *masi* cloth, whilst two side altar panels, one with indigenous Fijians and the other with Fijian-Indians, show unique cultural scenes of *tabua* and *yaqona* offerings to Christ. There is also a mural of St Peter Chanel, Fiji's first martyred saint, holding a symbolic war club.

Barotu to Korovou via the Kings Road

The quickest and most commonly travelled route between Rakiraki and Suva follows the 72km-long **Kings Road**, which heads inland at Barotu, only reaching the coast again at Korovou. From Savusavu Village the road clings to a deep valley carved out by the Wainibuka River. Along the way you may see locals heading downstream on precarious-looking *bilibilis*, rafts made from bamboo poles, sometimes laden with market goods.

Snake God Cave

Wailotua, Kings Rd, 25km northwest of Korovou • F$15 donation to villagers

At **Wailotua**, almost 50km south of Barotu, a large **cave** is cut into the steep mountain abutting the village. Inside you'll be shown its star attraction, a bulky stalagmite said to resemble a six-headed **snake god**. In pre-European times chiefs would meet and consult here. Sadly, the ancient stone is now coarsely scribbled with the names of local tourists.

Waimaro Waterfall

Kings Rd, 15km west of Korovou • F$23

The scenic **Waimaro Waterfall** is 11km along the Kings Road from Wailotua, past Dakuivuna village. Steps lead down to a stream and picnic bench surrounded by forest. If you arrive on a weekend or during school holidays the local kids will show you the best spots for jumping into the pool below the falls.

The Tailevu Coast

The most scenic route between Barotu and Korovou heads along an 80km dirt track hugging the remote **Tailevu Coast**. With its lovely coastal scenery, secluded villages, hiking tracks and offshore dolphin-spotting, this seldom visited region is an exceptional place to explore. In the southern portion, 10km from Korovou Town, **Natovi Landing** is the departure point for ferries to Ovalau and Vanua Levu.

Namarai to Bureiwai

Approaching from the north via the Nakorotubu Road, you hit the coast at **Namarai**, a neatly laid-out village in a small bay. You'll be warmly received by the locals, although note that this is a traditional, strongly Methodist area so dress appropriately. From Namarai, the most **scenic** section of the coastal road meanders south to Bureiwai around a series of beautiful bays covered in coconut palms. Two kilometres beyond Saioko village, keep an eye out for a small signpost for the Church of the Latter-day Saints. There's a small track on the opposite side of the road which heads out to a lovely **viewpoint** from a cliff overlooking the bay. Thirteen kilometres on is **Bureiwai**, where the daily bus from Suva terminates.

Nataleira

South of Bureiwai, the road cuts slightly inland for 10km passing over gently rolling hills interspersed with pine forests and grasslands towards the pretty village of **Nataleira**, a lovely base for visiting one of the area's great attractions, **Moon Reef**, forty minutes away by boat. As well as offering fantastic snorkelling, the reef is one of only a couple of reliable places in Fiji to spot and swim with bottlenose **dolphins**. Other local activities, which you can organize through your accommodation, include a two-hour hike through light forest to the summit of **Mount Tova** (645m), a volcanic plug with panoramic views.

South to Natovi Landing

Heading south from Nataleira Village the countryside becomes more densely vegetated, passing the scenic riverside setting of Dawasamu and Lawaki and eventually emerging to semi civilization at QVS boarding school, one of two prominent schools in the region set up in the early twentieth century for sons of Fijian chiefs. Ten kilometres south is **Natovi Landing**, departure point for a couple of ferry services (see opposite).

ARRIVAL AND DEPARTURE   **THE TAILEVU COAST**

By car Access to the Tailevu Coast road is easy to miss if travelling along the Kings Rd from Rakiraki: less than 1km south of Barotu, turn left onto the badly signposted

Nakorotubu Rd. Shortly afterwards turn left again at Luci's Shopping Centre, the last store you'll see until you reach Korovou. The steep road to the coast is best tackled by 4WD, although in dry weather it can be comfortably driven in a car with good tyres and high clearance.

By bus You can reach Nataleira by public transport from Suva, but not from Rakiraki. Lodoni Transport (☎ 339 2888) has two buses departing Suva on weekdays at 1.30pm and 2.30pm, and one bus on Saturday at 1pm, heading to Korovou, Natovi Landing and beyond Nataleira as far as Bureiwai (3hr), where both buses spend the night before returning early in the morning to Suva.

By minivan Buses run regularly from Suva and Nausori to Korovou, where you can hire a minivan to Nataleira or Takalana Bay Retreat for F$50.

By boat From Natovi Landing, passenger and car ferries operated by Patterson Brothers (☎ 666 1173 in Lautoka, ☎ 881 2444 in Labasa) depart for Ovalau (3.30pm, daily though not always on Sun) and Naubouwalu on Vanua Levu (7am on Tues, Thurs & Sat). Bligh Water Shipping (☎ 885 3191 in Savusavu, mobile ☎ 999 2536, ⓦ blighwatershipping.com.fj) departs three times a week for Savusavu on Vanua Levu.

ACCOMMODATION

Natalei Eco Lodge Nataleira ☎ 881 1168; map pp.104–105. Eight thatch bures alongside the beach, four of which are used as dorms, as well as two cottages with en-suite cold-water showers and flush toilets. Located right on the edge of the village, the lodge has little privacy but cultural interaction is without doubt the focus here. Activities include weaving lessons, *yaqona*-drinking, hiking and waterfall treks and, with larger groups, meke performances. A restaurant overlooks the beach – local-style meals are served at set times and cold drinks are sometimes available, but never alcohol. Dorms F$75; bures F$150

★**Takalana Bay Retreat** 1km north of Nataleira ☎ 991 6338, ⓦ takalana.blogspot.co.uk; map pp.104–105. There are just two bures here, connected by a communal sitting area where meals are served. Both bures are homely and well decorated with en-suite hot-water bathrooms and cooking stoves. The retreat is surrounded by 84 acres of private land descending to the coast with unobscured views towards Naigani and Ovalau islands. Rate (per person) includes meals. F$115

Korovou

The grubby, one-street town of **KOROVOU** forms the intersection of the Tailevu Coast Road and Kings Road. The southern portion of the Kings Road heads 30km south to Nausori and on to Suva. The town is essentially a convenient stop for **buses**, with a small market and a couple of stores.

ARRIVAL AND DEPARTURE

KOROVOU

By bus Apart from the Sunbeam express bus, several local buses head inland to Vunidawa and on to Suva.
Destinations Ba (7 daily; 4hr); Lautoka (8 daily; 4hr 45min); Suva (14 daily; 1hr 10min); Rakiraki (9 daily; 2hr 30min); Tavua (9 daily; 3hr 25min).

By minivan Public minivans beside the road run north to Natovi Landing for F$2, and you should be able to persuade the driver to continue 40min on to *Natalei Eco Lodge* (see above) or *Takalana Bay Retreat* (see above) for another F$25.

Suva and around

OUTDOOR MARKET, SUVA

Suva and around

Fiji's lively capital city, Suva, sits on a 5km-long peninsula in the southeast corner of Viti Levu, backed by steep mountains and fronted by a deep-water harbour. Visually it's one of the most attractive of all the South Seas ports, with pretty colonial buildings in the centre and moody weather rolling in off the ocean, covering the surrounding rugged peaks in thundery clouds. Despite the often humid and rainy climate, Suva has a lot going for it. Shopping is good and the nightlife is excellent, with cool bars, lively restaurants and busy nightclubs. With a population of 86,000 there are also all the facilities you could hope for, from banks to cinemas, along with all government departments. But a stream of country dwellers coming to the capital has put pressure on the municipal infrastructure, petty crime is an issue and tin shelters on the outskirts house increasing numbers of needy people.

Apart from the quaint **museum** and stately buildings there are few standout attractions in central Suva. However, spend some time here and you'll discover a vibrant **cosmopolitan** city with strong community bases from all corners of the Fijian archipelago and across the entire South Pacific. Organizations from throughout the region have their headquarters here and the University of the South Pacific attracts students from all over the world.

Inland, the lush tropical rainforest of Naitasiri quickly takes hold – the peaceful **Colo-i-Suva Forest Park** is only twenty minutes' drive from downtown. Suva's poorer neighbourhoods sprawl north along the Kings Road in an almost constant parade of busy satellite towns to Nausori, an industrial and farming centre home to Suva's domestic airport along the banks of the imposing **Rewa River**. The river and its surrounding mangrove estuaries have long been Fiji's tribal power-base, with both the Burebasaga Confederacy of Rewa and the Kubuna Confederacy of **Bau** based in the region.

Brief history

The name **Suva** means "little hill" and refers to a mound in the Botanical Gardens where the temple of Ro Vonu stood in Suva village. In the 1840s the village became embroiled in a dispute that was to have far-reaching consequences for the whole of Fiji.

The 1841 massacre

In 1841, **Qaraniqio**, a fearsome chief from Rewa, visited Suva and stole a pig. Qaraniqio and his warriors were caught in the act and one of his men was killed. In retaliation the Rewans attacked the village, killing over three hundred men, women and children; the bodies were carried by canoe to Rewa for a celebratory feast. On hearing of the massacre, **Cakobau**, chief of **Bau**, demanded retribution – Suva came under his protection as the chief of Suva Village had married a woman from Bau

TOBERUA ISLAND

Highlights

❶ Shopping in Mark Street Go bargain hunting for colourful Indian saris and other accessories along this historical shopping parade. **See p.137**

❷ Fiji Museum Come face to face with Fiji's cannibal past, including the half-chewed shoe of the Rev Thomas Baker. **See p.138**

❸ Fire walking at Mariamma Temple Experience this engrossing and hugely passionate Hindu fire walking ceremony held in August. **See p.140**

❹ Old Mill Cottage A scenic spot to enjoy some great Fijian dishes: just ask the staff for advice on what's fresh and delicious that day, from kokoda (fish marinated in lime juice and doused in coconut milk) to palusami (coconut cream slow cooked in *dalo* leaves). **See p.144**

❺ Suva nightlife Take a bar crawl along Victoria Parade to sample the best nightlife in the South Pacific. **See p.146**

❻ Toberua Island This warm and welcoming island resort is an ideal spot for diving, snorkelling, bird-watching and pure relaxation. **See p.149**

HIGHLIGHTS ARE MARKED ON THE MAPS ON P.134, P.136 & P.139

twenty years earlier. His revenge attack on Rewa eventually sparked the eleven-year **war** that decided the fate of the islands (see p.149).

Australia moves in

Having achieved victory and crowned himself King of Fiji, Cakobau faced even greater problems. On July 4, 1849 at Nukulau island off Suva, the house of US commercial agent **John Williams** (see p.222) accidentally caught fire during Independence Day celebrations. Following Fijian custom, the locals looted everything inside. The US Government held Cakobau accountable and demanded US$42,000 in compensation. In 1868, when the first instalment was due, the Australian-owned **Polynesian Company** offered to pay off the debt in exchange for 200,000 acres of land around Suva Point. Under threat of US naval attack, Cakobau had little choice but to accept and by 1870, 170 Australians had arrived to farm cotton in the area. However, they soon discovered the soil was too thin and the climate too humid and sugar was planted instead. Fiji's first **sugar mill** was built to process the crop, although this too failed to profit.

Suva becomes the capital

After Fiji was ceded to Britain in 1874, officials began to survey the islands to build a **new capital**. The Polynesian Company promised ample freehold land should they

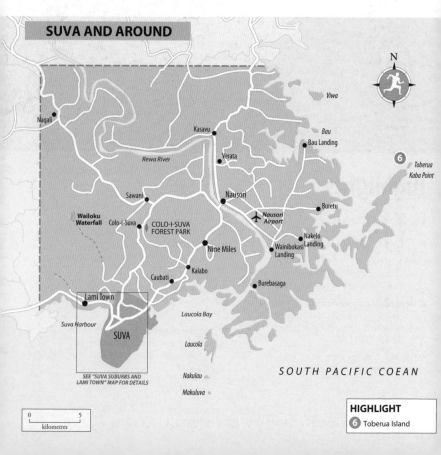

SUVA AND AROUND

Viwa

Naqali

Kasavu

Bau
Bau Landing

Rewa River

Verata

6 *Toberua*
Kaba Point

Sawani

Nausori

Buretu

Nausori Airport

Wailoku Waterfall Colo-i-Suva

COLO-I-SUVA FOREST PARK

Nakelo Landing

Wainibokasi Landing

Nine Miles

Kalabo

Caubati

Burebasaga

Lami Town

Laucola Bay

Suva Harbour

SUVA

Laucola

SOUTH PACIFIC OCEAN

SEE "SUVA SUBURBS AND LAMI TOWN" MAP FOR DETAILS

Nakulau

Makuluva

0   5
kilometres

HIGHLIGHT
6 Toberua Island

choose Suva and this, together with Suva's deep-water harbour, led the British to favour Suva over its nearest rival Nadi. By 1882 the move from the old capital of Levuka was completed. The dense jungle tumbling from the hills was cleared, the swamps were filled in and **Victoria Parade**, named after the monarch of the time, became the heart of the new town.

Twentieth-century and present-day Suva

In its early days as capital, Suva was little more than a backwater trading port but gradually it grew, securing wealth and new impressive **colonial-style buildings**. In 1914, gracious living finally arrived with the completion of the *Grand Pacific Hotel*, which boasted vintage champagne, haute cuisine and a manager from London's *Savoy*. Not quite as swish were the merchant quarters around **Cumming Street**, fronted by *kava* saloons and brothels. Many devout citizens called for the street to be cleansed of its evil, and just that happened in February 1923 when a rampant **fire** spread through the area.

By 1952 Suva covered an area of fifteen square kilometres and was proclaimed Fiji's first official city. A year later, a tsunami caused by an offshore earthquake smashed into the shoreline, killing eight people and causing damage to the city centre. In 1987 and again in 2000, Suva hit the world headlines after political **coups** threw the city into chaos with widespread looting. The 2006 coup was less fiery, with the army quickly assuming control of the streets. For more background on Fiji's political history see p.226.

City centre

4

The lively hub of the city, **Suva Central**, is not even half a square kilometre in size and runs south of Nubukalou Creek to Gordon Street. This is where the best of the city's eating, shopping and strolling opportunities are focused.

The Triangle and around

At the heart of Suva Central is **The Triangle**, a tiny park where locals meet to gossip under an impressive *ivi* tree. Fijian history buffs will notice three of the four inscriptions on the concrete historical marker here are incorrect: Cross and Cargill, the first missionaries to land in Fiji, arrived on October 12, 1835, not October 14, 1835; the government approved the move from Levuka to Suva in 1877 not 1882; and the Public Land Sales of 1880 were not proclaimed under the current *ivi* tree, but one further down the street towards Morris Hedstrom.

SUVA – A SELF-GUIDED TOUR

The following **walking tour** (9km) should take three hours – a taxi ride covering the same ground will cost F$25 with waiting time. Start from the **Old Parliament** on Victoria Parade and head north into the city turning left at Ratu Sukuna Park along the harbour wall of Stinson Parade and into the **market**. From the market, walk along Usher Street, bearing right at the traffic lights and into busy Cumming Street for shop browsing. At the end, walk uphill along Waimanu Road and at the fork, bear right up Toorak Road. Turn right on Amy Street, head past the Toorak mosque and continue along flame-tree-lined **Holland Street** with its fine city views, past the Laxmi Hindu Temple. At the roundabout, walk across Victoria Park to Pender Street and at the end, turn right and first left which takes you along winding Domain Road and past some expensive residences. When Domain Road eventually hits Ratu Sukuna Road, turn left and right again on Vuya Road, off which lies **Parliament House** where you should make a detour. Carry on down Vuya Road to Suva Point and then head right on Queen Elizabeth Drive along the picturesque foreshore, past the grand **Government House** and through Thurston Gardens to finish your tour at the **Fiji Museum**, or back on Victoria Parade.

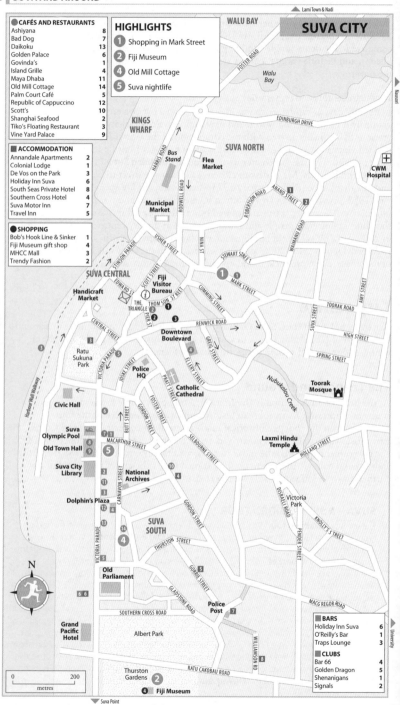

SUVA CITY

HIGHLIGHTS
1. Shopping in Mark Street
2. Fiji Museum
4. Old Mill Cottage
5. Suva nightlife

CAFÉS AND RESTAURANTS
Ashiyana	8
Bad Dog	7
Daikoku	13
Golden Palace	6
Govinda's	1
Island Grille	4
Maya Dhaba	11
Old Mill Cottage	14
Palm Court Café	5
Republic of Cappuccino	12
Scott's	10
Shanghai Seafood	2
Tiko's Floating Restaurant	3
Vine Yard Palace	9

ACCOMMODATION
Annandale Apartments	2
Colonial Lodge	1
De Vos on the Park	3
Holiday Inn Suva	6
South Seas Private Hotel	8
Southern Cross Hotel	4
Suva Motor Inn	7
Travel Inn	5

SHOPPING
Bob's Hook Line & Sinker	1
Fiji Museum gift shop	4
MHCC Mall	3
Trendy Fashion	2

BARS
Holiday Inn Suva	6
O'Reilly's Bar	
Traps Lounge	3

CLUBS
Bar 66	4
Golden Dragon	5
Shenanigans	1
Signals	2

Heading north from The Triangle, busy **Scott Street** is home to Village Six Cinemas (see p.146), showing the latest Hollywood and Bollywood flicks. Behind the post office, between Central and Edward streets facing Stinson Parade, is the **Handicraft Market**, with fifty stalls all selling pretty much the same stuff and vying for your attention. Prices here start high so you'll have to bargain to get a fair deal.

Ratu Sukuna Park

Heading towards the sea from The Triangle brings you to Stinson Parade, which runs parallel to the harbour walkway. At the southern end is **Ratu Sukuna Park**, venue for church meetings and pious preachers as well as being a hangout for drunks and prostitutes. Across the road on Victoria Parade is the **QBE Building**, with doctors and lawyers upstairs and the *Palm Court Café* (see p.144) and public phones in a quiet downstairs courtyard.

Sacred Heart Cathedral

Pratt St • Open access; services Mon–Fri 6.30pm, Sat 1pm, Sun 7am, 8.30am, 10am, 5pm & 7pm

Imposing **Sacred Heart Cathedral** is Fiji's only cathedral, and one of fourteen in the South Pacific. Construction of the twin-towered church commenced in 1895 with stone shipped in from the Hunter Valley in Australia and the timber flooring sourced from Quebec in Canada. The first mass was held in 1902 but the cathedral wasn't fully completed until 1935, 22 years after the death of its instigator, Bishop Julian Vidal from Australia.

4

North Suva

North of Nubukalou Creek, the Suva **bus stand** on Rodwell Road typifies Suva's bustle. By day, Indian peanut sellers and Fijian barrow boys run around amongst the black exhaust fumes frenetically plying their trade. By night, the area becomes desolate, save for a few drunks and homeless people, who sleep on the benches and rummage amongst the rubbish. Opposite the north end of the bus stand is the **Flea Market** (Mon–Sat 8am–6pm; see p.147), a great place to buy cheap clothes and souvenirs.

The Municipal Market

South end of Rodwell Rd • Mon–Sat 6am–6pm

Towards the city centre, the colourful **Municipal Market** (see p.147) is the largest in Fiji, with a huge variety of fruit and vegetables for sale. Upstairs are the *yaqona* and spice stalls, although note that *kava* drinking has been banned by the City Council. On Friday and Saturday mornings, Fijians from miles around visit the market, which spills out into the streets amongst the BBQ sellers and shoe-shine boys. Keep an eye out for pickpockets at these times.

Mark Street, Cumming Street and around

Southeast of the Municipal Market, a cluster of Chinese and Indian **merchant shops** can be found around **Mark Street** and **Cumming Street**. Crammed with an unbelievable array of homewares and astoundingly colourful clothing, these are great places to poke around in. At the eastern end of Mark Street, Toorak Road leads inland to the blossoming residential area of **Toorak**, home to the city mosque, while **Waimanau Road** – with the raucous bars of the *Kings Hotel* on its corner – heads north into the hills towards the Colonial War Memorial Hospital and beyond to grand Borron House, a government residence and ballroom used for ceremonial events.

South Suva

Sitting on reclaimed land dug out from the hill surrounding Albert Park, **Victoria Parade** is the administrative centre of Fiji, with modern high-rise office buildings lining the road. At the north end is the attractive whitewashed FINTEL Building built in 1922. Behind, the modern 1970s-style Civic Hall is the venue for occasional dance performances. Heading south on Victoria Parade is one of the prettiest buildings in Suva, the **Old Town Hall** with its cast-iron columned veranda. The building is now a Chinese restaurant downstairs while upstairs is the headquarters for Fiji's branch of Greenpeace. Next door is the imposing **Suva City Library** (see p.147).

A few hundred metres to the south, the solemn-looking **Old Parliament**, built in 1939, sits at the end of Carnarvon Street, facing Victoria Parade and Albert Park. It's now Fiji's judicial headquarters and houses various government departments.

Albert Park

There's usually a rugby game or cricket match going on at the muddy quagmire of **Albert Park**, used as a sports ground. The park also hosts provincial *soli*, or fundraising events, with handicraft stalls and meke performances, and in the August school holidays is the main venue for the Hibiscus Festival. Overlooking the park on Victoria Parade is the **Grand Pacific Hotel**, which at the time of writing was being revamped to its former glory after a period of dereliction.

The Fiji Museum

Thurston Gardens, accessible from Ratu Cakobau Rd • Mon–Fri 9am–4pm, Sat 9.30am–4pm • F$7 • ☎ 331 5944, ⊕ fijimuseum.org.fj

Suva's most rewarding attraction, the **Fiji Museum**, is set within **Thurston Gardens**, Suva's spacious and elegant botanical gardens. If you have even a slight interest in Fiji's history or want to see some of those wicked war clubs and **cannibal forks**, then it's worth the trip to Suva. The museum is neatly laid out with a grand hall displaying a double-hulled **war canoe**, some impressive 12m-long oars and lots of intriguing daily items such as tattooing tools and wigs. The adjoining gallery maps out the arrival of the first Europeans and includes part of HMS *Bounty*'s rudder, a piece of eight from the *Eliza* shipwreck (see p.220), and a small exhibition on the Reverend Thomas Baker, eaten by cannibals in 1864: don't miss the gnawed remnants of his shoes. Upstairs, the **Indo-Fijian Gallery** recounts the history of Indian indentured labourers brought to Fiji between 1879 and 1916. The gift shop on the ground floor has a good selection of books on Fijian history and culture.

Queen Elizabeth Drive

Opposite Thurston Gardens, where Victoria Parade becomes **Queen Elizabeth Drive**, is the beautifully-kept Suva Bowling Club, with fine ocean views across the harbour. Next door is the equally well-kept **Umaria Children's Park**, the best place in Suva to give kids a run around. A little further down is **Government House**, built in 1928 and now the private residence of the President of Fiji – its entrance is guarded by the much-photographed and long-suffering presidential guards in red tunic and white serrated *sulu*. Following Queen Elizabeth Drive is the paved **Nasele Walkway**, which hugs the stone seawall all the way to Suva Point, making a fine hour-long stroll. The roadside is a popular romantic spot for courting couples.

The suburbs and Lami Town

The four **Suva Suburbs** of Muanikau, Samabula, Tamavua and Cunningham are mostly residential areas but have several sights worth exploring. Beyond, to the west along the Queens Road, is seaside **Lami Town**, facing the attractive yachting anchorage of the Bay of Islands. Local buses run to the suburbs, Lami Town and the Orchid Island Cultural Centre regularly from 6am to 6pm, departing from the main bus stand.

Muanikau

Muanikau flanks the southern side of Suva Peninsula, southeast of the city. Nearby is the upmarket residential area of The Domain, sitting prettily on a hill with large houses hidden behind security fences and thick tropical landscaping.

Parliament House

Battery Rd · ☎ 330 5811

Suva's **Parliament House** was designed to resemble a traditional bure but made of steel with a bright orange roof. It was here that George Speight seized control of the government in the coup of 2000. Another coup instigator, Sitiveni Rabuka (1987), had the building commissioned and it was completed in 1992. The building lay idle after parliament was dissolved after the 2006 coup, but at the time of writing it was being restored in preparation for elections; to look around, phone in advance or ask the guard on the gate.

4

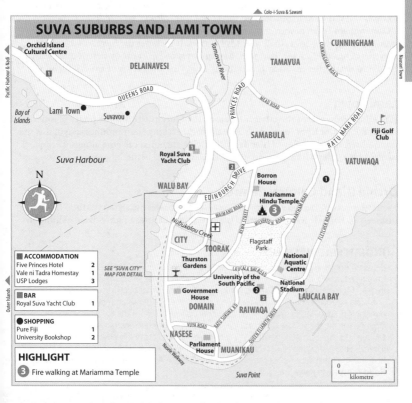

SUVA SUBURBS AND LAMI TOWN

Colo-i-Suva & Sawani

Pacific Harbour & Nadi

Nausori Town

Orchid Island Cultural Centre **1**

CUNNINGHAM

DELAINAVESI

Tamavua River

TAMAVUA

CUNNINGHAM ROAD

PRINCES ROAD

MEAD ROAD

QUEENS ROAD

Bay of Islands

Lami Town

Suvavou

RATU MARA ROAD

SAMABULA

Fiji Golf Club

Suva Harbour

Royal Suva Yacht Club **1**

VATUWAQA

N

2

EDINBURGH DRIVE

Borron House

Mariamma Hindu Temple **3**

VANI ROAD

GRANTHAM ROAD

FLETCHER ROAD

WALU BAY

WAIMANU ROAD

RENWA STREET

MILVERTON ROAD

Nubukalou Creek

CITY

TOORAK

Flagstaff Park

Outer Islands

ACCOMMODATION
Five Princes Hotel	2
Vale ni Tadra Homestay	1
USP Lodges	3

SEE "SUVA CITY" MAP FOR DETAIL

Thurston Gardens

LAUCALA BAY ROAD

National Aquatic Centre

BAR
Royal Suva Yacht Club	1

Government House

University of the South Pacific **2**

National Stadium

SHOPPING
Pure Fiji	1
University Bookshop	2

DOMAIN

RAIWAQA **3**

RATU SUKUNA ROAD

LAUCALA BAY

VUYA ROAD

HIGHLIGHT

3 Fire walking at Mariamma Temple

NASESE

Nasele Walkway

QUEEN ELIZABETH DRIVE

Parliament House

MUANIKAU

Suva Point

0 ————— 1
kilometre

University of the South Pacific

Laucala Bay Rd • ☎ 323 1000, ⓦ usp.ac.fj

East of the city centre on Laucala Bay is the Fiji campus of the **University of the South Pacific** (USP), established in 1968. The university's **public library** (Mon–Thurs 8am–10pm, Fri 8am–6pm, Sat 9am–6pm, Sun 1.30–6pm during term time; Mon–Fri 8am–4pm during holidays; ☎323 2402) includes the extensive Pacific Collection, for which visitors must pay a F$20 temporary membership fee to access. There's also an excellent bookshop where you can pick up the free monthly student magazine, *Wansolwara*.

National Stadium and Sports City

Close by the university is the **National Stadium** with a capacity of close to twenty thousand, while across the way in Sports City is the National Aquatic Centre and Vodaphone Indoor Sports Arena (see p.142 for details).

Tamavua, Samabula and Cunningham

Some of the most expensive residences in Suva are perched on the steep cliffs of **Tamavua**, with fantastic views of the harbour. They also look down on industrial Walu Bay, with its shipyards, oil storage tanks and car lots. **Samabula**, east of Central, is divided between the middle-class homes along Rewa Street and the appalling estates around Raiwaqa further south. A short distance up Rewa Street is the **Mariamma Hindu Temple** which has spellbinding fire walking ceremonies in August (see box below). To the west is the **Royal Suva Yacht Club**, a pleasant spot to have a beer and enjoy the views across the harbour towards the Viti Levu highlands and the prominent volcanic plug of Joske's Thumb.

Cunningham is the newest municipality on Suva's northern and eastern boundary, heading along the Kings Road towards Nausori. It includes the busy suburb of Nabua as well as Queen Elizabeth Barracks, headquarters of Fiji's army, where four rebels were beaten to death after an attempted mutiny following the events of the 2000 coup.

Lami Town

Five kilometres west of the city centre along the Queens Road is the pretty seaside residential area of **Lami Town**, with a small market selling fresh produce. Beyond is the tranquil setting of the **Bay of Islands**, with yachts anchored offshore alongside the rocky islets of Draunibota ("cave island"), and Labiko ("snake island").

Orchid Island Cultural Centre

Queens Rd (mountain side), 10km west of city centre • Mon–Sat 8am–4.30pm • Donation to villagers • ☎ 336 1128

Just west of Lami Town is the **Orchid Island Cultural Centre**, a rather dated exhibition

---

INDIAN FIRE WALKING

Between April and September every year, Dravidian Hindus around Fiji seek favourable omens from the gods during the replanting of crops. To test their faith and devotion, many take part in one of the eighty or so Indian **fire walking ceremonies** that occur throughout rural Fiji. The build up to any ceremony is a two-week long process of denial and self-discipline to attain purification, culminating in a night of passionate dedication when the fire pit is lit. Before crossing the pit, the yellow-clad participants undergo body piercings, notably through the tongue and cheeks, bathe in either a river or the ocean and are finally physically whipped into a frenzy before strutting across the hot embers – not surprisingly a few participants end up in hospital. The most accessible of the ceremonies is held in August at the **Mariamma Hindu Road Temple** off Rewa Street.

on Fijian culture set amongst landscaped gardens. You can enter a realistic *bure kalou* or temple or handle one of a dozen live pythons. A couple of giant leatherback turtles and several war clubs and other curios make up the other exhibits.

ARRIVAL AND DEPARTURE   SUVA

The most pleasant way to arrive in Suva is **by boat**, cruising into the deep-water harbour surrounded by majestic mountains – Walu Bay is the local shipping port for all outer island passenger ferries and cargo boats. The majority of visitors, though, arrive at and depart from the grimy **bus stand** in central Suva; from here, public buses travel from and to Lautoka, either along the north coast (Kings Rd) or south coast (Queens Rd), stopping at all towns en route. Nausori Airport is the departure point for all **flights** to Lomaiviti, Lau and Rotuma, and also serves Vanua Levu, Taveuni and Kadavu.

BY PLANE

Nausori Airport 20km north of Suva, Nausori Airport is often referred to as "Nausori Suva" (airline code SUV). There are few facilities and no lockers, although the Air Café (daily 5am–6.30pm) sells decent coffee.

Airlines Fiji Airways, Suva Travel Centre, BSP Life Building, Central St, Victoria Parade (Mon–Fri 8am–5pm, Sat 8am–noon; ☎672 0888); Air Nauru, Ratu Sukuna House, MacArthur St (Mon–Fri 8am–4.30pm; ☎331 731); Air New Zealand, Queensland Insurance Centre, Victoria Parade (Mon–Fri 8.45am–4.45pm; ☎331 3100); and Qantas Travel Centre, BSP Building, Victoria Parade (Mon–Fri 8am–5pm, Sat 8am–1pm; ☎331 3888).

Getting into town The taxi journey from Nausori Airport to Suva usually takes 30min and costs F$30. There's also a nine-seater public minibus operated by Nausori Taxis that runs to *Holiday Inn Suva* opposite the Old Parliament on Victoria Parade at 8.30am, 9.30am, 10.30am, 11.30am, 2.30pm, 5pm and 6.30pm (F$10 per person). To travel by local bus, you need to first head into Nausori town (every 30min 6am–6pm; F$1) and then catch a Suva-bound bus from there (every 15min 6am–6pm; F$1.80). Note that traffic can be bad along the Suva–Nausori road and the journey may take an hour at peak times.

Destinations Cicia (weekly; 1hr); Kadavu (daily; 30min); Labasa (2 daily; 40min); Lakeba (weekly; 1hr); Matei (2 daily; 45min); Nadi Airport (12 daily; 30min); Savusavu (2 daily; 45min); Taveuni (2 daily; 1hr); Vanua Balavu (weekly; 1hr).

BY BUS

With the exception of the Coral Sun tourist coach (see below), buses into Suva arrive at and depart from the hectic Suva bus stand beside the municipal market in Suva North.

Express buses Express bus services to and from Nadi (Queens Rd) and Lautoka (Kings Rd) are operated by Sunbeam Transport (6 daily each direction; F$15.70 to Nadi, 5hr; F$20.70 to Lautoka, 6hr) and Pacific Transport (☎330 4366; 5 daily each direction; F$15.10 via Queens Rd, 5hr). Alternatively, there's a comfortable tourist coach operated by Coral Sun (departs Nadi Airport 7.30am & 1pm, departs Suva 7.30am & 4pm; F$22; 4hr), which

arrives and departs outside *Holiday Inn Suva* opposite the Old Parliament on Victoria Parade.

Destinations Ba (7 daily; 6hr 10min); Bureiwai (2 Mon–Sat; 3hr); Korovou (14 daily; 1hr 10min); Laselevu (daily; 3hr 30min); Nadi (13 daily; 5hr); Navua (24 daily; 50min); Pacific Harbour (15 daily; 1hr 20min); Rakiraki (9 daily; 3hr 40min); Sigatoka (13 daily; 4hr); Tavua (9 daily; 4hr 40min); Vunidawa (6 daily; 1hr 45min).

BY MINIVAN

Minivans congregate around Stinson Parade behind the cinema or, if heading north to Nausori, behind the New World supermarket opposite the bus stand.

BY CAR

There are two main roads into Suva. From Nadi, the southern Queens Rd enters Suva via Lami Town, passing industrial Walu Bay, turning right at the roundabout and past the bus stand into the city centre. From Nausori, the Kings Rd heads through the congested suburbs of Nine Miles, Nabua and Samabula before descending down Edinburgh Drive to the same roundabout at Walu Bay (keep left for the city centre).

BY BOAT

Walu Bay Wharf All cargo boats and ferries dock at Walu Bay, west of the city centre. Passenger ferries ply the waters between Suva, Ovalau, Savusavu, Labasa and Taveuni, and also south to Kadavu, usually on a weekly run. Cargo boats (see p.180) serve the outer islands of Lau, Lomaiviti and Rotuma on an irregular monthly timetable – contact Fiji Shipping Corporation (☎331 9383) for the latest schedule.

Kings Wharf The more central Kings Wharf, overlooking the Suva Municipal Market, welcomes in overseas cruise liners and container ships.

Ferry operators Consort Shipping (☎331 3266), Patterson Brothers (☎331 5644), Suilven Shipping (☎331 8247) and Venu Shipping (☎339 5000).

Destinations Kadavu (weekly; 7hr 30min); Koro (2 weekly; 8hr); Northern Lau Group and Lakeba (weekly; 1–5 days); Ovalau (2 weekly; 6hr); Rotuma (monthly, 2 days); Savusavu (3 weekly; 10hr); Southern Lau Group (monthly; 2–6 days); Taveuni (2 weekly; 17hr).

4

SAFETY IN SUVA

Although Suva centre is safe during the day, you should exercise caution **after dark**, when taxis are the recommended way to get around, even if it's a matter of going a few hundred metres down the street. Female travellers should avoid going out unaccompanied after dark.

GETTING AROUND

On foot With a compact city centre and few attractions beyond, walking is the best way to get around Suva by day (see box above, for information on safety after dark). Thankfully, most streets have canopies to keep out the rain although the condition of the pavements is definitely not wheelchair- or pram- friendly.

By bus Local buses are exceptionally cheap – most inner city fares cost just F$1 – and meander around Suva to all satellite towns on a frequent schedule between 6am and 6pm, with a more limited service running until 10pm. All buses congregate at the Suva bus stand, but if travelling to Suva Point in the suburb of Nasese or to the university or National Stadium at Laucala Bay, you can wait at the bus stop beside Vanua House on Victoria Parade, which is more practical if you are in the city centre.

By taxi Taxis are exceptionally cheap and are the only really safe way to get around by night (see box above). Taxis are ubiquitous, with half a dozen taxi stands in the city centre alone: Carnarvon Taxis (☎ 331 5315) in Carnarvon St behind Dolphin Plaza, Black Arrow Taxis (☎ 330 0139) in

Central St opposite Westpac Bank and Usher Taxis (☎ 331 2977) in Usher St beside the market are the most convenient. Fares are calculated by a fixed-rate meter with a flagfall of F$1.50 (F$2 10pm–6am; F$5 from the airport) plus ten cents for every 100m travelled. A journey across the city shouldn't cost more than F$4.

By car There's nowhere to rent bicycles or mopeds in the city but a dozen companies offer car rental. The most convenient is Central Rental, 295 Victoria Parade (Mon–Sat 8am–5.30pm, Sun 8am–1pm; ☎ 331 1866, ⓦ www .central.com.fj); other reliable options include Budget, 123 Foster Rd, Walu Bay (☎ 338 1555, ⓦ budget.co.uk); Carpenters, 88 Foster Rd, Walu Bay (☎ 331 3644, ⓦ carprentals.com.fj); and Khans, 157 Ratu Mara Rd, Samabula (☎ 338 5033, ⓦ www.khansrental.com.fj). Metered parking spaces are available along most streets (20 cents for 15min), or there's longer-stay parking (F$1 per hour) along the vacant foreshore behind Civic Hall, accessible from either Stinson Parade or Victoria Parade beside Civic Tower.

INFORMATION

Tourist information There is no tourist information centre in the city, but major hotels operate tour and information desks.

Maps Free maps are available from hotel tour/info desks

but for more detail try the Henna Fiji map (F$10.50), available from the post office on Scott St or Bookmasters at 173 Victoria Parade.

ACTIVITIES AND SPORTS

Golf Fiji Golf Club, 15 Rifle Range Rd, North Samabula (☎ 338 1184) has a flat eighteen-hole course; non-members can play any day except Sat (daily 7am–5pm; F$30, trolley, clubs and shoes extra).

Massage If you're after a pampering, try Sundara Spa, 59 Gordon St, next to *Southern Cross Hotel* (daily 10am–10pm; ☎ 331 0288).

Swimming and sports centres Suva's most conveniently located swimming pool is the attractive

1925-built Suva Olympic Pool, off Victoria Parade (April–Sept Mon–Fri 10am–6pm, Sat & Sun 8am–6pm; Oct–March Mon–Fri 9am–8pm, Sat & Sun 7am–8pm; ☎ 330 5599), where you can swim all day for F$3. You can also swim at Laucala Sports City, Laucala Bay (☎ 331 2177), where there's an Olympic-sized indoor swimming pool at the National Aquatic Centre (daily 6am–7pm; F$5); nearby, the indoor Vodafone Arena offers badminton, judo and volleyball.

ACCOMMODATION

As you'd expect, the capital has a decent variety of **accommodation**, although it's the one place in Fiji you won't find palm-fringed resorts, thanks to the lack of nearby beaches. The only time it's difficult to find a room is at Christmas or during the Hibiscus Festival (usually the school holidays in Aug). **Suva South** and **Central** are the best options for most visitors, being close to the top restaurants and bars as well as the Fiji Museum. **Suva North** is distinctly seedier, with several hotels offering rooms by the hour. Heading out of the centre the **suburbs** offer a few more characterful options. Note that most of the budget motels and inns are quite shabby and serve the local clientele only. For **long-term rentals**, the classified pages of the *Fiji Times* or *Fiji Sun*, especially on Saturdays, are your best bet, with a good selection of houses, apartments and rooms. When enquiring, try and get a local to call as they are more likely to get a discount.

WATERSPORTS AROUND SUVA

The ocean around Suva is too polluted for swimming. The closest **snorkelling** reef is at Nukulau Island (see p.148) and a mediocre **surfing break** lies off Suva Point. For water activities it's best to head west to Pacific Harbour (see p.114), thirty minutes along the Queens Road, or to the offshore islands of Toberua (see p.149) or Caqalai (see p.176), both popular weekend destinations for city dwellers. You may find overnight skippered **yacht charters** and crew work advertised at The Royal Suva Yacht Club at Walu Bay.

CITY CENTRE

De Vos on the Park Ratu Sukuna Park ☎ 330 5005, ⓦ devosonthepark.com; map p.136. Dowdy on the outside but with a contemporary interior, this revamped hotel is set at the edge of Ratu Sukuna Park in the heart of the city. There are five floors with fine views of the ocean from the top two. Rooms are swish, catering to business travellers, with king-sized beds, a/c and broadband Internet access. The *Sea Salt* restaurant is a good option, with tasty surf and turf dishes. F$218

Southern Cross Hotel 63 Gordon St ☎ 331 4233, ⓦ southerncrosshotelfiji.com; map p.136. Close to the city centre and nightlife and with forty gleaming a/c rooms, a mock-marbled foyer and spacious lounge area, this six-storey hotel represents decent value for money. The pool is a bit claustrophobic, hemmed in by a courtyard on the ground floor. Up on the top floor is a Korean restaurant open till late. F$156

NORTH SUVA

Annandale Apartments 265 Waimanu Rd ☎ 331 1054; map p.136. Despite its location in Suva North this is an excellent deal, with clean rooms and harbour views. Accommodation for tourists is set aside from the locals' area and facilities include a/c, TV and hot-water bathrooms. Deluxe rooms have kitchens and are ideal for long-term stays. F$55

★**Colonial Lodge** 19 Anand St ☎ 330 0655, ⓦ coloniallodge.com.fj; map p.136. This charming and historic wooden house on a quiet cul-de-sac is run as a bed-and-breakfast for backpackers, students, volunteers and scholars. It feels homely, with an airy lounge area and wooden floors throughout: you choose from dorms, doubles or a fabulous self-contained studio in the garden. Guests can use the family kitchen, plus there's Internet access and discounts for longer stays. Rates include cooked breakfast; home-cooked dinners are F$15. Dorms F$33; doubles F$72; triples F$110; family room F$128

SOUTH SUVA

Holiday Inn Suva Victoria Parade ☎ 330 1600, ⓦ ihg .com; map p.136. The location is perfect for both tourists and business people, opposite the Old Parliament building and facing the ocean with beautiful harbour and mountain views. The 130 rooms are practical but rather uninspiring; sea-view rooms have small balconies. There's a swimming

pool and a decent tapas bar although the café and restaurant are overpriced. F$470

South Seas Private Hotel 6 Williamson Rd ☎ 331 2296, ⓔ southseas@fiji4less.com; map p.136. The cheapest accommodation in Suva, in a pleasant colonial-style wooden house, although its location down a side street north of Albert Park is a bit isolated. Rooms all share bathrooms down poky corridors and are furnished with plastic bunk beds. There's a communal kitchen and lounge area with TV. Dorms F$55; rooms F$66

Suva Motor Inn Corner of Mitchell and Gorrie streets ☎ 331 3973, ⓦ hexagonfiji.com; map p.136. Hidden at the end of Gorrie St, close to Albert Park, this is a good place for families, with a fun swimming pool and water slide and two-bedroom apartments sleeping up to six people. The thirty studio rooms have a/c and kitchenettes and are popular with business people. Rooms F$145; two-bedroom apartments F$225

Travel Inn 19 Gorrie St ☎ 330 4254, ⓔ travelinn @fiji4less.com; map p.136. Good location, quiet yet close to Victoria Parade, in a comfortable courtyard setting. All rooms are split into apartments with a shared bathroom, lounge with kitchenette and lockable communal door. You can take both rooms as an apartment or alternatively share the facilities with a stranger. Rooms F$60; apartments F$75

SUBURBS

Five Princes Hotel 5 Princes Rd ☎ 335 1575, ⓦ fiveprinceshotel.com; map p.139. Suva's boutique choice is on a colonial estate, with rooms, self-catering bures and a self-catering villa set in tropical gardens. It's a hike from downtown Suva, but there's a lovely saltwater pool and a gourmet restaurant. Rooms F$240; bures F$280; villa F$400

USP Lodges University Campus, Laucala Bay ☎ 323 2247, ⓔ talouli_m@usp.ac.fj; map p.139. Five studio flats on campus in two lodges, all with double bed, small kitchens and hot-water en-suite bathrooms. If you've come to study, or to immerse yourself into university life, this is a great base and there are plenty of buses into town, 10min away. F$75

Vale ni Tadra Homestay ⓦ wotif.com/hotels/vale-ni-tadra-homestay; map p.139. Located on the waterfront in Lami, this six-bedroom guesthouse with modern interiors enjoys a lovely beachfront location and a pool. The

4

owner also runs a good restaurant, *Eden*, a ten-minute taxi ride away. Breakfast, laundry and wi-fi are included in the rate. Garden view room A$100; ocean view room A$150; ocean suite A$350

EATING

The most popular **restaurants** in Suva are **Chinese**, and many of these whip up over-the-counter meals for around F$6. However, with variable hygiene standards, this kind of fast food is best avoided unless purchased from one of the two busy **food courts**: one at Downtown Boulevard off Renwick Rd; the other at Dolphin's Plaza on the corner of Victoria Parade and Loftus St – both are open between 8am and 5pm but closed on Sundays. Otherwise, there's a good variety of cuisine on offer from European to Indian and prices seldom exceed F$30. **BBQ hawkers** set up on Victoria Parade beside Ratu Sukuna Park from 6pm every day selling large portions of chicken and sausage with *dalo* and salad for F$5 – make sure the food is cooked in front of you as it often sits around for a while.

CITY CENTRE

Island Grille Downtown Boulevard Food Court; map p.136. One of five eating options in this busy food court and one of the few places in Suva you can buy Fijian food, albeit ready made. Try the delicious palusami and *dalo* for F$7 or rich octopus in coconut cream for F$9; the fatty meat dishes are best avoided. Mon–Sat 8am–5pm.

Palm Court Café QBE Courtyard, off Victoria Parade ☎ 330 4662, ⓦ palmcourtfiji.com; map p.136. Attractive bistro in a leafy courtyard setting, popular with the business crowd. The cooked breakfast costs F$15.30, steak or home-made fish burgers are F$8.20 or you can simply sit and relax over a coffee, herbal tea or thick shake. Mon–Fri 7am–4.30pm, Sat 7am–2pm.

Shanghai Seafood Corner of Thomson and Pier streets ☎ 331 4865; map p.136. Popular Chinese restaurant with an extensive numbered menu and food that's neither too spicy nor too salty. Make sure you bag a table on the veranda with views overlooking the busy Triangle. Mains such as steamed fish cost F$14–16. Daily 11.30am–2.30pm & 5.30–10.30pm.

★ **Tiko's Floating Restaurant** Stinson Parade ☎ 331 3626; map p.136. Not surprisingly, the focus of this floating restaurant is on freshly caught seafood, including mud crabs, king prawns, octopus and lobster, with a few steak and vegetarian dishes thrown in (from F$20). Service is impeccable. There's a wide selection of wines and the serenading guitarists along with the creaking noises of the ship all add to the South Seas atmosphere. Mon–Fri noon–2pm & 5.30–10pm, Sat 5.30–10pm.

NORTH SUVA

★ **Govinda's** 97 Mark St ☎ 330 9587; map p.136. Simple vegetarian café with a choice of twelve dishes with roti and ice creams. The most popular item is the great value "Combination Thali", which includes four curries, three vegetable dishes, chapati, samosa, three Indian sweets and juice for F$15. Mon–Sat 9am–5.45pm.

SOUTH SUVA

Ashiyana Old Town Hall, Victoria Parade ☎ 331 3000;

map p.136. Tiny, unpretentious restaurant that's a favourite with the Indian community, serving eye-wateringly hot curries. Mains such as *murgh tikka* cost from F$12. Tues–Sat 11.30am–2.30pm & 6–10pm, Sun 6–10pm.

Bad Dog Victoria Parade ☎ 330 2884; map p.136. If you've been in the Fijian sticks for a while, make a beeline for *Bad Dog*, with its designer decor, icy air-conditioning and eclectic cuisine: pizzas, steak, sushi and seafood (from F$12). The French-style puddings are a bit of a rarity, and you can move on to the bar for after-dinner drinks. Mon–Wed 11am–11pm, Thurs–Sat 11am–1am, Sun 5–11pm.

Daikoku FNPF Place Victoria Parade ☎ 330 8968; map p.136. Cosiest of the three Japanese restaurants in town, with five *teppanyaki* (griddle) tables, fresh sushi and reasonably priced *shabu-sabu* (hot pot); meals cost around F$30. Mon–Sat noon–2pm & 5.45–10pm.

Golden Palace 165 Victoria Parade ☎ 31 0318; map p.136. This upmarket Chinese restaurant decorated with colourful lanterns is a Suva institution. The food is good, albeit expensive, but the F$8 lunchtime specials are excellent value. Mains F$15–25. Mon–Sat 11.30am–2.30pm & 5.30–9.30pm, Sun 5.30–9.30pm.

★ **Maya Dhaba** 281 Victoria Parade ☎ 331 0045; map p.136. Fine Indian dining in an open-plan contemporary setting. There are 28 main dishes which makes selection difficult – try the subtle North Indian goat masala, on the bone with whole spices, or the South Indian chicken *dora*, rolled in rice pancakes. Mains cost around F$15–25. Licensed and BYO with F$10 corkage. Daily 11am–2.30pm & 6–10.30pm.

★ **Old Mill Cottage** 47 Carnarvon St ☎ 331 2134; map p.136. This unassuming-looking café with plastic tables is tremendously popular with Suva bigwigs – you may find yourself sitting next to an MP or top lawyer. The menu is broad, with several traditional Fijian favourites including palusami (F$7) and kokoda (F$8), as well as uninspiring but tasty Indian and Chinese dishes for around F$8. Ask about their daily specials if you can't decide. There's a pleasant wooden veranda where breakfast (F$10) and omelettes (F$7) are served. The home-made cassava chips are worth a try at F$1 a serve. Mon–Sat 7am–5pm.

Republic of Cappuccino Dolphin Plaza, Victoria

CLOCKTOWER, THURSTON GARDENS (P.138) >

Parade ☎330 8968; map p.136. Tiny and buzzy European-style corner café serving excellent coffee, plus smoothies, juices and croissants. Mon–Fri 7am–11pm, Sat 8am–11pm, Sun 8am–7pm.

★**Scott's Restaurant** 59 Gordon St ☎774 2226; map p.136. Tucked away in an obscure building next to the *Southern Cross Hotel*, this French restaurant is definitely the swankiest spot in town. Wood-panelling, antiques, alcoves and candles create a cosy yet elegant atmosphere. The classic French food is delicious and wines come from New Zealand, Australia and France. Mains cost F$35–45. Mon–Fri noon–2pm & 6–10pm, Sat 6–10pm.

Vine Yard Palace Old Town Hall, Victoria Parade ☎331 5111; map p.136. If you need a good feed on a budget, this all-you-can-eat lunchtime Chinese buffet (Mon–Fri 11.30am–2.30pm; F$15.80) is hard to beat, and is hugely popular with a ravenous Fijian crowd. Otherwise, the à la carte menu is best avoided. Mon–Sat 11.30am–10pm.

DRINKING, NIGHTLIFE AND ENTERTAINMENT

One of Suva's most enduring charms is its lively **nightlife**. Most of the bars and clubs are in one block around Victoria Parade and Carnarvon St, making it easy to hop from one to another and sample the different atmospheres. Fijians like to drink **communally**, as if drinking *yaqona* – if you buy a Fiji Bitter "long neck", which is more economical, it will be shared by passing round a small glass to down in one. It's a quick way of getting drunk and brawls occasionally break out in the wilder places. However, the locals are very protective of foreign visitors and on most occasions you'll be well looked after. **Taxis** are advisable for the ride back to your hotel (see box, p.142).

BARS

Holiday Inn Suva Victoria Parade ☎330 1600, ⓦihg .com; map p.136. If you're after a quiet drink, the lounge bar at the *Holiday Inn* is the best choice, although it's somewhat pricey. There's a pianist accompanied by light jazz musicians (Tues–Thurs) and a good R&B vocalist on Fri nights. Happy hour 5.30–6.30pm. Daily 4–9.30pm.

O'Reillys Bar 5 MacArthur St, corner of Victoria Parade ☎331 2322; map p.136. Popular with tourists and USP students, the bouncers here keep a tight grip on proceedings. There's loud music, plus a large-screen TV and pool table at the back; it's also the only place in Fiji you'll find Guinness on tap. The bar is connected to the *Bad Dog Café* (see p.144) on the corner, which has a wine bar serving overpriced but well-presented food. Mon–Sat 11am–midnight, Sun 5–11pm.

Royal Suva Yacht Club Queens Rd, Walu Bay ☎330 4201, ⓦrsyc.org.fj; map p.139. A bit out of the way – 2km from the city centre in Walu Bay – but with a lovely beer garden overlooking the sea it's an ideal spot to watch the sunset over a draught beer, and the bar snacks are good too. Happy hour Tues & Sat 6–7pm. Mon–Thurs 8am–10pm, Fri–Sun 8am–midnight.

★**Traps Lounge** 305 Victoria Parade ☎331 2922; map p.136. The main bar at the front is the place to be seen for an after-work tipple. There's a pool bar at the back, a non-smoking chill-out lounge at the top and a buzzing dance floor with live music Wed and Thurs from 10pm. F$5 admission some weekends. Mon–Sat 5pm–1am.

CLUBS

Bar 66 Dolphin Plaza, Victoria Parade, entrance on Loftus St ☎870 6071; map p.136. Hangout for the hip under-25s, with DJs playing pop and reggae and a small dancefloor. It doesn't get going until after 11pm and it's usually the last place to close, picking up the crowds from *Traps* after midnight. Tues–Sat 9pm–late.

★**Golden Dragon** 379 Victoria Parade ☎331 1018; map p.136. Long-standing favourite amongst the islanders with live music Wed and Thurs, mostly reggae-influenced, and lots of university students out for a laugh – you'll often see Polynesians dancing the hula here. Admission F$5 after 9pm Fri & Sat. Mon–Sat 7pm–midnight.

Shenanigans 5 MacArthur St ☎331 2322; map p.136. International beers and spirits alongside ubiquitous Fiji Golds, plus dance music, dancing and a lively atmosphere. Mon–Sat 11am–midnight, Sun 5–11pm.

Signals 255 Victoria Parade ☎331 3590; map p.136. Centrally located, this is the only club in Suva with any atmosphere before 10pm. You may wish to start your night here and then move on as it usually gets packed with drunken fishermen later in the evening. There's a long bar, dancefloor and cheap drinks. Watch your pocket. Mon–Sat 6pm–1am.

CINEMAS

USP Room NIII, SPAF Building, USP, Laucala Bay ☎323 2402. There are some Pacific screenings at the USP Campus in Laucala Bay.

Village Six Scott St ☎330 6006. Central cinema showing mainstream and Bollywood films. Tickets F$6.50. Daily 10am–11pm.

SHOPPING

Renwick Rd is the place to head for **malls**, which contain a variety of stores and amenities such as cafés and ATMS, while scruffy but characterful Cumming St (see p.135) has Suva's best selection of **clothes shops**, where you can buy fine Indian attire and fabric by the metre. One of the street's many tailors can then whip you up a suit or shirt, or try the Flea Market (see below).

BOOKSHOPS

Fiji Museum gift shop Thurston Gardens ☎331 5944; map p.136. Useful for historical titles and *Domodomo* (F$6), the museum's monthly journal. They also sell postcards with old photographs, wooden carvings, jewellery and souvenirs. Mon–Fri 9am–4pm, Sat 9.30am–4pm.

University Bookshop Laucala Bay ☎323 2500, ⓦuspbookcentre.com; map p.139. A selection of titles about the Pacific, on topics ranging from history and culture to law, legend, language and song. Mon–Fri 8am–5.30pm, Sat 8.30am–1pm.

CLOTHES

Trendy Fashion 9 Pier St ☎330 0313; map p.136. If you want to follow the local fashion for loud flowery shirts and sarongs, this is the place to come to get kitted out. The garments are affordable, 100-percent cotton and made in Fiji. Mon–Sat 9am–6pm.

COSMETICS

Pure Fiji Karsanji St; map p.139. A weekly factory outlet sale of Fiji's favourite products: lotions, potions, shampoos and sugar rubs made with coconut oil and other natural flower extracts. They make great gifts, though remember not to pack them in your hand luggage when leaving the country. Sat 10am–2pm.

DEPARTMENT STORES

MHCC (Morris Hedstrom City Center) Mall Renwick Rd; map p.136. Bland but useful a/c mall with an ATM, sports shops, fast food, coffee and a well-stocked supermarket. Daily 9am–10pm.

HANDICRAFTS AND JEWELLERY

Flea Market Usher St at Rodwell Rd; map p.136. This street market is where locals come to buy mats, *masi* and garlands for traditional ceremonies, and to get shirts and dresses tailor-made. Mon–Sat 8am–6pm.

Municipal Market South end of Rodwell Rd; map p.136. A cornucopia of seasonal fruit and vegetables, and great for a browse as well as to buy. Behind Usher St, with the rowdy *Ritz* bar and nightclub on its corner, are the fish stalls, with amazingly fresh seafood supplied direct by Suva's fishing fleet. At the far end of the market, the Women's Centre sells crafts, clothes and great shopping bags made from bright recycled fabrics. Mon–Sat 6am–6pm.

SNORKELLING AND FISHING EQUIPMENT

Bob's Hook Line & Sinker Harbour Centre, 14 Thomson St ☎330 1013; map p.136. Snorkelling gear and fishing equipment. Mon–Sat 9am–5.30pm.

DIRECTORY

Banks Westpac, corner of Scott and Central streets (Mon–Thurs 9.30am–3pm, Fri 9.30am–4pm); ANZ Bank, 25 Victoria Parade (Mon 9.30am–4pm, Tues–Fri 9am–4pm), also at Centrepoint and USP.

Dentist Shalom, First Floor Kadavu House, Renwick Rd (Mon–Fri 8am–5pm, Sat 8am–1pm; on call 24hr; ☎331 8477).

Doctors Dr Fatiaki, first floor Epworth Arcade, Nina St (☎330 2421); Fiji Care Medical Centre, 123 Amy St (Mon–Fri 8.30am–5pm, Sat 8.30–11.30am; ☎331 3355); Marie Stopes International, 157 Renwick Rd (Mon–Fri 10am–7pm, Sat 9am–1pm; ☎331 0101).

Embassies and high commissions Australia, Princess Rd ☎338 2211; France and EU Schengen States, Dominion House, Thomson St ☎331 2233; Federated States of Micronesia, Loftus Rd ☎330 4633; Indonesia, Gordon St ☎331 6697; Kiribati, McGregor Rd ☎330 2512; Nauru, Ratu Sukuna House, MacArthur St ☎331 3566; New Zealand, Pratt St ☎331 1422; Papua New Guinea, Gordon St ☎330 4244; Tuvalu, Gorrie St ☎330 1355; UK, Gladstone Rd ☎322 9108; USA, Loftus St ☎330 6243.

Hospitals Bayview Medical, 361 Waimanu Rd ☎331 1361; CWM Hospital Waimanu Rd ☎331 3444; Suva Private Hospital, 120 Amy St ☎330 3404.

Immigration Civic Tower Victoria Parade (Mon–Fri 8.30am–12.30pm; ☎331 2622).

Internet access Connect Internet café on Scott St (Mon–Fri 8am–midnight, Sat 9am–midnight, Sun 9am–8pm; F$3.60 per hr).

Libraries Suva Library, 196 Victoria Parade (Mon–8am–4.30pm, Fri 8am–4pm; F$20 non-Suva resident membership fee; ☎331 3433). University Library, USP Campus, Laucala Bay (F$20 temporary membership fee; ☎323 2402). The National Archives on Carnarvon St (Mon–Thurs 8am–4.30pm, Fri 8am–4pm; free; ☎330 4144) was once the print works for the *Fiji Times* and hosts a comprehensive collection of historical documents for public browsing, including *Fiji Times* newspapers dating back to the first issue in 1869 and many old photographic albums.

Pharmacy Superdrug Pharmacy, Central Building, Renwick Rd (Mon–Fri 8am–6pm, Sat 8am–3pm; ☎331 8755); Nasese Pharmacy, Ratu Sukuna Rd, 2km from city centre (Mon–Sat 8am–5pm & 7–9pm, Sun 10am–1pm & 7–9pm; ☎331 4450).

Police Corner of Pratt and Joske streets ☎991 or ☎331 1222. There are 24hr manned police posts at Market St

(📞331 1122) and Gorrie St (📞330 9822) overlooking Albert Park.
Post office Scott St (Mon–Fri 7.30am–5pm, Sat 8am–1pm).

Telephone Behind the post office on Scott St, in QBE Building, Victoria Parade. Phone cards are available from the post office.

Around Suva

There are plenty of attractions around Suva worth exploring on day-trips or by staying overnight. Off Suva Point is **Nukulau Island**, which has the only sandy beach and snorkelling reef in the vicinity. Inland, the tranquil forest park of **Colo-i-Suva** forms a boundary between Suva and the wet mountainous interior of Viti Levu. The mountains feed the impressive Rewa River, which drains to the north of Suva through Nausori town and into the vast, mangrove-lined **Rewa Delta**. This region, and the coast to the north, is home to the chiefly villages of Rewa and **Bau** – the latter once home to Cakobau, the only King of Fiji – and remains the most influential power-base in Fiji.

Nukulau

Lying 8km east of Suva Point, and barely 1km from Laucala Point is **Nukulau**, a tiny coral cay with good snorkelling and a pretty sandy beach. According to Fijian legend, the island is cursed by the devil god *Batidua*, who plagued the islanders for centuries. In 1846 the local Rewan people were only too happy to sell Nukulau to American **John Williams** (see p.134) who bought the island for US$30, paid in muskets and alcohol. The house he built here was burnt down and looted on July 4, 1849, an event which led to Fiji becoming a British colony; there are no remnants of the house today. Recently the island was the location of the makeshift prison which held the 2000 coup perpetrator **George Speight** before he was transferred to Naboro Maximum Security Prison after the Bainimarama coup of 2006. There are plans to turn Nukulau into a tourist attraction and introduce a ferry service from Suva harbour. For now, the only way to visit is to charter a small boat from the Royal Suva Yacht Club (see p.146).

Colo-i-Suva Forest Park

Daily 8am–4pm • F$5; guides F$30 for a 2hr walk • 📞 332 0211 • Take a Saweni- or Serea-bound bus from the Suva bus stand (hourly; 30min; F$2) or a taxi (20min; F$12)

Around 25 kilometres north of Suva is **Colo-i-Suva Forest Park**, a pristine area of low-altitude rainforest. It's a pretty place, dominated by mahogany trees, their trunks thick with parasitical tree ferns. There's a good chance of spotting **wild orchids** in the park as well as endemic **birds**, including the Pink-billed Parrotfinch. An easy one-hour **nature trail** leads to a couple of small **waterfalls** with pools good for swimming and nearby picnic benches.

Unfortunately, the park has a reputation for theft from cars and occasional muggings – the attendant at the park entrance can arrange a **guide**, and can look after valuables.

ACCOMMODATION   **COLO-I-SUVA FOREST PARK**

Raintree Lodge Just before the park entrance 📞332 0562, 🌐raintreelodge.com. A pleasant retreat with three large dorm lodges with small rooms and kitchens and five quaint wooden cottages embedded in the surrounding forest. The lodge has an excellent restaurant, which puts on a BBQ lunch every Sun (F$17), popular with Suva residents. If you're just here for the day, stop in for morning coffee or afternoon tea. Restaurant open daily 7am–10pm. Dorms **F$25**; rooms **F$65**; studios **F$135**; bures **F$165**

The Rewa River Delta

East of Suva, the landscape is dominated by the snaking tributaries and mangroves of the **Rewa River delta**, dotted with small fishing villages. At the eastern end of the river

THE RISE OF BAU ISLAND AND KING CAKOBAU

Despite its modest size **Bau Island** played a key role in the history of Fiji. Up until the eighteenth century, Verata, 10km north of Nausori, and its rival **Rewa** had ruled the archipelago, the latter being the head of the aristocracy of Burebasaga, one of the three founding clans. In 1760, a tiny island named Ulu-ni-Vuaka ("the head of the pig"), barely 300m from the shore of Viti Levu, was settled by warriors of Verata lineage and in time became known as Bau. The island's first chief erected **sea walls** to protect it from invasion and built stone canoe docks, making the island a powerful seafaring base. In 1808 a Swedish "beachcomber" (see p.220) named **Charlie Savage** – who five years later would end up in the cannibals' pot – visited Bau and brought with him **firearms**, until then never possessed by Fijians. Using these new, terrifying weapons, the ruling chief, Naulivou, fought a series of wars with Verata, 15km to the north. When Verata was weak Rewa grew in strength and between the two, they battled the upstarts from Bau for supremacy. Bau grew more powerful under the rule of the brutal cannibal chiefs of **Tanoa** and later **Cakobau**. The chiefs seized upon the right of *vasu* (see p.230), claiming wide support from villages throughout Fiji. At its peak, the island boasted three thousand inhabitants and twenty temples.

By 1871, with the backing of the European merchants of Levuka, Cakobau had proclaimed himself **King of Fiji**. Three years later he ceded the islands to Britain. Today, the chief of Bau remains one of the most powerful in Fijian political life. As for Rewa, the aristocrats managed to retain their hold over their far-flung subjects and the Burebasaga Confederacy remains the largest and most powerful of Fiji's three ancient confederacies.

is **Kaba Point**, where the great war between Rewa and Bau came to its bloody conclusion in 1855 with a battle involving five thousand warriors and a hundred war canoes (see p.221).

Bau Island

Seven kilometres north of Kaba Point is Bau Landing, access point for the chiefly island of **Bau**. To visit the tiny island, reached by punt from here (F$6), you need to ask the *Turaga-ni-Koro* or village spokesman (☎362 4028) for permission. If you receive an invitation you should bring *yaqona* roots and dress respectably. The island is small in size but has over two hundred houses and a fascinating history (see box above). The mound in the centre is where the chiefly families live, while around the perimeter are sub clans: craftsmen from Lau, warriors from Botoni and fishermen from Kadavu. The island's Methodist **church**, dating from 1859, was the first to be built in Fiji. It was erected under the orders of King Cakobau, the fierce chief of the island who converted to Christianity in 1854. All the ancient temples on Bau were destroyed, and their stone used in the construction of the church. The baptismal font beside the altar is reputed to be Cakobau's killing stone, where the skulls of his captives were smashed before being eaten.

Toberua Island

Three kilometres off Kaba Point is the four-acre **Toberua Island**, home to one of Fiji's first boutique island resorts (see below). There are colourful coral formations and **reef sharks** at nearby Toberua Passage, which is excellent for both snorkelling and scuba diving. The resort will organize your transport to the island, as well as twice-weekly boat trips to **Mabualau**, a tiny limestone islet 5km to the east, dedicated as a nature reserve and packed with large white fluffy **boobies**.

ACCOMMODATION TOBERUA ISLAND

★Toberua Island Resort ☎347 2777, ⊕toberua .com. This delightful resort has built its reputation around its friendly staff, many of whom have worked here their entire lives, and guests often return year after year. The fifteen bures have wonderfully spacious, traditionally decorated interiors with outdoor airy showers. The resort's PADI dive outfit runs trips to over twenty dive sites, from coral heads to walls and crevasses. F$495

Beqa,
Vatulele
and Kadavu

TAPA CLOTH

Beqa, Vatulele and Kadavu

Beqa, Vatulele and Kadavu, the three main islands south of the Fijian mainland, present world-class scuba diving, hair-raising reef surfing and record-breaking game fishing. If that's not enough to entice you, several of Fiji's most beautiful beaches are located here, with shallow lagoons offering fabulous sea-kayaking and deep bays sheltering fishing villages.

The rugged island of **Beqa** is famed for its fire walkers and, just offshore in its huge lagoon, adrenaline-pumping shark dives accessed from Pacific Harbour (see box, p.116). West of Beqa is the delightful limestone island of **Vatulele**, a centre for **tapa cloth** making and home to several unusual attractions including ancient rock carvings and a cave full of bizarre red-coloured prawns. The farthest of the southern islands from Viti Levu and the largest of the three is **Kadavu**, barely a forty-minute flight from Nadi, and closer still from Suva, but a world away from the tourist trail. With its twisting **Astrolabe Reef** and dramatic mountain scenery, this is the place to visit for adventure on the water, and to immerse yourself in Fijian culture.

Beqa and around

If not shrouded by clouds, the roughly contoured profile of **BEQA** (pronounced "Mbenga") can be seen clearly from Suva. It's closer still to Pacific Harbour, from where small boats bump across 12km of open sea to reach it. The island is roughly circular in shape, with steep forest-clad mountains rising sharply from a meandering coastline. Its large lagoon, protected by a 30km-long barrier reef, is renowned for **shark dives** and deep-sea game fishing, as well as the famous **surfing break** of Frigates Passage opposite the small island of **Yanuca**; most diving and game fishing trips leave from Pacific Harbour and are covered in Chapter Three (see p.116).

Beqa's most distinctive feature is its **fire walkers** (see box, p.155). You can often see them perform on Viti Levu, especially at the Arts Village in Pacific Harbour (see p.114), but nothing beats witnessing the real thing on home soil – Rukua, Naceva and Dakuibeqa on the southeastern side are the main fire-walking villages.

The island's 1400 inhabitants live in nine coastal villages. There are no roads on the island but several **walking tracks** between villages make for pleasant exploring. The easiest route runs from Waisomo on the northern tip of the island to Rukua along the west coast. You can also hike to one of the island's **three mountains** – Korolevu (439m), towering over Lalati Village on the north coast, is the most challenging and highest. The best way to sample the coastline is from a kayak and *Lalati Resort* (see p.154) runs a delightful kayaking trip to tranquil Malumu Bay, which bites deep into the west coast, almost severing it from the main bulk of Beqa.

ARRIVAL AND DEPARTURE

BEQA

By boat Many visitors reach Beqa on a pre-arranged resort transfer from Pacific Harbour but there's also a public ferry which departs from Navua every day except Sun sometime between noon and 2.30pm (30min; F$45 per person one way).

Highlights

❶ Surfing, Frigates Passage Surfers shouldn't miss the strong left-hand break at Frigates Passage on the little island of Yanuca. **See p.154**

❷ Beqa fire walkers Watch the locals amble over white-hot stones during traditional ceremonies in the village of Dakuibeqa. **See p.155**

❸ Tapa cloth making, Vatulele Try your hand at tapa cloth making with the women of Lomanikaya Village on Vatulele. **See p.157**

❹ Kayak around Kadavu Explore the indented bays, mangrove forests and traditional villages along Kadavu's rugged coastline. **See p.160**

❺ Astrolabe Reef, Kadavu One of the best dive sites anywhere, home to colourful soft corals, fast channels and large fish. The reef is the third biggest in the world. **See p.162**

❻ Manta rays, Vuro With a span of over six metres, these vast but harmless creatures are one of the biggest fish species in the ocean. Snorkelling trips to Vuro allow you to see them at close range. **See p.163**

HIGHLIGHTS ARE MARKED ON THE MAP ON P.154

5

ACCOMMODATION

Lalati Resort Malumu Bay ☎347 2033, ⓦlalati-fiji
.com. Of the handful of upmarket dive resorts on Beqa,
which cater mostly to the North American market, the pick
is *Lalati Resort* on the northeast coast, with six spacious
bures, a swimming pool, spa and gourmet meals. F$440
★**Lawaki Beach House** ☎331 8817, ⓦwww
.lawakibeachhouse.com. The only affordable place to

stay on Beqa is on the west coast at the end of a long
stretch of beach. The two bures have en-suite hot-water
bathrooms, while the six-bed dorm lodge and pre-
fabricated tents with mattresses share a cold-water
bathroom. Rates include meals. Tents F$93; dorms F$139;
bures F$298

Yanuca

By comparison with Beqa, **Yanuca**, 12km west, is a relatively low island, with
light forest, gentle hills and a solitary village on the east coast. The main reason to
visit is the excellent **surfing** available at **Frigates Passage**, an extremely consistent
and powerful left-hand break that's one of the best surfing spots in the South

KADAVU, BEQA AND VATULELE

HIGHLIGHTS

1. Surfing, Frigates Passage
2. Beqa fire walkers
3. Tapa cloth making, Vatulele
4. Kayak around Kadavu
5. Astrolabe Reef, Kadavu
6. Manta rays, Vuro

0   20
kilometres

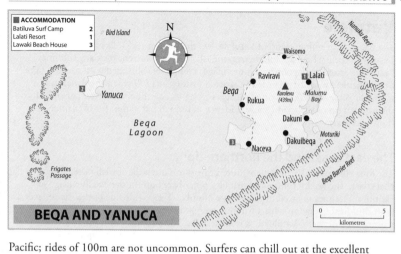

ACCOMMODATION
Batiluva Surf Camp	2
Lalati Resort	1
Lawaki Beach House	3

N

Bird Island

Waisomo

Raviravi ¦ 1 Lalati

Yanuca 2

Beqa Korolevu Malumu
Rukua (439m) Bay

Dakuni

*Beqa
Lagoon*

Moturiki
3 Dakuibeqa
Naceva

Nanuku Reef

Beqa Barrier Reef

*Frigates
Passage*

BEQA AND YANUCA

0 _____ 5
kilometres

Pacific; rides of 100m are not uncommon. Surfers can chill out at the excellent
Batiluva Surf Camp on the island's west coast; the coarse coral beach adjacent to the
surf camp has lots of hammocks strung between coconut palms and a deep lagoon
with good snorkelling.

ARRIVAL AND DEPARTURE   YANUCA

By boat The 45min boat trip to Yanuca departs from Pacific Harbour every day at 3pm and costs F$50 return.

ACCOMMODATION

★**Batiluva Surf Camp** ☎345 0384, ⓦbatiluva
.com. Hemmed in on the west coast by the island's
steepest hills, this appealing place is run by a Hawaiian
couple. There are two A-frame wooden lodges, one with
two rooms for couples and the other with a four-bed
dorm, all sharing two cold-water showers and four
toilets. With kerosene lamps enhancing the secluded
atmosphere, this is one of the most laid-back surfing
destinations in the South Pacific. Surf trips depart every
day at 8.30am and, depending on the group, return
sometime in the afternoon. Rate (per person) includes
meals, snorkelling and fishing gear, and surfing
transfers. **F$175**

THE LEGEND OF BEQA'S FIRE WALKERS

Unlike Hindu fire walking (see p.34), **Beqa's fire walkers** perform purely for entertainment
rather than religious purification. The legend of how the islanders obtained mastery over fire
has been passed down through the generations.

Once there was a famous storyteller named **Dredre** who lived in the ancient mountain
village of Navakeisese on Beqa. His tales would captivate the villagers throughout the night
and it was customary to bring small gifts as a token of appreciation. One evening, Dredre
requested all present to bring him the first thing they encountered when out hunting the
next day. The following morning, a young warrior named **Tui** went fishing in a mountain
stream and pulled out what he thought was an eel from the mud. To his surprise, the eel
assumed the shape of a *Vu*, or spirit god, and Tui knew that Dredre would be most pleased
with his gift. The spirit god pleaded for its life offering all sorts of tempting powers but only
when Tui was promised the **power over fire** did he succumb. The spirit god dug a pit,
lined it with stones and lit a huge fire upon it. When the stones were white hot, the spirit
god leaped in showing no effect from the heat. Tui followed and to this day his
descendants from the Sawau tribe re-enact the same performance of walking on
white-hot stones.

5 Vatulele

The flat yet intriguing island of **Vatulele**, or "the ringing rock", lies 32km south of Viti Levu. Covering 31 square kilometres, the island boasts ancient rock art, sublime beaches, a sparkling lagoon and four villages completely absorbed with making **tapa cloth**. Vatulele was first recorded in written history in 1799 when the American schooner *Anne and Hope* spotted villagers along its coastline. However, petroglyphs on the western tip of the island show evidence of human habitation for over three thousand years.

The east coast and the northern tip

The four villages on Vatulele lie within a thirty-minute walk of each other along the flat **east coast**. The **health centre** and primary school are both in the chiefly village of **Ekubu**, sometimes referred to as "Village Number Two". This side of the island faces a bountiful fishing lagoon with a fringing reef 3km from shore and several small islets within. One of them, **Vatulevu**, was nicknamed "Bird Island", as it used to host thousands of nesting **red-footed boobies**. Unfortunately, when the landowner introduced goats in 2002 it took less than a year for them to strip the vegetation and leave the island barren. The birds now nest on the sharp limestone cliffs between **Long Beach** and the limestone passages of the **Grotto** along the **northern tip** of Vatulele. Guests staying at *Vatulele Island Resort* (see p.157) can kayak for twenty minutes along the coast to spot the boobies and their adorable fluffy offspring.

The west coast

Vatulele's famous **petroglyphs**, carved into the limestone cliffs at a height of 10m, are on Vatulele's **west coast**, south of *Vatulele Island Resort*. The designs include hands, faces and animals such as roosters. Just south of here is another island icon, the **sacred red prawns** in the tidal cave of Korolamalama. The prawns are known as *ura buta* or "cooked prawns" owing to their extraordinary deep red colour. Eating the prawns is strictly forbidden – the islanders believe anyone who harms them will be shipwrecked.

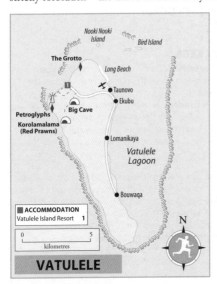

For a fabulous view of the lush green carpet of forest that covers Vatulele, and of the eagles and swiftlets that thrive amongst the craggy cliffs, climb the ninety steps of the solar-powered **lighthouse**, perched on the cliff edge. The fifteen-minute trail to the lighthouse starts just beyond the gates of *Vatulele Island Resort*.

Inland to Big Cave

Ten minutes' walk along the bumpy road connecting the *Vatulele Island Resort* and the villages along the east coast brings you to a trail branching south to **Big Cave**, in the heart of the island. There's a cool freshwater swimming pool at the cave's entrance and, with a torch and guide, you can explore the network of tunnels which eventually connect through to the sea.

5

THE MAKING OF TAPA CLOTH

From sunrise to sunset, the deep resonating thump of wood beating against wood echoes around the villages of Vatulele. This is the sound of **tapa cloth** production, a fine paper made from the bark of the **mulberry tree**, or *masi* in Fijian. The cloth was traditionally used as clothing, wrapped around the waist and draped over the shoulder of people with chiefly status. It also represented a conductor between the spirit and living world, and was hung from the high ceiling of the *bure kalou*, or temple, and used by the priest to mediate with the gods. Today, it is used in decorative **artwork** and gift wrapping sold in boutique shops around Fiji.

The production of tapa is almost exclusively done by women. The first step is to slice and strip the long thin bark of the mulberry tree into single pieces which are then soaked in the sea for four nights. Once supple, the bark is beaten into a **pulp** using hardwood slabs and heavy wooden sticks and joined with other strips to make a single piece of cloth. Dried in the sun, the cloth is eventually **decorated** using patterned stencil designs depicting the origin of the artist and figurative icons relevant to a clan's totemic god – often a turtle or shark. Once stencilled, the cloth is known in Fijian as *masi*. Only two or three colours are used – brown dye is obtained from the bark of the mangrove tree; the black dye comes from charcoal; while the red dye that is sometimes used is obtained from seeds. For the villagers on Vatulele, tapa is the main **cash crop**, generating an average annual income of F$2000 per household, although for some tapa artists this can reach F$6000, equalling the basic salary of a Fijian civil servant.

ARRIVAL AND DEPARTURE
VATULELE

By air The grass airstrip on the east side of Vatulele is used exclusively to bring in guests staying at *Vatulele Island Resort*. The daily 25min flight from Nadi Airport departs at 11.30am, returning at 12.50pm, and costs F$150 each way.

By boat Anyone else visiting the island will need to rely on the small outboard village boats which leave from Korolevu (see p.162) on the Coral Coast every Tues, Thurs and Sat, generally around noon. The 45min boat journey costs F$30 one-way.

ACCOMMODATION

Vatulele Island Resort 📞 672 0300, 🌐 vatulele.com. This exquisite resort offers fine dining, nineteen private villas and a ratio of four staff to every guest. Straddling a beautiful white-sand beach and with its own tiny offshore island used as a picnic spot, the resort ranks as one of the finest in Fiji. US$1800

Kadavu and around

KADAVU (pronounced "Kan-davu") is the fourth-largest island in Fiji, snaking 57km from east to west with a rugged coastline littered with deep bays. The island is divided into three sections, each connected by a narrow isthmus. **West Kadavu** is dominated by the volcanic cone of Nabukelevu at its western end while to the east is Kadavu's only expanse of flat land, taken up by the small airstrip and the government centre of **Vunisea**. **Central Kadavu**, east of Vunisea, has the island's best **beaches**, as well as the fantastic Namalata Reef off the north coast. **East Kadavu** overlooks part of the immense Astrolabe Reef and is home to a handful of **dive resorts** backed by steep tropical rainforest and a sprinkling of waterfalls. The resorts will be able to arrange a guide to help you spot Kadavu's four **endemic bird species**: the Kadavu Fantail, Kadavu Honeyeater, Velvet Fruit Dove and Kadavu Musk Parrot.

There are just over ten thousand inhabitants on Kadavu, primarily engaged in subsistence farming and fishing, making it one of the best places to immerse yourself in **Fijian culture**. Most of the 75 coastal villages are hidden in bays or amongst mangrove estuaries and obscured from view when travelling along the coast by boat. Every third village has a primary school and all are connected by walking trails.

5

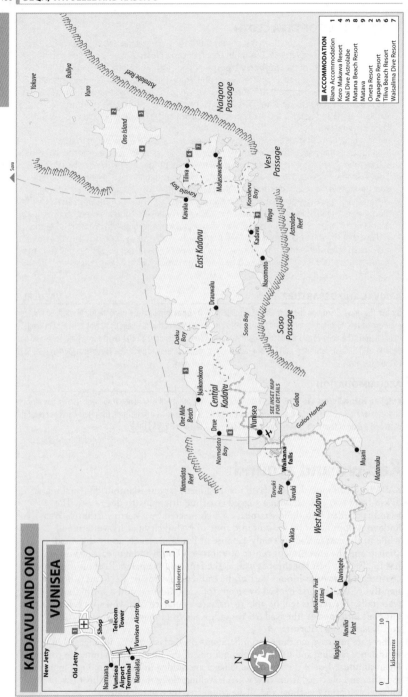

KADAVU AND ONO

Yakuwe

Buliya

Varo

Astrolabe Reef

Ono Island

2

3

4

Sava

Naigoro
Passage

7

6

Matasawaleva

Tilliva

Kavala

Vesi
Passage

Korolevu
Bay

9

Woya

Astrolabe
Reef

Kavala Bay

Kadavu

East Kadavu

Nacomoto

Drauwalu

Doku
Bay

Soso Bay

Soso
Passage

One Mile
Beach

5

Naikorokoro

Central Kadavu

Drue

8

Vunisea

Galoa

Galoa Harbour

SEE INSET MAP
FOR DETAILS

Namalata
Bay

Waikana
falls

Muani

Namalata Reef

Tavuki
Bay

Tavuki

West Kadavu

Matamuku

Yakita

Davingele

Nabukelevu Peak
(838m)

Nagigia

Navilia
Point

0 ———— 10
kilometres

ACCOMMODATION
1 Biana Accommodation
4 Koro Makawa Resort
3 Mai Dive Astrolabe
8 Matana Beach Resort
9 Matava
2 Oneta Resort
5 Papageno Resort
6 Tiliva Beach Resort
7 Waisalima Dive Resort

VUNISEA

New Jetty

Old Jetty

1

Namuana

Telecom
Tower

Shop

Vunisea
Airport
Terminal

Namalata

Vunisea Airstrip

0 ———— 1
kilometre

N

5

Brief history

In 1792, William Bligh became the first European to chart Kadavu and its dangerous coral reefs, but for the next few decades the islanders had little contact with the outside world. This peaceful isolation was shattered in 1829 when the island was **conquered** by warriors from Rewa from southeastern Viti Levu. As such, Kadavu was brought under the influence of the powerful Burebasaga Confederacy and forced to assist Rewa in the 1840s war against Cakobau.

Thirty-five years after Bligh's encounter, French commander Dumont d'Urville almost ran aground on the reefs north of Ono and so named them after his ship, *L'Astrolabe*. After publishing his journals which described the discovery of endless supplies of the Chinese delicacy **bêche-de-mer** (sea cucumber), Kadavu began to attract overseas traders. Galoa Harbour, on the southern side of present-day Vunisea Town, became a busy port and it wasn't long before American **whalers** moved into Tavuki Bay on the north coast. Land was briskly traded with the locals for firearms and alcohol and Chinese and European merchants set up stores and began planting cotton. Galoa reached its peak in 1871 but within a few years it had become a virtual ghost town when Levuka, backed by Cakobau, established itself as the main port for trade.

Many of the **Chinese** traders remained, marrying into local Fijian families, and the Chinese link remains strong today. Kadavu's largest export is *kava*, reputed as the finest and strongest in Fiji. The fourteen provincial chiefs on Kadavu remain relatively autonomous from the Burebasaga Confederacy and are amongst the most powerful local chiefs in Fiji.

Vunisea and west Kadavu

You're most likely to be swept in and out of the township of **VUNISEA** on your way to one of Kadavu's resorts, which is a shame as it makes a convenient base for exploring the attractions of **west Kadavu**. It has a pretty setting between Namalata Bay on the north coast of Kadavu and Galoa Harbour on the south coast. In pre-European days, warriors would slide their war canoes on rollers over the isthmus separating the north and south bays to save themselves the long journey around the coast.

Namuana village

Beside the airstrip and fronting the beach at Namalata Bay is pretty **Namuana village**, famous for its **turtle calling ceremony**, an event that now occurs only occasionally. The turtles, said to represent two maidens of the village lost to sea, are summoned to the surface by a chant sung by the women. If a turtle doesn't appear, it's said a person from its bitter rival village of Nabukelevu is present. A twenty-minute trail from the village leads up to the saddle of the hill, with great views of both bays, and continues to secluded **Waikana Falls**, where you can swim in a shallow pool.

The south coast road

A rough but scenic dirt road heads across the isthmus from Vunisea along the **south coast** of west Kadavu all the way to Nabukelevu-i-Ra Village on the western tip of the island. Along the way it passes several beautiful bays and the towering peak of **Nabukelevu**, also known as Mount Washington. It's possible to climb to the 838m-high summit in a full day, starting out from Davinqele Village on the south coast. From the top you'll see the dramatic north face of the peak tumbling down to the sea.

Central Kadavu

East of Vunisea, a dirt road, better for walking than driving, meanders inland to the dense tropical rainforest of **central Kadavu**. Roughly 8km in, the road splits in two. The right-hand track heads north following an undulating valley to a series of five beautiful

5

DIVING AND WATERSPORTS ON KADAVU

Life on the water is such an integral part of Kadavu that it's little wonder watersports are the main attraction for visitors – in particular scuba diving, thanks to the phenomenal 100km-long **Astrolabe Reef**. Snorkelling can be arranged at your resort.

DIVING

The Astrolabe Reef can be divided into two distinct sections: the 50km northern loop, forming a figure of eight shape, is all in open water, entwined with canyons, arches and other spectacular seascapes; while the section of reef hugging the east and south coast of Kadavu to Galoa Harbour has five rich current-fed passages all featuring a profusion of **soft corals**. There are strong drift dives at Naiqoro, shallow corals at Vesi, **sharks** at Nacomoto, **fans** at Soso and **manta rays** at Galoa.

Viti Watersports (☎670 2413, ⓦvitiwatersports.com), offers PADI Open Water **dive courses** (4 days; F$695) (2-tank dive F$225) at the three resorts facing the Astrolabe: *Tiliva*, *Waisalima* and *Matava* (not to be confused with *Matana Beach Resort* in central Kadavu). It also runs daily dive excursions (2-tank dive F$225) for all but *Matava*, which operates its own fully certified dive boats.

Dwarfed by the Astrolabe, the equally impressive and diverse **Namalata Reef** off the north coast of Vunisea is used by *Matana Beach Resort* and *Papageno Resort*, which both operate their own private dive boats. Note that there are no independent dive operators for those staying in Vunisea.

SURFING

The passages at Soso and Vesi have unpredictable but sometimes massive **surfing breaks**, most easily accessible from *Matana Beach Resort* on the southeast coast. The best spot for surfing, though, is off the western tip of Kadavu. Here you can surf the gnarly left at King Kong, or, if on the rare occasion it's blown out, head around the point to Daku Beach where there are both reef breaks and a beach break for beginners.

KAYAKING

It's possible to **kayak** around Kadavu in nine days or Ono Island in seven days, camping on beaches, staying in villages or bedding down at a budget resort along the way. New Zealand outfit *Tamarillo Tropical Expeditions* (☎360 3043, ⓦtamarillo.co.nz; 7-day all-inclusive packages start from NZ$2295 per person) have well-organized itineraries and great contacts with the local villages, with guided two-person sea kayaks and support boats. It can be hard work, with a minimum of five hours of paddling in sometimes choppy seas working muscles you never knew existed, but it's a great way to experience the island's remote coastlines and villages. Less strenuous overnight packages and day-trips exploring the mangrove estuaries run on demand from the base camp at Korolevu Bay on the southeastern corner of Kadavu.

FISHING

Game fishing charters using top-of-the-range gear are available from *Matava* on the southeast coast of Kadavu. You can cast in the surrounding reefs for Giant Trevallys or trawl between 1000m and 3000m of water for marlin, tuna and sailfish. More casual hand-line fishing can also be organized from all resorts.

sandy **cove beaches** beside the picturesque village of **Naikorokoro**. Around the point, west of the village, is the enviably located *Matana Beach Resort* (see p.163), set back from the beach and screened by thick vegetation.

Heading east from *Matana*, a ten-minute walk around the rocky point leads to **One Mile Beach**, a secluded beauty with deep sand and massive coconut palms. The beach marks the start of a 10km-long **trail** along the northern coastline, passing a couple of small rocky headlands and Naivakarauniniu Village on the way, and ending up at *Papageno Resort* (see p.163) and its forests. High up in the forest there's a sweeping lookout over **Daku Bay** and, forty minutes' walk inland, a small **waterfall** with swimming pool.

PREPARING FOR A DIVE, KADAVU >

5

East Kadavu

Beyond Daku Bay lies the heavily indented coastline of **east Kadavu**, difficult to access other than by sea. Kavala Bay on the north coast and Korolevu Bay on the south coast form great basins surrounded by steep mountains. Their river estuaries are lined in **mangrove forests** and you can explore these incredibly peaceful environments by **kayak**. However, it's the underwater spectacle of the **Astrolabe Reef** that attracts most visitors here; the reef hugs the southeast side of Kadavu all the way to Galoa Harbour and extends 40km north in open sea. Divers are well catered for at East Kadavu's **dive resorts**.

Kadavu village

The village of **Kadavu** lies hidden behind mangrove estuaries and hemmed in by steep mountains. At the back of the village, a high **waterfall** has carved and hollowed a russet-coloured rocky chamber into unusual shapes with a deep swimming pool below – when visitors arrive, energetic village kids swarm in to show off their courage by jumping from the 20m-high rock faces surrounding it.

Nacomoto

From Kadavu you can hike for an hour through rainforest to **Nacomoto**, where village stays can be arranged (see opposite). If you want to see grey **reef sharks** and large schools of barracuda, jacks and emperors, Nacomoto Passage is as good a bet as anywhere in Fiji, with dive boats from *Matava* (see opposite) diving the site frequently.

Kavala Bay and Tiliva village

A strenuous full-day hike from either Kadavu Village or Nacomoto crosses over to **Kavala Bay** on the north coast, passing several waterfalls along the way. The trail continues east along the coastline to the village of **Tiliva**, where there's a small resort (see opposite). From here, a pretty **coastal trail** heads east to the only backpacker dive resort on Kadavu (see opposite).

ARRIVAL AND DEPARTURE   KADAVU

By plane Vunisea has the island's only airport, connected by flights (daily except Sun) from both Nadi (45min) and Nausori (30min), operated by Pacific Sun.

By boat The weekly cargo boat operated by Venu Shipping (☎ 339 5000; F$50 one way, F$75 for a bed in a six-berth cabin) departs from Walu Bay in Suva every Tues at 10.30pm, arriving at 6am on Wed at Vunisea, where it unloads for a few hours before heading

east to Kavala Bay for its second stop on Kadavu. The boat leaves Kavala Bay at 2pm on Wed and heads back to Suva. You could also try Western Shipping (☎ 331 4467; lounge F$50 one-way), which operates the *Cagi-Mai-Ba*, an aged cargo boat that visits Vunisea and various bays along the northeast coast, including Daku Bay (9hr), once or twice a month but to no fixed schedule.

GETTING AROUND

By resort boat Each resort has its own fleet of boats, which meet pre-booked guests at Vunisea airport or at one of Vunisea's two ferry jetties, the Old Jetty and the New Jetty just to the north.

By village boat You should be able to pick up a village boat from Vunisea – go to Galoa Bay for boats heading along the south coast, or alongside the airport for the north coast. Note that the seas can be rough, especially along the exposed south coast, and that boats do not carry life

jackets. It takes 35 minutes to reach the west point of Kadavu from Vunisea and an hour to reach the Astrolabe Reef in good weather, double if seas are rough.

By road The two winding roads on Kadavu are unsealed, making them impassable after heavy rains. There are no buses, and no rental cars available, but several minivans and trucks shuttle around Vunisea between the airstrip and jetties and can be hired for exploring further.

INFORMATION

Services Apart from at the resorts, facilities are limited: there is no tourist information, no banks or restaurants and

only a few basic shops selling mostly tinned food and kerosene. In Vunisea, heading up the hill from the north coast, you first pass the imposing hospital (☎ 362 0788) on the right-hand side. Continuing up the hill and bearing left, the post office and police station (☎ 368 1268) are on the left side of the road.

ACCOMMODATION

Note that the airport terminal building is the only place on the island to buy **takeaway food**, but only with incoming flights around lunchtime. You'll be reliant on your accommodation place for food, though you can pick up fresh fruit and veg from the market in Vunisea. **Village homestays** in Nacomoto in East Kadavu can be organized through either *Matava* (see below) or Tamarillo Expeditions (see p.160). Homestays can also be arranged at Solodamu Village in West Kadavu (☎ 362 3009); a contribution of at least F$35 per person should be given to help pay your way.

VUNISEA AND WEST KADAVU

Biana Accommodation Vunisea ☎ 368 6010. This basic cottage overlooking the old jetty has three rooms, mostly used by government workers, sharing a lounge, kitchen and cold-water bathroom. The owners cook and serve meals (F$8). The beach here is sandy, and there are good snorkelling reefs in the bay but you'll need to bring your own gear. Rate (per person) includes breakfast. F$65

CENTRAL KADAVU

Matana Beach Resort ☎ 368 3502, ⓦ matanabeachresort.com. With the Namalata Reef offshore, *Matana* is primarily a dive resort, and the owners' dive business, Dive Kadavu, is often used as the resort name. Offers ten bures with polished timber floors and large windows, in a beautiful setting. Rates include meals. F$125

★ **Papageno Resort** ☎ 603 0466, ⓦ papagenoresort.com. Set in 346 acres of serene tropical forest, this is a nature lover's paradise. Accommodation is in rooms, villas and colonial-style bures, and food is outstanding, sourced from locally grown organic ingredients. Divers have the option of either the Astrolabe or Namalata reefs and there are regular snorkelling trips to visit the manta rays at Vuro Island, plus game fishing off Nabukelevu. Rates include meals. Rooms F$392; villas F$455; bures F$515

EAST KADAVU

★ **Matava** ☎ 333 6222, ⓦ matava.com. Tucked into a small beachless bay enclosed by rocky Waya Island, *Matava* is fantastically well organized but retains a village-style atmosphere. The bures are slightly rough around the edges but with welcoming hosts and a fine blend of European and Fijian cuisine, it's excellent value for money. Apart from its own dive operation, *Matava* has some of the finest snorkelling in Fiji just ten minutes away by boat at Vesi Passage, with soft coral gardens and thousands of exotic reef fish. Rates include all meals and snorkel gear. F$325

Tiliva Beach Resort ☎ 333 7127, ⓦ tilivaresortfiji.com. A tiny and unassuming Fijian-owned retreat with just six bures and a small dive operation. The village visits are a highlight, and you can also surf, kayak, fish and take guided hikes. Rates include meals. F$535

Waisalima Dive Resort ☎ 603 0486, ⓦ waisalima.com. Accommodation is in thatched bures, either with shared facilities or en suite. The resort is located just 5min from Naiqoro Passage, which has the most varied scuba diving reef along the Astrolabe, with brilliant corals and swift drift dives, and you can also hike, kayak and fish here. Rates include meals. F$460

Ono Island and around

Off the northeastern tip of Kadavu and surrounded by the Astrolabe Reef is **Ono Island**, home to two small villages and several beautiful beaches. Surrounding Ono Island are a dozen smaller islands including **Vuro**, where **manta rays** congregate.

ACCOMMODATION

Koro Makawa Resort ☎ 603 0782, ⓦ koromakawa.com.fj. This private upmarket retreat offers a spectacular two-bedroom thatched cottage perched on a small hill with fabulous views overlooking the ocean. Hearty home-cooked meals are included, and there's a fully certified PADI dive operation on site. Children cost an extra US$80. All-inclusive packages (per couple) US$500

★ **Mai Dive Astrolabe** ☎ 603 0842, ⓦ maidive.com. An Aussie-Fijian option that's a great choice for dive fanatics, who may want to opt for the week-long package.

ONO ISLAND

Accommodation is in inviting bungalows with lots of timber, verandas and hammocks. The food is excellent, especially given the remote location. Four-night minimum stay. Rates include meals. F$270

★ **Oneta Resort** ☎ 603 0778, ⓦ onetaresort.com. This resort enjoys a wonderful beachside location, where you can lounge in a hammock or wander the tropical garden around your bure. The food – and the nearby fishing – is sensational. Rates include meals. Dorms F$280; bures F$470

Lomaiviti and Lau

BAY OF ISLANDS

Lomaiviti and Lau

A world away from the beach resorts of the Mamanucas and Yasawa Islands, the historically fascinating Lomaiviti and Lau groups radiate from the east coast of Viti Levu, eventually dissipating before a massively deep ocean trench separating Fiji from Tonga. Those who visit these enchanting islands step into the Fiji of old, where islanders fish the lagoons as a matter of necessity and travel the open seas in small boats.

6

As a tourist destination, the inner islands of the **Lomaiviti Group** are relatively developed, particularly Ovalau, home to Fiji's charming former capital, **Levuka**. In comparison, the Outer Lomaiviti and the entire expanse of the **Lau Group** offer few facilities but will captivate the minds of the most curious of travellers. The area has a rich **Tongan heritage** and is popular with visiting yachts drawn to its spectacular limestone islands and bays. With over sixty islands to visit across a wide expanse of ocean, virtually no accommodation and limited transport, time and patience are the main requisites for successfully exploring this region.

Brief history

The Lomaiviti and Lau islands played a key role in the struggle for supremacy over the Fijian archipelago. By the mid-nineteenth century the ruthless **Ratu Seru Cakobau**, high chief of Bau, had brought much of Fiji under his control. However, the Tongans held a long association with the Lau Group, which in most parts are closer to their islands than Viti Levu. In 1848, **Enele Ma'afu**, a Tongan prince, was sent to Lakeba in Lau under the guise of protecting the missionaries established there. By supporting Cakobau's enemies and plying his own brand of fierce warfare, Ma'afu soon began to dominate the region, even gaining control of Vanua Levu and Taveuni. By the 1870s, Cakobau concluded that Ma'afu had the upper hand. Fearful of a direct confrontation he decided to cede Fiji to Britain, which he believed would halt the Tongan's conquest. The British were reluctant to accept Cakobau's terms as he didn't represent the united people of Fiji. So, in 1871, Cakobau rallied a few white settlers in Levuka, and, with the backing of his allied chiefs, announced himself **King of Fiji**. After much debate and tension, **cession to Britain** was completed on October 10, 1874 and **Levuka** became the administrative capital of the new colony. Ma'afu, his aspirations of control of Fiji halted, reluctantly accepted administration over the Lau Group.

Lomaiviti Group

The sixteen islands of the **Lomaiviti Group** form a neat triangular cluster in the heart of the Fijian archipelago, 20km east of Viti Levu and 50km south of Vanua Levu. In the nineteenth century the island of **OVALAU** became the centre of European trade, with whalers and merchants setting up camp beside the village of **Levuka**, eventually to

Activities around Levuka p.172
Cakobau and the Lovoni tribe p.175
Diving around Makogai and Wakaya p.177

Cargo boats p.180
Lau crafts p.183

LEVUKA

Highlights

❶ Historic Levuka Soak up the colonial atmosphere of Fiji's hugely welcoming old capital, with its colourful Wild West-style facades. **See p.169**

❷ Bobo's Farm Eco retreat on Ovalau with an organic farm, waterfalls and fantastic hiking. Food is a particular highlight here. **See p.175**

❸ Lovoni Hike your way up to the historic village of Lovoni, dramatically sited in a volcanic crater and once home to a famously fierce hill tribe. **See p.175**

❹ Caqalai Island Snorkel amongst reef sharks and take it easy at this tiny backpackers' resort. **See p.176**

❺ Journey by cargo boat Intrepid travellers should take a trip into the past aboard a cargo boat, mingling with locals and exploring the tiny remote islands of the Lau Group. **See p.180**

❻ Bay of Islands Marvel at the unusual limestone formations and explore caves and hiking tracks at these remote islands off Vanua Balavu. **See p.181**

HIGHLIGHTS ARE MARKED ON THE MAPS ON P.168 & P.169

become Fiji's first capital. Levuka remains the region's main tourist draw, yet visitor numbers are blissfully insignificant. Surrounding Ovalau, a handful of **small islands** lie within a 15km radius, entwined within stunning coral reefs and boasting secluded white sandy beaches and **hillforts**: **Naigani** is home to a small resort and several large hillforts, while a handful of beautiful small islands with **backpacker resorts** lie off the south coast. Further east, the **Outer Lomaiviti** consist of half a dozen high volcanic islands with virtually no tourist infrastructure.

6

Ovalau

From a distance, **OVALAU** resembles a giant meringue with its top bitten off. The missing top of the island is, in fact, a blown-out crater, 400m deep with three lakes and the proud village of **Lovoni** lying at the bottom. Just under eight thousand people live on the island, over half of them based in and around the characterful seaside town of **Levuka**, basking in its new UNESCO World Heritage status, and hemmed in by sheer rainforest-covered mountains midway along the east coast. The drier coastline of **North Ovalau** has rolling grassy hills, and a beautiful beach at Arovudi, while forested **South Ovalau** has few specific attractions, although you are likely to pass through to access the island's airstrip and the road to Lovoni.

ARRIVAL AND DEPARTURE   OVALAU

BY PLANE
The small airstrip at Bureta on the southwest side of Ovalau is used only by Northern Air Services (☎ 347 5005, ⌨ northernair.com.fj) for flights from Nausori (12min). A minibus meets all incoming flights and shuttles passengers to Levuka for F$10. When departing Levuka for the airport,

request the minibus service at your hotel.

BY FERRY
From Natovi Landing Patterson Brothers (☎ 331 6544) have regular departures (daily, though not always on Sun, around 3.30pm; 4hr; F$35 one way) from Natovi Landing, a rather isolated spot midway up the east coast of Viti Levu,

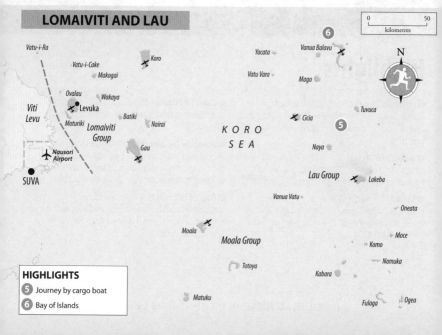

LOMAIVITI AND LAU

0 — 50 kilometres

Vatu-i-Ra

Vatu-i-Cake

Koro

Makogai

Ovalau · Wakaya

Viti Levu

Levuka

Moturiki · Batiki

Lomaiviti Group

Nairai

Gau

Nausori Airport

SUVA

Yacata

Vanua Balavu **6**

Vatu Vara

Mago

Cicia

Tuvuca

K O R O
S E A

Naya **5**

Lau Group

Lakeba

Vanua Vatu

Oneata

Moala

Moala Group

Moce

Komo

Namuka

Totoya

Kabara

Matuku

Fulaga · Ogea

HIGHLIGHTS
5 Journey by cargo boat
6 Bay of Islands

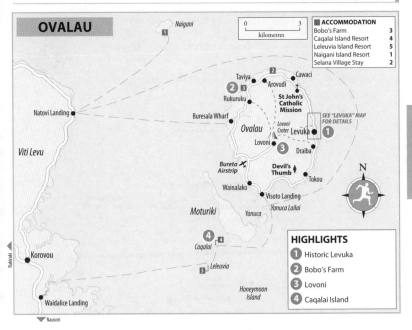

to Buresala on the west coast of Ovalau, from where there is a connecting bus into Levuka; the ferry returns to Natovi at 5am the following morning. A Patterson Brothers bus runs to Natovi Landing from Bay 6 at the Suva bus stand at 1.30pm (F$10).

From Suva Venu Shipping (☎ 339 5000) has twice-weekly departures from Walu Bay in Suva direct to Levuka (6hr; F$20 passenger one-way, F$171 car plus

driver one-way), although there is no fixed timetable (phone for details).

From Caqalai or Leleuvia If you're heading from Viti Levu direct to the small backpacker resorts on Caqalai or Leleuvia (see p.176), onward small boat passage from either island to Levuka costs around F$35 and takes 40min. The boat journey can be done in either direction, making a round trip a popular option with budget travellers.

GETTING AROUND

By bus The only public bus on Ovalau is the school service, which runs from Bureta at 6am (daily except Sun; F$2) to St John's Catholic Mission via Levuka, returning along the same route around 3pm.

By taxi, carrier van or 4WD To explore further, taxis and carrier vans have a base beside the seawall opposite the Church of the Sacred Heart in Levuka.

Levuka

Once a wild whaling outpost, diminutive **LEVUKA** is now a charming seaside town. Its laid-back atmosphere is epitomized by its weathered yet colourful clapboard buildings, most of which now function as Chinese or Indian-run **stores**, so packed full of goods and groceries it's difficult to poke around without bumping into someone. Outside, the pillared pavement is where the town's residents meet for a gossip. The town has a rich Fijian and colonial heritage and the best way to learn about it is by walking and talking with the genuinely hospitable locals, either on a guided walking tour (see box, p.172) or on a home visit arranged through the museum at the Morris Hedstrom building on Beach Street (see p.171).

The main thoroughfare of Levuka town, misleadingly named **Beach Street**, passes between the rocky seawall and the town's most historic buildings. It's a simple tar-sealed track where dogs roam and people wander back and forth unconcerned about the occasional carrier van that trundles along.

6

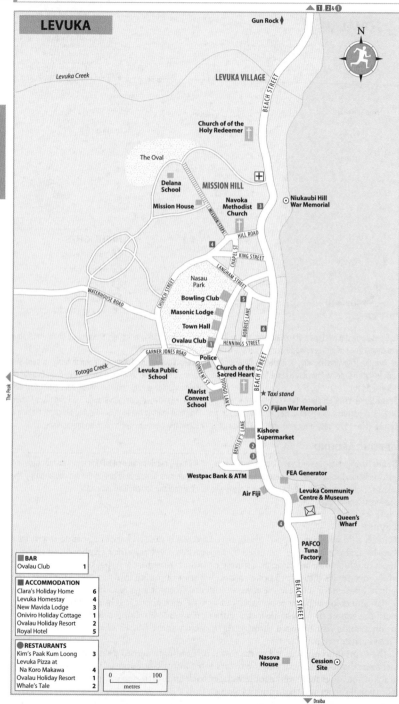

Brief history

With a protected harbour and a welcoming chief, Levuka Village hosted a small band of British and American **whalers** during the 1830s. In return for shelter, the whalers gave gifts of muskets which the villagers used to fend off the fierce hill people from Lovoni in the centre of the island. Soon to follow the whalers were a motley crew of fugitives, blackbirders and beachcombers, with zealous Victorian **missionaries** hot on their heels. In the 1860s, following speculation that Fiji would soon become a British colony, Levuka grew rapidly, with traders arriving from New Zealand and Australia. By 1871, when the great warrior Cakobau declared Levuka the **capital of Fiji**, there were over two thousand European residents and 52 hotels and bars. It was joked that ships would navigate into port by following the bobbing rum bottles drifting on the tide.

Levuka's short life as a South Pacific metropolis came to an abrupt end in 1881 when the British moved the capital to Suva, which offered more land for expansion. The town suffered a second blow in 1895 when the north side was flattened by a **hurricane**. After the collapse of the copra trade which briefly occupied Levuka in the 1920s, the settlement gained a new lease of life thanks to the PAFCO **tuna cannery** set up here in 1976. During the 1980s, with the emergence of **tourism**, Levuka found itself as a curio, a relic of Fiji's colonial past. It also realized its unique status as a town of Fijian firsts: the first Methodist church, the first hotel, the first bank, school and newspaper are but a few of its proud claims. In 2013, the town's colonial architecture became protected as a UNESCO **World Heritage Site**.

The port

At the southern end of Beach Street is the large tuna cannery and **port**. There's a lovely view of the seafront from the port, although the smell from the factory and the persistent noise of whirring generators from the power station spoil the atmosphere. At the junction of Beach Street and Queens Wharf is a drinking fountain on a small island in the road; this was once the site of a pigeon loft used to send post between Levuka and Suva in less than thirty minutes.

The Morris Hedstrom building

Beach St • Museum Mon–Fri 8am–1pm & 2–4.30pm, Sat 8am–1pm • F$2 • ☎ 344 0356

Beach Street is dominated by the **Morris Hedstrom building**, standing proudly at the southern end of town a hundred metres north of the power station. Opened in 1868 as a grocery store, Morris Hedstrom built up a trading empire which thrived during the colonial era, finding its way to every corner of the archipelago. You'll still find Morris Hedstrom supermarkets in most Fijian towns but this original store was dedicated to the National Trust in 1980 and today houses the **Levuka Community Centre**, as well as a tiny **museum**. The latter houses a rather sad collection of chemist's bottles, clay pipes and shells – a printing press and photographic equipment being the only tangible relics of the colonial era. There is a useful library, though, and the museum's curators are hugely knowledgeable about Levuka's history. They can also help arrange **home visits** to local residents.

Church of the Sacred Heart

Midway along Beach Street is the **Church of the Sacred Heart**. This picturesque Catholic church with a domed roof was built in two stages: the main section for worship was crafted from local timber in 1858 with the arrival of the first Catholic missionaries, while the imposing **clock tower** was erected forty years later, using thick limestone blocks baked from coral. The blue light on top of the tower acts as a beacon for ships together with another on top of the hill. The church is worth a peek inside for its gruesome yet humbling series of fourteen **paintings** depicting Christ's crucifixion.

North of the church, beyond Hennings Street, are the newer and less intriguing quarters of Levuka, rebuilt after the devastating hurricane in 1895.

6

ACTIVITIES AROUND LEVUKA

There are a couple of worthwhile **hikes** around Levuka, including **The Peak trail**, an arduous two-hour hike through forest culminating in a panorama of the eastern coastline from the large hill which rears up behind Levuka. Hikes are available with the affable Nox, who is best contacted through *Levuka Homestay* (☎ 344 0777; The Peak F$25; plantation walk including information on local medicine and a swim in a natural pool F$20).

The Levuka Community Centre (Mon–Fri 8am–1pm & 2–4.30pm, Sat 8am–1pm; ☎ 344 0356) organizes ninety-minute **walking tours** (from F$10) on demand. A more impromptu walking tour is offered by Nox (book via *Levuka Homestay* on ☎ 344 0777; from F$10), who will guide you round the less-explored parts of town.

The nearest **diving** operators are *Leleuvia Island Resort* (see p.176) and *Naigani Island Resort* (see p.176). Otherwise, there's excellent **snorkelling** off Caqalai Island, which can be visited as a day-trip from your resort.

Nasau Park and around

Inland from Beach Street along Hennings Street are the playing fields of **Nasau Park**, once the venue of King Cakobau's headquarters on his visits to Levuka. Before you reach the park, a small bridge crosses Totoga Creek. Tucked away behind a delightful white picket fence and abutting the creek is the **Ovalau Club**, built in 1904 and now Fiji's oldest social club. Next door is the double-storey **Town Hall**, built in 1898 to commemorate the silver jubilee of Queen Victoria. The neighbouring burnt-out Neoclassical building is the old **Masonic Hall**, desecrated in 2000 by a mob of two hundred villagers from Lovoni. During the spiralling events of the Speight Coup, Lovoni's firebrand Methodist priest told his congregation that the hall was a centre for devil worship. It was also rumoured that secret tunnels under Nasau Park connected it to the *Royal Hotel*, Nasova House and, bizarrely, the Grand Lodge of the Masonic Order in Scotland. The culprits were later pardoned in court for their naivety. The tunnels turned out to be drainage outlets to the sea.

Continuing on past the Bowling Club leads to the back of the colonial-era *Royal Hotel*, a pleasant spot for afternoon tea; to reach the hotel entrance turn right at the intersection of Langham Street. Otherwise, continue north to the quaint maroon-and-white **Navoka Methodist Church**, founded in 1862. The church conducts its services (Sun 10.15am & 4pm) solely in English to encourage Fijian and European communal worship.

Mission Hill

From Navoka Methodist Church, 199 steps lead up to the summit of **Mission Hill**, named after Fiji's first mission school, built here in 1852 by the Reverend John Binner. From the top a path continues to **Mission House**, where Cakobau was proclaimed King of Fiji in 1871. Beyond is the flat hilltop known as the **Oval**, where colonial residents gathered on Saturdays for a spot of horse racing. There's a fabulous unobstructed **view** from here overlooking the old quarters of Levuka and out towards the offshore islands of Makogai, Batiki and Wakaya. Keep an eye out for **pilot whales**, which are present year-round in the Koro Sea – if you're exceptionally lucky you may spot a humpback whale between May and October. A dirt road continues on from the top of the Mission Hill, past Delana Public School to the hospital at the northern end of Beach Street.

The back alleys

At the southern end of the Oval you'll find a small bush track that winds its way back down the hill to the alluring **back alleys** of Levuka. A confusing network of pathways and small bridges meander back and forth connecting the old wooden houses where many of Levuka's residents live. There's no obvious track to follow but as long as you keep heading downhill you'll eventually end up at Nasau Park.

Niukaubi Hill

Jutting out into the sea splitting Levuka town and Levuka Village is **Niukaubi Hill**, a small bluff where the Supreme Court and parliament were located before the capital moved to Suva. In its place now stands a **war memorial** listing all Fijian soldiers who died fighting for Britain during World War I. The adjacent bay is where the *Leonadis* docked on March 3, 1879, bringing with it Fiji's first shipload of indentured Indian labourers.

Levuka Village and Gun Rock

Three hundred metres north of Niukaubi Hill, beyond the hospital, is **Levuka** Village where the first Europeans set up camp. The small village is backed by a large exposed rockface known as **Gun Rock**, used as target practice by the cannons of HMS *Havanah* to impress and intimidate Cakobau and other chiefs. Ask around the village for a guide to accompany you on the twenty-minute hike to the top.

Nasova House and the Cession Site

The grand **Nasova House**, once the residence of the British Governor, lies at the southern end of Levuka, beyond the tuna cannery. Across the road is the ceremonial spot where King Cakobau signed the **Deed of Cession** on October 10, 1874, handing over not only sovereignty to Great Britain but also his iconic warclub. A public re-enactment of this occasion is performed every year on the same date, coinciding with the week-long festival, "Back to Levuka" (see below). A stone embedded with a plaque was laid to mark the **Cession Site** in 1935, and two further stones accompanied this – one in 1970 to commemorate Independence, and the second in 1974 to mark the centenary of the original deed. Prince Charles presided over the 1970 Independence Ceremony and used the beautiful **thatch bure** across the road as his temporary home.

ACCOMMODATION   LEVUKA

Small guesthouses make up the majority of Levuka's accommodation options. Although there are less than fifty rooms in total, the only time you will struggle to find a place to stay is during "Back to Levuka Week", the town's heritage festival (mid-Oct), when booking is essential.

Clara's Holiday Lodge Beach St ☎ 344 0013. This quaint colonial-style home with a cream-coloured picket fence is a little deceiving from the outside – this is by far the cheapest accommodation in town. The tiny rooms are a little musty, lack screens on the windows and share cold-water bathrooms. Rates include breakfast. Dorms F$20; rooms F$50

★**Levuka Homestay** Church St ☎ 344 0777, ⓦ levukahomestay.com. This delightful modern homestay ranks amongst the best in Fiji. Run by an Australian couple, it has just four a/c guest rooms staggered up the hillside, with simple furnishings and cosy bathrooms. The breakfast is an event in itself, with freshly made fruit smoothies, fruit, home-made muesli, a cooked breakfast, fresh tea or brewed coffee. Rates include breakfast. F$170

New Mavinda Lodge North Beach St ☎ 337 0995, ⓔ newmavindalodge@connect.com.fj. This mock-palatial modern building – with high ceilings complete with glittering chandeliers, and shiny ceramic floors that give off an echo as you walk – seems completely out of place in Levuka. All eleven rooms have TV and a/c, and the clinical eight-bed dorm has its own his-and-hers hot-water

en-suite bathrooms – not bad for the price. There's even a laundry service and Internet access. Rates include breakfast. Dorms F$30; rooms F$80

Oniviro Cottage Vakaviti, North Levuka ☎ 344 0166, ⓦ owlfiji.com/holidaycottage.htm. This tiny one-bedroom bungalow located just over 1km north of Levuka is the only holiday home on Ovalau and sits in a spacious landscaped garden under the looming Gun Rock cliff. The lounge-cum-kitchen is well furnished but the hot-water bathroom and toilet is accessed from outside. Weekly rate F$650

Ovalau Holiday Resort North Levuka ☎ 344 0329, ⓦ owlfiji.com/resort.htm. Although this bungalow-style resort is not the most practical base, being 5km north of Levuka town, it does boast a small sandy beach with fair snorkelling across the road, a swimming pool and a good restaurant serving tasty, well presented food. The five basic cottages sleep up to six people, making them handy for families. F$77

Royal Hotel Robbie's Lane ☎ 344 0024, ⓦ royal levuka.com. Originally constructed in the 1860s and rebuilt in 1916 after a devastating fire, the *Royal* is the oldest hotel in Fiji. The main building has plenty of colonial character, and the fifteen rooms upstairs come with slanted wooden floorboards, creaking four-poster beds and tiny bathrooms. The five modern cottages in front of the swimming pool overlooking Beach St are a lot more comfortable. The staff can appear rather aloof, but with a full-sized billiard table, Internet café, bicycles and laundry there's a lot going for this place. Rooms F$53; cottages F$94

EATING AND DRINKING

Levuka has just enough **restaurants** to keep you happy on a short visit, but with only a trickle of tourists and few residents dining out, they lack panache. **Groceries** can be bought at Kishore Supermarket (Mon–Sat 6.30am–6.30pm, Sun 7–11am), next to the *Whale's Tale* restaurant on Beach St. For **drinking**, the century-old *Ovalau Club* is your best bet; alternatively, the courtyard in front of the *Royal Hotel* is a good choice for a quiet afternoon tipple.

★**Kim's Paak Kum Loong** Beach St ☎ 344 0059. This place has a bit of everything: Chinese, Indian, European and Fijian. Meals are hearty and cheap, starting from F$8 for vegetarian stir-fry and going up to F$15 for lamb curry or fish in *lolo* sauce. There's outdoor dining on the wooden veranda with views of the waterfront, but the drone from the town's electricity generators may irritate. Mon–Sat 7am–2pm & 6–9pm, Sun 6–9pm.

Levuka Pizza at Na Koro Makawa Beach St ☎ 344 0429. Located almost opposite the tuna cannery, the speciality here is tuna pizza (F$8.50), something of an acquired taste; other popular toppings include prawn and lobster. If you don't fancy pizza, fish and chips and stir-fry are also on the menu. Daily 7am–2pm & 6–9pm.

Ovalau Club Nasau Park. Long-established social club where you can chat with the friendly regulars over a beer or play snooker on a full-sized table for twenty cents a game. Local bands sometimes play at weekends, when the club's at its liveliest; otherwise visit on a Tues for the weekly residents' get together (from 6pm). Mon–Thurs 4–10pm, Fri 2–11pm, Sat 10am–1am, Sun 10am–9pm.

Ovalau Holiday Resort North Levuka ☎ 344 0329. This resort restaurant is run by an Indian family, so the curry dishes are nicely authentic. They also offer tasty seafood including lobster and crab. It's 5km north of town, but if you call ahead they'll offer free pick-up and drop-off to your hotel. Daily noon–2pm & 6–9pm.

Whale's Tale Beach St ☎ 344 0235. A charming nautical ambience and delightful home cooking make this a top choice – they're a local legend for their fish and chips. The lunchtime burgers are also spot-on, and the set dinner at F$25 is good value. Mon–Sat noon–2pm & 6–10pm.

DIRECTORY

Banks Westpac Bank (Mon–Fri 9.30am–12.30pm & 1.30–4pm) at the southern end of Beach St has the town's only ATM machine.

Hospital Beach St, at the northern end of town (☎ 344 0164).

Police On the corner of Totoya Lane and Garner Jones Rd (open 24hr; ☎ 344 0222).

Post office On Queens Wharf Lane leading down to the port (Mon–Fri 8am–1pm & 2–4pm).

Telephones Outside the post office, in front of Kishore Supermarket on Beach St and at the *Royal Hotel*.

North Ovalau

North of Levuka, it's a pleasant 7km walk along the dirt road passing Vatukalo Village to the large Catholic mission and boarding schools of **St John's College** at **Cawaci**. On the southern boundary of the mission, sitting on a bluff overlooking the sea, is the **Bishop's Tomb**, final resting place of Bishop Julien Vidal from France, Fiji's first bishop. From the tomb there's an impressive view north along the coast towards Cawaci's centrepiece, the twin-towered **Church of St John the Baptist**, its thick whitewashed coral stone walls standing out against the green mountains.

Arovudi Village

At the northern point of Ovalau, 14km from Levuka, there's a beautiful white sandy beach alongside the village of **Arovudi**. Between the beach and the village is an impressive rock foundation where once stood a *bure kalou* or priest's temple. At the western end of the beach is a large collection of jet-black **volcanic stones** used by the women of the village to make an unusual flavouring known as *kora*: grated coconut is wrapped in banana leaves and placed under the stones, where it ferments slowly for four days, a salty flavour being added with each incoming tide. The women are also renowned for catching **sardines**, which are chased by giant trevally into awaiting nets.

ACCOMMODATION

NORTH OVALU

★**Bobo's Farm** North coast, between Taviya and Rukuruku villages ☎362 3873, ⍵bobosfarm.com. A five-hundred-acre private farm, run by energetic Bobo and his German wife Karin. It's in a beautiful spot, surrounded by rainforest; Bobo will talk passionately about the medicinal values of vines, roots and leaves. The single wooden A-frame cottage has two rooms, a shared lounge, solar power and a cold-water bathroom; delicious organic meals are served in the farmhouse. A 5min trail alongside a stream leads to an unusual black-sand beach with good swimming and snorkelling, but you'll need to bring your own snorkel gear. Bobo can also organize fishing trips, a three-hour hike to Lovoni Crater (see

below) and trips to Naigani Island (see below). The superb meals made with Bob and Karin's own organic produce cost extra: breakfast (F$12.50), lunch (F$14), dinner (F$20). The farm is accessed along a 300m track leading down to the coast; a taxi from Levuka will drop you at the turn-off for F$30. **F$74**

★**Salana Village Stay** Northeast of Arovudi Village ☎835 9260, ⍵sala_nagalu@yahoo.com. Basic but clean accommodation with shared cold-water bathrooms and Fijian-style food. There's a range of activities on offer including traditional mat weaving and a hike to a large hillfort on top of Tomuna Peak (F$30 including lunch, minimum two people). Rate includes meals. Dorms F$70

South Ovalau

The coast of **South Ovalau** is rugged and covered in thick tropical forest. Jutting out above Tokou Village is the dramatic volcanic plug nicknamed the **Devil's Thumb**. Heading up the west coast, flanked offshore by Moturiki Island, you'll find the village of **Wainalako**, founded by freed Solomon Island slaves in the middle of the nineteenth century. A few kilometres beyond Wainalako is the Bureta airstrip.

Lovoni

From the Bureta airstrip, a dirt track winds inland, following the Bureta River to **Lovoni** village, one of the island's star attractions. The village was made infamous by the fierce tribe (see box below) who lived behind an impregnable hillfort in the centre of the volcanic crater here (they've since moved to a more practical location just to the side).

The easiest way to visit is by road with Epi's Tours (☎763 7546 or 923 6011, ⍵owlfiji.com/epi.htm; F$45 includes lunch), although note that this involves a bone-crunching ride from Levuka in the back of a carrier van followed by a two-hour lecture on the history of Lovoni. A more rewarding alternative is to take a **guided hike** with Nox (see p.172) starting from Draiba village, a few kilometres south of Levuka. This is the shortest trail from the coast but it still takes a tough couple of hours through thick rainforest before you reach the dramatic setting of the crater – arrange for a carrier van to bring you back by road. You can also approach Lovoni from *Bobo's Farm* or *Salana Village Stay* (see above), although these are both full-day hikes.

Naigani Island

The history of **Naigani Island**, 10km off the northwest coast of Ovalau, is typical of the region's volatility. The islanders trace their roots back to **Verata** on Viti Levu, to which they

CAKOBAU AND THE LOVONI TRIBE

During 1870 and 1871, **Cakobau** tried time after time to subdue the fierce **Lovoni tribe** who had been constantly menacing the European settlers around Levuka. Unable to break through the ring of defences protecting the village in Lovoni Crater, Cakobau sent a Methodist missionary to Lovoni, inviting the tribe to a **reconciliation** in Levuka. Tired of being pursued by Cakobau, the Lovoni chief consulted his priest and accepted the invitation. On June 29, 1871 the entire village came down to Levuka. A meal was prepared, but as soon as the tribe set down their weapons to eat, Cakobau's warriors surrounded and subdued them. In time the majority were sold off as **slaves** and dispersed throughout every corner of the archipelago. Those that remain are a stoutly proud group, believing their village to be the only one in Fiji not to have been conquered by Cakobau.

remain politically aligned. Verata was one of the two traditional enemies of Bau, so when the island was invaded by Cakobau in 1860 a thousand of the islanders were killed and carried off to Bau to be eaten – only two people were left alive. A few years later, an Australian named **Riley** was given a portion of the island as a dowry, having married the daughter of a Verata chief. Today, Naigani has a population of around fifty, descendants of the two surviving islanders and Riley's offspring. They live in a village on the north coast, lodged between two volcanic peaks. The **original village** is found on the northernmost peak, protected by a rim with a killing stone at its entrance. A large **hillfort** higher up was used for additional security at times of war. Large amounts of Lapita pottery have been discovered around the island dating back more than two thousand years.

ARRIVAL AND DEPARTURE   NAIGANI ISLAND

By boat You can visit Naigani by boat on a day-trip from Ovalau, from either *Bobo's Farm* or *Salana Village Stay* (see p.175), but the most practical way to visit is to stay at the island's resort, which arranges guest transfers from Natovi Landing on Viti Levu or Taviya Village on Ovalau, both around a 30min journey.

ACCOMMODATION

Naigani Island Resort ☎ 603 0613, ⓦ naiganiisland .com. This intimate resort is built around Riley's old plantation house on the south coast. Popular with both families and scuba divers, it offers eighteen two-bedroom plantation-style cottages, a swimming pool with water slide, three-hole golf course, good snorkelling off the beach and certified PADI scuba diving. **F$220**

Caqalai and Leleuvia

Two small islands along Ovalau's south coast, **Caqalai** and **Leleuvia**, possess beach resorts and are becoming popular with **backpackers** keen to avoid the increasingly commercial Yasawa Islands trail. The nicest is **Caqalai Island**, where at low tide you can wade out to nearby **Snake Island**, which offers good **snorkelling** and the chance to spot black-and-white **sea snakes**. Although they are extremely venomous, the snakes are so timid and agile that you will have little chance of getting near them. Even better snorkelling is available at **Honeymoon Island**, a sand spit 5km to the east where you'll likely spot small reef sharks hiding amongst the coral.

ARRIVAL AND DEPARTURE   CAQALAI AND LELEUVIA

By resort transfer Both resorts arrange guest transfers from Viti Levu (at Waidalice Landing north of Nausori) or from Levuka port. Costs from Waidalice are F$40 per person one-way, with a minimum of two people. You can reach Waidalice by taxi from Suva (F$55) or by bus/minivan via Nausori (F$7). From Levuka, the 40min boat journey costs F$35 to Caqalai or Leleuvia.

ACCOMMODATION

★**Caqalai Island Resort** ☎ 343 0366, ⓦ owlfiji.com /caqalai.htm. This appealing resort is run by the Methodist Church of nearby Moturiki Island. The twenty bures are beautifully thatched and hidden amongst palm trees on the edge of the beachfront, and the bathrooms, painted in colourful murals, have cold-water showers and flush toilets. The only drawback is that no alcohol is sold on the island, but it's fine to bring your own. Rates include meals. Camping (with hired tent) **F$55**; dorms **F$65**; bures **F$150**

★**Leleuvia Island Resort** ☎ 368 0721, ⓦ leleuvia .com. Caqalai's close rival, 2km to the south, is slightly larger and has an equally stunning beach setting. Choose from traditional thatched bures or the male and female dorms. The sand-floor restaurant is well positioned overlooking the beach and there's fantastic snorkelling, paddleboarding and kayaking. Sat night is lovo night. Rates include meals. Dorms **F$35**; bures **F$160**

Outer Lomaiviti

Few travellers reach the six islands of **Outer Lomaiviti** other than to scuba dive the exceptional coral reefs around **Makogai** and **Wakaya**, accessible from live-aboard dive boats (see box below). Rising out of the Koro Sea some 50km east of Ovalau are the large volcanic islands of **Koro** and **Gau**, the fifth and sixth largest landmasses in Fiji respectively. Both are blessed with rich agricultural land and large indigenous populations, but they are difficult to get to, even harder to explore and seldom visited by foreigners except on organized working holidays.

Makogai and Wakaya

In 1911, the small hilly island of **Makogai** became a **leper colony** for sufferers of the disease from throughout the South Pacific. Under the care of Mother Mary Agnes, a community was built consisting of a large hospital, cinema, shops and a church, as well as a cemetery where 1241 leprosy sufferers now rest in peace. The colony closed in 1969, twenty years after an effective treatment for the disease was found. In 1986, Makogai was declared a **marine reserve** and is now run by the Ministry of Fisheries as a research centre, with a large hatchery breeding giant clams, trochus and sea turtles. To the south of Makogai lies the upmarket private island resort of **Wakaya**.

6

ACCOMMODATION   WAKAYA

Wakaya Club Resort ☎344 8128, ⓦwakaya.com. You'll need to cough up a pretty vast sum to stay at this fabulously opulent resort, with just ten luxurious bures. The resort has its own small aircraft flying in guests from Nadi and Nausori airports (transfers US$960 per couple). Packages include meals, alcohol and scuba diving. **US$1900**

Koro

The triangular-shaped island of **Koro** lies 70km northeast of Ovalau and less than 50km south of Vanua Levu. Rising to a peak of 560m, this volcanic island has splendid views from its inland road, with bush tracks, **waterfalls** set among tropical forests and herds of wild horses in the grassy inland plains. The largest village is Nasau, midway along the east coast about 5km north of the airstrip, home to a hospital, post office and government headquarters. The women of Koro are renowned for their finely woven **handicrafts**, particularly mats and fans.

ARRIVAL AND DEPARTURE   KORO

By plane Northern Air Services (☎347 5005, ⓦnorthernair .com.fj) fly to Koro from Nausori every Sat (F$190 one-way). **By boat** Consort Shipping (☎331 3266; F$50 one-way) departs Walu Bay in Suva at 6pm on Mon and Fri, calling in at Muanivau Landing on the south point of Koro around 2am before heading off to Savusavu on Vanua Levu.

ACCOMMODATION

Dere Bay Resort ☎331 1075, ⓦderebayresort.com. Located on Dere Bay on the northwest coast, Dere Bay Resort primarily sells private beachside real estate to wealthy investors. There are three bures though (each sleeping four) and you have access to the restaurant, bar and pool. **F$200**

Koro Beach Resort ☎368 3301. These six simply furnished bures adjacent to *Dere Bay Resort* have en-suite hot-water bathrooms facing a narrow beach, and a casual beachfront restaurant. Bure rates include meals. Camping (with own tent) **F$20**; bures **F$150**

Gau

The substantial 140-square-kilometre island of **Gau** lies 60km south of Koro and is characterized by dense rainforest on its high ridges, grasslands in the lower hills, sandy

---

DIVING AROUND MAKOGAI AND WAKAYA

The figure-of-eight coral **reef** that wraps around Makogai and Wakaya offers phenomenal scuba diving. Live-aboards diving the reef include *Fiji Aggressor* (7-day package from US$2995; ⓦaggressor.com) and the slightly more intimate *Nai'a* (10-day package US$4914; ☎345 0382, ⓦnaia.com.fj). The exclusive *Wakaya Club Resort* (see above) also offers scuba diving.

beaches along the south coast and mangroves in the north. There is **no accommodation** but you can visit with the UK-based organization, Frontier (⊚frontier.ac.uk; minimum four weeks £895), either working as a volunteer school teacher and staying in one of the eighteen local villages around the coast, or conducting research on the Reef Conservation Programme. The largest village is Qarani, home to internationally acclaimed rugby superstar **Waisale Serevi**. Qarani has the safest anchorage for yachts and the island's only doctor. The disused road around Gau has long been overgrown so travel between villages is by small boat or bush track. The village of **Nawaikama** on the west coast beside the island's jetty has a hot-water stream, fed by a **thermal spring** in the hills, where the village kids bathe.

Lau Group

Like the flick of a paint brush, sixty tiny dots in a canvas of deep blue make up the **LAU GROUP**, a widely dispersed collection of islands forming the distant eastern border of Fiji. Only half the islands are inhabited and the people who live here are almost completely reliant on the reef-strewn sea that surrounds them. Cargo boats from Suva bring in essential supplies and connect the islands with the outside world. Otherwise, they remain untouched, **undeveloped** and seldom visited by outsiders. For those that do venture here, a warm welcome awaits as well as the chance to sample a unique **culture** – a mixture of Polynesian **Tonga** and Melanesian Fiji.

The Lau Group can be split into three regions: Moala, Northern Lau and Southern Lau. The three high volcanic islands of the **Moala Group** lie to the south of Lomaiviti and are the closest to Viti Levu and the least influenced by Tongan culture. **Northern Lau** is the region most appealing to tourists, thanks to the historic island of Vanua Balavu which has access to the spectacular Bay of Islands. **Southern Lau** is the most isolated part of the group, in places closer to Tonga than Suva. These islands hold the region's seat of power at the traditional village of Tubou on Lakeba.

If you're coming to the Lau Group, bring plenty of cash – there are no banks, only a handful of small village stores and food and fuel costs are inflated due to their isolation.

Brief history

Before **Captain James Cook** chartered the island of Vatoa in Southern Lau in 1774, the Lau Group was a little-known group of remote islands where Tongans and Fijians traded, occasionally fought and often intermarried. The Tongans came for the giant *vesi* trees that flourished around the islands of Fulaga and Lakeba. These were hollowed out to make large double-hulled canoes used for exploration, trade and war around the Tongan empire. In 1800, the *Argo*, one of the first Western merchant ships to enter Fijian waters, was **shipwrecked** on the Bukatatanoa Reef east of Lakeba. Its survivors were rescued in canoes by people from Lakeba and became the first white people to live amongst Fijians. Items from the ship including ceramic plate and buttons moved briskly around the islands, providing much curiosity. Sadly the ship also brought with it a strain of **cholera** which caused many deaths throughout the group.

In 1835, two Wesleyan Methodist **missionaries**, the Rev William Cross from England and Rev David Cargill from Scotland, landed at Tubou on Lakeba, becoming the first missionaries to arrive in Fiji. The pair had already worked in Tonga for several years and were accompanied by several envoys of the **Taufa'ahau**, the Christian King of Tonga. During the great **wars** of the 1840s between Bau and Rewa, fierce Tongan warriors fought for both sides in different parts of the islands. By 1848, their reputation had begun to embarrass Taufa'ahau, so he sent the headstrong **Prince Ma'afu** to Lakeba to control his people. Ma'afu excelled at his task and soon began to dominate the Lau Group. He moved his seat of power to Lakeba and by 1869 had declared himself *Tui Lau* or "**King of Lau**". With the islands pacified and a Christian ruler in place, European planters moved in,

6

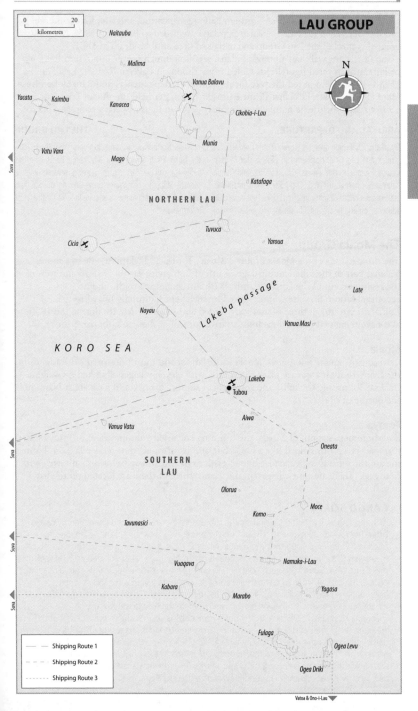

LAU GROUP

0   20
kilometres

N

Naitauba

Malima

Vanua Balavu

Yacata   *Kaimbu*

Kanacea

Cikobia-i-Lau

Vatu Vara

Mago   *Munia*

Katafaga

NORTHERN LAU

Tuvuca

Cicia   *Yaroua*

Late

Nayau   *Lakeba passage*

Vanua Masi

KORO SEA

Lakeba

Tubou

Aiwa

Vanua Vatu

Oneata

SOUTHERN LAU

Olorua

Moce

Komo

Tavunasici

Namuka-i-Lau

Vuaqava

Kabara   *Yagasa*

Marabo

Fulaga   *Ogea Levu*

Ogea Driki

Vatoa & Ono-i-Lau ▼

Suva ◄

— Shipping Route 1
-- Shipping Route 2
··· Shipping Route 3

purchasing the fertile islands of Northern Lau to grow cotton, and later for coconut oil production. When the entire Fijian archipelago was ceded to Britain in 1874, Ma'afu was granted control of the Lau Group and remained here until his death in 1881.

Today, Lauans walk tall amongst Fijians, retaining much power in political life. Two of Fiji's most revered figureheads hailed from Tubou on Lakeba: Ratu Sir Lala Sukuna (1888–1958), who paved the way for the nation's independence; and **Ratu Sir Kamisese Mara** (1920–2004), Fiji's first Prime Minister. The latter held the title of President from 1993 to 2000 before being unceremoniously deposed by the Speight coup (see p.226).

6

ARRIVAL AND DEPARTURE
THE LAU GROUP

By plane Pacific Sun operates weekly flights from Nausori Airport direct to Cicia, Northern Lau (Thurs; 1hr; F$263); Lakeba, Southern Lau (Thurs; 1hr; F$275); and Vanua Balavu, Northern Lau (Wed; 1hr; F$275), but no flights between the islands. Flights are often booked out months in advance, especially around Christmas and other school holidays. Northern Airways flies to Moala (Wed; 1hr; F$100).

By boat From Suva's Walu Bay, cargo boats (see box below) travel various routes, leaving several times a month. Shipping companies come and go quickly, and routes change frequently, so enquire in Suva for the latest information.

The Moala Group

The three islands of the **Moala Group** – Moala, Totoya and Matuku – lie in a rather isolated part of the Fijian archipelago, south of Lomaiviti, east of Kadavu and west of the main portion of the Lauan islands. With infrequent sea traffic and no accommodation, they are seldom visited by travellers. Culturally linked to the Lomaiviti Group, all three islands were raided and seized by Ma'afu during the 1850s and have remained under the administrative control of the Lau Group ever since.

Moala

Covering 66 square kilometres, **Moala** is the largest and most populated of all islands in the Lau Group. It's an easy place to explore, with eleven villages all linked by walking tracks crisscrossing the hills. The government station, airstrip and jetty are at Naroi on the northeast tip.

Totoya

Forty kilometres south of Moala, the stunning collapsed volcanic crater of **Totoya** has formed a steep rim shaped like a horseshoe and is surrounded by a deep lagoon. From the air, the setting is spectacular but access into the horseshoe bay is difficult even with calm seas. There are four villages on the island; three of these are located on the bay.

CARGO BOATS

An intriguing way to visit the islands of the Lau Group is to travel around the region by **cargo boat**. The round-trip journey from Suva on all routes takes between six and seven days, offering a wonderful opportunity to mingle with the locals and to get a feel for the vastness of the region. Although there is no fixed schedule, there's usually at least one departure a week to the islands from **Suva**, with each boat visiting between three and eight islands before heading back to the capital. Three to six hours are spent at each port, giving you enough time to disembark and have a quick look around. It may be tempting to linger on an island a little longer but bear in mind it may be several weeks before the next boat turns up.

Conditions on board are basic. A few boats have **cabins**, each with five bunk beds, but these are often stuffy, stink of diesel fumes and come crammed with luggage. Instead you'll probably be sleeping under the stars on the open deck. It's wise to take at least a pillow for resting your head on and preferably a mat to spread out on. Note that meals provided on board are basic and it's worth bringing plenty of drinks and snacks. Toilet paper is another necessity – and be prepared for the sometimes vile conditions of a cargo boat bathroom.

Matuku

Matuku, the southernmost of the islands, is slightly smaller than Moala. Graced with lush tropical forests rising to a peak of 388m, the rich volcanic soil on its slopes is ideal for farming and some of the finest *dalo* is grown here. Three of the island's four villages sit alongside one of several long, white sand beaches which flank the south side of the island – you'll usually find the village women here engaged in basket weaving using spiky *voi voi* leaves (*Pandanus Thurstoni*).

Northern Lau

For an off-beat adventure, exploring **Northern Lau** is an unforgettable experience. The most appealing of all the Lauan destinations, **Vanua Balavu**, lies in the heart of the region, surrounded by the dramatic, uplifted limestone islands of the **Bay of Islands** – a popular yachting destination. If you plan carefully, you get to Vanua Balavu by plane, spend a few days exploring and then catch the **cargo boat** back to Suva via other Lauan islands. Be warned, though, that boat schedules and sometimes even flights may change last-minute or become delayed due to bad weather and both are overbooked during Christmas holidays.

Vanua Balavu

On a map, the long, thin curving island of **Vanua Balavu** looks uncannily like a sea horse with Masomo Bay as its eye and the small islets of Malata and Susui forming its hooked tail. Vanua Balavu is the second most populated island of the Lau Group, with 1800 people in fourteen coastal villages, farming copra or gathering bêche-de-mer from the lagoons as an income. In 1855, the Tongan prince Ma'afu invaded Vanua Balavu, the first of his Fijian conquests, and based his court in the village of **Lomaloma**, now the main village on the island. The island remains heavily influenced by **Tongan customs**, with the local dialect formed mostly of Tongan words and bures following the rounded Tongan style of architecture.

On foot you can **hike** the 5km from Lomaloma to the southern tip of the island, passing the cliffs flanking Nakama Village. Ask around for a guide to show you the **hot springs** and burial caves in the hills. It's possible to wade across a sand spit from the southern tip of Vanua Balavu to explore Malata island. Hugging Malata's southeast tip is **Susui Island**, a favourite local picnic spot, with an inland lake where turtles can be spotted; the protected Raviravi Lagoon is off its northern shore.

The **northern half** of Vanua Balavu, beyond the grass airstrip, is rocky with sharp limestone pinnacles along the coast and mostly inaccessible. The coastal road ends at Mavana Village, where the deposed prime minister Laisania Qarase comes from.

The Bay of Islands

Off the northwestern tip of Vanua Balavu is the pretty **Bay of Islands**, known locally as Qilaqila, a collection of deep indented bays, islands and islets, secluded beaches and limestone cave, with excellent snorkelling

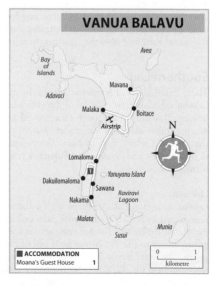

VANUA BALAVU

Bay of Islands

Avea

Mavana

Adavaci

Malaka • • Boitace

Airstrip

N

Lomaloma

Yanuyanu Island

Dakuilomaloma

Sawana

Raviravi Lagoon

Nakama

Malata

Munia

Susui

■ ACCOMMODATION
Moana's Guest House 1

0   1
kilometre

6

available in its brilliant turquoise lagoon. The bay makes an exceptional anchorage for visiting **yachts** between May and October (for permission to anchor, contact the government station in Lomaloma on VHF channel 16). The islands themselves are mostly impenetrable – difficult to approach by boat and covered in a tangled mass of shrubs and ironwood trees. However, there are a couple of walking tracks worth exploring, as well as easy access to **Vale ni Bose**, "the Meeting Place of the Gods". This huge cathedral cave, over 40m high, is full of stalactites and has several windows letting in dashes of light – note that at high tide you'll be wading chest-high in water.

ACCOMMODATION	VANUA BALAVU

Moana's Guest House A 15min walk south of Lomaloma ☎ 889 5006, ⓦ moanasguesthouses.com. The only official accommodation on Vanua Balavu offers two simple beachside bures with mosquito nets, shared toilet, cold-water shower and solar power. You'll be well fed with local vegetables and fish, although note there are also several small stores in Lomaloma Village where you can buy snacks. *Moana's* can organize village visits, hiking trips and boat trips to both Raviravi Lagoon and the Bay of Islands (bring snorkelling gear); a vehicle for sightseeing costs F$50 for half a day. Rates (per person) include meals. **F$95**

Vatu Vara and the private islands

To explore the Northern Lau islands **beyond Vanua Balavu**, you could try hitching a ride on one of the yachts anchored in the Bay of Islands. Alternatively, with some persuasion and around F$400 in cash, you could ask a boatman from Lomaloma Village to take you on a day-trip. One of the most dramatic islands to visit is forest-covered **Vatu Vara**. Its 305m plateau is the highest point in the Lau Group and can be seen from Vanua Balavu, 60km to the east. Up close, the limestone cliffs of the plateau cascade down to a coral terrace with rich farming land and palm-fringed beaches. It's rumoured that a treasure chest of gold coins was buried on the island by Joe Thompson, an American eccentric who lived and died here in the late 1800s.

Several islands in Northern Lau have been bought as **private islands** by foreign millionaires: **Mago**, less than 20km off the south tip of Vanua Balavu, was acquired by Hollywood star Mel Gibson in 2005 for US$15 million. Fifty kilometres west of Vanua Balavu are the twin islands of **Yacata** and **Kaimbu**, owned by Japanese investors. Kaimbu was once home to the most expensive resort in Fiji but it closed down shortly after the 2000 coup. Thirty kilometres northwest of Vanua Balavu, and a mere 60km from Taveuni (see Chapter 7) is **Naitauba**, once the island hideaway of 1970s actor Raymond Burr and now the "spiritual hermitage" of the Adi Dam religious cult.

Southern Lau

The diffuse islands of **Southern Lau** are the most remote in Fiji. The main island, **Lakeba**, administrative capital of the entire Lau Group, lies in its northern sphere, leaving all islands to the south far removed from shipping and air services. The southernmost islands of Vatoa and Ono-i-Lau lie 200km south of Lakeba, a journey that can take several days by boat. The two most intriguing islands to visit are Lakeba, rich in history and culture, and **Fulaga**, a rugged coral atoll with unusual limestone formations.

Lakeba

Lakeba, almost circular in shape with a diameter of 8km, has the region's only **airstrip** (connected by weekly flights from Nausori) and is the main link with the Fijian mainland. Before the Tongan conquest of Lau, Lakeba was the dominant power in the group, home to the *Tui Nayau* or "Lord of Nayau", which refers to a small island to the north. The most recent *Tui Nayau* was former prime minister Ratu Sir Kamisese Mara, who also held the *Tui Lau* title created by Tongan prince Ma'afu.

LAU CRAFTS

The people of Southern Lau are renowned as fine **artisans**, with the women skilled makers of *tapa* cloth (see p.157) and the men, particularly from Kabara, well-known as the best **woodcarvers** in Fiji. You'll find examples of their work, mostly in the form of *tanoa* bowls, readily available in the handicraft markets around Suva or in the more expensive souvenir shops in Nadi. Unfortunately, most of the region's hardwood *vesi* trees – the best species for woodcarving – have been cut down and the islanders are being encouraged to plant the faster-growing sandalwood, known locally as *yasi*, as an alternative.

As well as *tapa* cloth and woodcarving, Lau islanders produce the coarse twine known as **magimagi**. Commonly seen binding together bures, *magimagi* comes from the fibres of a coconut husk, baked in the sun, soaked in the sea and briskly rubbed together to make long threads. The threads are meticulously braided to form a strong twine, often several kilometres in length. *Magimagi* was once used to lash together the parts of a canoe, although today it is most often seen extending from a *tanoa* or *kava* bowl towards the person of highest rank, or attached to either end of a *tabua* or whale's tooth (see p.231).

6

Tubou

The island's main village is **Tubou**, located on the southwest coast. With a population of around six hundred, it forms Lakeba's heartbeat and is home to the government and provincial headquarters, hospital, post office, several stores and jetty. The village has a strong Tongan influence, with people living in rounded thatch bures and wearing *ta'avala* (woven mats) around the waist. The graveyard behind the provincial office has a small stepped platform where the Tongan prince and warrior **Ma'afu** lies buried.

The rest of the island

A well-maintained dirt road hugs much of the flat **coastline**, making it easy to get around by foot. Several impressive **caves** with stalactites and stalagmites can be explored including Delaiono, south of Tubou on the southern tip, and Oso Nabukete along the uplifted west coast. Slightly inland, close to the airstrip, are more caves, originally used as refuges in times of war or for banishment. In the centre of the island is the largest **hillfort** in Fiji. Situated on top of the 360m-high Keketeke Peak, the fort was capable of sheltering over 2500 people, although today most of its stone walls lie buried in the undergrowth. Off the east coast is a myriad of tiny islands ideal for exploring by punt – you should be able to hire a boatman from the village of Nukunuku for around F$40 an hour.

ACCOMMODATION   LAKEBA

Homestay accommodation The Lau Provincial Council in Tubou (☎822 0329) can help arrange homestay accommodation. You should present a *sevusevu* (see p.31) when you arrive as your traditional request for assistance. Expect to pay F$50 per person per night for board and meals.

Fulaga

The crescent-shaped limestone island of **Fulaga** lies in the distant southern part of the group, 100km south of Lakeba. The low-lying, three-tiered island has an unusual flooded basin in its centre which is littered with eroded mushroom-shaped rocks and cove beaches. There are three small villages on Fulaga but no accommodation. There is no accommodation on Fulaga, but you can visit by cargo ship (see box, p.182).

Vanua Levu and Taveuni

TAVEUNI SUNSET

Vanua Levu and Taveuni

The northern islands of Vanua Levu and Taveuni are Fiji's forgotten frontier. Once the centre of European exploration and the ensuing copra (coconut oil) trade, they are far removed from mainstream tourism and offer a great opportunity for adventure travel. Vanua Levu, Fiji's second-largest island at 5587 square kilometres, is dominated by rambling countryside and has just two towns, Labasa and Savusavu. Labasa has a hilly rural hinterland worth exploring by bus while the serene yachting anchorage of Savusavu boasts quaint drinking holes and restaurants as well as plenty of nearby hikes and snorkelling beaches. Off Vanua Levu's southeast coast is the rugged, forest-covered Taveuni, the third-largest island in Fiji, yet not even a tenth the size of its neighbour. Dubbed the "Garden Island", Taveuni is dominated by the stunning Bouma National Heritage Park, a magnet for hikers and bird-watching enthusiasts.

Between the two islands is one of the world's best **dive sites**, the Rainbow Reef, while off Vanua Levu's north shore is the **Great Sea Reef**, the world's third-largest coral reef system, covering over two hundred thousand square kilometres.

Vanua Levu and Taveuni are often dubbed "The Friendly North" owing to the hospitality of the region's people, although the reality of life here is not quite so sweet. Battered by **hurricanes** and flooding in recent years and hit by the falling prices of both sugar and copra, the islands offer few opportunities for the younger generation, many of whom have moved to Viti Levu in search of work. **Tourism** is the region's greatest hope, although it is hindered by the lack of infrastructure, particularly sealed roads and long runways capable of handling jets. A real-estate boom around Savusavu has given some local land-owning Fijians hope of riches, but most profits from developments tend to end up abroad.

ARRIVAL AND DEPARTURE | VANUA LEVU AND TAVEUNI

Vanua Levu and Taveuni are served by passenger **ferries** and **flights** from Viti Levu. It's relatively simple to combine a trip to **both islands**, as most ferry routes call in at both Vanua Levu and Taveuni. Ten days should give you plenty of time to get a feel for the islands; one itinerary would be to arrive by plane in Labasa, travel by bus to Savusavu and then over to Taveuni by boat.

BY PLANE

Flights to the islands are in small propeller planes from either Nadi or Suva. Note that seats often fill up quickly, especially when dive groups and their equipment take over the entire plane, so book as far in advance as possible. The baggage allowance is 20kg per person so call

TAVORO WATERFALL, BOUMA NATIONAL HERITAGE PARK

Highlights

❶ **Labasa countryside** Mingle with the locals on an open-sided bus ride into the pretty Labasa hills. **See p.193**

❷ **Savusavu** Hike in the hills, marvel at the hot springs, snorkel in the clear waters and end the day with a sundowner drink overlooking the bobbing yachts in the bay. **See p.194**

❸ **Rainbow Reef** Explore soft corals and tropical fish at this pristine section of reef between Vanua Levu and Taveuni; the diving is world-renowned. **See p.200**

❹ **Kioa and Rabi Islands** Sample two South Pacific cultures, one from Polynesia, the other from Micronesia, living on these adopted islands. **See p.202**

❺ **Bouma National Heritage Park** Fiji's most varied national park, offering walks in lush forest, high waterfalls, historical sites and an intriguing marine reserve. **See p.208**

❻ **Lake Tagimaucia** Spot the elusive orange dove or the even rarer Tagimaucia flower at this mountain lake on Taveuni. **See p.213**

HIGHLIGHTS ARE MARKED ON THE MAP ON P.188

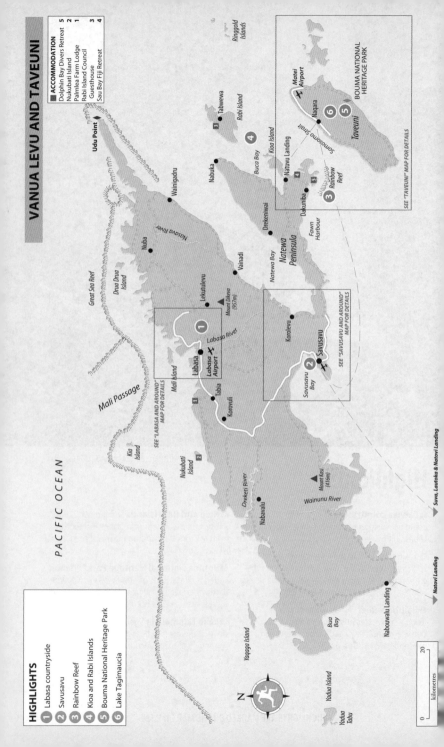

VANUA LEVU AND TAVEUNI

HIGHLIGHTS

1. Labasa countryside
2. Savusavu
3. Rainbow Reef
4. Kioa and Rabi Islands
5. Bouma National Heritage Park
6. Lake Tagimaucia

ACCOMMODATION

Dolphin Bay Divers Retreat	5
Nukubati Island	2
Palmlea Farm Lodge	1
Rabi Island Council Guesthouse	3
Sau Bay Fiji Retreat	4

PACIFIC OCEAN

Great Sea Reef

Udu Point

Ringgold Islands

Wainigadru

Nuba

Nabuka

Tabwewa

Rabi Island

Nasogu River

Drekeniwai

Vainadi

Lekutulevu

Mount Dikeva (957m)

Drua Drua Island

Mali Island

Mali Passage

Kia Island

Nukubati Island

Drekeri River

Yaqaga Island

Nabavalu

Mount Kasi (416m)

Wainunu River

Bua Bay

Yadua Island

Yadua Tabu

Nabouwalu Landing

Natovi Landing

Suva, Lautoka & Natovi Landing

Labasa

Labasa Airport

Tabia

Koroivuli

Korolevu

Savusavu

Savusavu Bay

Natewa Bay

Natewa Peninsula

Fawn Harbour

Dakuniba

Rainbow Reef

Buca Bay

Kioa Island

Natuvu Landing

Somosomo Strait

Taveuni

Matei Airport

Naqara

BOUMA NATIONAL HERITAGE PARK

SEE "TAVEUNI" MAP FOR DETAILS

SEE "LABASA AND AROUND" MAP FOR DETAILS

SEE "SAVUSAVU AND AROUND" MAP FOR DETAILS

N

0   kilometres   20

TUI TAI ADVENTURE CRUISE

One of the best ways to explore Vanua Levu and Taveuni is on the luxurious ★**Tui Tai Adventure Cruise** (📞885 3032, 🌐tuitai.com; seven nights from US$2895 per person, includes meals and activities). The cruise takes place on a 42m, three-masted schooner with air-conditioned cabins, en-suite bathrooms, spa treatments and on-deck daybeds. Along the way you can **dolphin-watch** off Vanua Levu, snorkel or dive the **Great Sea Reef** and kayak up the mangrove-lined Nasavu River to a remote village. Probably the only time you'll run into other travellers is on the visit to Bouma National Heritage Park on Taveuni. The cruise also calls in at the gloriously remote **Ringgold Islands** and the fascinating cultural enclaves of Kioa and Rabi (see p.202). Pre-booked guests are picked up from both Savusavu on Vanua Levu and Matei on Taveuni.

ahead if you are bringing your own scuba gear.

Pacific Sun 📞672 3555, 🌐pacificsun.com.fj. Offers seven daily flights to Labasa in a 44-seater ATR – five from Nadi (1hr 5min; F$277) and two from Suva (45min; F$217); three daily flights to Savusavu in small 12-seater twin-propeller Twin Otters from Nadi (1hr; F$417); and four daily flights to Taveuni, two from Nadi (1hr 25min; F$401) and two from Nausori, Suva (1hr).

BY FERRY

To Vanua Levu Passenger ferries to the islands depart from Lautoka, Suva and Natovi Landing (on the east coast of Viti Levu). The Patterson Brothers daily ferries from Natovi Landing offer the fastest journey time (3hr 30min) although they arrive at the remote Nabouwalu Landing on the west coast of Vanua Levu; most travellers prefer to head direct to Savusavu. Seas are often rough, particularly across the perpetually choppy Bligh Water – ferries from Suva or Natovi Landing miss the worst of this section.

To Taveuni For Taveuni, ferries from Suva arrive at the wharf at Nayalayala, known locally as the Wairiki Wharf, between Wairiki and Waiyevo on the west coast of Taveuni; the ferry calls in at Savusavu along the way, giving you the option of getting off and catching the next ferry to Taveuni at a later date. Small boats journeying across Buca Bay from Vanua Levu arrive at the old wharf in Lovonivonu, known as the Korean Wharf, 3km south of Naqara town and also on the west coast.

FERRIES FROM VITI LEVU

Bligh Water Shipping 📞666 8229 in Lautoka; 📞885 3191 in Savusavu, mobile 📞999 2536, 🌐blighwater shipping.com.fj. Departs Lautoka twice a week for

Savusavu (11hr 30min; from F$55); and departs Natovi Landing three times a week for Savusavu (7hr; from F$55).

Consort Shipping 📞331 3266 in Suva, 📞881 1454 in Labasa, 📞885 0279 in Savusavu. Operates the comfortable two-hundred-passenger *MV SOFI* departing Suva for Savusavu (12hr; F$60, cabin bunk F$90) on Mon & Fri at 6pm, and Wed at 1pm, stopping on the way at Koro island on the Wed & Fri runs and connecting on to Taveuni (16hr; F$70, cabin bunk F$100) on the Mon & Fri runs. Charter buses meet passengers arriving at Savusavu Wharf for connections to Labasa Town. Travel between Savusavu and Taveuni costs F$37 one-way and takes 4hr 30min.

Patterson Brothers 📞666 1173 in Lautoka, 📞881 2444 in Labasa. Ferry departing 7am Tues, Thurs & Sat from Natovi Landing, 60km north of Suva and crossing Bligh Water to Nabouwalu (3hr 30min; F$50) on the southwest tip of Vanua Levu. A charter bus connects between Nabouwalu and Labasa (2hr 30min; F$15).

INTER-ISLAND FERRIES

A small inter-island ferry connects the islands across Buca Bay, with services starting in Taveuni and crossing over to Vanua Levu, where they pick up passengers from Savusavu and Labasa for the return leg.

Venu Shipping 📞885 0466 in Savusavu, 📞820 3391 in Taveuni. Departs from Wairiki Wharf in Taveuni at 9am on Mon, Wed, Fri and Sat, crossing to Natuvu Landing on the eastern tip of Vanua Levu (1hr 30min; F$18). A bus from Savusavu (departing at 7.30am) arrives at Natuvu Landing at 10.30am in time for passengers to catch the ferry to Taveuni; the same bus picks up passengers alighting from Taveuni and drops them into Savusavu (3hr; F$14).

Vanua Levu

VANUA LEVU is about half the size of its big brother Viti Levu, but in terms of tourist facilities it pales by comparison. There are few white sandy beaches and little accommodation outside of Labasa and Savusavu, which are connected by the island's only sealed road. However, the lack of other tourists makes it a joy to explore, especially on an inland bus ride, and the spectacular setting of Savusavu Bay is worth the trip alone.

As with Viti Levu there are distinct leeward and windward sides to the island. The dry north coast is strewn with sugarcane farms, pine forests and mangroves with the Fiji-Indian-dominated **Labasa Town** as its focal point, while the hillier south is dominated by tropical rainforest and huge coastal coconut plantations. Midway along the south coast is **Savusavu**, a picturesque sailing town which makes a lovely base for a few days.

Three remarkable islands lie off Vanua Levu's coast: **Yadua Taba** to the west, home to the endemic crested iguana; and to the east, facing Taveuni, the two culturally unique islands of **Rabi** and **Kioa**, each home to a displaced South Pacific community.

Brief history

Vanua Levu was the site of the initial European rush into Fiji in the early nineteenth century, fuelled by the discovery of **sandalwood** in Bua Bay on the southwestern coast of the island. Opportunist merchants from Port Jackson (Sydney) and London first began arriving in 1804, loading up with sandalwood before sailing on to the ports of Asia, where their cargo was sold at a great profit. In return the Fijian landowners received muskets, pans, mirrors and other trinkets, until every tract of the prized resource had been cut down.

During the 1860s more Europeans began to arrive, this time in search of land for the **cotton trade**. The chief of Vanua Levu and Taveuni, Tui Cakau, sold fifty thousand acres of fertile land on Vanua Levu to European traders at just two shillings per acre. The balance was paid in the form of credit to buy liquor and luxury goods from the new landowners. After the collapse of cotton prices at the end of the 1860s, the Europeans switched to the **copra trade**, which flourished until the 1940s. Huge areas of coconut plantations still stand tall amongst the coastal landscape and a few die-hard *kai loma* planters, mixed-blood descendants of the original Europeans, continue to eke out a living from the crop. Recently some of the old European and *kai loma* families have begun to carve up their huge plantations, selling them off in small chunks to **expat investors**. The most popular properties are located around Savusavu, which has seen prices rise to as much as F\$200,000 (US\$110,000) an acre.

Labasa and around

The hot and dusty market centre of **LABASA** on Vanua Levu's north coast is Fiji's largest town outside of Viti Levu but receives virtually no tourists. The administrative centre of Vanua Levu, it has a purposeful bustle during the day, but by sundown, with the departure of the last local bus, the streets become deserted. On the outskirts is the town's lifeline, the Labasa Sugar Mill, which perpetually hisses, creaks and bellows out smoke during the sugar-crushing season between May and December. Labasa's surrounding hilly **countryside** is the main attraction for visitors and exploring this area by open-sided bus offers great mountain vistas. Also nearby are two resorts with diving access to the fabulous, uncharted **Great Sea Reef**.

The Municipal Market and around

The town centre is flanked on its east side by the flood-prone Labasa River, which flows 5km north to the coast through mangrove forest. Beside the Labasa bridge is the delightful **Municipal Market** (Mon–Fri 7.30am–4.45pm, Sat 7am–1pm), a good place to mingle with the locals. In the small park overlooking the river are six small open-sided huts where locals gather to drink *yaqona* – you can join in by offering a F\$1 donation towards the grog bowl.

Nasekula Road

Heading east from the bridge is Labasa's main street, **Nasekula Road**, lined by colourful Fiji-Indian shops. The busiest spot along the street is Dragon Entertainment, a pool hall with blaring reggae music where Fijians and Fiji-Indians congregate. South of the bus

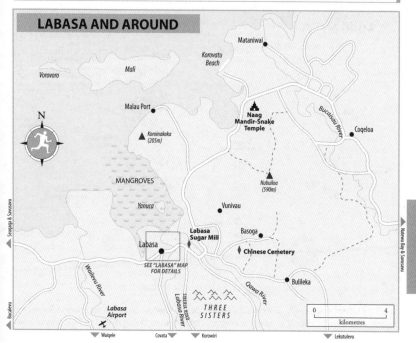

LABASA AND AROUND

Mataniwai

Korovatu Beach

Vorovoro

Mali

N

Malau Port

Naag Mandir–Snake Temple

Bucaisau River

Coqeloa

Koroinakoka (205m)

MANGROVES

Nubuiloa (590m)

Yanuca

Vunivau

Labasa Sugar Mill

Labasa

Basoga

Chinese Cemetery

SEE "LABASA" MAP FOR DETAILS

Waileuu River

Qawa River

Buileka

Seaqaqa & Savusavu

Natewa Bay & Savusavu

Bucalevu

SIBERIA ROAD Labasa River

Labasa Airport

THREE SISTERS

0   4
kilometres

7

Waiqele   Covata   Korowiri   Lekutulevu

stand, a pleasant **riverside walk** leads from Reddy Place to Guru Nanak School beside Nacula village. From the village you can head back to Nasekula Road via Vunimoli Road.

ARRIVAL AND DEPARTURE
LABASA

BY PLANE

Airport With the only tarmac runway outside Viti Levu, miniscule Labasa Airport is located 10km southwest of town. Taxis into the centre of Labasa cost F$12; minivans (every 30min; 5.45am–5pm) pass along the main road near the terminal and cost F$1 to Labasa.

Destinations Nadi (daily; 1hr 5min); Nausori, Suva (2 daily; 45min).

BY BOAT

Labasa's port at Malau is 8km east of town and generally open only for container ships. Ferry passengers arriving at Nabouwalu are met by a connecting bus to Labasa.

BY BUS

All public buses arrive at and depart from the Labasa bus stand, adjacent to the Municipal Market.

To Savusavu From Labasa there are regular buses to Savusavu (6 daily; F$8; 2hr 30min) heading west along the Seaqaqa Highway. You can also reach Savusavu the long way round via Natewa Bay. This route follows the sealed Wainikoro–Dama Road east of Labasa and then switches to dirt roads through the mountains to Wainigadru village. From Wainigadru another dirt road heads south along the coast to Savusavu. A daily service run by Waiqele Buses covers the route, leaving Labasa at 9am and arriving in Savusavu at around 4.30pm (7hr 30min).

To Nabouwalu Heading from Labasa to the Patterson Brothers ferry terminal at Nabouwalu takes around 5hr by bus (departures 6.30am, 10.30am, 1pm & 2pm; F$12).

Destinations Basoga (8 daily; 20min); Coqeloa (10 daily; 45min); Dreketilialia (6 daily; 45min); Lekutulevu (3 daily; 1hr 20min); Nabouwalu (4 daily; 5hr); Savusavu (7 daily; 2hr 30min–7h 30min).

GETTING AROUND

On foot Labasa is a small town and most places are within walking distance.

By taxi Taxis cost twenty cents per 200m within the town area, plus a flag fall of F$1.50. If hiring a taxi to tour the

countryside, you should negotiate a price before departing; expect to pay F$20 for an hour's tour.

By car Renting a car is a good way to explore the countryside around Labasa. Carpenters Motors

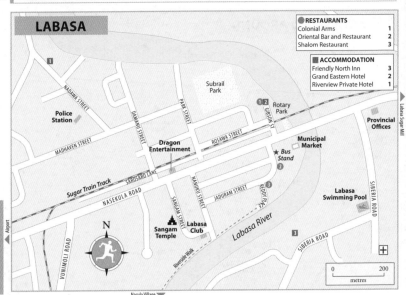

($\textcircled{T}$ 881 1522, $\textcircled{W}$ carpmotors.com.fj) on Rosawa St has the cheapest 4WD Jeeps at F$230/day (limited selection). Otherwise try Vanua Rentals ($\textcircled{T}$ 881 1060; from F$260/ day) in the Mobil station on the corner of Nanuku and Jadaram streets, or Budget ($\textcircled{T}$ 881 1999) at Vakamaisuasua Industrial, a few kilometres west of town.

ACCOMMODATION

Labasa's **hotels** are mostly aimed at Fijians travelling on business. You shouldn't have a problem finding a room and discounted rates are usually available at weekends. If you're looking for a quieter base, consider *Palmlea Farm Lodge* (see p.194), 14km west of town, overlooking the ocean.

Friendly North Inn Siberia Rd $\textcircled{T}$ 881 1555, $\textcircled{E}$ fni @connect.com.fj. Not quite as far out of town as its address suggests, but still a 20min walk. This is the best option if you're staying awhile as most of the sixteen duplex cottage rooms have kitchenettes. There's a pleasant garden, bar and restaurant and the Labasa swimming pool is a short walk along the road past the hospital. **F$80**

Grand Eastern Hotel Gibson St $\textcircled{T}$ 881 1022, $\textcircled{E}$ grest @connect.com.fj. Labasa's smartest hotel, popular with business people – you should get walk-in rates at

weekends or quiet periods. The 24 rooms are a little tired but the setting is lovely, in a quiet cul-de-sac close to the busy bus stand. The hotel has a swimming pool and slightly expensive restaurant and bar. 24hr reception. **F$120**

Riverview Private Hotel Nadawa St $\textcircled{T}$ 881 1367. Pleasant house overlooking the river a 15min walk north of town past the police station. The spacious dorm room has five single beds and a private balcony but the private rooms are a bit poky, with dingy bathrooms and no hot water. Dorms **F$30**; rooms **F$80**

EATING AND DRINKING

Colonial Arms Grand Eastern Hotel, Gibson St $\textcircled{T}$ 881 1022. If you're after decent European cuisine this is the only place to go, with salads and beef burgers at lunch and a full mixed grill, steaks and pizzas at dinner (mains F$25–35). Daily 7–9.30am, 11.30am–2pm & 4–10pm.

Oriental Bar and Restaurant Jaduram St. Labasa's best place to eat out, this a/c Chinese restaurant has pleasant decor and background music and serves over two hundred dishes, from *chilli taufu* (F$8) to pizzas (F$10). It's also a popular bar, with beer served by the jug. Come early

at lunchtime to get one of the window tables overlooking the bus stand. Mon–Sat 10am–3pm & 6.30–10pm, Sun 6.30–10pm.

Shalom Restaurant 9 Jaduram St $\textcircled{T}$ 995 2638. Just beyond the bus station, this little place is one of many serving curries, chop suey and snacks such as *dalo* chips. With mains costing from F$6.50, it's cheap and cheerful, and the hand-painted signs and bright benches and tables make for an endearing interior. Daily 10am–8pm.

DIRECTORY

Banks ANZ, corner of Nasekula Rd and Gibson St (Mon 9.30am–4pm, Tue–Fri 9am–4pm); Westpac, corner of Nasekula Rd and Sangam Ave (Mon–Thurs 9.30am–3pm, Fri 9.30am–4pm). Both have ATMs.

Doctors Singh's Medical Centre, Reddy Lane (Mon–Fri 8am–4pm & Sat 8am–noon; ☎ 881 3824).

Hospital Northern District Hospital, off Siberia Rd on the east side of the river (open 24hr; ☎ 881 1444).

Internet access Govinda's on Nasekula Rd next to Pacific Sun has twelve terminals and serves coffee (Mon–Sat 8am–5.45pm).

Pharmacy My Chemist, 5 Nasekula Rd (Mon–Thurs 8am–6pm, Fri 8am–7pm, Sat 8am–3pm, Sun 9.30–11am; ☎ 881 4611).

Police Nadawa St (open 24hr; ☎ 881 1222).

Post office Nasekula Rd (Mon–Fri 7.30am–4.30pm, Sat 8am–noon).

Telephone Plenty outside the post office, although you'll need a calling card. Skype calls are available from Govinda's internet café.

East of Labasa

Some of the most attractive countryside around Labasa lies to the east of the sugar mill across the Qawa River. Past the river, the main Wainikoro–Dama road turns north towards the coast. Five kilometres along is the turn-off for **Malau Port**, protected by the large offshore island of Mali.

The snake temple

Buses from Labasa heading to Natewa Bay pass the temple (30min; F$1.20); a taxi should cost F$18

Twenty kilometres northeast of Labasa is the Hindu shrine of Naag Mandir, better known as the **snake temple**. Inside is a peculiar attraction: a cobra-shaped rock that devotees claim has grown by 3m over the space of seventy years – the roof has had to be raised four times. Visitors are welcome to visit the shrine (remove shoes first).

Korovatu Beach and beyond

Two hundred metres past the snake temple is the turn-off to palm-backed **Korovatu Beach**, the nearest sandy beach to Labasa. It's 3km from the main road to the beach and cars are charged F$5 access. Beyond the turn-off, the main road continues in a perfectly straight line for 3km, the longest stretch of straight road in Fiji. The surrounding **scenery** – with big mountains to the south and unusual rocky outcrops to the north – is an excellent place to **explore** by foot, with opportunities to wander along dusty roads through Indian settlements and climb hills for panoramic views.

Lekutulevu

Regular buses run to Lekutulevu from Labasa (daily except Sun at 7am, 10am & 2.45pm; F$3.50); the road is extremely rough and the journey takes over an hour – if the road is bad, the bus stops at Dreketilialia and you'll need to walk the remaining 4km

Twelve kilometres south from Labasa, accessible along the Bulileka Road, is the remote village of **Lekutulevu**. The village offers a delightful guided one-hour hike to a **waterfall** (local guide F$12). Along the way you'll pass a natural stone *tanoa* (drinking bowl) 3m

---

SIGHTSEEING BY LOCAL BUS

Hopping on and off Labasa's charming **open-sided buses** is a great way to see the countryside and meet the locals The following routes are highly recommended, each departing hourly from Labasa bus stand from 6am to 6pm, with increased services during peak hours.

Labasa to Basoga or Vunivau (20min; F$1.20). After passing the sugar mill and turning left up Valebasoga Road, get off the bus at the brow of the hill before the Chinese Cemetery. Walk towards the telecommunication tower (15min), following the ridge for stunning mountain views. Head back down via the tower access road, past Indian houses to Bulileka Road

(20min). From here, frequent buses head back into Labasa. **Labasa to Coqeloa** (50min; F$1.60). This route passes the sugar mill and snake temple and travels through Indian sugarcane settlements around the Bucaisau River Valley. Plenty of dirt roads branch out from the valley, making tempting walking diversions amongst beautiful mountain scenery.

FIJI CRESTED IGUANAS

The seldom seen **Fiji crested iguana** (*Brachylophus* vitiensis) is one of the few large reptiles living in the South Pacific and found only on a handful of islands in Fiji. Averaging 40cm in length (split evenly between body and tail), they are distinguished from the more common and slightly smaller banded iguana by three thin white stripes around the body and a mohican-style head-dress. If aroused, their skin turns from a pale green colour to jet black.

These fascinating creatures were first discovered by Australian zoologist John Gibbons in 1979 on the tiny island of **Yadua Taba**, which nuzzles its larger sister Yadua 20km off the western tip of Vanua Levu. The 170-acre uninhabited island, declared as Fiji's first wildlife reserve in 1981, is home to around twelve thousand crested iguanas, which eat the leaves and flowers of the island's wild hibiscus trees. Other habitats include Monuriki in the Mamanucas and several small islands in the Yasawas, although populations at these locations are small. The only way to **visit** Yadua Taba is on a scientific research project, but you can view the iguanas without disturbing their natural habitat at Kula Eco Park on the Coral Coast (see p.112).

in diameter which is reputed to be used by the ancient god Dakuwaqa. A thirty-minute detour from the waterfall leads to the summit of **Mount Uluinamolo**, from where you can see Taveuni on a clear day.

West of Labasa

Fourteen kilometres west of Labasa the tar-sealed Wainikoro–Dama Road branches towards the coast at Tabia, where a couple of remote resorts allow you to explore the **Great Sea Reef**. This is the third longest continuous barrier reef system in the world, boasting 44 percent of Fiji's endemic marine life and 74 percent of its corals. Forty minutes by boat to the north in the far reaches of the Great Sea Reef sits **Kia Island**, where surfers can enjoy impressive **breaks**.

ACCOMMODATION — WEST OF LABASA

Nukubati Island ☎881 3901, Ⓦnukubati.com. The best access to the massive Great Sea Reef is available from this private island retreat. The upmarket resort is aimed at honeymooners and divers and offers seven luxury bures, as well as game fishing, sailing and trips to the breaks around Kia Island (Nov–March). Rates include meals. US$790

★**Palmlea Farm Lodge** Naduri–Tabia Rd ☎828 2220, Ⓦpalmleafarms.com. This simple and inviting eco-resort grows its own organic fruit and vegetables and has three elegant bures, all overlooking the ocean. Scuba diving trips to the Great Sea Reef can be arranged. Rates include breakfast. F$295

Savusavu and around

SAVUSAVU, Vanua Levu's main tourist centre, is a small one-street town squeezed between rolling hills and a silvery ocean. Sitting alongside a bay that was once a giant volcano, Savusavu is Fiji's most popular anchorage for visiting **yachts**. With several excellent **restaurants** and bars, splendid walks in the **Savusavu Hills** and fabulous nearby snorkelling at **Lesiaceva Point**, the town makes for a pleasant short stay.

From Savusavu, the sedate **Hibiscus Highway** passes old coconut plantations, hugging the south coast of Vanua Levu, while to the north are two picturesque waterfalls hidden amongst tropical rainforests, one at the village of **Vuadomo**, the other at the **Waisali Nature Reserve**.

FESTIVALS IN SAVUSAVU

Two of the best times to visit Savusavu are during **Savusavu Festival Week** in November, when local arts, music and culture are promoted, and during the annual **Hindu Krishna Lele Festival**, which features fire walking and is held at the Khemendra School just before Christmas.

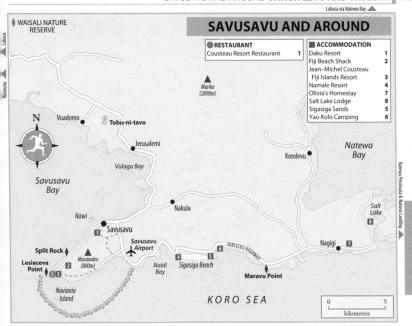

The town centre
The town is strung along Ratu Suliano Street, better known simply as **Main Street**. The commercial centre with the bus stand, municipal market, post office, banks and shops lies at the eastern end of the street; this area springs to life on Fridays and Saturdays with an influx of visitors from the countryside, who come to trade at the **market**, where there's the usual wonderful display of fresh produce.

Copra Shed Marina
To the west of the commercial centre is the **Copra Shed Marina**, which marks the beginning of the town's quieter quarters where Main Street hugs the foreshore. Here you'll find the **Yacht Club**, which has beautiful views overlooking the bay across to distant blue-tinted mountains. You can sip a drink at the water's edge here, eat at one of two lovely waterfront restaurants or shop in the posh boutiques nearby.

The hot springs
Nakama Rd, across from the playing field

Two hundred metres south of the marina up Nakama Road are Savusavu's **hot springs**. The three small bubbling pools are too hot to bathe in and are often full of sacks of *dalo* being slowly cooked. The boiling water trickles into a small stream below the pools where it cools sufficiently to dip a toe in.

The pearl farm on Nawi Island
Nawi Island • Farm tours (1hr 30min) Mon–Fri 9.30am & 1.30pm • F$25 • ☏ 885 0821, ⓦ pearlsfiji.com

West from the town centre along the gritty beachfront is the jetty for the underwater **pearl farm** at Nawi Island, which you can visit to learn about the unique multi-hued pearl production in Savusavu Bay. Tours take place on a glass-bottomed boat and there's usually time for a quick snorkel (bring your own gear). If you're visiting between October and November or April and May you'll get to see the harvesting of the pearls by hand.

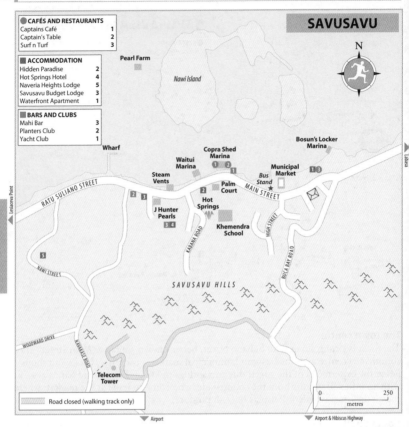

CAFÉS AND RESTAURANTS
Captains Café	1
Captain's Table	2
Surf n Turf	3

ACCOMMODATION
Hidden Paradise	2
Hot Springs Hotel	4
Naveria Heights Lodge	5
Savusavu Budget Lodge	3
Waterfront Apartment	1

BARS AND CLUBS
Mahi Bar	3
Planters Club	2
Yacht Club	1

Road closed (walking track only)

7

ARRIVAL AND DEPARTURE

SAVUSAVU

BY PLANE

Airport Flying in to Savusavu Airport involves a dramatic descent over the hills to land at a short runway fronting the ocean. Pacific Sun flies in several times daily from Nadi and Suva.

Getting into town It's a 5min ride from the airport to town. Buses run hourly (F$1); otherwise a taxi will cost F$4.50.

Destinations Matei (1 weekly; 20min); Nadi Airport (5 daily; 1hr); Nausori, Suva (2 daily; 45min).

BY BOAT

Ferries Passenger and car ferries arrive at Savusavu Wharf, a 5min walk west of the town centre.

Destinations Lautoka, Viti Levu (2 weekly; 11hr 30min); Natovi Landing, Viti Levu (3 weekly; 7hr); Suva, Viti Levu (3 weekly; 12hr); Wairiki Wharf, Taveuni (5 weekly; 4hr 30min).

Private yachts If you are arriving by private yacht you should contact Customs House (Mon–Fri 8am–1pm &

2–5pm; ☎885 0727, VHF16) on the west side of Main Street. There are three privately run marinas running east–west: Waitui Marina (☎885 30301, ✉waituimarina @connect.com.fj), The Copra Shed (☎885 0457, ⊛coprashed.com) and Bosun's Locker (☎885 0122, ✉curly@connect.com.fj). All offer moorings costing from F$8 to F$12 per day depending on the season, with weekly and monthly rates available.

BY BUS

All buses arrive at and depart from the Savusavu bus stand.

To Labasa From Savusavu there are regular buses to Labasa heading north via the Waisali Nature Reserve. You can also reach Labasa via Natewa Bay, a rough journey with Waiqele Buses departing Savusavu at 9am and reaching Labasa around 4.30pm.

To Nabuka Vishnu Buses head east along the Hibiscus Highway to Nabuka on Buca Bay (F$6.65).

To Natuvu Landing Those travelling to Taveuni can catch a charter bus from Savusavu at 7.15am to Natuvu Landing,

A WALK TO SAVUSAVU HILLS AND LESIACEVA POINT

To marvel at the fine views over Savusavu Bay, take a **walk** around **Savusavu Hills**. The best **route** starts from the eastern end of town, turning right up Buca Bay Road towards the airport. After a steep fifteen-minute walk, turn right again up the imaginatively named "Access Road" and follow the ridge westwards for nice **views** overlooking the town and Nawi Island.

There are three routes **back into town**. The **shortest** trail, which takes around thirty minutes, diverts off the road to the telecoms tower perched on the hilltop. From the far end of the clearing above the tower, a small grassy track leads down to a dirt road within five minutes. Follow this road and take the second turning on the left, heading uphill again on Nawi Street. From here, the ridge walk has views over the southern end of the bay and winds its way through light forest, past corrugated iron lean-tos back into town.

The other two options continue along Access Road for thirty minutes south towards the **airport**. From here you can either catch a bus or taxi back into town (see below) or continue for thirty minutes along the south coast via Nukubalavu Village to **Lesiaceva Point**. Near the point, on the north side of the *Cousteau Resort* (see p.207), is a public beach with excellent **snorkelling** at Split Rock, 500m offshore. It's a 7km walk along the coastline back into town, or you can catch a bus or taxi (see below).

Alternatively, **guided hikes** around the Savusavu Hills are available with Sharon from *Naveria Heights Lodge* (3–7hr; F$55–120; min 2 people; ☎ 885 0348).

7

where the ferry departs for its 1hr 30min journey across the Somosomo Straits to the west coast of Taveuni.

Destinations Labasa (6 daily; 2hr 30min); Nabuka (3 daily; 4hr); Natuvu Landing (3 daily; 4hr).

GETTING AROUND

By car or scooter The best way to explore the Hibiscus Highway and Natewa Peninsula is by renting a car. Carpenters Rentals (☎ 885 0122) rent out small 4WD vehicles for around F$140 per day. They also offer scooters, although these are suitable only for driving along the sealed section of road which extends for the first 20km. Otherwise try Budget Rent A Car (☎ 885 0377).

By bus Buses depart from the Savusavu bus stand on Main Street and can drop you off at points along the Hibiscus Highway and at the Waisali Nature Reserve, though they only run infrequently. Buses to Lesiaceva Point leave at 7.15am, noon or 4pm (get off when you see the signboard "Aunty Bui's Place"), returning at 7.45am, 12.30pm and 4.30pm.

By taxi It's easy to flag down taxis around town. A taxi to Lesiaceva Point costs F$8 to *Cousteau Resort*, F$3 to *Daku Resort*.

By bike Mountain bikes can be rented from *Naveria Heights Lodge* (see p.198) for F$25 per day; they also offer mountain bike tours for experienced cyclists (from F$65 including lunch).

INFORMATION

Tourist information There is no official tourist information centre in Savusavu but the Savusavu Tourism Association (ⓦ fiji-savusavu.com) distributes a brochure on the town which you can pick up from Trip N Tour (Mon–Fri 9am–4.30pm, Sat 9am–noon; ☎ 885 3154, ⓔ tripntours @connect.com.fj) in the Copra Shed Marina. The helpful staff here can book snorkelling and diving trips (see box, p.198).

ACCOMMODATION

Accommodation in Savusavu ranges from basic guesthouses in town to the lavish *Cousteau Resort* out on Lesiaceva Point. Hotels in Savusavu town are dull but adequate for exploring the restaurants and sometimes rowdy bars. Staying in the hills or at Lesiaceva Point is a lot more interesting and only a few dollars' taxi ride away.

SAVUSAVU TOWN

Hidden Paradise West Main St ☎ 885 0106; map p.196. Just west of the Copra Shed, this friendly guesthouse has a handy location and is the only place with a backpacker atmosphere. It's fronted by the cute shack-like *Seaview Café*. Rates include breakfast. Dorms F$25; rooms F$60

Hot Springs Hotel Off Kabana Rd ☎ 885 0195, ⓦ savusavufiji.com; map p.196. This four-storey hotel isn't the most attractive building in town but the views from the top two floors are great. Rooms are uninspiring but there's a pool, restaurant and 24hr reception. Heavily discounted walk-in rates of around F$95 are often available. F$195

SNORKELLING AND DIVING AROUND SAVUSAVU

The best place to **snorkel** around Savusavu is at **Split Rock** close to *Cousteau Resort*. You can get a public bus or taxi from town (see p.197). Snorkel out towards the pearl buoys for the best coral patches. Long-established **dive** operator **Koro Sun Divers** (☎ 885 2452, ☒ korosundive .com; two-tank dive F$230) offer daily pick-ups from the Savusavu area and dive the reefs in the Koro Sea off the south coast as well as the Rainbow Reef. Once a week they run trips to the remote reefs of Namena Island.

In the busy sailing season between May and October one of the visiting yachts may offer day or overnight **sailing charters** – check at the Copra Shed or Waitui marinas. **Tui Tai Adventure Cruise** (see box, p.189) have their head offices in Savusavu, between the *Planters Club* and the J Hunter Pearl Office on Main Street.

Savusavu Budget Lodge West Main St ☎ 885 3127, ☒ savusavubudgetlodge.com; map p.196. Located at the quiet west end of town and above the owners' tiny Indian restaurant, this affordable lodge has simple rooms, most with a/c, tiny TVs and small en-suite hot-water shower rooms. Non a/c rooms F$40; a/c rooms F$60

Waterfront Apartment East Main St ☎ 920 2161; map p.196. Open-plan self-contained apartment above the *Surf n Turf* restaurant with a/c, kitchen, hot-water bathroom and a view over the veranda roof to the bay. A great spot for long stays, when discounted rates are given. F$85

SAVUSAVU HILLS

★**Naveria Heights Lodge** Council Ave, Savusavu Hills ☎ 885 0348, ☒ naveriaheightsfiji.com; map p.196. Superb homestay in the hills offering three rooms with a view, each featuring polished wooden floors and a sun deck. It's a steep and puffy 15min walk uphill to get here from town but the owner happily picks up guests. A healthy, home-made breakfast is served on the wooden veranda which has a little plunge pool and serene views over the bay; other meals can be cooked on request. You can also book massage, facials and yoga, plus jungle trails and hikes to traditional villages. Rates include breakfast. F$250

LESIACEVA POINT

Daku Resort 1km along Lesiaceva Point Rd ☎ 885 0046, ☒ dakuresort.com; map p.195. Excellent-value villas, cottages and bures built around a swimming pool and overlooking the ocean in spacious landscaped gardens. This versatile resort specializes in holiday study courses featuring birdwatching, singing, poetry and local craft. F$295

★**Fiji Beach Shack** 6km along Lesiaceva Point Rd ☎ 885 1002, ☒ fijibeachshacks.com; map p.195. Two boutique holiday homes blending Fijian architecture with contemporary furnishings, both with saltwater plunge pools. Perched on a steep hill a hundred steps up from the road with fabulous views overlooking the bay – handy for snorkelling at Split Rock. F$340

Jean–Michel Cousteau Fiji Islands Resort Lesiaceva Point ☎ 885 0188, ☒ fijiresort.com; map p.195. Owned by the son of Jacques Cousteau, this luxurious and environmentally sensitive resort boasts 25 beautifully hand-crafted thatch bures plus a fabulously opulent villa. The beach isn't great, but there's fine snorkelling off the pier and kids are spoilt with their own play centre, swimming pool and personalized carers. As you'd expect, scuba diving is brilliantly managed and there also are well-organized kayaking and waterfall trips. Rates include meals, activities and excursions. Bures A$1116; villa A$3300

EATING AND DRINKING

Savusavu is a wonderful place for dining out, rivalling Nadi for choice and with several good **restaurants** on the water's edge. Although the town has a genteel feel by day, don't be surprised to see drunks staggering around on Friday and Saturday nights – one notorious place to avoid is the *Tavern Bar* next door to the *Planters Club*. After around 8pm it's probably best to take a **taxi** back to your accommodation.

RESTAURANTS AND CAFÉS

Captains Café Copra Shed Marina ☎ 885 0511; map p.196. Shakes, cakes and coffees with views over the water. Light meals include Caesar salad and curry of the day for F$8 or pizzas from F$15. Daily 8am–9pm.

Captain's Table Copra Shed Marina; map p.196. A tad expensive, but the seafood and meat dishes such as teriyaki tuna (F$18) are superbly cooked and the lunch specials are

great value. The glamorous setting on the water's edge is outstanding. Daily 11am–2.30pm & 5.30–9.30pm.

Cousteau Resort Restaurant Lesiaceva Point ☎ 885 0188; map p.195. Exquisitely presented food served in the elaborate setting of a 20m-high thatch bure. The set lunch (F$53) and dinner (F$70) menus offer two courses, with a choice of around three mains. Book in advance. Daily lunch and dinner only.

★**Surf n Turf** East Main St ☎885 3033; map p.196. Trendy café-restaurant with a cute wooden veranda on the foreshore. It serves excellent coffee and cooked breakfasts (F$8), as well as offering a heartier lunch and dinner menu of European and Fijian mains (around F$18), including sophisticated dishes such as parrot fish in coconut oil with pineapple fried rice. Mon–Sat 9am–9pm, Sun 4.30–9pm.

BARS AND CLUBS
Mahi Bar At the Hot Springs Hotel ☎885 0195; map p.196. There are sweeping views of the bay from the veranda of this hotel bar, but drinks are pricey. There's live music and (usually drunken) dancing on Fri and Sat night from 7pm. Daily 1pm–midnight.

Planters Club West Main St ☎885 0233; map p.196. Old boys' hangout where you can sit in peace with a draught beer and watch the sunset. The main lounge displays interesting memorabilia recounting the bygone copra days. Mon–Sat 10am–10pm, Sun 10am–8pm.

★**Yacht Club** Copra Shed Marina ☎885 0457; map p.196. Refined watering hole with cheap beer on draught, great sunset views and live reggae music on Sat at 5pm. Happy hour 5–7pm. Daily 10am–10pm.

DIRECTORY

Banks ANZ and Westpac are both on Main St, opposite either side of the bus stand.
Doctors Dr Taoi, Palm Court, West Main St (Mon–Fri 8.30am–1pm & 2–4.30pm; ☎885 0721).
Hospital Savusavu District Hospital is 2km east of Savusavu on the road to Labasa (Mon–Fri 8am–1pm & 2–4.30pm; outside these times on-call for emergencies only; ☎885 0444).
Internet access Savusavu Computers, opposite the Ministry of Education at east end of town (Mon–Fri 8.30am–5pm, Sat 8.30am–1pm; F$4 per hr).
Pharmacy Siloah Chemist, Palm Court, West Main St (Mon–Sat 8.30am–1pm & 2–4.30pm; ☎925 0062).
Police There's a multi-coloured painted Tourist Police Unit inconveniently located 2km east of town on the road to Labasa (☎855 0222).
Post office East Main St, almost on the corner of Buca Bay Rd (Mon–Fri 8am–4pm, Sat 8am–noon).
Telephone Opposite Copra Shed Marina and in front of post office.

Tobu-ni-tavo Waterfall
18km north of Savusavu, off the Labasa Rd • Buses from Savusavu to Labasa can drop you at the turn-off to Vuadomo; a taxi will cost around F$30

North of Savusavu, the attractive **Tobu-ni-tavo Waterfall** makes a pleasant day-trip. Head north on the road to Labasa, past the pretty village of Jerusalemi, keeping an eye out for Vuadomo Road on the left, 16km from Savusavu. A steep 2km dirt track leads down to **Vuadomo Village** on the coast, where you pay a small entrance fee to visit the waterfall, an easy twenty-minute hike up the valley.

Waisali Nature Reserve
31km north of Savusavu, off the Labasa Rd • Mon–Sat 9am–3pm • F$8 • Buses from Savusavu to Labasa can drop you at the Reserve; a taxi will cost around F$50

Around 30km north of Savusavu is **Waisali Nature Reserve**, administered by the National Trust but in a rather neglected state. From the car park, the thirty-minute **waterfall trail** leads down through lush tropical rainforest. Look out for orchids en route to the waterfall: there are around thirty species in the area. The reserve is also perhaps the last remaining home of the endangered Fiji ground frog.

The Hibiscus Highway
Heading south from Savusavu, past the airport, the Buca Bay Road turns eastward, hugging the southern coastline of Vanua Levu to the eastern tip of the island at Buca Bay. The first 20km of road out of Savusavu – nicknamed the **Hibiscus Highway** – is tar sealed, and passes old copra plantations, colonial-style homesteads and several quiet **resorts** along the coast, although there are no restaurants or shops. There is generally good **snorkelling** off the coast, especially around the mushroom islets of Maravu Point, but you'll have to walk out some way from shore over a raised platform of dead exposed coral to get to the reefs. A decent public **sandy beach** backed by rows of massively tall coconut palms is accessed through a gate at *Sigasiga Sands*.

By bus The Hibiscus Highway is served by buses travelling between Savusavu and Nabuka on Buca Bay (3 daily).

ACCOMMODATION

Namale Resort ☎ 885 0435, ⊕ namalefiji.com; map p.195. Exclusive retreat with luxury bures and a spa centre overlooking a beautiful beach. Owned by American life coach Tony Robbins; "life mastery" courses are taught here Jan–April. Rates include meals. US$1130

Olivia's Homestay Nagigi Village ☎ 885 3099; map p.195. A good village homestay experience, with the energetic Olivia encouraging interaction with her relatives. Rooms are basic and cold-water showers are shared by all. F$30

Sigasiga Sands ☎ 885 0413, ⊕ theultimateparadise .com; map p.195. Private plantation resort set among coconut palms, with a huge lawned area beside a beach.

There are two pretty thatch-roof bures available for short stays, plus a two-bedroom holiday villa for long-term rent. Both come with kitchen facilities. Bures US$60; villa US$175

Yau Kolo Camping ☎ 885 3089, ⊜ yaukolo@yahoo.com; map p.195. Basic dorm lodge with ample room in the spacious gardens to pitch a tent, although there are no kitchen facilities – home-cooked meals can be arranged. There's fair snorkelling and a narrow beach across the road, and a 15min trail leads to a small waterfall. Sometimes closed around Christmas. Rates include breakfast. Camping (with own tent) F$12; camping (with hired tent) F$20; four-bed dorm F$20

The Natewa Peninsula

The **Natewa Peninsula** is almost severed from the main chunk of Vanua Levu, connected only by a kilometre-wide sliver of land east of Savusavu. To the north of the peninsula is Natewa Bay, while to the south is the Somosomo Strait separating Vanua Levu from Taveuni. At the eastern end of the peninsula, ferries to Taveuni and the two smaller islands of **Kioa** and **Rabi** depart from **Buca Bay**.

Salt Lake

Twenty seven kilometres east of Savusavu, the Buca Bay Road reaches the narrowest part of the peninsula and the turn-off to **Salt Lake**, a brackish lake fed by the mangrove-lined Qaloqalo River which boasts excellent **fishing** and birdwatching.

ACCOMMODATION   **SALT LAKE**

Salt Lake Lodge ☎ 828 3005, ⊕ saltlakelodge.com; map p.195. Overlooking the Qaloqalo River, accommodation here consists of a lodge, a beach house for couples and a bure. As well as fishing from the pontoon, kayaks are available for drifting up and down the river. Lodge F$356; beach house F$300; bure F$124

Natewa Bay

East of Salt Lake, the Natewa Peninsula broadens and features increasingly dense rainforest teeming with endemic birdlife – it's one of the few places in Fiji to spot the rare **silktail**, a tiny black bird with a speckled blue head. A 4WD vehicle is needed to explore the region as the roads here are terrible, especially during the rainy season. Two side roads branch off to the fishing villages of Drekeniwai and Vuasivo on **Natewa Bay**; ask around at either village to hire a boat and guide to search for **spinner dolphins**, commonly sighted in the bay – expect to pay around F$120 for an hour.

Buca Bay

The Buca Bay Road finally hits **Buca Bay** at Loa village, from where dirt roads branch off north and south along the coast. The road north heads through a dozen fishing villages to **Nabuka** at the tip of Natewa Bay, facing Rabi Island. Two kilometres south of Loa is **Natuvu Landing**, departure point for ferries to Taveuni. Twelve kilometres south of Natuvu you can see **petroglyphs** etched into stone boulders alongside the creek bed at the village of Dakuniba (ask to see them). A couple of **dive resorts** are hidden in the heavily indented southeastern tip of the peninsula, which has the closest access to the stunning **Rainbow Reef**.

VIEW FROM MATANGI ISLAND RESORT (P.208) >

By bus Buses connect Savusavu with Natuvu Landing (3 daily; 4hr), linking with the ferry crossing to Taveuni, and continue on to Nabuka.

By boat Ferries to and from Taveuni dock 2km south of Loa

at Natuvu Landing (1 daily; 1hr 30min). Boat charters for Kioa depart from Vatuvonu, and for Rabi from Karoko village, 2km south of Nabuka. *Dolphin Bay Divers Retreat* and *Sau Bay Fiji Retreat* (see below) send boats to collect visitors.

ACCOMMODATION

Both of the resorts listed below are set in remote bays, inaccessible by road, and pick up guests across the straits from Taveuni.

★**Dolphin Bay Divers Retreat** ☎888 0531, ⓦdolphinbaydivers.com. Half the pleasure of this resort is in the motorboat trip to get to Dolphin Bay (F$55 transfer fee), but arriving is a treat too: the simple but appealing bamboo bures and safari tents sit beside the beach. The dive instructors are adept, and the coral reef just offshore is a paradise for snorkellers. Excellent meals are enjoyed communally at a central bure: meal plans (F$60/90) are a

must as there's nothing else for miles. Safari tents F$65; bures F$125

Sau Bay Fiji Retreat ☎992 0046, ⓦsaubayfiji.com. This resort has four simple wooden cottages with fans and en-suite bathrooms, plus a deluxe suite with outdoor shower and a glamping-style safari tent. Spectacular diving and snorkelling, plus kayaking, fishing, massage and village visits. Cottages F$395; suite F$715; safari tent F$840

Kioa Island

Just offshore from Buca Bay, the small, hilly island of **Kioa** is home to four hundred Tuvaluans. Back in the 1940s the people of Vaitupu, the largest of the nine coral atolls in Tuvalu, were faced with a stark choice: cling on as rising sea levels began to erode their tiny island, or look for a new home. In 1947, the freehold island of Kioa, 1000km to the south in Fiji, was purchased by the people of Vaitupu for £3000. The first migrants arrived almost immediately and a steady trickle has continued ever since. The islanders live in the solitary village of **Salia** on the south coast. In 2005, they were formally granted Fijian citizenship. The fair-skinned Polynesian Tuvaluans have a lifestyle and language quite different from the Fijians. They are known as skilled fishermen and are often seen handline fishing from outrigger canoes way out to sea.

By boat To get to the island ask the captain of the ferry (see above) to drop you off on its run between Natuva Landing and Taveuni, or catch the daily Nabuka bus departing Savusavu at 10.30am to Vatuvonu village, where you can charter a boat for the 15min journey to Kioa (F$50).

Homestay accommodation ☎850 0387, ⓦkioaisland .org. There is no official accommodation on Kioa but you can arrange a homestay visit through the Kioa Island Council. F$25

Rabi Island

Rabi Island, 66 square kilometres in size, is home to the displaced **Banaban Islanders** from faraway Kiribati in Micronesia. Their tiny five-square-kilometre original homeland, Banaba Island, was systematically stripped of its **phosphate** deposits by British mining interests between 1902 and 1942. Soon after, during World War II, the island was captured by the Japanese, who slaughtered many of the islanders. At the end of the war the British Government relocated the remaining Banabans to Rabi Island in Fiji which it had purchased shortly before the Japanese occupation. The islanders received formal Fijian citizenship in 2005, and today almost five thousand Banabans live on Rabi. **Tabwewa**, halfway along the north coast, is the largest village on the island.

By plane The seldom used airstrip is at Tabiang Village on the southern tip of the island.

By boat Catch the daily Nabuka bus departing Savusavu at 10.30am to Karoko village, 2km south of Nabuka, where you should be able to charter a boat over to the island for F$80.

Rabi Island Council Guesthouse Tabwewa ☎330 3653 (in Suva). Used mostly by visiting government workers, but it also accepts tourists by prior arrangement. Beds are in plain four-bed rooms, and food is provided by the villagers. F$50

Taveuni

Across the strait from Vanua Levu, the smaller island of **TAVEUNI** is a stunning combination of luxuriant forest, soaring mountains and colourful coral reefs. Much of the island's pristine rainforest is protected by the Bouma National Heritage Park and tourism is handled sensitively, making it one of the best places to sample Fiji's varied **wildlife**. Geologically, Taveuni is one of Fiji's youngest islands, and its dramatic volcanic scenery, wild flowers and laid-back atmosphere bring to mind Hawaii as much as Fiji.

Most visitors arrive at the small settlement of **Matei** on the north coast, home to the airstrip, plenty of accommodation and a series of pretty beaches. South of here, along the rugged east coast is the access point to the huge **Bouma National Heritage Park**, which features world-class birdwatching and hikes through a series of waterfalls. Just offshore are the thriving coral reefs of the **Waitabu Marine Park**. Across the knife-edge ridge splitting the 42km-long island lies the smoothly sloping **west coast**, where most of the island's eleven thousand inhabitants live. Here, **Somosomo**, head village of the powerful Cakaudrove Province, merges into the modern trade centre of **Naqara**. The peaceful Catholic Mission at Wairiki lies to the south, with **De Voeux Peak**, accessible by 4WD or by a long trek on foot, towering high above. Close by, in the heart of the island, is **Lake Tagimaucia**. The west coast also has the most direct access to the phenomenal **Rainbow Reef** just across the Somosomo Straits.

Brief history

Archeological evidence indicates that Taveuni was first inhabited around 250 BC and that ring ditches and **hill forts** around the volcanic cones were first built around 1200 AD. In 1643 **Abel Tasman** was the first European to record sighting the island, though he made no attempt to land. This is probably fortunate as the Taveunians were renowned as fierce warriors. In the early nineteenth century they sent great **war canoes** to help the alliance of Bau in its struggle with the Rewans. By the 1840s, they faced a battle on home turf as the Tongan Prince **Ma'afu** threatened to take over the island. Allegiances were split, with some Taveunians supporting the prince and the remainder sticking with the **Tui Cakau**, high chief of the island. In 1862, after much wrangling, Tui Cakau's army defeated Ma'afu in a bloody sea battle off the coast near Somosomo.

Lured by the rich soils and gentle slopes ideal for growing **cotton**, Europeans soon began buying up large tracts of Taveuni's west coast. After the collapse in cotton prices following the American Civil War, copra took over as the most viable cash crop and the organized lines of coconut palms still loom high on the west and south coast plantations. Some of the original **colonial families** remain on the island and have moved tentatively into the tourism industry; this in turn has attracted a growing number of expats.

GETTING AROUND   **TAVEUNI**

Bear in mind that **getting around** Taveuni can prove a little unpredictable. You won't get lost as there's only one road following the coast, but heavy downpours cause frequent **flooding**, particularly at the bridge at Qeleni, which separates the two tourist hubs of Matei and the Bouma National Heritage Park. Floods generally subside in a few hours and seldom last for more than a day, although **landslides** along the steep and muddy roadside may cause longer delays. The only section of **sealed road** extends for 20km along the northwest coast from Matei to Wairiki. Potholes and fallen coconuts on the dirt coastal road are notorious hazards.

By minivan or carrier van With few taxis on the island, the most convenient way to get around is by minivan or carrier van. These can be found at Matei Airport, Naqara or, with a bit of luck, waved down on the roadside. The fare from Matei to Bouma is around F$50 one way.

By bus Pacific Transport (☎ 888 0278), based at Naqara, runs the island's limited bus service. Buses run to

Navakawau in the south (Mon–Fri 9am, 11.30am & 4.40pm; 2hr; F$5) and between Wairiki and Lavena on the northeast coast via Matei and Bouma (Mon–Sat 8.45am, 12.05pm & 4.40pm, Sun 11.05am & 4.05pm; 1hr 45min; F$4). The last bus from Wairiki spends the night at Lavena and departs the following morning at 5.45am – useful for those who want to spend a lazy

7

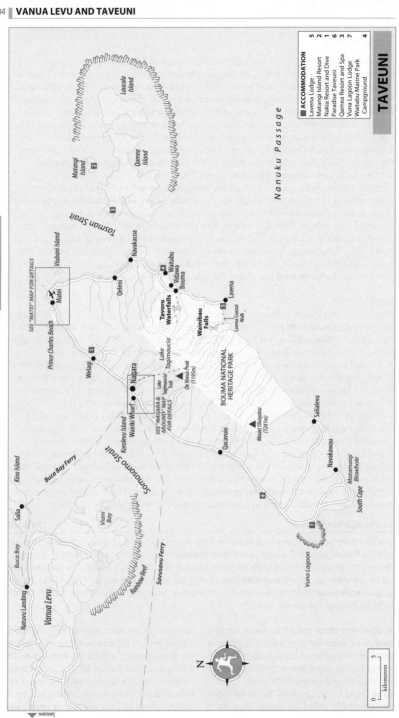

TAVEUNI

Nanuku Passage

Laucala Island

Matangi Island

Qamea Island

Tasman Strait

Navakacoa

Waitabu
Vidawa
Bouma

Qeleni

SEE "MATEI" MAP FOR DETAILS

Viubani Island

Matei

Prince Charles Beach

Tavoro Waterfalls

Lavena

Lavena Coastal Walk

Wainibau Falls

Welagi

Waiyevo

Lake Tagimaucia

De Voeux Peak (1195m)

Naqara

SEE "NAQARA &
AROUND" MAP
FOR DETAILS

Lake Tagimaucia Trail

BOUMA NATIONAL HERITAGE PARK

Wairiki Wharf

Korolevu Island

Mount Uluigalau (1241m)

Somosomo Strait

Qacavulo

Salialevu

Navakawau

Buca Bay Ferry

Kioa Island

Matamaiqi Blowhole

South Cape

Salia

Buca Bay

Naturu Landing

Vanua Levu

Viani Bay

Rainbow Reef

Savusavu Ferry

Vuna Lagoon

N

0   5
kilometres

afternoon on the beautiful Lavena Coastal Walk and overnight in the village.

Van and driver hire For F$140 you can hire a local driver and van for the day which generally works out cheaper than renting a car. Unfortunately van drivers are reluctant to venture off the coastal highway and into the bush.

Car rental Budget Car Rental in Naqara (Mon–Fri

8am–5pm; ☏ 888 0291, ✉ gardenstate@connect.com.fj; 4WD only, F$145–185 per day) is the only car rental company on island. If you plan on scaling De Voeux Peak, you'll certainly need a 4WD vehicle.

Sightseeing tours Most hotels and resorts on Taveuni offer private sightseeing tours (usually with a minimum of four guests).

Matei

MATEI, jutting out on the northernmost tip of Taveuni, is the ideal base for exploring the island: lying midway between the Bouma National Heritage Park and Rainbow Reef, it offers plenty of water-based activities (see box, p.207), pleasant **beaches** and a good selection of restaurants. This modern settlement of around five hundred people is a mix of old colonial families, Indian entrepreneurs and a new wave of foreigners living the dream in luxury oceanfront villas. The settlement stretches along the main coastal road either side of the small bluff known as **Naselesele Point**.

Two kilometres west of Naselesele Point is **Beverley Beach**, a deep sandy gem backed by lush hardwood trees. The coral reef here lies close to shore and offers great **snorkelling** along a 30m-deep drop-off, with reef sharks occasionally paying a visit. Confident swimmers can also reach the snorkelling reef off Natadrua Island, in the sheltered **lagoon** 700m off the north side of Matei, but it's best to paddle out on a **kayak**.

Peckham Pearl Farm

Farm tours (1hr 30min) Mon–Fri 10am • F$25, minimum 2 people • ☏ 888 2789

Based out in the lagoon, **Peckham Pearl Farm** operates tours which include a brief introduction to pearl farming and a chance to snorkel in the lagoon. Tours depart from the beach, normally at high tide.

ARRIVAL AND DEPARTURE MATEI

By plane There are regular flights to Matei from both Nadi (2 daily) and Nausori, outside Suva (2 daily), as well as a weekly flight (Wed; F$130) from Savusavu. The flights give awesome views on clear days. In bad weather, turbulence can be a problem, especially with the frequent crosswinds at Matei. A small, much photographed wooden hut welcomes visitors to the airport. There is usually a taxi waiting for incoming flights – the fare to Matei is around F$3. Most guests with pre-booked accommodation are met

by their hosts.

Destinations Nadi Airport (2 daily; 1hr 25min); Nausori; Suva (2 daily; 1hr); Savusavu (1 weekly; 20min).

By bus A rather erratic and infrequent bus service links Matei with locations to the west and east; you can flag down the bus from your accommodation place, but as it's often late this may mean hanging around.

Destinations Lavena (3 daily; 1hr 15min); Naqara (3 daily; 30min).

ACCOMMODATION

Matei is one of the few places in Fiji where you can rent a **self-catering** holiday home or cottage. There are also several excellent small **boutique resorts** around Matei, and an excellent **campsite**.

RESORTS

Bamboo Resort Taveuni West Matei. Book through Bamboo Travellers in Nadi ☏ 672 2225, ⓦ bamboobackpackers.hostel.com. This stylish resort with an open-plan central hall was once a high-end resort, but has been taken over by Fijians and turned into an excellent backpacker destination. It's set on a 90-acre coconut plantation on the mountain side of the coastal road and offers informal but hugely enjoyable speedboat

trips incorporating village visits, snorkelling and surfing. Back at the resort you can learn about Fijian medicine and jewellery making, and there's copious *kava* drinking and fire dancing. The 21 bures have a warm, colonial feel, with dark wood furnishings and thatch roofs; there's sporadic wi-fi but no a/c, and the electricity supply is limited. Rates include breakfast. Dorms F$25; bures F$90

Taveuni Island Resort West Matei ☏ 888 0441, ⓦ taveuniislandresort.com. Exclusive resort set on a

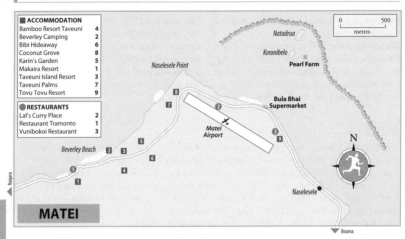

ACCOMMODATION

Bamboo Resort Taveuni	4
Beverley Camping	2
Bibi Hideaway	6
Coconut Grove	8
Karin's Garden	5
Makaira Resort	1
Taveuni Island Resort	3
Taveuni Palms	7
Tovu Tovu Resort	9

RESTAURANTS

Lal's Curry Place	2
Restaurant Tramonto	1
Vunibokoi Restaurant	3

MATEI

7

landscaped hilltop with perfect ocean views across the straits to Vanua Levu. The twelve villas are rather box-like from the outside, but interiors are spacious and come with luxury fittings, fine white linen and private rainforest showers. Steps from an infinity pool lead down to a delightful sandy beach. Rates include meals. US$830

Taveuni Palms West Matei ☎888 0032, ⓦtaveuni palms.com. This is one of the most expensive resorts in Fiji, and at this price you may be left wondering why the two-bedroom villas are located smack opposite the airstrip. However, each comes with its own swimming pool, seven personal staff and a private cove beach. Rates include meals. US$1500

Tovu Tovu Resort East Matei ☎888 0560, ⓦtovutovu .com. This locally owned budget retreat with an excellent-value restaurant and dive operation is just beyond the supermarket at the eastern end of Matei. The five bamboo cottages come with old-fashioned furniture and tiny bathrooms but are clean and comfortable. There's no beach, although the lagoon across the road is good for kayaking. F$114

HOLIDAY HOMES, COTTAGES AND CAMPING

★**Beverley Camping** West Matei ☎888 0326. The cheapest and best located place to stay in Matei, right beside the beach: simple but idyllic sums it up. There's a basic kitchen with cooking facilities and fridge, two flush toilets, 24hr electricity and also a simple thatch bure with

two tiny rooms and private cold-water shower. The warm-hearted owner shares fruit from the surrounding trees. Camping (with own tent) F$15; camping (with hired tent) F$17; rooms F$50

Bibi Hideaway West Matei ☎888 0443. Five cottages, very reasonably priced and delightfully rustic, set in a large hillside plantation full of flowering shrubs and fruit trees (the fruit is free to guests). The beach is just a 3min walk away. F$100

★**Coconut Grove** East Matei ☎888 0000, ⓦcoconut grovefiji.com. Three well-kept cottages set on a hillside overlooking Matei Beach, with exceptional views over the lagoon. The restaurant serves some of the best food on Taveuni and the staff are very welcoming. Rates include continental breakfast. F$360

Karin's Garden West Matei ☎888 0511, ⓦkarins gardenfiji.com. Owned by German couple Karin and Peter, this two-bedroom wooden cottage makes an affordable base for exploring. If you don't feel like cooking in the small kitchen, Karin will knock up mostly organic meals on the covered gazebo at the cliff's edge for an extra charge. F$270

Makaira Resort Matei ☎888 0680, ⓦfijibeachfront atmakaira.com. Owned by a lovely Hawaiian couple with a passion for deep-sea fishing, this two-acre hilltop property has two bungalows with stunning sea views plus access to Beverley Beach across the road. Both cottages have quality furnishings with decorative art work. There's a massage bure and sundeck, and Roberta, the owner, puts on a delicious seafood buffet every Tues. F$335

EATING AND DRINKING

There are several **grocery stores** along the roadside in East Matei, the most comprehensive being on the main seafront strip, but none sells alcohol. There are a couple of good independent **restaurants**, which on the outer islands is something of a rarity.

Lal's Curry Place ☎888 0705. Tiny Indian restaurant with home-style cooking served from the wooden veranda of Mrs

Lal's house. It's a bit hard to find, tucked away down a driveway opposite the supermarket, but the chatty Mrs Lal cooks the

SNORKELLING, DIVING AND OCEAN SPORTS AROUND MATEI

From Matei it takes roughly forty minutes by boat to reach the superb dive sites along the **Rainbow Reef** off the south coast of Vanua Levu. The rich current-fed waters off Matei are also fantastic for big **game fishing**, with marlin, swordfish and yellowfin tuna plentiful. As well as the operators listed below, *Makaira Resort* (see opposite) can also organize game-fishing trips (US$360 per half-day) in a 24ft aluminium boat.

OPERATORS

Jewel Bubble Divers Beverley Beach ☎888 2080, ⓦjeweldiversfiji.com. Diving and snorkelling trips. Two-tank dive US$120.

Swiss Fiji Divers Beverley Beach ☎888 0586, ⓦswissfijidivers.com. Long-established outfit offering diving and snorkelling trips. Two-tank dive F$150.

Taveuni Dive Waiyevo ☎828 1063, ⓦtaveunidive .com. Diving and snorkelling trips to the Great White Wall on Rainbow Reef. Two-tank dive F$265.

Taveuni Ocean Sports Nakia ☎867 7513, ⓦtaveunio ceansports.com. Family-owned operation, offering snorkelling, kayaking, surfing, fishing and scuba diving. Activities cost from F$40 per day; 2-tank dive US$120.

finest curries in the north. She will also offer deliveries if you call a few hours in advance. Mon–Sat dinner only.

★**Restaurant Tramonto** ☎888 2224. Perched on a hilltop at the southernmost point of Matei, this pizza restaurant offers the most spectacular waterside dining in Fiji from a wooden veranda overlooking the placid waters of the Somosomo Straits. The pizzas are thin crusted and delicious (from F$30) and there's a bar serving cocktails.

Daily 10am–9pm.

★**Vunibokoi Restaurant** At Tovu Tovu Resort ☎888 0560. Resort restaurant specializing in delicious Fijian food, with mains starting at F$15. The creamy *rourou* (vegetable leaf) soup is divine, and there's usually fresh *qari* (crab) and *kari* (prawns) cooked in *lolo* (coconut cream). They also offer home-made burgers for the less adventurous. Daily 7am–2pm & 6–9pm.

7

The offshore islands

The three offshore islands of **Qamea**, **Matangi** and **Laucala**, scattered across the deep Tasman Straits from Matei, possess some of the best private island resorts in Fiji. Almost 30km north of Taveuni, the remote **Ringgold Islands** (see box, p.208) pop out of the horizon, just about visible from Matei on a clear day.

Qamea

Just over 2km offshore, **Qamea** is the closest and largest of the islands, with a rugged coastline and hilly peaks thick with tropical forest. It boasts a picturesque beach although note that it's exposed to the strong southeasterly trade winds between May and October. Much of the island is freehold land and there are no roads.

Matangi

Matangi was purchased in 1853 by the Mitchell family, planters from England, who farmed copra here for over a century. The Mitchells' fifth-generation descendants have turned the island into one of the finest resorts in Fiji, making the most of the horseshoe-shaped island's usual sandy beach and snorkelling lagoon.

Laucala

Laucala, another freehold island at the northern tip of Qamea, was once owned by publishing tycoon Malcolm Forbes, who created an idealistic model plantation on the island in the 1970s. A small luxury resort was built along with an airstrip and staff village, complete with a church. After his death, the island became neglected and was eventually sold for US$11 million in 2003 to Dietrich Mateschitz, founder of Red Bull energy drinks. He has constructed a new multi-million-dollar **private resort** (ⓦlaucala.com), where visiting celebs fork out US$7000 per night. The island boasts pristine beaches and the 30km-long **Heemskerck Reef** lying off its north coast is a great spot for fishing.

THE RINGGOLD ISLANDS

Almost 30km northwest from Taveuni, the remote **Ringgold Islands** are a collection of small islands supporting thousands of breeding **seabirds**, including the red-footed booby and black noddy on Vetaua island. The only inhabitants live on rolling Yanuca island where farming is viable. To visit these enchanting islands you need to join the Tui Tai Adventure Cruise (see box, p.189) which spends a day exploring the sunken crater of Cobia Island with hiking and snorkelling in the lagoon. **Nuku**, an atoll surrounded by tiny coral islets, has some of the finest white sand in Fiji, where hundreds of sea turtles lay their eggs between September and January.

ARRIVAL AND DEPARTURE   THE OFFSHORE ISLANDS

By boat Boats for the islands leave from the black-sand beach at Navakacoa village, 12km south of Matei, served by three daily buses between Lavena and Matei.

ACCOMMODATION

★**Matangi Island Resort** ☎ 888 0260, ⓦ matangi island.com. What really sets this superb resort apart are the beautiful treehouse bures set in forest that is home to orange doves, silktails and parrots. Bures, both treehouse and beachside, are spacious, with high ceilings, en-suite bathrooms and outdoor rainforest showers. There's a swimming pool and delightful restaurant and the scuba diving nearby is first-class. Rates include meals and boat transfers from Navakacoa. US$950

Qamea Resort and Spa ☎ 888 0220, ⓦ qamea.com. The central grand bure restaurant here is very impressive, replicating a traditional Fijian temple, and the bungalow-style accommodation is screened by foliage. Daily snorkelling trips, plus hikes, kayaking and snorkelling – and highly recommended spa treatments. US$425

Bouma National Heritage Park

Fifteen kilometres south of Matei is the northern boundary of the **Bouma National Heritage Park**, an important wildlife reserve, protecting forty thousand acres of ancient **rainforest** laced with waterfalls and home to rare birds and plants. The park was established in 1990 by the people of Bouma District, with assistance from the Fijian and New Zealand governments.

Within the park are four villages, each running a specific eco-attraction: **Waitabu**, the first of the villages encountered along the road from Matei, has a protected **marine park**; 4km further into the park, **Vidawa** offers a rewarding rainforest hike to ancient ruins in the hills; neighbouring **Korovou** (also known as Bouma) maintains the spectacular Tavoro Waterfall Trail through three sets of falls; and the last of the four villages, **Lavena**, 15km to the south and at the end of the road, has a beautiful coastal walk with kayaking and another refreshing waterfall at its end. Also within the park are **Lake Tagimaucia** and **De Voeux Peak**, although these are best accessed from the west coast.

Waitabu Marine Park

Guided snorkelling trip F$20 • Bookings ☎ 888 0451

Waitabu Marine Park, set in a secluded bay off the main road, is the first attraction you'll come to. There's no sign indicating the village – keep an eye out for the access road heading towards the coast from the brow of a steep hill, about fifteen minutes' drive south of Navakacoa. Waitabu translates as "sacred waters", and in 1998 the seven Fijian communities here signed an agreement to neither fish nor anchor in a one-kilometre stretch of coastline up to the fringing reef. Consequently, the coral and fish here are thriving and can be visited on a **guided snorkelling trip**. The **visitor centre** at the end of the access road beside the beach has cold-water showers and an extensive selection of snorkelling equipment. If you turn up unannounced it may take a while before someone from the village wanders down to help out so it's worth calling in advance; hotels will arrange this if you're visiting on an organized day-trip. You can stay at their **campground** (see p.210).

Vidawa Rainforest Hike

Guided hike (6–7hr) F$50 • Bookings essential on ☎ 990 5833

A kilometre beyond the Waitabu turn-off, the road passes through the smallest of the four villages, Vidawa. Here, the community has organized the **Vidawa Rainforest Hike**, a full-day trek to the pristine upper forests. The guided hike departs from the small **visitor centre** in the village. The earlier you start, the more chance you have of spotting the **native birds** which forage in the fruit trees of the lower slopes before heading back to the cover of the high forest – golden whistlers, silktails, red shining parrots and blue-crested broadbills are commonly sighted. Once you start ascending the hills into the forest, the foliage becomes thick with tangled vines and there are only fleeting views of the surrounding mountains. It was in the deep jungle, away from the exposed coasts, that Taveuni's first inhabitants used to live, protected from warring tribes and cannibalism. Today the only evidence of their existence is a series of **stone platforms** hidden in the undergrowth. After trudging through the sweaty and often muddy rainforest, the hike emerges in the lower forests at the first Tavoro waterfall (see below) where you can take a refreshing swim.

7

Tavoro Waterfall Trail

Daily 8am–5pm • Trail access F$15 • ☎ 888 0390

The most popular of the four adventures in the park is the **Tavoro Waterfall Trail**. The self-guided walk starts from the **Tavoro visitor centre**, in Korovou village, often referred to as Bouma village; the centre has toilets and sells souvenirs and cold drinks.

To the first waterfall

From the visitor centre, an easy ten-minute stroll through gardens leads to the first of the three **waterfalls**. The first falls are arguably the most picturesque and have the best pool for swimming. Boulders on the left side of the pool lead to a 5m-high rock ledge which cuts in behind the cascading water – if you summon up the courage, you can throw yourself through the falls and into the deep pool beneath. You could easily spend a few hours splashing around here (changing huts are provided) or cooking yourself a **barbecue** on the grills provided. However, most visitors generally push on for the more adventurous trail to the second and third falls, returning to the first falls for a swim at the end of the hike.

To the second waterfall

The section of trail to the **second falls** is the prettiest, starting with a steep ten-minute climb up, helped along by wooden steps and a crushed coral path to the ridge above the first set of falls. From the top there's a covered platform with a view over Thurston Point towards Qamea Island. The track then heads into light forest and crosses the Tavoro River, where there are large boulders to hop across and a rope for hanging onto. Another ten minutes brings you to the photogenic 30m-high second falls, which cascade over numerous ledges into a natural pool.

To the third waterfall

The trail to the **third falls** offers the most demanding hiking and can be very slippery after heavy rain. It's worth the effort, though, as most day-trippers only visit the first and second falls, leaving the third blissfully uncrowded. The trail starts 30m downstream from the second falls, and climbs a steep bank on the far side of the stream into thick forest. It takes another thirty minutes to reach the falls. At only 10m high, they are the smallest of the three, but the wide pool below is great for swimming and deep enough to jump into. It's possible to climb up the slippery rock ledges of the falls and continue upstream, following the river (you'll need sturdy shoes for walking along the river bed) to reach a succession of smaller falls. Allow yourself an hour to return from the third falls to the roadside.

Lavena Coastal Walk

Trail access F$15 • ☎ 920 5834

The pretty beach at **Lavena**, 6km south of Tavoro, marks the start of a scenic **coastal walk** to another set of waterfalls hidden in forest. Accommodation is available at *Lavena Lodge* (see below), at the entrance to the village where the coastal road from Matei ends; the lodge also doubles as the **visitor centre** where you pay your entrance fee for the coastal trail (3hr return).

The first forty-minute section is a flat amble with wonderful views along the coast, passing a black-sand beach and a lagoon littered with rocky pedestals resembling giant mushrooms. About halfway you'll reach the tiny settlement of **Naba**. It's respectful not to wander through, so follow the path down to the beach to the small stream at the far end of Naba from where the trail continues. After meandering around several cliffs and over a suspension bridge, the trail gradually ascends inland under a light forest canopy to a rocky stream. The two waterfalls, known as **Wainibau Falls**, are obscured from view by a 10m-high rock face on either side. To get to the falls you'll need to swim through the passage – keep to the left side, where there's a small ridge just under the waterline to follow. You can jump from the top of the smaller waterfall into the pool, which is deep and full of prawns. Another way to explore this section of the park is on a guided **kayak tour** (see box below).

ARRIVAL AND DEPARTURE   BOUMA NATIONAL HERITAGE PARK

By car The only road access to the park's four main attractions is from the north, along the winding dirt coastal road from Matei via Navakacoa. The majority of people visit on a day-trip organized by their accommodation.

By bus You can get to the park by public bus on the Pacific Transport service (3 daily) running between Lavena and Naqara (1hr 45min) via Matei (1hr 15min). Note that the last bus back towards Matei leaves at 2pm so if you are departing later than this you will have to order a taxi back from the park; note also that this 2pm bus doesn't always start out at Lavena, so it's worth checking, and wait at the Korovou Village bus stop rather than the waterfall one.

INFORMATION

Entry General access to the park is free. However, to participate in the four village enterprises, a small fee is paid at each village visitor centre.

Information For more information, see ⓦ bnhp.org, or enquire at the visitor centres at Waitabu Marine Park (☎ 888 0451), Vidawa (☎ 920 5833), Korovou (☎ 888 0390) or Lavena (☎ 920 5834).

ACCOMMODATION

Lavena Lodge Lavena Village ☎ 820 3639. Sitting on the beachfront at Lavena, this is the only accommodation in the national park. The three twin rooms are screened and have mosquito nets but are otherwise very basic, and the shared bathroom is rather dingy. However, it's worth staying here in order to make an early morning start on the Lavena Coastal Walk. Meals (around F$10) can be arranged with one of the villagers or you can use the lodge's kitchen facilities. Dorms F$30; rooms F$60

Waitabu Marine Park Campground ☎ 888 0451, ⓦ bnhp.org. The marine park campground provides a great opportunity for a remote night under the stars. There are toilets and showers, and you can pre-order simple Fijian meals. Camping (with own tent) F$13; camping (with hired tent) F$17

KAYAKING AROUND LAVENA

A great way to explore the coastal scenery around Lavena is on a **guided kayak tour** (4hr; F$50, includes lunch), which you can arrange at *Lavena Lodge* (see above). Experienced guides from the village will accompany you on a one-hour paddle south from Lavena before trekking inland to the falls for lunch. The guides will then tow your kayak back to the village, allowing you to return along the **Lavena Coastal Walk** (see above). Keen kayakers can hire a guide for the day and paddle further down the coast where the cliffs become steeper and several waterfalls tumble directly into the sea – though note that it's a gruelling six-hour trip across open sea to view this spectacle and conditions can be rough.

The west coast

The **west coast** of Taveuni, protected from the trade winds, overlooks the Somosomo Straits towards Buca Bay on Vanua Levu. Most of the coastline is rocky, with few beaches and no fringing reef. The land was cleared of its hardwood trees by colonial farmers and planted instead with neat rows of **coconut palms**. Today, the 6km stretch of road between the chiefly coastal village of **Somosomo** and the Catholic mission at **Wairiki** is the population centre of the island, home to the only town, **Naqara**, and the hospital and police headquarters at Waiyevo. Naqara's accommodation is pretty low key, so you're better off staying at one of the coastal resorts such as *Nakia* to the north, or the popular *Aroho Taveuni Resort* at Wairiki (see p.214).

The bulk of travellers visit the region solely for its close access to the **Rainbow Reef** (see box, p.207, for details of dive operators). However there are also a few land-based attractions nearby including the hair-raising **natural waterslide** at Waitavala and the **180 Degree Meridian** line which passes through Taveuni here. Also nearby is the access road to **De Voeux Peak**, the island's second-highest mountain, and **Lake Tagimaucia**.

7

Somosomo

Eighteen kilometres south of Matei along the west coast is the village of **SOMOSOMO**, home to the **Tui Cakau**, high chief of an area encompassing all of Taveuni and much of Vanua Levu. Compared to the surrounding homes along the roadside, the **chief's house** with its adjacent meeting hall (*bure bose*) looks imposing but elsewhere it would appear rather ordinary. This disregard of monetary wealth yet strict observation of stately rank is found throughout Fijian villages and is at the very core of Fijian tradition. There's little reason to stop at Somosomo other than to shop at the Morris Hedstrom store, the largest **supermarket** on Taveuni (Mon–Fri 8am–6pm, Sat 8am–noon).

Naqara and around

Across the bridge from Somosomo is **NAQARA**, a rather disorganized collection of wooden shacks and corrugated-iron buildings that passes for the island's main town. Looking completely out of place in the centre of town is the three-storey Garden State building, site of several handy services. Food is available from several supermarkets and street-side shacks.

A kilometre south of Naqara at the village of **Lovonivonu** is Taveuni's old wharf, now known as the **Korean Wharf** and used only by small boats, including those crossing to and from Buca Bay on Vanua Levu (see p.200). Ten minutes' walk south is the village of **Vuniuto**, where you can hire a guide to visit the **Kula-na-Wai Waterfall**, an hour's walk inland (F\$10 per person; minimum 2 people).

Waitavala Sliding Rocks

The most popular attraction along the west coast is **Waitavala Sliding Rocks**, a fun 200m-long natural waterslide where you chute down the rapids of a narrow stream on

---

CAKOBAU'S WAR CANOE

Ra Marama, the last great double-hulled **Fijian war canoe** to grace the South Seas, was built at Somosomo during the 1830s to 1840s. The canoe, measuring 30m long and 6m wide, took seven years to complete and could carry over 130 warriors. At the keel-laying ceremony, several young warriors were clubbed to death to increase the canoe's *mana*, or spiritual power; missionaries intervened at the canoe's launch when more warriors were due to be sacrificed. The canoe was presented as a gift to **Cakobau** of Bau who used it as a powerful symbol of strength in his wars against Rewa which eventually crowned him King of Fiji. After Cakobau's death in 1882, the canoe was returned to Somosomo where, beached, it perished to the wind and sea – no trace of it remains.

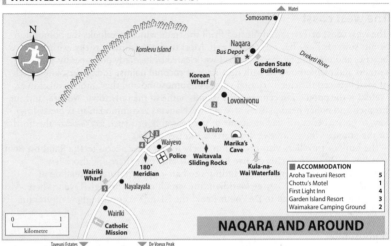

your backside. Old clothes are recommended, and if the water is foaming in the lower pool at the bottom it means the currents are fast – in these conditions it's wise to watch a local slide down before giving it a go yourself. The water slide, lying south of Vuniuto, is a little tricky to find: walk north from *Garden Island Resort* for five minutes and turn into the hills at the wide dirt track beside a wooden bus shelter. From here it's a twenty-minute walk to the bottom of the waterslide – fork left just past the sign for the prison, then right after 100m on the narrow path which leads up to the pools.

Waiyevo

Three kilometres south of Naqara, the hillside settlement of **WAIYEVO** makes up the island's administrative centre. There's no beach here, but it's a good base for **diving** – access to **Rainbow Reef** is only ten minutes away by boat, and non-divers can snorkel at **Korolevu Island**, a five-minute paddle by kayak from the coast; kayaks can be rented from the *Garden Island Resort* (see p.214).

The 180 Degree Meridian

On the unsigned road leading from central Waiyevo up to the hospital and police station

At Taveuni's quirkiest attraction, a small information board covered by a tin roof marks the exact spot of the **180 Degree Meridian**. Fiji is one of only two places in the world where this line of longitude passes through land, the other being at the far eastern tip of Russia. The meridian theoretically marks the beginning and end of each day, although for the sake of convenience the International Date Line kinks eastwards to avoid splitting Fiji into two time zones and two different days. In colonial times, several unscrupulous planters justified the working of labourers on Sunday by claiming they were actually working on Monday's side of the dateline.

Wairiki

The new **wharf** of Nayalayala, where all large ships dock on Taveuni, marks the division between Waiyevo and **WAIRIKI**, which otherwise seamlessly merge. The pretty settlement revolves around the imposing **Catholic Mission**, where a two-hour Mass is celebrated every Sunday at 7am – it's said that the congregation sing with such enthusiasm that cracks have appeared in the windows. Located on a hill, the Mission overlooks the ocean where the island's warriors fought thousands of invading Tongans in a **sea battle**, fighting with clubs from their canoes. The Taveunians won the day, promptly ate their adversaries and halted the Tongan invasion of Fiji.

De Voeux Peak and Lake Tagimaucia

From Wairiki, a dirt road heads to the telecoms station at **De Voeux Peak** (1195m). If you're fit it's not difficult to walk to the top, but it will take a couple of hours from the turn-off just before the Catholic Mission. Once at the **summit**, the view overlooking Taveuni, Vanua Levu and south to Gau and Koro is incredible on a fine day. Be warned, though, clouds often obscure the peak and whilst it may be sunny by the coast, rain could easily be falling on the mountain. The **birdwatching** up here is excellent, with regular sightings of silktails and orange doves, especially in the nesting season (Aug & Sept).

From the summit, it's possible to continue for another two hours, hacking through bush along the northern ridge to **Lake Tagimaucia**, a crater lake 823m above sea level where the endemic **Tagimaucia flower** (see box, p.213) blooms. A relatively well-maintained but arduous trail leads to the lake from Waiyevo (7hr return) – a guide is essential and can be arranged through most west coast resorts.

ARRIVAL AND INFORMATION

THE WEST COAST

By boat Ferries from Suva arrive at Wairiki Wharf, between Wairiki and Waiyevo. Small boats crossing Buca Bay from Vanua Levu arrive at the old wharf in Lovonivonu, known as the Korean Wharf, 3km south of Naqara.
Destinations Natuvu Landing (4 weekly; 1hr 30min); Suva (2 weekly; 16hr).
By bus Ancient and rickety buses operated by Pacific Transport (☎ 888 0278) run from Naqara in both directions on a limited service. Expect late departures.
Destinations Lavena (3 daily; 1hr 45min); Matei (3 daily;

30min); Navakawau (3 daily except Sat & Sun; 2hr).
By car Budget Car rental (Mon–Fri 8am–5pm; ☎ 888 0291, ✉ gardenstate@connect.com.fj; 4WD only, F$145–185 per day) is in the Garden State building in Naqara.
Services There's a branch of Colonial Bank, with an ATM machine, on the ground floor of the Garden State building in Naqara (Mon 9.30am–4pm, Tues–Fri 9am–4pm). Waiyevo has a hospital and police station, which sit on a small hill 200m from the main road; there's also a post office in the centre of town.

ACCOMMODATION

NORTH OF NAQARA

★**Nakia Resort** ☎ 888 1111, ⊛ nakiafiji.com; map p.204. This low-carbon resort is run by dive specialists, and their trips and tutoring are outstanding. Nakia has only four bures – all furnished with local materials and decked out with fresh flowers – making for an intimate experience. The food is organic and grown in the garden; if you're eating here it's cheaper to buy the meal plan. F$240

NAQARA AND AROUND

Chottu's Motel ☎ 888 0034, ✉ chottus@connect.com.fj; map p.212. This long-standing place has the cheapest rooms on Taveuni, with shared bathrooms. Larger self-contained units are equally affordable and have basic kitchen facilities, fridge and en-suite bathrooms. Rooms F$60; units F$70

Waimakare Camping Ground ☎ 993 0319; map p.212. A ten-minute walk south of the Korean Wharf, this secluded campsite is set in light forest within the grounds of a Fijian family home. There's a plain wooden dormitory with a kitchen: beds consist of a mat and mattress laid on the floor. The family will cook for you if required, and are generous with the abundant fruit from the garden – pawpaws, bananas, pineapples and avocados. Camping (with own tent) F$10; dorms F$25

WAIYEVO

First Light Inn Above the post office ☎ 888 0339, ✉ firstlight@connect.com.fj; map p.212. Five pastel-coloured motel rooms, which are clean and simple with a/c, satellite TV and telephone. There's a restaurant next door. F$60

THE WEEPING TAGIMAUCIA FLOWER

The beautiful **Tagimaucia flower** – or *Medinilla waterhousei* – grows only at high altitude near water and, apart from at a few isolated locations on Vanua Levu, Lake Tagimaucia on Taveuni is the only place in the world you can see it. The beautiful flowers, which hang in bright clusters from a liana vine, have two red waxy outer petals and four white inner petals resembling a bell; they bloom in profusion between September and January. This being Fiji, there is a romantic legend attached: the tumbling flowers represent the tears of a maiden forbidden to marry her true love.

Garden Island Resort Next door to the post office ☎ 888 0286, ⓦ gardenislandresort.com; map p.212. The pleasant oceanfront setting of this resort is pleasant enough once you're inside the landscaped gardens, and rooms (some with ocean views) are modern and attractive. A large sea almond tree at the north end of the resort hosts hundreds of fruit bats. **$366**

WAIRIKI
★Aroha Taveuni Resort ☎ 888 1882, ⓦ arohataveuni.com; map p.212. Set up by expat New Zealanders, this is a welcome addition to the Taveuni resort scene, with a comfortable but relaxed vibe. There are two bures, both with great outdoor showers, plus an infinity pool, excellent restaurant and landscaped gardens edging the beach. Good diving trips can be arranged. **F$250**

Southern Taveuni

Southern Taveuni is dominated by rows of coconut palms growing on the rich volcanic soil. Inland, a series of volcanic cones pop out from the gentle slopes rising to the island's highest point, the inaccessible Mount Uluiqalau (1241m). Right at the southern end of Taveuni is the rocky **South Cape** and, just up the east coast, the **Matamaiqi Blowhole**.

Nabogi Ono Farm

Full day tour F$80, half-day tour F$50, birdwatching F$40 • ☎ 828 3677 • The bus from Naqara to Navakawau Village passes the farm (3 daily except Sun)

South of Waiyevo, and an hour and a half by road from Matei, is **Nabogi Ono Farm**, a hundred-acre fruit farm run as an ecological reserve. This is the most accessible place on the island for regular **bird-spotting** and the only place outside Bouma National Heritage Park where the native forest almost reaches the coast. Offshore is a pristine section of reef which you can visit on a guided half- or full-day tour (book in advance) which includes a **snorkel safari**; the full-day option also features birdwatching and a rainforest trek.

Vuna Lagoon

Three kilometres south of Nabogi Ono Farm is *Paradise Taveuni*, the main resort in the area. There's no beach but the resort's **dive operation** visits both the Rainbow Reef and the rarely explored dive sites off **Vuna Lagoon**. The lagoon is a good site for novice divers with lots of coral heads and reef fish but without the steep drop-offs or strong currents found at Rainbow Reef. The picturesque **Namoli beach** is fifteen minutes' walk north and you can also reach the blowhole at Matamaiqi in about ninety minutes.

ACCOMMODATION   **VUNA LAGOON**

★Paradise Taveuni ☎ 888 0125, ⓦ paradiseinfiji .com. The beautiful hand-crafted bures here are made from coconut palms, and the restaurant serves local cuisine blended with European flavours. The on-site diving facilities are excellent. **F$750**

Vuna Lagoon Lodge ☎ 888 0627. This family-owned guesthouse has a peaceful location facing the lagoon. There are three rooms, one with private bathroom, and a larger occasionally-used dormitory. Dorms **F$25**; rooms **F$75**

The Matamaiqi Blowhole

Buses from Naqara heading to Navakawau Village pass the blowhole but head back to Naqara via the inland road; it's possible to walk from the *Vuna Lagoon Lodge*

South of Vuna Lagoon and its village, jet-black rocks litter a promontory known as the **South Cape**, where Taveuni's last volcanic eruption spilled into the sea around 500 years ago. The highlight of the area is the **Matamaiqi Blowhole**, an unpredictable beast which occasionally spouts jets of sea water 15m or more into the air – it's most likely to perform on the turn of the low tide. Watch to see what the seas are doing for at least five minutes before getting too close to the blowhole.

7

ROTUMA

The most remote of the Fijian islands, 43-square-kilometre **Rotuma** lies over 600km north of Suva in a lonely stretch of ocean south of Tuvalu. Its Polynesian culture and language are significantly different from that of the Micronesian Fijians, and the island is only part of Fiji at all thanks to an accident of history.

In 1881, tired of internal friction, the seven chiefs of Rotuma decided it was in their best interests to cede their island to Britain, following the example of the Fijians. Unfortunately for the Rotumans, the island was deemed too isolated to justify its own governor. Instead it was decided that Rotuma should politically become part of Fiji, its remote neighbour to the south. On May 13, 1881, at a spot in Motusa marked by a stone wall embedded with a brass plaque, Rotuma relinquished its sovereignty to Fiji. Movements for independence from Fiji have been mooted since Fiji's independence from Britain in 1970, but today, with over five thousand Rotumans based in Suva, Rotuma's independence movement has little support.

The islanders do, though, want to keep Rotuma **free from mass tourism**. In 1985, 85 percent of Rotumans voted to keep tourist development at bay, making the island a challenge to visit without a personal invitation.

7

AROUND THE ISLAND

The government headquarters for Rotuma have been stationed at **'Ahau** since 1902. Colonial-style buildings house the hospital, police and judiciary as well as a small cement jail with two tiny cells. The island's post office is also located here.

Rotuma is enclosed by a lagoon fringed by a reef and is almost completely surrounded by stunning white sandy **beaches** set off by jet-black volcanic rock. Two of the best are **Oinafa Beach** on the northeastern point of the island, which is also a good spot for body surfing and snorkelling in the turquoise lagoon around the twin islands of Haua; and isolated **Vai'oa Beach**, one of the prettiest in the South Pacific, and usually deserted, with towering palm trees and fabulous snorkelling.

A handful of impressive **archeological sites** can be found inland – including the ancient **burial site** of the kings of Rotuma on top of **Sisilo Hill** and an ancient stone tomb near **Islepi Village** – as well as over a dozen **volcanic cones**. The highest of these rises to 256m, protruding from the gently rolling hills which are extensively planted with *taro*, yams, *kava* and numerous varieties of fruit trees, particularly oranges.

FARA

Without doubt the liveliest time to visit is over Christmas, a period noted for the singing and dancing festivities of **Fara**. The party begins on December 1 (Dec 24 for Juju and Pepjei districts) and lasts until mid-January. Each evening children wander around their villages singing *fara* songs and clapping their hands for a beat. When the kids stop at a house, the family comes out to watch, rewarding them with gifts of perfume, talc and fruit, usually watermelon. If the singing is poor, water is thrown to chase the group away. As the evening progresses, the rest of the villagers join in, grabbing guitars, ukuleles and perhaps a bucket of orange wine. If you visit Rotuma during *fara* you will certainly be invited to take part.

ARRIVAL AND DEPARTURE

By plane The grass airstrip at Malhaha on the north coast of Rotuma is served exclusively by Pacific Sun from Nadi (departs Fri; 30min; F$630 one-way). There are always plenty of small trucks meeting incoming flights at the airstrip and you should be able to negotiate a ride.
By boat Western Shipping runs a cargo boat between Suva and Oinafa wharf on the northeast coast of Rotuma (monthly, usually on Sat; 2-day journey; deck F$118, cabin F$180).

INFORMATION AND ACCOMMODATION

Visiting Rotuma without a personal invitation is tricky. One option is to post a message to ⓦrotuma.net, the island's **community website** and bulletin board: someone locally may be willing to organize a **homestay** for you. Tourism Fiji (ⓦfiji.travel) are more used to dealing with mainstream destinations, but may be able to assist. Otherwise, try asking around in Suva to locate expatriate Rotumans who may put you in contact with a relative back home.

DETAIL OF TRADITIONAL FAN

Contexts

History

Feared for its cannibal tendencies and avoided by mariners for its treacherous reefs, Fiji was one of the last island groups in the world to be encroached upon by the West. When the *kaivalagi*, the men from far away, finally arrived in 1803 they found a deeply hierarchical tribal culture characterized by allegiance to village chiefs, fierce warfare and pagan religion. Europeans exploited the Fijians' natural resources, particularly sandalwood, coconuts and bêche de mer (sea cucumber), and brought with them firearms and alcohol with which to pay off the local chiefs.

The arrival of firearms sparked several bloody wars between tribes, particularly the powerful clans of Rewa and Bau on eastern Viti Levu. This turbulent state of affairs eased in 1874 after **Cakobau**, the self-proclaimed "King of Fiji" converted to Christianity and renounced cannibalism, events which would lead to Fiji becoming a **British colony**. The Fijians, however, proved a reluctant workforce for the new authorities and so indentured labourers from India were shipped in to work the land and make profitable this curious outpost of the empire. This situation continued for almost a hundred years until the country secured its independence in 1970 and was faced with the challenging task of forming a harmonious national identity, a struggle that continues today.

The first Fijians

With no written record, the movement and lifestyles of the first Fijian peoples have been revealed only with the advent of accurate archeological research, particularly the discovery of **Lapita pottery**. Many Fijians, however, give credence to the legend of **Lutunasobasoba** as the first settler of the islands.

Lapita migration

Scientific findings place **Bourewa**, north of Natadola Beach on the west coast of Viti Levu, as the earliest site of human habitation in Fiji, dating back to 1220 BC. Distinctive **Lapita pottery** (see box, p.110) found all around the Melanesian archipelago, suggests that the settlers originated from Southeast Asia, most probably Taiwan or the Philippines. Thought to be lighter skinned than modern Fijians, they inhabited Papua New Guinea, then the Solomon Islands before settling on Vanuatu, New Caledonia, Fiji and Tonga. This migration was followed by a more dynamic flow of people, likely to be darker-skinned Melanesians who reached Fiji between 1000 and 500 BC. The Melanesians continued east to Tonga, the remote islands of Rarotonga and Tahiti, before eventually reaching Aotearoa (New Zealand) and Hawaii, all part of present-day Polynesia, around 800 AD.

Date unknown	1220 BC	1000–500 BC
The Fijian myth of the first settler, snake god Lutunasobasoba, is born.	Settlers from Southeast Asia arrive on western Viti Levu.	Melanesians arrive in Fiji, on a migration that would take them on to Hawaii.

Lutunasobasoba

The majority of Fijians recognize **Lutunasobasoba** as the first person to settle the islands and as founder of the tribal system. However, the story of his discovery of Fiji only entered the national consciousness in 1892 after a competition in a local newspaper to find the best explanation for Fijian evolution. Supposedly, the great chief Lutunasobasoba landed on the west coast of Viti Levu at Vuda, arriving by canoe from Tanzania in East Africa. Either his spirit or one of his clan moved north to Ra where he was immortalized as **Degei**, the supreme god of Fiji who is said to have lived in a cave in the form of a **snake**. Today, it's common for Fijians to claim an impressive genealogical network of around twelve generations tracing their tribe (*yavusa*) back to either Lutunasobasoba or Degei.

Tribal culture

Very little is known about the Fijian islanders in the centuries before European contact, although it's clear that they built extensive hill fortifications and stone fish traps around the coastline. They also created beautiful **wood carvings** including war clubs, *yaqona* bowls and head rests, wove *tapa* cloth to adorn the body and made jewellery. **Tattooing** or *qai* was commonplace, often around the mouth and conducted with a chipped *kai* shell to form a raised scar.

Tribes seldom ventured beyond their territorial boundaries unless to hunt or pay homage to their superior neighbouring chiefs. Consequently, a variety of distinct tribes evolved in relative isolation, each with their identifying customs, gods and dialects (see box opposite).

European encounters

Bypassed by the early Spanish explorers who had headed north to the Philippines, Fiji had to wait until the seventeenth century before European ships reached Fijian waters. In 1643, Dutch navigator **Abel Tasman**, who had discovered New Zealand and Tasmania the previous year, sailed past the Fijian island of Taveuni on his way back to Jakarta in Indonesia. He narrowly avoided shipwreck off the Nanuku Reef east of Vanua Levu and quickly made a northward passage away from the islands. Another 130 years were to pass before European explorers returned.

William Bligh and the Bounty, 1789

During his celebrated voyage of 1774, **Captain James Cook** made a note of the remote Vatoa Island in the southern Lau Group. Although he didn't explore the region further he later met Fijians while in Tonga. Greater recognition goes to **William Bligh**, who in 1789 found himself passing through the heart of the Fijian archipelago aboard a small wooden launch along with seventeen men and just six rowing oars. Having captained his ship, **HMS Bounty**, to Tahiti, Bligh was famously the victim of a mutiny led by Fletcher Christian on April 28 just off Tofua in Tonga. Mindful of the dreadful stories of the warlike, cannibalistic people from Tonga, Bligh and his small crew anxiously paddled for five days past Gau and between Vanua Levu and Viti Levu. On the sixth day, in the Yasawas, two war canoes set out in pursuit of their vessel but, thanks to a timely squall, Bligh escaped and eventually

1000 (AD)	**1643**	**1774**
As Tongans and Samoans attack the islands, the Fijians become a warrior people.	Dutch navigator Abel Tasman sails past Taveuni.	Captain Cook writes of the existence of Vatoa Island.

EARLY RELIGION AND CUSTOMS

Two tiers of **gods** ruled the living: the highest-ranked gods, the *kalou-vu*, were universally venerated immortals. For everyday affairs, the people sought blessings from a collection of localized gods known as the *kalou-yalo*. These were ancestral spirits who in the living world had been respected chiefs or triumphant warriors. These gods commanded the weather, had powers over war and sickness and were called upon to bless the people with abundant fish and fruits, but were otherwise not invoked. Contact with these gods was conducted through the **high priest** (*bete*), a member of the priestly clan or *bete mataqali*. The *bete* sat in a high-roofed temple known as the *bure kalou* and, possessed with *yaqona*, would call the spirits to descend down the *tapa* cloth hanging from the temple roof and speak through his body.

MANA

Blood spilling was an integral part of Fijian custom and imbued items with what was known as **mana**, or spirituality. *Mana* was especially important for warriors and chiefs; their personal war clubs were anointed in human blood in order to bring them mystical powers. War canoes were launched over the bodies of sacrificial victims and the building of temples and chiefly houses required people to be buried alive within the foundations. **Cannibalism** (see box, p.123) was the apotheosis of such blood lust, with war parties constantly scouting for unsuspecting victims. Direct tribal confrontations were less frequent, though when they occurred they tended to take the form of the sacking of entire villages by uprooting crops and burning houses, usually once the survivors had surrendered and moved on to new land.

POLYGAMY AND WIDOW STRANGULATION

Polygamy was commonplace among the early Fijians. On a man's **death**, his spirit was believed to linger in the village for four days to haunt his enemies, during which period it was also customary for the widows to be strangled to death in order to accompany the husband's spirit to the afterlife or *Bulu*.

WITCHCRAFT AND SUPERSTITION

Witchcraft and **superstition** were similarly deeply ingrained in Fijian culture. Certain people had the power to invoke the spirits to taunt their enemies, most notably through illness, in which case the village **sorcerer** would perform an elaborate *yaqona* ceremony (see p.40) to chase the spirit away and reveal the perpetrator.

made it to the Dutch settlement at Coupang on Timor forty days later. Bligh had managed to successfully chart 39 Fijian islands and the section of sea where he made good his escape is known as Bligh Waters.

The Argo and the arrival of beachcombers 1800–1810

The first white people to land on Fijian soil were probably the crew of the schooner **Argo**, who were shipwrecked off Lakeba in Lau in 1800. They brought with them Asian cholera which promptly annihilated much of the local population. A few years later, a steady stream of merchant ships from Sydney Harbour began to arrive, attracted by the fragrant **sandalwood** newly discovered at Bua Bay on the remote southwestern coast of Vanua Levu.

1789	1800	1804
Cast onto a small rowing boat by mutineers, William Bligh successful navigates Fiji.	The schooner *Argo* is shipwrecked and the first white people arrive in Fiji.	Europeans discover – and decimate – Fiji's sandalwood trees.

A few Europeans, mostly escaped convicts or mercenaries, chose to settle on the islands. Known as "**beachcombers**", they aligned themselves with local chiefs and acted as go-betweens for the merchants and Fijians. One particular beachcomber, a Swede named **Charlie Savage** (see below) had a strong influence on the tribal balance of power in Fiji. Shipwrecked aboard the *Eliza* in 1808, he was presented as a hostage to the chief of **Bau**, a tiny island off the east coast of Viti Levu. Over the following

THE CANNIBAL ISLES

And now the drums beat pat, pat, pat, pat, pat. What is the signal? It means that a man is about to be cut up and prepared for food, as is a bullock in our own country. See the commotion! The majority of the population, old and young, run to gaze upon the intended victim. He is stripped naked, struck down with the club, his body ignominiously dashed against a stone in front of a temple, and then cut up and divided amongst a chosen few, ere the vital spark is extinct.

Rev Joseph Waterhouse, *The King and People of Fiji*, Pasifika Press, 1886

Cannibalism in Fiji wasn't something that happened every so often, it was a routine part of life. In crudely pragmatic terms, human flesh served as a much-needed source of protein, especially amongst the hill people, for Fiji was almost devoid of meat-bearing animals. But its real power lay in **intimidation** – by eating the flesh of an enemy, a Fijian was consuming the *mana* or strength of their foe. **Warfare** was usually a tit-for-tat process. Small bands of marauding warriors would prowl the countryside looking for easy prey. If a stand-off between two warring parties ensued, taunts would be cast but seldom was there a full confrontation – securing just one victim was enough for a wild orgy back home.

With the procurement of a **bokola**, or uncooked human, men performed a *cibi* or war dance and unmarried girls responded in an erotic *wate* dance around the captive. The humiliation of the victim didn't usually end there. Young boys were given sharpened sticks and encouraged to taunt and torture the captive, a practice echoed today when a pig is brought down from the plantation for eating. In some severe accounts recorded by missionaries living amongst the Fijians in the 1800s, the tongue was cut out while the victim was still alive and eaten whilst his blood was drained and drunk. Eventually, the *bokola* was placed at the **killing stone** and the head smashed using a war club. The body was cleaned and cooked. The heart and tongue were considered the choicest parts and given to the chief, who would consume the flesh using a specially carved cannibal fork with four prongs, whilst other body parts were distributed amongst the villagers.

Understandably, in the early days of encounter, Europeans were afraid of the "Cannibal Isles" although most often, visitors, however strange looking, were treated gracefully and generously. A few did end up in the pot: Charlie Savage met his end on the island of Vanua Levu in 1813. It is said his bones were later made into sail needles. The most notorious case of cannibalism in the islands, though, rests with the unfortunate **Reverend Thomas Baker** who was killed and eaten by the Colo hill people of Viti Levu (see p.123) in 1867.

By the mid-1800s, with the introduction of firearms and the ensuing power struggle of Cakobau over his Rewan enemies, cannibalism hit its peak. Some first-hand accounts of missionaries stationed at Bau claimed that as many as three hundred people were brought back as the spoils of a single war and body parts hung off every house waiting for consumption. By the 1870s, Cakobau had converted to **Christianity** and ceased to practise cannibalism; following his lead, so did the majority of the Fiji islanders.

1813	1822	1835
Swedish mercenary Charlie Savage is eaten on Vanua Levu.	The town of Levuka is established.	Wesleyan missionaries arrive on Lakeba.

years his unscrupulous demeanour and knowledge of muskets soon saw the island's opportunist chiefs – Naulivou and later Cakobau (see p.210) – with whom Savage had aligned himself, begin to dominate the region. The possession of **firearms** soon became a matter of survival for rival villages. With gun in hand and mercenaries by their sides, they turned the previous petty marauding style of warfare into full-blown genocidal campaigns with entire villages being laid waste and their inhabitants shot, cooked and eaten.

The arrival of the missionaries, 1835

In 1835, after a lull in visiting European merchant ships, Cross and Cargill of the Wesleyan London Missionary Society arrived on Lakeba in the Lau Group and established the first mission in Fiji. Though they found little resistance to their efforts they managed to convert only a few Tongans living on the island. Other **missionaries** soon followed and set up base around **Levuka**, where a few hardened European merchants had huddled together in a small trading outpost. Appalled at the entrenched traditions of cannibalism and widow strangulation, the missionaries soon realized that the spread of Christianity would depend on the powerful pagan chief of Bau.

Cakobau's war with Rewa

Bau's ruling chief, **Cakobau**, was a particularly ruthless warrior and received homage from many islands in Fiji, from Kadavu in the south to Taveuni in the north. But having waged an unsuccessful war with Qaraniqio, chief of bitter neighbour **Rewa** since 1840, Cakobau had overstretched his domain and accrued too many dangerous enemies. He had also lost the support of the white traders of Levuka and had to endure a trade and ammunition blockade.

In 1853, several disaffected chiefs and five hundred warriors rebelled at Kaba Point, a few kilometres south of Bau, and stole the sails of Cakobau's prized 72-ton **gunboat** which he'd recently acquired from the Americans. In retaliation Cakobau led a raid on Kaba, but the heavily fortified stronghold proved resilient. In March the following year Cakobau's status was further eroded by a devastating fire which destroyed many houses on Bau as well as his sacred war temple. The chief took this as a sign that his gods had abandoned him.

On April 30, Cakobau received a letter from his old adversary, King George of Tonga, encouraging him to accept **Christianity**. After a long conversation with Joseph Waterhouse, the resident Methodist missionary on Bau, he decided to *lotu*, or convert. There were so many subsequent conversions throughout the islands that there were not enough missionaries to baptize all the newly faithful, let alone instruct them in the scriptures. Such mass conversion was a seismic social shift, necessitating not just the widespread acceptance of the Christian God and the rejection of all other gods, but also the destruction of the temples and the cessation of cannibalism and widow strangulation.

In early 1855, Qaraniqio, chief of Rewa, died. Weary of war, the Rewans sued for peace. Cakobau's other enemies, however, hearing of his abandonment of Fijian traditions, now rallied at **Kaba Point** to wage war not only on Bau, but on Christianity. King George of Tonga came to Cakobau's assistance with two thousand Tongan

1840	1853	1855
The US navy arrives in Fiji, with violent results – 70 Fijians die at Malolo.	Cakobau, the powerful chief of Bau, converts to Christianity.	Cakobau declares himself King of Fiji.

warriors led in part by **Ma'afu**, ruler over the Lau Group. Their intervention proved decisive, with the Tongans leading the main assault and Bauan warriors holding back any retreat. After victory was assured, Cakobau, keeping faith with his new religion, forbade celebratory feasting on his enemies. With Rewa and Verata finally subdued, he arrogantly declared himself *Tui Viti* or **King of Fiji** although it was to be years before the title was formally recognized.

The path to colonialism

It soon became apparent that King George's assistance in the Kaba victory had come at a price – the control of northern Fiji. The Tongan prince **Ma'afu** had already established his seat of power on Vanua Balavu in the Lau Group and was making steady inroads into the province of Cakaudrove, hitherto home of Cakobau's strongest allies. Ma'afu, full of confidence after his leading role in the assault on Kaba, now became a serious threat to Cakobau's kingdom and over the nineteen years leading up to cession, the two chiefs **battled** indirectly for absolute control over Fiji, with Ma'afu steadily gaining the upper hand.

The American claims

While dealing with the Tongans, Cakobau faced a new problem – a **debt** to the US Government. Back in 1849 on Nukulau island off Suva, the house of **John Williams**, the US commercial agent, had accidentally burned to the ground during US Independence Day celebrations. What remained of his stockpile of supplies was subsequently ransacked by locals. Ever since the fire, Williams had been pressing the US government to claim compensation from the Fijians. In 1851 he had asked the captain of a US warship to demand US$5000, but the claim was dismissed as unfounded. However, the next time a US Navy ship visited in 1855, Williams was successful in gaining the support of its captain for his and a number of other American claims for compensation.

Cakobau, now the most powerful local chief, was held accountable to the impossible tune of US$42,000. Taken aboard the warship, he was bullied into signing acceptance of these claims and forced to promise payment within a year. Afraid of being taken prisoner to the US, Cakobau appealed to Pritchard, the British consul in Levuka, and promised **sovereignty of Fiji** to the British along with thousands of acres of land if the debt to the US was paid off and Ma'afu could be persuaded to relinquish his pursuit of power. Pritchard, hopeful of cession, managed to stall the American demands, and at a gathering of chiefs in Levuka in 1859, he persuaded Ma'afu to cease his war with Bau. Despite his efforts, cession was initially rejected by Britain in 1862 on the grounds that Cakobau, despite claiming kingly *status*, did not represent the united peoples of the islands. There were also concerns that the colony would prove unprofitable and a hindrance in times of war.

The second wave of European migration

Although Britain had rejected taking on Fiji as a colony, the following decade saw a new **rush** of Europeans to the islands, fuelled by rumours of imminent cession. A further hundred thousand acres of land were sold to white traders by rogue chiefs eager

1860s	1867	1871
Blackbirders, obtaining Fijian slaves through fraud, flourish.	The Reverend Thomas Baker is attacked and eaten by hill tribes in Viti Levu.	Cakobau declares his government in Levuka.

BLACKBIRDING

Blackbirding, the recruitment of slave labourers through trickery, flourished in Fiji during the 1860s, driven by labour shortages in the cotton plantations. European merchants would drop anchor at remote islands, particularly Vanuatu and the Solomon Islands, and persuade the illiterate locals into signing papers which legitimized a work contract to take them off to far-away islands as labourers. The locals usually knew nothing of what they had signed and were lured onto the merchant ships by trinkets and locked in the hold to prevent them jumping overboard.

As trade in this "black ivory" flourished, merchants became more unscrupulous, succumbing to blatant kidnapping, rape and murder along the way before selling their human cargo in Levuka for £10 per head. By 1872, when the trade was put to a stop by the presence of British warships, roughly four thousand overseas labourers were working in Fiji's plantations, each man being paid £6 a year under a three-year contract. Most of the labourers were eventually **freed**, some returning to their homelands, but many stayed on, establishing new settlements on Ovalau and Viti Levu, or being adopted into nearby Fijian villages.

to obtain firearms and alcohol. Plantations of **cotton** were established on Taveuni, Vanua Levu and the Lau Group, and **blackbirding ships** (see box above) began to bring in captives from the Melanesian Islands to deal with the shortage of labour. As more traders arrived, the small whaling outpost of Levuka began to take on the role of Fiji's capital. Beyond the control of the authorities, it soon developed into a debauched frontier-like town characterized by vice and alcoholism.

Meanwhile, Ma'afu continued his advances on Bau and the Americans again pursued their claim with Cakobau. In 1867, with an American warship threatening to bombard Levuka, Cakobau turned to the newly formed Australian-owned **Polynesian Company**, which guaranteed payment of the claim by instalments in return for land around Suva.

The deed of cession, October 10, 1874

With the Americans off his back, Cakobau declared the formation of a **government** in Levuka in 1871 with the backing of a few chiefs, and gained formal recognition of his claim to be **king**. Of the many bills passed, most concerned regulations in the sale of land, alcohol and firearms, and a poll and land tax was introduced to raise funds. These laws didn't go down well with some parts of the lawless society in Levuka, who immediately incited riots. Meanwhile, the local Fijians, unable to pay their taxes, were coerced to work on plantations as their penalty. After two years of government, Cakobau had lost the trust of his people, divided the Levuka traders and accrued a **financial deficit** of £87,000. If that wasn't enough, Ma'afu and his allies in the north had refused to pay their taxes and the wild Colo hill people of Viti Levu had begun to attack Christian villages.

With the situation looking bleak, Cakobau once again offered to cede Fiji to Britain. This time, the new consul, James Goodenough, reported favourably, and with other foreign powers – notably the Americans, Prussians and French – keen to annex the islands, the British government agreed. On **October 10, 1874**, in a pompous ceremony

1872	1874	1875	1876
Blackbirding is outlawed.	Heavily in debt, Cakobau cedes Fijian sovereignty to Britain.	Measles kills a third of the population.	The Great Council of Chiefs is established.

in Levuka, Cakobau, Ma'afu, other high chiefs and representatives of Queen Victoria signed the deed ceding sovereignty to Britain.

One of the first and most significant acts to be passed by the first Governor General, Sir Arthur Gordon, was the indefinite **suspension of land sales** in order to protect the Fijian system of *vanua* or tribal land ownership. The British were keen to preserve the Fijian tribal system in order to rule more efficiently. In 1876 the **Great Council of Chiefs**, or *Bose Levu Vakaturaga*, was established to advise the colonial government on Fijian matters, with Queen Victoria recognized as the most powerful chief.

Indenture and development

Immediately after cession Cakobau and his two sons made a stately visit to Sydney. They returned carrying **measles**, and swiftly passed it on to chiefs from all around Fiji who had come to learn about their adventures overseas. Within two months almost a third of the Fijian population had died from the outbreak. Faced with this crisis, those opposed to cession and Christianity reverted to their heathen ways. A longer-lasting effect of the outbreak was a decimated workforce, and one unwilling to toil in the plantations to add to the coffers of empire. In response Sir Arthur Gordon proposed to bring in **indentured labourers** from India – a move that would have lasting consequences for the evolution of Fijian society.

The first shipment of Indian labourers arrived aboard the *Leonadis* in Levuka in 1879. Between then and 1920 when the scheme was abolished, 60,553 Indians, mostly men, arrived in Fiji. Their working contract or "**girmit**" (from the word "agreement") was to last for five years, after which time the labourer could return home. Life was harsh on the sugar and copra plantations, but having endured five years of serfdom, the majority preferred to stay on in Fiji working as farm hands or clerks and eventually setting up trading stores or leasing small tracts of farmland with the savings they had made; many had also broken caste rules by intermarrying, making life back in India impossible. Word of these new opportunities soon reached India and by 1904, **Indian merchants**, mostly Gujarats and Punjabis of all castes and religions, began to arrive.

The largest employer and backbone of the Fijian economy was the Australian-owned **Colonial Sugar Refining Company** (CSR), established in 1880. But once the indenture programme ceased in 1920, a series of strikes for better living and working conditions of the existing Indian labourers eventually forced CSR to transform its huge plantations into smallholdings, leased by aspirational Indians. By the 1930s indigenous Fijians were becoming resentful of the wealth and status accrued by the Indians and began to refuse to renew their leases. Pressure was exerted by CSR but it was **Ratu Sir Lala Sukuna**, high chief and Oxford graduate, who persuaded his people to work with the Indians. To protect indigenous interests, the Native Land Trust Ordinance (later to become the present-day Native Land Trust Board) was established to negotiate land tenure leases on the behalf of Fijian landowners.

A small but economically influential group, the **Fijian Chinese**, began to arrive from China in the 1850s: the first community was in Levuka. Chinese immigrants were the first to open shops in rural Fiji.

1879	1882	1904	1920
Indian indentured labourers arrive in Levuka.	Suva becomes capital of Fiji.	Indian merchants come to seek their fortunes in Fiji.	Indentured labour is abolished: 60,553 Indians have been brought to Fiji.

World War II

During World War II, Fiji's strategic position saw it being used as a base by Allied forces. With the British occupied in Singapore and Burma, Fiji's defence was initially placed under the control of **New Zealand**. Three airfields were built at Nadi and a series of gun batteries were erected overlooking Nadi Bay and Suva Harbour. After the Japanese attack on Pearl Harbor in December 1941, the **US Navy** was given control of Nadi Bay.

With the Japanese encroaching into Papua New Guinea and the Solomons, Fijian soldiers volunteered for combat duty. The Americans immediately recognized their aptitude for **jungle warfare** and sent Fijians to assist in the Solomons, notably at Guadalcanal and Bougainville, where they served with distinction. Fiji-Indians were not encouraged to enlist under the orders of the British who were fearful of giving them military training in light of the independence movement in India.

Independence

As the war ended, politics in Fiji split along ethnic lines. The majority of **indigenous Fijians** remained content with the colonial administration, ruled in essence by their village chiefs and with both their land and chiefly system protected. **Fiji-Indians** had always wielded economic clout, as demonstrated through sporadic trade union strikes against the CSR, but as their population increased, so too did their political power. Disenchanted with low sugar pay-outs, their inability to buy freehold land, and growing antagonism fuelled by India's independence from Britain in 1947, they became more vocal and determined to oust the colonial government. The British, too, wanted to move on from their control of the islands, but were reluctant to let the Fiji-Indians take their place.

An initial move towards **self-government** occurred in 1953, with the expansion of powers of the Legislative Council. Half its members were elected, a third of whom were Fijian, a third European and a third Fiji-Indian. By 1963, the Legislative Council became an entirely elected council, except for two members appointed by the Great Council of Chiefs to ensure Fijian political dominance. But this was not enough for dissident Fiji-Indians. At the forefront of this group was A.D. Patel, founder of the National Federation Party. He demanded independence for Fiji with a government elected by universal suffrage.

The Fijians became increasingly wary of the Fiji-Indian influence, and fearing loss of land they lobbied Britain for support. As a compromise, the British introduced a form of self-government in 1967, with **Ratu Kamisese Mara** appointed the first Chief Minister and seats allocated ethnically. In April 1970, the Legislative Council was replaced by a parliament with a 52-member House of Representatives. Indigenous Fijians and Fiji-Indians would each be allocated 22 seats, with the rest elected by "general voters", European, Rotumans and other minority groups. The general voters tended to vote for indigenous Fijian candidates, so Fiji-Indian dominance was held in check.

Full **independence** from Britain was granted on October 10, 1970, ending 96 years of colonial rule. The Alliance Party, headed by **Ratu Sir Kamisese Mara** of the Lau Group, ruled the nation for the first seventeen years of independence and set in motion

1930s	1940s	1953
Ratu Sir Lala Sukuna attempts to resolve growing conflicts between ethnic Fijians and Indians.	Fiji used as an Allied base during World War II.	Limited moves towards Fijian self-government, with the establishment of the Legislative Council.

policies to prioritize **Fijian affairs** over those of the Indian population. The most contentious policy of the era was to restrict land leases to a maximum thirty-year tenure.

The four coups

Simmering ethnic tension, a large, well-funded military and a relatively recent transition to democracy have seen Fiji experience **four coups** since independence. Although all were relatively peaceful in nature, they have permanently altered the political landscape and caused immense damage to Fiji's international reputation.

Rabuka and the first two coups, 1987

Ratu Mara's Alliance Party dominated Fijian politics in the post-independence years. However, in 1987 a **coalition** of the Fiji-Indian-supported Labour Party and the Fijian breakaway National Federation Party won a historic victory in the April elections. Headed by **Dr Timoci Bavadra**, a chief from the west of Viti Levu, this new-look government seemed to promise a bright and harmonious future. Unfortunately, this hope proved premature, and the government was dogged by the insecurities of the Fijian chiefly system, which opposed the political power of both Indians and the western chiefs. Influenced by the fascist Taukei Movement, which sanctioned a "Fiji for Fijians only" policy, and encouraged by the authoritarian Methodist Church, **Sitiveni Rabuka**, a little-known colonel from the military, stormed parliament on May 14, 1987, and took over the country in a **bloodless coup**. He handed power to the Governor General, **Ratu Penaia Ganilau**, high chief of Cakaudrove.

To Rabuka's surprise, Ratu Ganilau, a strong supporter of parliamentary democracy, ruled the military takeover unconstitutional and attempted to form a government of

---

COUP CAST LIST

Ratu Sir Kamisese Mara Lauan high chief and leader of the Alliance Party, which ruled Fiji from 1970 to 1987. Accused of being behind the first coup of 1987.

Dr Timoci Bavadra Ethnic Fijian from western Viti Levu and founder of the multiracial Fiji Labour Party. Served as prime minister for one month before being ousted by the Rabuka coup.

Sitiveni Rabuka Ethnic Fijian and colonel in the Fiji Military Forces. Carried out Fiji's first military-led coup in May 1987 and was suspiciously silent during the 2000 coup events.

Mahendra Chaudhry Ethnic Indian leader of the Fiji Labour Party, which defeated Rabuka in the 1999 general elections. Appointed as minister of finance in 2007.

George Speight Fijian businessman who stormed parliament with rebel militants on May 19, 2000, holding Chaudhry and 35 government officials hostage for almost two months.

Laisenia Qarase Ethnic Fijian banker appointed by Bainimarama as interim prime minister in 2000. Introduced contentious ethnically-biased parliamentary bills favouring ethnic Fijians. Removed from power in a coup led by Bainimarama on Dec 5, 2006 after a year of continuous political tension.

Commodore Frank Bainimarama Commander of the Fiji Military Force (FMF) and currently interim prime minister following his coup of 2006.

1958	1960s	1970	1987
Death of popular statesman and founder of the Native Land Board Trust, Ratu Sir Lala Sukuna.	Fiji-Indians ramp up their opposition to British rule.	Full independence is granted.	Two coups: the first headed by chief Bavadra, the second by colonel Sitiveni Rabuka.

national unity comprising both parties. In response Rabuka staged a **second coup** on September 23, 1987. He proclaimed Fiji a **republic**, with the intention to serve only the interests of the Fijian people and to sever all links with the Commonwealth. Under a new **constitution** legalized in 1990 government seats were allocated solely along racial lines and heavily weighted towards Fijians. Rabuka won the nominally democratic elections which followed in 1992. Flushed with victory, he now set himself above the chiefly hierarchal system that he had initially intended to uphold.

Internal conflict led to Josefata Kamikamica walking out of Rabuka's government with his five seats, causing Rabuka to lose his majority. Elections were forced in 1994 and this time, failing to homogenize the Fijian voters, Rabuka made a coalition with the independent General Voters Party promising a new constitution removing the ethnically biased voting system. Subsequently, Fiji was **readmitted to the Commonwealth** in 1997.

Speight and the third coup, 2000

Whilst Fijian politicians bickered over provincial power struggles, **Mahendra Chaudhry**, the grandson of an indentured labourer, rallied the Indians into a combined force under the Fiji Labour Party and won a resounding victory in the 1999 elections. Aware of the ethnic tension that could result, Chaudhry appointed eleven of the eighteen cabinet posts to indigenous Fijians. Unfortunately, even this was not enough to appease the extreme right.

On May 19, 2000, **George Speight**, a failed Fijian businessman, stormed parliament with a gang of armed thugs and took Chaudhry and his government hostage. Whether Speight worked alone in the coup remains uncertain, but it is unlikely. Ratu Mara, at that time president, tried to assume control over the country in a coup within a coup, but was removed by the army commander, **Frank Bainimarama**, on the advice of his colleague and 1987 coup perpetrator Sitiveni Rabuka. Rabuka claimed that it was Ratu Mara who had instigated the Speight coup in the first place. Ratu Mara in turn accused Rabuka of being behind Speight. Bainimarama, caught in the middle, declared martial law and appointed **Laisenia Qarase**, an ethnic Fijian, as the interim prime minister.

On July 12, 2000, 56 days after storming the parliament, Speight released the hostages, having been assured sanctuary by Bainimarama. However, he was later arrested and found guilty of treason – he remains locked up in a high-security prison. On September 2, 2000, an attempted **mutiny** of the army was quashed by Bainimarama with the loss of eight lives – again Rabuka was accused of being its instigator. Ten days later, a High Court ruling officially found the interim government illegal and returned power to Chaudhry. The decision was challenged by the ousted prime minister, Laisenia Qarase, and in March 2001 the ruling was overturned. Afraid it wouldn't hold, Qarase immediately resigned as prime minister to ensure the dissolution of parliament and to force a general election. Five months later, campaigning under a newly formed SDL party, **Qarase** was returned legally as prime minister. The country regained economic stability but the government introduced several extremely controversial policies, including the **Reconciliation, Tolerance and Unity Bill** (2005) which would pardon all preceding coup perpetrators, and the **Qoliqoli Bill** (2006) which entrusted all beaches, lagoons and reefs to indigenous land owners with strong implications for the tourist industry.

1992	1997	1998
Democratic elections won by Rabuka.	Fiji readmitted to the Commonwealth.	Mahendra Chaudhry becomes the first Fiji-Indian prime minister.

Bainimarama and the fourth coup, 2006

Commodore Frank Bainimarama, head of Fiji's oversized military forces, had publicly disapproved of Qarase's contention of the 2001 elections, claiming that it had been a condition of his appointment as interim prime minister after the 2000 coup that he would not stand for re-election. Bainimarama was hell-bent on prosecuting all those involved in the previous coups, regardless of chiefly status, and on undertaking the even greater task of weeding out the **corruption** and nepotism rife amongst Qarase's highly paid and bumbling senior civil servants. Despite a very public war of words between the two, Qarase and his SDL party were returned to power in the general elections of May 2006.

By October, Bainimarama had issued a number of demands to the Qarase government relating to corruption and bringing the 2000 coup perpetrators to justice. A three-month deadline was set and when it came and went he announced that the Fijian military was taking control of the country in a televised address on **December 5, 2006**. Qarase was flown to his home island of Vanua Balavu. The coup, Fiji's fourth, had been widely expected and there was little disruption to daily life apart from army roadblocks. Foreign governments, particularly **Australia** and **New Zealand**, condemned the coup as illegal and issued stern advisories against all travel to Fiji, paralyzing the country's tourist industry.

Post-coup Fiji

In order to appease the international community, Bainimarama promised **democratic elections** for March 2009 and established a multiracial interim government that included Mahendra Chaudhry as minister of finance, with Bainimarama acting as interim prime minister. But instead of elections, 2009 saw a major constitutional crisis for the country. Bainimarama's government was declared illegal by the Court of Appeal, and he and the government resigned, only for the president to promptly dismiss the Court of Appeal ruling and reinstate Bainimarama as prime minister. **Public Emergency Regulations**, clamping down on the media and curtailing Fijians' freedom of speech and assembly, were put in place, and only lifted in 2012. The media remains parochial and bland, and it's rare to hear criticism of the government.

But Bainimarama has gained genuine popularity by trying to put an end to Fiji's coup culture (an aim ironically achieved via a coup) and by attempting to reduce the power of the archaic chiefdoms. His government's **People's Charter** aims to "rebuild Fiji into a non-racial, culturally vibrant and united, well-governed, truly democratic nation that seeks progress and prosperity through merit-based equality of opportunity and peace." Long-promised elections are finally scheduled for September 2014: in March, 2014, Bainimarama stepped down from the military in order to run as a legitimate candidate.

Tourism and the economy

Fiji's great economic hope lies in **tourism** and, fickle though the industry can be, visitor numbers have bounced back after each coup. However, with the proliferation of overseas investors in the industry it is increasingly difficult to ensure that tourist profits are reinvested in Fiji. One solution seems to be the development of community ecotourism as seen at Bouma National Heritage Park (see p.208).

2000	2000	2006
George Speight stages a third coup, imprisoning prime minister Chaudhry.	Army commander Frank Bainimarama intervenes and removes Speight.	Bainimarama stages a fourth coup in attempt to prosecute previous insurgents.

Tourism aside, the future of industry on the islands looks bleak. The country's dependence on imported produce has crippled Fiji's balance of trade. **Sugar**, once the mainstay of foreign income and the exclusive domain of Indian commerce, has slipped desperately in price, and preferential price agreements from the EU are set to expire in 2017. **Fishing** rights within Fiji's huge Exclusive Economic Zone (EEZ) offers some hope for sustained development, but with many of the fishing permits being sold to Taiwanese fishing boats, and without a policing unit to rid its waters of illegal longline fishing vessels, there is great fear of rapid depletion of fish stocks. Fiji's greatest success in recent years has been the export of bottled drinking **water**: several brands, especially Fiji Water, now compete successfully on global markets.

2009

Promised elections do not materialise, and Fiji is suspended from the Pacific Islands Forum and the Commonwealth.

2014

Bainimarama resigns from the military in order to stand in democratic elections.

Society and culture

Fijian society is essentially split into two groups: indigenous or ethnic Fijians, and the large Indian or "Fiji-Indian" minority. Ethnic Fijian culture is a unique blend of Melanesian and Polynesian tradition influenced by rigid Methodist Christianity introduced in the nineteenth century. Fiji-Indians maintain Hindu, Sikh and Muslim customs that were brought to the islands by indentured labourers from the Indian subcontinent. Other smaller minority groups include the Chinese, as well as other Pacific Islanders such as the Rotumans and Banabans.

Indigenous Fijians

Indigenous Fijians are bound in a strict hierarchal order based on a loyalty to their home village and tribe, an attachment which connects them in a broader sense to the land or *vanua*. At the pinnacle of ethnic Fijian hierarchy sit the **chiefs** or *ratu*, whose titles are inherited through the paternal lineage.

The tribal structure

Fiji is split into three **confederacies** or tribal unions: Burebasaga (southern Viti Levu and Kadavu); Tovata (northern Fiji and the Lau Group); and Kubuna (eastern Viti Levu and Lomaiviti). Kubuna is traditionally considered the most powerful as it was once ruled by Ratu Seru Cakobau (see p.210), who became King of Fiji in 1871. Tovata is the smallest but has been the most politically successful, contributing two post-independence prime ministers (Ratu Sir Kamisese Mara and Laisenia Qarase), while Burebasaga is the largest, incorporating Suva, Lautoka and Nadi; Burebasaga is also the only one permitting a woman to be its paramount chief.

Each confederacy is made up of a collection of **yavusa** or tribes. Each tribe usually lives in one village and is sub-divided into **mataqali** or clans. There are usually between three and six *mataqali* in a tribe. Each has a prescribed role within the village – the chiefly *mataqali* is known as the *turaga* and it is from here that the *yavusa*'s high chief is selected. The final order in the hierarchy is the **tokatoka**, or extended household, which binds closely related families. Within the *tokatoka* are individual households known as *vuvale*, and these are presided over by the senior male. All ethnic Fijians can thus define their position in society by declaring their family name, *tokatoka*, *mataqali* and *yavusa*.

VASU AND TAUVU

Two important concepts can influence the tribal hierarchy: *vasu* and *tauva*. **Vasu** is a special Melanesian privilege held by a nephew over his uncles on the mother's side. The extent of this privilege is limited by the rank of those concerned but a son born to both a chiefly mother and father can expect rights over the property of his uncles on the mother's side. Cakobau famously used this privilege to extend his powerbase from Bau.

The term **tauvu** literally means "sprung from the same spirit" and is the special relationship between two tribes sharing the same totemic god, usually an animal such as a turtle or shark. Every tribe knows its corresponding *tauvu* around the country even though the actual *vu*, or spirit, may well have been forgotten by the younger generation. The relationship of the *tauvu* enables free access to food and hospitality between the respective tribes and once meant allegiance in times of war.

TABUA

The **tabua**, the tooth of a sperm whale, is a much prized possession in Fijian culture. Usually fashioned into a necklace with coconut fibre, *tabua* were traditionally given for atonement or as a gift between chiefs to request a bonding relationship. Before the whaling days of the 1820s, whales' teeth were extremely rare and other items such as the barb of a stingray or the shell known as *cava* were used as the *tabua*. But with the slaughter of thousands of whales during the mid-nineteeenth century, whales' teeth began to circulate around the islands and their symbolic status was established as the norm. Today, *tabua* are still used to settle disputes between villages and are often presented at wedding ceremonies.

Administration and village law

For administrative purposes, the colonial government divided Fiji into four geographic areas – Western, Central, Eastern and Northern – made up of fourteen **provinces**, or *yasana*. These divisions still apply today. Within each province are a number of districts known as *tikina* which share a common pool of amenities such as health centres and schools. Villages are each expected to elect an administrator or **turaga ni koro** to enforce government rules. It is the *turaga ni koro* whom visitors should address when first entering a village, and not the chief, who is considered above such matters.

In most instances, **village law** takes precedence over the law of the land. For example, if a theft takes place, the suspect's family is advised and expected to punish the wrongdoer and seek forgiveness for the crime, usually by presenting food to the victim. Should this fail to resolve the matter, the *tokatoka* are gathered at a formal *yaqona* ceremony at which the individual is shamed and held accountable. Persistent offenders are dealt with by the leader of the *mataqali*, who in extreme cases may insist on a public flogging. For serious crimes, for example drug dealing, murder or rape, the *turaga ni koro* steps in to enforce government law.

Land rights

The issue of **land rights** is central to ethnic Fijian culture and identity. The vast majority (87 percent) of Fiji's land is owned by indigenous Fijians and classed as "native land" under a tenure system introduced by the British. Clan chiefs distribute land among their members for building homes or planting gardens for personal use. Should an individual wish to make a profit from the land, an official **government lease** must be obtained through the Native Land Trust Board (NLTB). It is from these land leases that the majority of rural Fijians receive an income to support their traditional lifestyles.

Traditional customs

One of Fiji's great achievements has been the retention of **traditional customs** in everyday life, not only within the village community but also throughout the business and political world. The most visible of these traditions is **yaqona drinking** (see box, p.31). The drink, known as *kava* across the rest of the South Pacific, is obtained by pouring water through pounded roots of the *Piper methysticum* plant. It was once a tradition reserved only for high priests and chiefs as a means of communicating with the ancient spirits. In times gone by, the *yaqona* roots were chewed by young maidens to make them soft and then grated and squeezed through hibiscus fibres into a wooden or clay bowl known as the *tanoa*. By the late 1800s, *yaqona* drinking had become the social event it is today and it remains very much at the heart of traditional Fijian culture. Ceremonial *yaqona* gatherings are usually followed by **feasting** and a traditional **meke** performance of dance and song (see box, p.62).

Yaqona is always drunk to mark the most important **celebrations**: the first birthday of the first-born child, puberty, marriage and death. Each features elaborate feasts and gift presentations, which all *mataqali* members should attend and contribute towards.

Money for village necessities is usually raised by a **soli**, a community fundraising event, which takes place in the nearest city or town and involves a meke dance performance or the selling of handicrafts.

Fiji-Indians

First brought to Fiji as indentured labourers, **Fiji-Indians** today make up 38 percent of the population. Indian influence can be seen throughout the islands, especially in the towns and cities of Viti Levu and Vanua Levu where small shops and businesses are almost exclusively run by Fiji-Indians. You'll also find Indian food is extremely popular in Fiji, with almost every small town boasting a curry house. However, despite repeated campaigns for equal rights, Fiji-Indians cannot buy freehold land or even call themselves "Fijian" (see box below). Given these circumstances, this large minority tends to operate as a society within a society and today many Fiji-Indians are looking for new opportunities overseas.

A key factor separating Fiji-Indians from Indians from the subcontinent is the more relaxed social structure seen in Fiji. When Indian labourers first arrived from the subcontinent under the *girmit* contract, the **caste system** which regulated life back home was instantly shed. Those of different castes were forced to live and work together and inter-caste marriage was common owing to the lack of female immigrants. In time, a form of pidgin Hindi became the universal language of both Hindus and Muslims, with words, phrases and accents borrowed from both English and Fijian. The resulting language, now known as **Fiji-Hindi**, is today almost unintelligible to Indians from the subcontinent.

Fiji's Hindu and Muslim populations share the same **religion** as their forefathers and celebrate all the major festivals. There are noisy celebrations at *Diwali* (October), face-painting at *Holi* (March) and enthralling fire-walking ceremonies regularly held at temples (April and September). The most notable Muslim celebrations are Ramadan and Eid.

During much of the postwar period Fiji-Indians outnumbered native Fijians, although the reverse is now true owing to mass emigration and a higher ethnic Fijian birthrate. Many well-educated Fiji-Indians have moved to Canada, Australia and New Zealand in response to Fiji's repeated political instability. The remainder struggle to get by on the **sugarcane farms**, hit by falling prices and the expiry of land leases.

Women in Fiji

Unless born of chiefly status, **women in Fiji** hold few positions of authority and the general attitude amongst both indigenous Fijians and Fiji-Indians is that a woman's place is at home or as a menial worker. Women received the right to vote in 1963 but appreciation of women's rights and equal opportunities is mostly overlooked by politicians. The non-governmental Fiji Women's Rights Movement (🖰 fwrm.org.fj) has aimed to redress this balance since its establishment in 1986 and has set up programmes to encourage women in leadership. By far the greatest concern to women of Fiji is **domestic violence**, accounting for sixty percent of cases reported to the Fiji Women's Crisis Centre (🖰 fijiwomen.com).

WHAT'S IN A NAME?

Under the Fijian constitution anyone who can trace their ancestry back to the Indian subcontinent is classed as "**Indian**" rather than "Fijian". Alternative names such as "Indian Fijian", "Indo-Fijian" and "Fiji-born Indian" have all been proposed but all have proved too controversial to be accepted by nationalist politicians. This is often due to the issue of property whereby only "Fijians", ie ethnic Fijian tribal members, can claim rights to native land. One of the more widely accepted terms is **Fiji-Indian** and we have used this name to refer to Fijians of Indian descent throughout this guide.

Modern culture

Modern Fijian culture preserves aspects of traditional Fijian and Indian life whilst being strongly influenced by globalization. Brought up with the Internet and satellite TV, young Fijians, both ethnic Fijian and Fiji-Indian, tend to mimic the trends in modern music and fashion of the West, especially Australia and New Zealand. In addition, interaction with tourists has led some Fijians to question their strictly religious and hierarchical culture.

Music

A few **Fijian musicians** have established themselves over the past two decades, including female singer Laisa Vulakoro, who blends Fijian folk with R&B in a style of music known locally as *vude*; and Rotuman/Irish Daniel Rae Costello, who has released over thirty albums and created a fusion style of calypso, latin and reggae known as "Aqualypso". The most successful Fijian band of recent years are **Rosiloa** (formerly Black Rose), who started out performing covers at tourist resorts in Nadi and now sell out gigs across the South Pacific. Their biggest hit, *Raude*, a blend of traditional meke music mixed with high-tempo dance beats, can be heard on their debut album *Voices of Nature* (2000); they have released a couple of albums since. The current music trend in Fiji is **hip-hop**, gentler than the US urban version and with a definite reggae influence, but the soundtrack blasting from buses and cars tends towards cheesy **pop**.

Film

Fiji's first and most celebrated native **film**, *The Land Has Eyes*, premiered at the Sundance Film Festival in 2004. Directed by Vilsoni Hereniko and filmed mostly on Rotuma, the film is a fabulous low-budget depiction of the islanders' conflicting attitudes to change. Focusing on the struggle of a young Rotuman girl caught between two worlds – the traditional life on Rotuma and a possible scholarship to the Fijian mainland – the film shares parallels with the internationally successful Maori film *Whale Rider*. Fiji has also proved a popular location for **Hollywood films** including *Blue Lagoon* (1979), *Return to the Blue Lagoon* (1991) and *Castaway* (2001), as well as the forgettable sequel to snake horror *Anaconda* (2004) and the suspense thriller *Boot Camp* (2008).

Art and craft

Contemporary Fijian **art and craft** reflects tradition, with paintings made upon *tapa* cloth and the wooden designs of war clubs, priest dishes and *tanoa* bowls providing inspiration. You can view displays and sometimes performing arts at the Oceania Centre for Arts and Culture (☎323 1000), part of the University of the South Pacific in Suva.

Sport

For a tiny nation, Fiji has had a significant impact in the world of **sport**. **Rugby Union** is a particular obsession and fills the back (and often front) pages of all the daily newspapers. The Fijian team won the Rugby World Cup Sevens in 1997 and 2005. The full fifteen-a-side team has also excelled but never quite matches the high expectations of the people – the national team reached the last eight of the 2007 Rugby World Cup, and were prevented from reaching the quarter finals in 2011 by a thumping Welsh victory. Several **Fiji-born players**, Lote Tuqiri and Sitiveni Sivivatu to name a couple, have been poached to play for Australia and New Zealand, although they still remain local heroes in their homeland.

Another international star is golfer **Vijay Singh** who claimed the world number one title from Tiger Woods between 2004 and 2005. He has also won three major championships (The Masters, 2000; PGA Championship, 1998 and 2004) – not bad considering he used to practise with coconuts on the beach as a child in Nadi. Other sports Fiji has excelled at on the world stage include netball, lawn bowls and judo.

Wildlife

The most obvious natural wonders of Fiji are to be found in its vast ocean habitats, littered with diverse coral reefs and bursting with over four thousand species of fish. Equally fascinating are the islands' steamy rainforests and mangroves, thick in vegetation and home to an elusive and vivid collection of native birds, though, with the exception of bats, devoid of any native mammals.

As with many isolated island groups, Fiji's terrestrial and freshwater ecosystems are particularly rich in **endemic species** (unique occurrences of species within a limited geographic area). Almost a thousand have been documented and over half of the country's plant species are unique to the islands.

Coral reefs and marine life

Fiji has some of the most accessible **coral reefs** in the world, often starting just metres from the beach and extending along veins or passages to the steep drop-offs of the fringing reefs where **reef sharks** or spinner dolphins can often be spotted. Deep, rich currents support large pelagic fish including tuna and trevally as well as bull, tiger and hammerhead sharks. Humpback **whales**, once frequent visitors between May and October, are now seldom encountered, with only a handful of sightings each year mostly around Lomaiviti, though smaller **pilot whales** can be seen year-round.

Extensive **barrier reefs** flank most of the larger volcanic islands. The longest is the Great Sea Reef off Vanua Levu, which has been ranked as globally significant owing to its unique diversity and exceptional level of endemic species. Other globally important **reef system**s include the Lomaiviti Triangle in the Koro Sea as well as the isolated reefs of Rotuma which support unique coral species. Smaller **patch reefs** can be found within the huge lagoon system of the Mamanuca Group and make popular snorkelling and diving spots. In the shallow lagoons of Viti Levu, those reefs not damaged by fishing are increasingly becoming bleached as a result of rising sea temperatures.

The reef

The building block of all coral reefs is the **coral polyp**, a small spineless animal similar to an anenome with a series of six or eight tentacles. In **hard corals**, the polyp uses

---

THE RISING OF THE BALOLO

This fascinating annual natural event occurs at various locations around the Pacific, but most prolifically in Fiji. The **balolo** (*Eunice viridis*) is a long spaghetti worm that lives deep in the coral reef. On two nights each year the male and female worms release their tails, containing sperm or eggs, to the surface in a perfectly synchronized spawning event. Amongst Fijians the worm's tail is a delicacy. Villagers head out to the reefs to gather the tails before the sun rises when they melt into a gooey mess. The worm is eaten raw or fried and said to taste like caviar. The larger of the two risings is known as the *Vula i Balolo Levu*, and occurs at high tide at the last quarter of the moon in either October or November.

On Vanua Levu, the appearance of the *balolo* coincides with the arrival of a deep-water fish called **deu** which swims up the mangrove estuaries to lay its eggs. Fijian women from villages along the southeast coast gather in the rivers to catch the *deu* with nets – if a lady doesn't catch one she's believed to have committed adultery and may be banished from the village for a year.

calcium carbonate from seawater to build itself a tough, cup-shaped skeleton. Polyps grow together in colonies of thousands, gradually constructing the reefs we see today. **Soft corals**, particularly common in Fiji, do not build skeletons and are soft or leathery in texture. They are found only in rich nutrient-fed currents and at lower light intensities.

Coral reefs are extremely sensitive to climatic conditions, partly due to their symbiotic relationship with a type of algae known as **zooxanthellae**. These algae live within the coral polyp and convert ocean nutrients through photosynthesis into food. Zooxanthellae also produce a range of pigments which give the otherwise clear, white coral its beautiful colour. Zooxanthellae depend on **light** for photosynthesis which is why corals can only thrive in clear waters less than 50m deep. Ideal water temperatures range between 24°C and 29°C, hence the large profusion of reefs in Fiji. If water temperatures suddenly change, the polyps stop growing and may expel the zooxanthellae, leading to the effect known as **coral bleaching**.

Reef fish

In almost every lagoon you'll find a huge range of small **reef fish**, some darting in and out of the coral, others coalescing in great schools.

Perhaps the most iconic reef fish is the orange and white **clown anenomefish**. Clownfish are found weaving through the tentacles of stinging sea anenomes with which they form a symbiotic relationship. Although they live in pairs as lifetime partners, you may notice a third, smaller clown fish hanging around. This is a non-mating male who functions as a kind of insurance policy. If the female clown fish dies, the dominant male changes sex and the smaller fish takes over as the male. Surprisingly feisty, clown fish will rush up to your mask if you get too close.

Closely related to the clownfish is the ubiquitous **damselfish**. Only around 5cm from nose to tail, damselfish come in a huge range of colours, the most vivid being the golden and black-and-white striped versions. Larger but just as colourful are the elegant **butterflyfish** and **angelfish**. Difficult to tell apart, these species both whizz around the reef in pairs. If you can get up close you may notice a small spine by the gills that indicates an angelfish rather than a butterflyfish. Also possessing a sharp spine is the aptly named **surgeonfish**, a streamlined version of the angelfish often found in large schools.

One of the few fish you can hear underwater is the **parrotfish**, who munch away at the reef making a distinctive scraping sound with their sharp, beaked mouth. Larger reef fish found in lagoons include the thick-lipped, grumpy-looking **grouper** and the long, streamlined **barracuda**, who often file past in squadrons.

Sharks

Of the dozens of shark species found in Fijian waters, by far the most common are the smaller **reef sharks** (blacktips, whitetips and, to a lesser extent, grey reef). These elegant shallow-water predators seldom reach over 2m in length and feed on small reef fish, squid and crustaceans. Of the **big sharks**, bulls, tigers and hammerheads are present in Fiji but rarely enter the lagoons, preferring the deep current-fed passages along the outer edges of the reefs, or, as is the case with bull sharks, lurking in the murky coastal waters and mangrove estuaries. Bull sharks have beady eyes and a blunt snout and are considered the most aggressive shark species, owing to their high levels of testosterone. Tiger sharks have a distinct mottled skin tone and are occasionally encountered on the shark-feeding dives carried out in Beqa Lagoon. Hammerheads are the most timid of the three and stick to deeper waters. **Shark attacks** in Fiji are incredibly rare. Those that have occurred have almost always involved local spear fishermen carrying bloody, injured fish.

DO NOT DISTURB!

Triggerfish Fiercely territorial, the brightly coloured triggerfish has an unnerving habit of rushing full speed towards divers encroaching on its space. It has small but sharp teeth and can give a nasty nip.

Lionfish Named after its large mane of feathers, this beautiful fish is often seen hovering at reef walls. Between the feathers is a set of sharp, venomous spines that can deliver a painful sting.

Moray eel Growing up to 3m in length, moray eels are nocturnal predators with sharp teeth and large, gaping jaws. By day they rest in crevices and holes in the reef, occasionally poking their heads out to have a look around. They will only bite humans if provoked.

Pufferfish The most poisonous marine animal in the world, puffer fish blow themselves up into a ball when threatened – an obvious sign to leave well alone.

Rays

Three types of rays are found in Fiji. The largest are the bat-like **manta rays** that can grow to over 4m in width and are often seen around the Yasawa Islands. The smaller **stingray** is harder to spot, preferring to bury itself in the sandy bottom of lagoons. Armed with a razor-sharp venomous barb, stingrays only present a danger when stood upon – always look before settling on a patch of sand. The rarest type of ray in Fiji is the beautiful **spotted eagle ray**. This species, which features numerous white spots on an inky blue body, hunts in the open ocean.

Turtles

Four species of **sea turtle** – loggerhead, leatherback, green and hawksbill – lay their eggs deep in the sand of Fiji's coral cays. Hawksbill turtles are the most common, and can be found in Fiji's oceans year-round while greens and leatherbacks only visit during the nesting season (Nov–Feb) – the latter is the largest type of sea turtle and is sadly becoming a rare sight.

Invertebrates

Marine **invertebrates** include crustaceans, molluscs and starfish as well as sponges and sea anemones. One of the most fascinating is the colourful **nudibranch** or "sea slug". Tiny creatures, barely the width of a fingernail, nudibranchs come in over three thousand varieties. Their Latin name means "naked gills" and refers to the feather-like appendages above their bodies. Also found crawling across the reef are tiny **coral shrimps**. Certain species of shrimp creep into the mouths of reef fish to clear away parasites. Found on the bottom of shallow lagoons is the leathery **sea cucumber**. Also known as "bêche de mer", sea cucumbers are considered a delicacy in China and are gathered by local fishermen for export.

The islands' seagrass beds and coral reefs also provide habitats for three species of **sea snakes** including the distinctive black and white banded sea snake. **Hermit crabs** in stolen shells can be seen crawling around most beaches leaving curious trails in their wake, while massive **coconut crabs**, whose claws are so powerful that they can rip through the husk of a coconut, make a tasty meal if caught – a tin strip is often wrapped around the trunk of coconut palms to stop the crab from climbing up to scavenge the nuts.

Sea birds

Nineteen species of endemic **sea birds** are found in Fiji's lagoons, most nesting on tiny coral and limestone islands or on cliff edges along the larger islands. The stately **frigate bird** is the largest of this group and its distinctive split tail outline is often seen high in the sky and near the coastline when stormy weather is approaching. Strikingly white **tropicbirds** with long tail feathers are also prolific, as are clumsy-looking oversized

boobies, along with the smaller terns and noddies which follow each other around on fishing expeditions and dive bomb the lagoons in spectacular fashion. Shearwaters and **reef herons** can be spotted island-wide, cautiously prancing along the beach edge in search of fish.

Mangrove forest

Fiji's eighteen thousand hectares of **mangrove forest** buffer much of the coastline along Viti Levu and Vanua Levu and provide important breeding grounds for many of Fiji's reef fish. They also perform an invaluable role in protecting the coastline from hurricanes and wave erosion. With thick tentacle roots draping from the forest canopy and stumps thrusting upwards from the murky blend of fresh and salt water, these forests are unforgiving environments but incredibly productive. **Birdlife** abounds, with mangrove herons, kingfishers, lories and orange-breasted honey-eaters the most commonly found species. For the Fijians living around the river deltas, the *tiri* (mangrove) offer a plethora of foodstuffs, with an abundance of **small fish** caught in reed traps, shrimps and, most delicious of all, **mud crabs** scooped up in fishing nets.

Rainforests and terrestrial wildlife

Fiji's tropical **rainforests** are incredibly dense, with tall, thin trees entangled with vines and creepers crowding upwards towards the elusive light. Below the canopy, impressive prehistoric-looking **tree ferns** grow in profusion while several beautiful species of **wild orchids** can be found on the forest floor. Of the 1600 known plants found in Fiji, 56 percent are endemic, most found only within the rainforest.

More than forty percent of the forest cover of the islands remains intact, and some islands, such as Taveuni, still have contiguous forest stretching from the high-altitude cloudforest all the way to the coast. The largest tract of virgin primary forest is the Sovi Basin on Viti Levu, which has become an important area for sustaining birdlife. The remainder of Fiji's rainforest has usually been influenced by people, either through logging or farming. On the wet **windward** sides of the islands, Fijian hardwood species

COCONUT – A LIFELINE

The **coconut palm** (*Cocos nucifera*) is a symbol of paradise and lines the shores of most Fijian beaches. For the islanders, it's a symbol of life and once accompanied the early Polynesians on their epic journeys across the Pacific. Its practical uses are considerable: the **leaves** are woven to make hats and baskets and used to thatch roofs, whilst the rigid discarded midrib of the leaf is gathered to make *sasa* brooms. **Milk** from the young nuts is drunk while the meaty **flesh** is eaten or scraped to make coconut cream. The mature nut has a hard flesh which is dried and cut to make **copra**, from which commercial grade coconut oil is produced. The hard inner **shell** of the coconut makes a handy bowl traditionally used for *yaqona* drinking (see box, p.31) and to make earrings and other jewellery. The dry stringy fibres of the outer husk are rolled to make *magimagi* (see p.183), a coil used for binding bures and for decorative art. Coconut fibres are also perfect for use as kindling and the husks often fuel the village kitchen stove.

Coconut palms often reach 30m in height and you'll frequently hear the dull thud of a nut falling to the ground. In fact, the threat of **death by falling coconut** has become something of an urban myth, with a figure of 150 fatalities per year often reported by journalists (often used in comparison to, say, shark attacks or plane crash statistics). This story can be traced back to an article in the *Journal of Trauma* which focused on coconut injuries in Papua New Guinea. Although there were four reported injuries and two deaths, these included people who had died whilst climbing the trees. Given deaths caused by falling coconuts are not recorded, the 150 figure is likely to have been plucked out of thin air.

such as *kauvula* and *kadamu* are common as well as *dakua*, a softer conifer from the kauri family used locally for furniture making. The heavier hardwoods of *damanu*, *vesi* and *rosawa* have been cut extensively for timber export and craft. Perhaps the most beautiful of trees found in the forest is the **banyan**, a member of the fig family. The banyan initially grows as a vine on a host tree before its aerial prop roots descend and embed themselves in the ground, creating huge buttress roots which meander along the forest floor.

The dry **leeward** sides of Fiji's islands were once home to large tracts of casuarinas, ironwood and sandalwood forests. Most of the land is now covered in **grassland** or planted with imported Caribbean pine. The most fertile soil is found along the river valleys, particularly on the larger islands, and this is almost always converted to **sugarcane farmland**.

Several rogue species are beginning to dominate Fiji's native forests, notably the soft-wooded and fast-growing **African Tulip** found along riverbeds and the **mahogany tree** introduced over forty years ago. Over forty thousand acres of mahogany plantation are now ready for cultivation, the largest supply of the lucrative hardwood outside Brazil.

Terrestrial birds and animals

Most impressive of the 57 native breeding terrestrial **birds** is the crimson **Kadavu shining parrot**, unique to the islands of the Kadavu Group. Other large parrots can be found on Taveuni, Gau and Koro. Most common of the smaller forest species are fruit doves, fantails and white-eyes, with the fabulously vivid **orange dove** and golden dove being the most striking. The velvet-black silktail and dusky coloured long-legged warbler are the most elusive of Fiji's birds and listed as critically endangered. The dry grasslands are the preferred hunting grounds for Fiji's **birds of prey**, which include the Fiji goshawk, Pacific harrier and peregrine falcon. Collared lories, parrot finches and honey-eaters can be spotted in urban gardens.

The only terrestrial **mammals** native to Fiji are **bats**, of which there are two endemic species – the Fijian flying fox and the small Fiji blossom bat. Otherwise the islands' largest land-based species are comprised solely of reptiles and amphibians. These include the crested iguana (see p.194), two snakes – the Pacific boa and the mildly poisonous but seldom seen Fijian burrowing snake – two frogs and a variety of tiny geckos or skinks. Fiji's forests support a huge range of **insects** including 44 recorded varieties of **butterflies**; most have simple brown and black colourings in order to blend in with the dark foliage. Much more vivid are the **dragonflies**, which are commonly seen at streams within the forest.

The **mongoose**, often seen scuttling across roads between cane fields, was introduced from India in the 1880s to control rats that were damaging sugar plantations. Without a natural predator they thrived and along with the **mynah**, an aggressive and chatty black and white bird introduced at the same time, they have been responsible for chasing much of Fiji's native birdlife away from the coastal areas and into the deep forest. The best islands for **birdwatching** are Kadavu and Taveuni which remain free of the mongoose. The introduction of the exceptionally ugly **cane toad** from South America in the 1930s to check the spread of cane beetles was similarly short-sighted. When threatened, the cane toad and its tadpoles excrete a milky poison from glands on the back which can kill native wildlife. Unfortunately, the toad is now prolific around Fiji's countryside.

Books

Fijian literature has focused mostly on political analysis, with numerous critical writings confronting the country's ethnic problems and military coups. Fiction makes for slim pickings and Fijian books can be hard to find outside of the country. The most reliable source is the University Book Centre at the University of the South Pacific (☎321 2500, ⓦuspbookcentre .com), which will ship books internationally. Other bookshops are listed in the Guide.

HISTORY

R. A. Derrick *A History of Fiji* (Government Press, Fiji). Originally written in 1942, this classic of early Fijian history up to cession in 1874 is arranged thematically, which makes it much more interesting than the usual trawl through dates.

Kim Gravelle *Fiji's Heritage – A History of Fiji* (Tiara Enterprises, Fiji). Thoroughly readable history highlighting fifty important events that have shaped the destiny of the country.

Rajendra Prasad *Tears in Paradise* (Glade, New Zealand). Documenting the Indian struggle for acceptance and identity, this book is the best of a collection of contemporary writings giving the Indian perspective on the last 125 years.

David Routledge *The struggle for power in early Fiji* (Institute of Pacific Studies, Fiji). An academic perspective tracing events from early Fijian history to independence in 1970 – historical photos and engravings keep things lively.

★**Baron Anatole von Hügel** *Fiji Journals 1875–1877* (Fiji Museum Press). Wonderful diary of a young half-British, half-Austrian rogue who tramped around Fiji in the late nineteenth century. Von Hügel made several expeditions into the interior of Viti Levu, collecting many artefacts and drinking vast quantities of *yaqona* along the way. A lively insight into Fijian life during early colonial times.

CULTURE AND SOCIETY

Mensah Adinkrah *Crime, Deviance and Delinquency in Fiji* (Fiji Council of Social Services). If you can't quite believe Fiji has a dark side, this thought-provoking collection of essays, balanced with sociological reasoning, makes for essential reading.

Solomoni Biturogoiwasa *My Village, My World; Everyday Life in Nadoria, Fiji* (University of the South Pacific). Refreshingly simple insight into everyday village life, packed with colourful detail.

★**Winston Halapua** *Tradition, Lotu & Militarism in Fiji.* An insider's view of local politics and ethnicity, revealing the deceptive world of self-interest and fascism amongst Fiji's elite.

Asesela Ravuvu *The Facade of Democracy: Fijian Struggles for Political Control* (Reader Publishing, Fiji). An insight into the mind of a Fijian nationalist, critical of both European and Indian involvement in Fijian society.

Sir Vijay R. Singh *Speaking Out* (Knightsbrook, Australia). Not to be confused with the golfer of the same name, the author of this bold collection of thought-provoking articles is one of Fiji's most prominent Fiji-Indian politicians. Focusing on the events of the 1987 and 2000 coups, the book ruffled quite a few feathers, prompting several nationalist politicians to call for it to be banned.

★**Peter Thomson** *Kava in the Blood* (Tandem Press, UK). A recollection of life growing up in Fiji, of serving in the government administration and of confronting and ultimately accepting the hard realities of the coups.

NATURE AND THE ENVIRONMENT

Clare Morrison *Herpetofauna of Fiji* (University of the South Pacific). A little book covering a pretty slim subject in scientific detail, with colour photos of Fiji's reptiles and amphibians.

Ian Osborn *Beautiful Fiji* (Pacific Travel Guides, Fiji). Photographic journey through Fiji's pristine environment.

Dick Watling *A Guide to the Birds of Fiji & Western Polynesia* (Environmental Consultants, Fiji, ⓦpacificbirds .com). The birdies' bible, with colour plates and detailed accounts of 173 species found throughout the region.

Dr Michael A. Weiner *Secrets of Fijian Medicine* (University of California Press, US). Records some of Fiji's dying knowledge of traditional medicine. Arranged by type of illness and listing Fijian and English plant names.

TRAVELLERS' TALES

★**Kim Gravelle** *Romancing the Islands* (Graphics Pacific, Fiji). Written by one of the South Pacific's leading photojournalists, Gravelle recounts 44 of his liveliest tales of adventure, all featuring a refreshing hint of humour.

Paul Theroux *Happy Isles of Oceania* (Penguin, US & UK). A good read from one of the few big-name travel writers to have written about the South Pacific. His account of Fiji, one of several island nations covered, portrays some of the less-than-democratic aspects of Fijian society and was felt by many to have cut a little too close to the bone.

J. Maarten Troost *Getting Stoned with Savages* (Broadway Books, US). A witty tale of misadventure that begins in Vanuatu and ends with a candid view of Fiji in the modern world.

FICTION

Robert Campbell *Tradewinds & Treachery* (Steele Roberts, New Zealand). A clash of cultures and ideologies haunts this tale of love in the turbulent years leading up to colonial rule.

Allan Carson *Pacific Intrigue* (Durban House, US). A fast-paced American detective story of Islamic terrorist activity set between Seattle and Suva, touching on the simmering tensions between Fijians and Indians.

★**Daryl Tarte** *Fiji: a Bloody and Lustful Story of Fiji's History* (Pascoe Publishing, Australia). Renowned local writer Tarte permits himself a little bit of fantasy entwined with the facts to produce this fine tale of intrigue in grand Michener-style proportions.

Joseph C. Veramu *Moving through the Streets* (Mana Publications, Fiji). This Suva-set novel by a lecturer at the University of the South Pacific provides a realistic account of the pressures and temptations facing Fiji's urban youth.

DICTIONARIES AND LANGUAGE

A. Capell *The Fijian Dictionary.* Comprehensive dictionary with Fijian/English and English/Fijian.

A.J. Schütz *Say it in Fijian.* Well-written guide to Fijian; includes a small dictionary.

G.B. Milner *Fijian Grammar.* Detailed text covering all grammatical aspects of Fijian.

Language

English is the official language of Fiji, taught and spoken in schools and used in parliament and in business. Throughout the upper strata of Fijian society the language is spoken with great fluency, with an accent not dissimilar to British Received Pronunciation or "Queen's English". Young people speak their own casual blend of English, spoken with a hint of a South African accent, and with words and phrases borrowed from both Fijian and Fiji Hindi.

At home, indigenous Fijians speak **Fijian**, Rotumans speak **Rotuman** and Fiji-Indians speak **Fiji Hindi**, a unique form of Hindustani. Some Fiji-Indians, especially in the rural areas around north Viti Levu, Vanua Levu and Taveuni, speak Fijian as a third language and a few Fijians speak Fiji Hindi but the two ethnic groups tend to converse in English. Learning a few basic phrases in either language will raise a smile among the locals and prove especially useful for travellers staying in rural areas.

Fijian

Fijian is part of the Malayo-Polynesian branch of the huge Austronesian family of languages, which stretches from Madagascar to Easter Island, and from Taiwan and Hawaii to New Zealand. Within Fiji, regional isolation has led to the formation of nine distinct dialects. For example, the commonly used word "*vinaka*", which in its simplest form means "good", has many variations: "*vinaduriki*" in the Yasawas, "*vina'a*" in Taveuni and "*malo*" in Lau. In the 1840s, the dialect known as **Bauan** was the first version of Fijian to be transcribed into the roman alphabet (by Scottish missionary David Cargill). This has lead Bauan to become the most universally accepted type of Fijian, and it is the version taught in schools and used at formal occasions.

The two most difficult aspects of Fijian to a foreign ear are the pronunciation of consonants and the difficulty in differentiating words. Fijian sentences sound as if they are spoken as one long jumbled word with syllables rolling into each other. It is common for Fijians to speak in a **monotone**, with one person talking uninterrupted before the second person speaks – bouncing conversations back and forth is considered impolite. See opposite for details of Fijian **dictionaries** and language textbooks.

Pronunciation

The majority of letters are pronounced as in spoken English, although the first **vowel** in a word is usually emphasized. Some vowels are drawn out, in which case they are marked with a macron (ā). More awkward to pronounce are the **consonants**:

b is pronounced "mb" with a soft m as in nu**mb**er
c is pronounced as a "th" sound as in mo**th**er
d sounds like the "nd" in sa**nd**y

g has a soft "ng" sound as in si**ng**er
q has a harder "ngg" as in fi**ng**er
r is usually rolled

Once the above system is mastered, **place names** begin to make sense. For example, Lakeba is pronounced "Lakemba", Nadi becomes "Nandi" and Beqa is pronounced "Mbenga".

> **BULA!**
> **Bula** literally means "life" in Fijian. You'll hear it everywhere and from everyone. It is used as a greeting, and in its simplest form translates as "hello". "*Ni sa bula*" is a more polite form of greeting, with the reply being "*bula vinaka*".

BASIC PHRASES

hello (polite)	(nī sā) bula	when?	naica?
yes	io	how many?	vica?
no	sega	it's ok	sa vinaka
please	yalo vinaka, mada	no problem	sega na leqa
thank you (very much)	vinaka (vakalevu)	excuse me	tulou
good morning (polite)	(nī sā) yadra	I'm sorry	lomana
what is your name? (polite)	o cei na yacamu (nī)?	go away	lako tani
my name is …	na yacaqu o …	stop!	kua!
where are you from?	o nī lako mai vei?	slow down!	malua!
I'm from …	au lako mai …	one more	dua tale
who?	cei?	see you again	sota tale
where?	vei?	see you tomorrow	sota ni mataka
what?	cawa?	goodbye (polite)	(nī sā) moce

NUMBERS

1	dua	13	tini ka tolu
2	rua	14	tini ka vā
3	tolu	15	tini ka lima
4	vā	16	tini ka ono
5	lima	17	tini ka vitu
6	ono	18	tini ka walu
7	vitu	19	tini ka ciwa
8	walu	20	ruasagavulu
9	ciwa	21	ruasagavulu ka dua
10	tini	30	tolusagavulu
11	tini ka dua	100	dua na drau
12	tini ka rua	1000	dua na udolu

GETTING AROUND

where is the …?	e vai (beka) na …?	farm, garden	teitei
where are you going? (also used as how are you?)	o lai vei?	forest	veikau
		house	vale
nowhere particular (general response)	sega, gāde gā	island	yanuyanu
		mountain	qulunivanua
near	vōleka	road, path	sala
far	yawa	school	koronivuli
let's go	daru lako	shop	sitoa
I am going to …	au lai na …	sleeping house	bure
beach	matāsawa	village	koro

TIMINGS

today	ni kua	late	bera
tomorrow	ni mataka	night	bogi
yesterday	nanoa	ready	vaka rau

USEFUL VOCABULARY

beautiful	totoka	diarrhoea	coka
big, many	levu	difficult	drēdrē
busy, full	osooso	dirty	duka
clean	savata	fishing	siwa
cold	batabatā	hot	katakata
cup	bilo	knife	isele
delicious	maleka	money	ilavo

old	makawa	strong	kaukaua
perhaps	beka	sunny	siga
photo	taba	swim	qalo
possible	rawa	tired	oca
rain	uca	toilet	vale lailai
request	kerekere	too much	rui
sanitary towel	qamuqamu	turtle	vonu
shark	qio	walk	gādē
single, alone	taudua	wind	cagi
small, little	lailai		

FOOD AND DRINK

bele	green vegetable	qari	cooked crab
bulumakau	beef	rourou	spinach
dalo	taro, a root crop	saqa	boiled
ika	fish (general)	tapioca	cassava, root crop
jaina	banana	ura	cooked prawn
kokoda	fish marinated in	uvi	yam
	lime juice	vakalolo	pudding made from
lolo	coconut cream		*dalo* and coconut
lovo	underground oven		cream
mai kana!	come and eat!	vua	fruit
niu	coconut	wai	water
ota	seaweed	weleti	papaya/pawpaw

Fiji Hindi

Fiji Hindi, spoken by all Fiji-Indians, is a unique blend of several Hindustani dialects with a smattering of Arabic, English and Fijian words and phrases thrown in. In religious worship, classical Sanskrit written in Devanagari is used and Devanagari is taught in Indian schools. Gujaratis and Sikhs retain closer ties with their traditional languages when speaking amongst each other.

BASICS

hello (casual)	ram ram	please	thoraa
hello (polite)	namaste	thank you, goodbye	dhanyewaad
hello (Muslim)	salaam walekum	good, I see	achaa
how are you?	kaise?	bad	kharab
fine	theek	ok	ha or rite
what is your name?	kon naam tumhar?	come and eat	aao khana khao
my name is ...	hamar naam hai ...	drink, smoke	pio
what's this?	honchi he?	tea	cha
how much?	kitna?	warm, hot	garam
yes	ha	wait	sabur karo
no	nahi or na	sit	baitho
too much	bahut	perhaps	shayad
I don't want it	nahi magta	photograph	tasveer
excuse me, sorry	maaf karna	see you again	phir milenge

NUMBERS

1	ek	5	paanch
2	do	6	cha
3	teen	7	saat
4	chaar	8	aat

| 9 | no | 100 | sao |
| 10 | das | 1000 | hazaar |

FIJI-INDIAN FOOD

archaar	pickles		baked in a tandoor
baigan	eggplant		oven
bhaath	cooked rice	pilau	rice, gently fried with
bhindii	okra		spices
biryani	rice dish of meat or	puri	puffed up bread,
	vegetables baked		deep-fried and crispy
	with turmeric and	roti	round unleavened
	whole spices		flat-bread, cooked on
chapatti	unleavened		a hot plate
	flat-bread	samosa	stuffed pastry cooked
dhal	lentils, often cooked		in oil
	in soup	thali	combination of
ghee	clarified butter		vegetarian and
gulgula	pancake		sometimes meat
halwa	Indian sweet		dishes with chutney,
korma	meat braised in		pickles, rice, roti and
	yoghurt		dhal; served as a
	sauce (mild)		single meal
masala	curry powder	vindaloo	meat, usually pork,
murga	chicken		seasoned in vinegar
naan	white leavened bread		(hot)

Rotuman

Rotuman is spoken exclusively by the people of Rotuma, a Polynesian island in the far north of Fiji. It has a distinctive word structure featuring metathesis (two vowels following each other but creating two separate quite abrupt sounds) and an extensive use of diphthongs (vowel clusters). To confuse matters further, many words have been borrowed or adapted from Samoan and Tongan. The apostrophe is used between vowels to indicate a glottal stop while the macron (ā) indicates extended vowels as in Fijian. The use of diaeresis (ä) means that a vowel should be pronounced apart from the letter which precedes it.

If you're interested in **studying Rotuman** it's worth getting hold of Elizabeth Inia's *A New Rotuman Dictionary* available from ⓦpacificislandbooks.com. Alternatively, the excellent Rotuman website ⓦrotuma.net has links to sound files of spoken Rotuman.

BASICS

hello	faiäksia noa'ia	please	figalelei
where are you going?	'äe la'se tei?	thank you	faiäksia
what is your name?	sei ta 'ou asa?	yes	'i
my name is ...	'otou asa le ...	no	'igka
what's this?	ka tese te?	goodbye	nonoam

USEFUL WORDS

dance	mak	rest	au'ua se
drink	īom	sea	sasi
eat	āte	sit down	päe se lopo
fishing	hagoat	sleep	mös
hurry up	rue la mij	slow down	ariri'se
plantation	vekaogta	swim, shower	kakou

ROTUMAN DISHES

fekei	sticky, starchy sweet	**tāhroro**	fermented coconut milk
porasam	*taro* leaf cooked in coconut cream		flavoured with chili

Glossary

Adi female chiefly title

balabala the trunk of a tree fern, used decoratively in villages and gardens

balolo marine worm living in coral reefs and considered a delicacy

bati warrior

bete priest

bilibili bamboo raft

bilo coconut shell used for drinking yaqona

boso slang for "boss"

bure bose meeting hall

bure kalou traditional Fijian temple

chautaal traditional songs sung at the Hindu Holi festival

cobo clapping with cupped hands

copra the dried, oil-yielding kernel of the coconut

dakua popular wood for carving

Daquwaqa Fijian shark god

Degei most revered of the Fijian gods

Diwali Hindu celebration, festival of lights

drua war canoe

Eid Muslim holiday marking the end of Ramadan

Fara Rotuman Christmas festival

girmit labour contract given to Indian indentured labourers

Holi Hindu celebration, festival of colours

ivi Tahitian chestnut tree believed to have spiritual connotations and found in ancient villages

kai colo hill people from the interior of Viti Levu

kai loma people of part Fijian, part European descent

kai viti people of Fiji

kai vulagi people from overseas

kava Polynesian word for yaqona

kerekere communal borrowing

lali slit drum hollowed from a hardwood tree

Lapita ancient Pacific Ocean culture named after their distinct style of pottery

loloma affectionate greeting

lotu in broad terms, Christianity or the Church

lovo traditional food cooked in an underground oven

magimagi plaited coconut fibre

mana spiritual power

manumanu the three totems of a clan, usually a fish, an animal and a fruit or tree

masi tapa cloth decorated with stencilled designs

masu prayer said before meal

mataqali land-owning clan

meke traditional song and dance performance

qai tattoo

qoliqoli area from high tide mark to the reef edge, perceived by some as public access and others as mataqali-owned

Ramadan the Islamic holy month of fasting

rara village green

Ratu male chiefly title

reguregu sniff to the cheeks, used as a greeting between clan members

Ro chiefly title of Rewa, Naitasiri, Namosi and Serua provinces

Roko chiefly title of the Lau Group

salwar kameez traditional dress worn by Muslims

sari traditional Indian dress

sere chant at a yaqona ceremony

sevusevu ceremonial offering of yaqona

solevu large ceremonial gathering

soli fundraising event

sulu Fijian sarong

suluka home-made, rolled tobacco leaf

tabu forbidden, sacred

tabua traditional gift, usually a whale's tooth, given in return for a favour or to ask for atonement

tanoa wooden bowl with four or more legs used for preparing yaqona

tapa paper cloth made from the mulberry tree, used as traditional dress

taukei original inhabitant; movement for indigenous rights

tauvu tribes sharing the same totemic god

tiri mangrove forests

tokatoka extended household

tualeita ancient pathway connecting villages

Turaga ni vuvale head of the house

Turanga ni koro head of the village

Turanga respected title donating the head of a group of people; old-fashioned address similar to "gentleman"

vanua land to which Fijians are spiritually bound

vasu the concept of a nephew or niece having privileges over an uncle

vesi popular wood for carving

voivoi leaf of the pandanus plant used for weaving

vude Fijian music blending folk and R&B

waqa yaqona roots in powder form

yaqona mildly narcotic ceremonial and social drink strained from the root of the *Piper* methysticum plant

yavusa tribe

Small print and index

A ROUGH GUIDE TO ROUGH GUIDES

Published in 1982, the first Rough Guide – to Greece – was a student scheme that became a publishing phenomenon. Mark Ellingham, a recent graduate in English from Bristol University, had been travelling in Greece the previous summer and couldn't find the right guidebook. With a small group of friends he wrote his own guide, combining a highly contemporary, journalistic style with a thoroughly practical approach to travellers' needs.

The immediate success of the book spawned a series that rapidly covered dozens of destinations. And, in addition to impecunious backpackers, Rough Guides soon acquired a much broader readership that relished the guides' wit and inquisitiveness as much as their enthusiastic, critical approach and value-for-money ethos.

These days, Rough Guides include recommendations from budget to luxury and cover more than 120 destinations around the globe, as well as producing an ever-growing range of ebooks.

Visit **roughguides.com** to find all our latest books, read articles, get inspired and share travel tips with the Rough Guides community.

Rough Guide credits

Editor: Claire Saunders
Layout: Anita Singh
Cartography: Katie Bennett
Picture editor: Emily Taylor
Proofreader: Stewart Wild
Managing editor: Keith Drew
Assistant editor: Prema Dutta

Production: Charlotte Cade
Cover design: Nicole Newman, Emily Taylor, Anita Singh
Editorial assistant: Rebecca Hallett
Senior pre-press designer: Dan May
Programme manager: Helen Blount
Publisher: Joanna Kirby
Publishing director: Georgina Dee

Publishing information

This second edition published November 2014 by
Rough Guides Ltd,
80 Strand, London WC2R 0RL
11, Community Centre, Panchsheel Park,
New Delhi 110017, India
Distributed by Penguin Random House
Penguin Books Ltd,
80 Strand, London WC2R 0RL
Penguin Group (USA)
345 Hudson Street, NY 10014, USA
Penguin Group (Australia)
250 Camberwell Road, Camberwell,
Victoria 3124, Australia
Penguin Group (NZ)
67 Apollo Drive, Mairangi Bay, Auckland 1310,
New Zealand
Penguin Group (South Africa)
Block D, Rosebank Office Park, 181 Jan Smuts Avenue,
Parktown North, Gauteng, South Africa 2193
Rough Guides is represented in Canada by Tourmaline
Editions Inc. 662 King Street West, Suite 304, Toronto,
Ontario M5V 1M7
Printed in Singapore by Toppan Security Printing Pte. Ltd.

© Rough Guides, 2014
Maps © Rough Guides
No part of this book may be reproduced in any form
without permission from the publisher except for the
quotation of brief passages in reviews.
256pp includes index
A catalogue record for this book is available from the
British Library
ISBN: 978-1-40935-133-7
The publishers and authors have done their best to
ensure the accuracy and currency of all the information
in **The Rough Guide to Fiji**, however, they can accept
no responsibility for any loss, injury, or inconvenience
sustained by any traveller as a result of information or
advice contained in the guide.
1 3 5 7 9 8 6 4 2

MIX
Paper from
responsible sources
FSC
www.fsc.org FSC™ C018179

Help us update

We've gone to a lot of effort to ensure that the second edition of **The Rough Guide to Fiji** is accurate and up-to-date. However, things change – places get "discovered", opening hours are notoriously fickle, restaurants and rooms raise prices or lower standards. If you feel we've got it wrong or left something out, we'd like to know, and if you can remember the address, the price, the hours, the phone number, so much the better.

Please send your comments with the subject line "**Rough Guide Fiji Update**" to ✉ mail@uk.roughguides .com. We'll credit all contributions and send a copy of the next edition (or any other Rough Guide if you prefer) for the very best emails.

Find more travel information, connect with fellow travellers and plan your trip on Ⓦ roughguides.com.

ABOUT THE AUTHOR

Helena Smith is a freelance writer and photographer who specializes in independent travel and community projects. She blogs about food and her home borough at eathackney.com.

Acknowledgements

Vinaka to all the incredibly kind and hospitable people I met in Fiji, especially Sharon in Savusavu; Tilly and Juli in Matei; and Sudesh, Margaret and Suzie in Suva. Also to Ian Osborn who wrote the first edition of this guide and was generous with his advice. Plus thanks to old friends Claire Saunders who edited this book, and Keith Drew who commissioned it.

Photo credits

Index

Maps are marked in grey

Map symbols

The symbols below are used on maps throughout the book

✈	International airport	⊤	Wind farm	— —	Ferry
✈	Domestic airport/airstrip	☀	Lighthouse	– – – –	Footpath
♦	Place of interest	⚑	Viewpoint	═══	Road
⊠	Post office	⌒	Mountain range		Unpaved road
ⓘ	Information office	▲	Mountain peak		Pedestrian road
⊞	Hospital	/◣	Volcano	▭▭▭	Steps
★	Transport stand	⋀	Spring	══	Railway
⚓	Anchorage	⍣	Reef	▥	Building
⛽	Fuel station	⌓	Cave	⊞	Church (town)
⊥	Gardens	⚶	Waterfall	▢	Market
⚓	Swimming pool	♆	Mosque	◯	Stadium
⛳	Golf course	⛪	Temple	♦	National Reserve/park
⊙	War memorial	☦	Church (regional)	▢	Beach
				▢	Mangrove

Listings key

■	Accommodation
●	Restaurant/café
■	Bar/club
●	Shopping